GENESIS

A LIVING CONVERSATION

ALSO FROM BILL MOYERS AND PUBLIC AFFAIRS TELEVISION

The Language of Life: A Festival of Poets

Healing and the Mind

A World of Ideas

A World of Ideas II

Joseph Campbell and the Power of Myth

The Secret Government: The Constitution in Crisis

Report from Philadelphia: The Constitutional Convention of 1787

Listening to America

GENESIS

A LIVING CONVERSATION

BILL MOYERS

Betty Sue Flowers, Editor
Judith Davidson Moyers, Executive Editor
Elizabeth Meryman-Brunner, Art Research

BROADWAY BOOKS
NEW YORK

BROADWAY

A previous edition of this book was originally published in 1996 by Doubleday, a division of Random House, Inc. It is here reprinted by arrangement with Doubleday.

Text design by Stanley S. Drate/Folio Graphics Co. Inc.

Broadway Books titles may be purchased for business or promotional use or for special sales. For information, please write to: Special Markets Department, Random House, Inc., 280 Park Avenue, New York, NY 10017.

PRINTED IN THE UNITED STATES OF AMERICA

Visit our website at www.broadwaybooks.com

First Broadway Books trade paperback edition published 2002.

The Library of Congress Cataloging-in-Publication Data has cataloged the Doubleday edition as:
Moyers, Bill D.
    Genesis : a living conversation / Bill Moyers. — 1st ed.
        p.   cm.
    1. Bible. O.T. Genesis—Criticism, interpretation, etc.
2. United States—Interviews.   I. Title.
BS1235.2.M68   1996
222'.1106—dc20   96-15318
                                                 CIP

ISBN 0-385-49043-7

13 12 11 10 9 8 7 6 5 4

This book is dedicated to

Eli Evans
William Flynn and Thomas Moran
Burton Visotzky and Charles Halpern
and
Judy Doctoroff O'Neill,

present at the creation

CONTENTS

ACKNOWLEDGMENTS

Like the television series from which it grew, this book owes its existence to the collaboration of a creative team. Catherine Tatge produced the PBS series, as she did my earlier series with Joseph Campbell, and she had, in coordinating producer Michael Epstein, researcher Eliza Bayard, and production assistant Lisa Ammerman, a formidable combination of intelligence and energy. I am also indebted to the intelligence and precision of my researcher, Michael Smith. Judith Moyers and Judy Doctoroff O'Neill were executive producers of the series, responsible from beginning to end for one of the most difficult endeavors we have ever attempted; Judith, the president of Public Affairs Television, once again poured her unique imagination into the design and execution of this book, as she did for *The Language of Life*. Betty Sue Flowers, as editor, brought to *Genesis* the coherence and clarity with which earlier she so wisely shaped *Joseph Campbell and the Power of Myth*, *A World of Ideas*, and *Healing and the Mind*. PAT's Debbie Rubenstein, as project manager, created order in a production process that at times edged close to primordial chaos. Art researcher Elizabeth Meryman-Brunner was again invaluable and Jim Linderman and George Viener assisted her admirably. Robert Miller offered essential help in preparing the Epilogue. We had the further assistance of Jane Rosenthal, Evelyn Cohen, and Massumeh Farhad, our art consultants. Bruce Tracy of Doubleday never faltered in his support of our efforts or his knack for good judgment at just the right time. I owe a very special salute to Eli Evans and Lisa Goldberg of the Revson Foundation for their courage in supporting the *Genesis* project when I first raised it several years ago; without them, and Charles Halpern and Rabbi Rachel Cowen of the Nathan Cummings Foundation, I likely might never have left Ur. Ervin Duggan, the president of PBS, offered immediate inspiration when he heard about the project, and the participants in the conversations were moved when I read them his letter urging us "to break the awful taboo against intelligent, reflective discussions of religious subjects in our denuded public square." Of the participants themselves I cannot say enough. Talking about such matters on television is so rarely done I could offer them no precedent as a guide and no assurance of the outcome. But they came in good faith—no pun intended—and the series and this book are indelibly their creation. They became deeply involved in the process, acting as a splendid advisory group. And two contributed special talents: Hugh O'Donnell's cover art and Liz Swados's music for the series reflect the beauty and power contained in the stories.

EDITOR'S NOTE

A lively discussion, with its laughter, raised eyebrows, significant silences, and voices speaking at once, is almost impossible to capture on paper. But there are reasons for trying. One reason is to encourage thoughtful reflection about the original conversations. These conversations were cut to fit the time constraints of television—but here, they appear in fuller form, allowing readers to stop and ponder a statement, or to think about it in relation to a larger context. Sometimes, when participants saw an edited draft of the discussion, they added clarifying comments, which, of course, do not appear in the televised version. I'm grateful, though, that the participants let me keep a sense of spontaneity in their comments, resisting the urge to edit themselves out of speech and into "prose." I'm also grateful to Bill Moyers, whose ear was always tuned to the human dimension of the conversation, and who often took my edited work back to the screen in order to recapture the flavor of the original. His edits were both incisive and enlivening.

Debbie Rubenstein, my partner in this work, was a never-failing source of support and good humor. She and Judith Moyers, along with Judy Doctoroff O'Neill, are largely responsible for the way the many components of this book—art, Genesis text, and conversation—have come together. Once again, we were lucky to have Elizabeth Meryman-Brunner as art researcher.

I'm grateful, too, for the many kinds of support I received from Margaret Flowers, Linda Jinks, John Michael Flowers, and, most of all, John Flowers.

Our hope is that, as you read these conversations, you will be inspired to revisit the original Genesis text and to form a discussion group of your own. We have reprinted abridged versions of the stories from either the *New Revised Standard Version* or the new *Schocken Bible* translated by Everett Fox. But the stories, in all their richness, are worth rereading in a number of different translations, and well reward many hours of discussion. They are, after all, the narrative foundations for our Western culture.

—BETTY SUE FLOWERS
University of Texas at Austin

INTRODUCTION

BY BILL MOYERS

It was reported to be "the best conversation" in town. Deciding to check it out for myself, late one afternoon I made my way up to the Jewish Theological Seminary of America at the corner of Broadway and 122nd Street, across from Union Theological Seminary and a few blocks north of Columbia University. There, around a long plain table in a modest basement room, sat a score of people, talking. I recognized among them a film critic, a screenwriter, a poet, an editor, an essayist and novelist, and a smattering of biblical scholars, Jewish and Christian. Their leader was a bearded man whose intense dark eyes moved swiftly from speaker to speaker, as if he had scored so many tennis matches he could instinctively anticipate the action. And action there was, if the play of ideas is the game you love.

They were talking about Genesis, the first book of the Bible, whose stories have inspired three of the world's enduring religions and the spiritual, ethical, and literary imagination of Western civilization. What stories they are! We are swept from the creation of the world through the founding of Israel, from the architecture of the cosmos to the intrigues of the patriarchs, from Adam and Eve naked in the Garden to Joseph strutting in his coat of many colors. From fratricide to reconciliation they carry us, in a narrative saga that opens with "In the beginning God" and concludes "in a coffin in Egypt."

The participants this evening were making the most of it. No speeches, proclamations, or declamations: This was conversation, the kind you wish would happen at Sunday dinner. They were listening, responding, questioning, amending, inquiring, challenging—sometimes with wit, a wink, an eyebrow lifted; never with feigned agreement for agreement's sake and always with good-natured civility. I heard them wrestling not only with what the stories might have meant to the first people who heard them thousands of years ago, but with how those ancient stories connect to everyday life today. As they talked, this ordinary, unadorned room became for these few hours a place of creative incubation. The writer Cynthia Ozick has said of her experience there: "What goes on in this room is more exciting to me than anything that ever happened. It's as if the text really matters."

This is what their leader, Rabbi Burton Visotzky, had intended when he organized the Genesis seminar in the early 1980s. By shrewdly constructing these monthly sessions as workshops where people do midrash—the Jewish tradition of "searching out," through commentary, the contemporary application of the Bible to life—Rabbi Visotzky challenged his participants to ask of the stories, "What do they mean for us, now, in our lives, nearing the end of the twentieth century? How do they help us make sense of the world today?" Even now, he explains to newcomers, "the communal study of the Bible can continue to provide us with a means for clarifying our ideas about the world around us and for linking them historically to a long-standing tradition." It is in this shared reading and rereading that the Bible "ceases to be just another book, gathering dust on the shelf. In a community of readers a conversation takes place. The give-and-take of interpretation creates an extra voice in the room, the sound of Reading the Book."* When this happens, the Bible speaks "not only to each community of readers, be they Jewish, Christian, or any other flavor, but to all humanity."

To test these ideas, Rabbi Visotzky opened his Genesis seminar to a motley assortment of readers—laity and biblical scholars alike. All interpretations would be given a hearing, so that different points of view might expand every participant's ability to hear the nuances of the text. "It doesn't matter whether the reading of Scripture is traditional or modern, fundamentalist or critical, Christian or Muslim or Jewish, whether it comes from an adult or a child, an agnostic or a believer, a professor or a cabdriver. Every group, every person has something unique to offer in the interpretation of the Bible—all we need to do is learn how to listen."

The conversation takes surprising twists and turns. A question to the screenwriter and film director, Robert Benton (*Bonnie & Clyde*, *Kramer vs. Kramer*, *Places in the Heart*) caused the participants to see Joseph in a different light. Rabbi Visotzky had asked Benton whom he would cast as the femme fatale, Potiphar's lustful wife, who tried in vain to seduce her husband's handsome and trusted young slave. Would he choose Meryl Streep or Glenn Close? Before Benton could answer, novelist Nessa Rapoport responded, "No, Joseph is the femme fatale." It was, Visotzky later said, "a stunning insight as well as wicked humor," illuminating the extraordinary beauty of the youthful Hebrew and pointing to "the metaphysical quality that accompanies God's favor and leaves us uneasy, unable to categorize such a one."

---

*Rabbi Visotzky employed this term for the title of his own work. *Reading the Book*, originally published by Anchor Books, is an ebullient tour through the rabbinic imagination. The distinguished scholar Raymond Brown has urged both Christians and Jews to read it "in order to appreciate their respective heritages." I agree. It has added immeasurably to my own reading of the Bible.

In another session the group was discussing God's command and promise to Abraham in Genesis 12: "Go from your land and your birthplace and your father's house to the land I will show you. I will make you a great nation . . ." The writer Max Apple announced, "I wouldn't have written it that way!" As everyone looked at him, he somewhat sheepishly explained that God "gives it away at the outset; it is not a test of Abraham's faith if he is promised a reward from the very start." For Visotzky, this was a valuable commentary on the story; for the participants, it was an icebreaker, liberating them to challenge the scripture with their own intellect, from their own experience.

Listening to the seminar, I remembered my first visit to the cathedral in Chartres, where I had come upon a sculpture so striking it stopped me in my tracks. The artist depicts Adam, the first human, emerging as an idea from the side of God's head. God was *thinking* us into existence. With such a beginning, how could we not be destined ever after to think upon the implications of our own existence, to imagine and argue what it means to be made in God's image? That very likeness guarantees that human beings could never be coerced into thinking alike; imagination, conscience, and choice—the glory and grief of free will—were there from the beginning.

Small wonder there are as many methods of interpreting the Bible as there are interpreters. Each of us arrives at our interpretation through an intricate path of inherited memories, personal experiences, convictions, doctrines, habits, knowledge, tastes, and mores, not to mention politics. The Word—I forget now who said this—is to be found neither in the text nor the reader, but in the relationship where the two meet. In this intimacy—of one-on-one or in a community of readers—the timeless Word appears, bearing with it as well revelation for the day.

Or so it seemed as I eavesdropped on the Genesis seminar, and I came away resolved then and there to test whether the communal reading of these stories could happen on television. Of talk *about* religion we have no shortage on television, but religious conversation is rare, and religious conversation in the democratic spirit—committed but civil—rarer still. Mostly religion is discussed on television nowadays in a political context: one more interest group stalking the corridors of power, like the AARP or the National Association of Manufacturers. I reckoned that if a television series could reflect the dynamics of the Genesis seminar, where people do not shy away from the Bible as a religious document and can speak from a principled position while listening respectfully to others, the result might prove refreshing to an audience hungry for a discussion of values, demonstrate how strongly opinionated people can talk about their beliefs in public without proselytizing or polemics, and inspire ecumenical imitations in communities around the country.

The Visotzky seminar was too large for the small screen to treat kindly, even if the participants had been willing to surrender the intimacy of that room to an unseen audience of millions. For our PBS series, my colleagues and I settled on a circle of eight people for each program, including Rabbi Visotzky, who over the months had become not only my personal rebbe but just plain Burt, my friend. The others came from far and wide, bringing to the circle a diversity of experience from various stations of life and learning. There were journalists, scholars, literary critics, a psychotherapist, an artist, a composer, a lawyer, a college president, a psychologist, a translator—all with quite different angles of vision on the stories.

Our time together was notably enriched because the participants did not come from the same religion or neighborhood, but from all three of the great monotheistic faiths that trace their origins to Abraham—Judaism, Christianity, Islam. A Hindu took part, too, and a practitioner of Zen Buddhism; their comments opened us to new insights on the stories. Often, we disagreed with each other, and sometimes, the more we talked, the more we disagreed. But while talking together exposed our differences, it also brought us closer together. And sometimes we discovered that, despite our differences, we shared our deepest values with people who seemed most unlike us.

I marvel at the power of these stories and have never tired of them—God walking in the Garden in the cool of the evening, the wily logic of the serpent, the violent jealousy of Cain, Jacob's bold lie to his father, the unbearable moment of Isaac under the upraised knife of Abraham. They have been familiar to me since childhood, although they were sanitized in Sunday school by elders who thought it best to protect the fragile sensibilities of the innocent (if only they had known what we were reading between the covers of those hymnals during the sermons!). So it was not until much later that I noticed just how imperfect were the human instruments God had chosen—Abraham, who offers Sarah to the Pharaoh to save his own skin, the deceitful Jacob, the vain Joseph, the drunken Noah, who cruelly curses his grandson.

The dysfunctional family is not a modern invention, and it is because these stories ring so true about human nature that they retain their hold on us. They tell about the rise of a community of faith and the struggle of real men and women to know what it means to be the people of God. History, for these storytellers, was the unfolding of divine action and human reaction—"God in search of man," in Rabbi Abraham J. Heschel's famous description. The realness of God was never an issue in these stories, and the task, said Rabbi Heschel, was "how to live in a way compatible with His presence." Down through the ages, the stories have been told again and again so that each ensuing generation could lay claim to them, for the sake of remembrance, redemption, and the future. "The faith," says *The New Interpreter's Bible*, my favorite commentary, ''was not fundamentally an idea, but an embodiment, a way of life. The language and experience of faith thus remained concrete and personal . . . It does not dissolve into myth, into some mystical world of the gods that suppresses the human or the natural, or some religious world far removed from the secular sphere. By and large, the world reflected in these stories is ordinary, everyday, and familiar, filled with the surprises and joys, the sufferings and the troubles, the complexities and ambiguities known to every community.''

I find my own life's adventures in these stories. Deep in the night, wrestling with my fantasies, disillusionments, and failures, I recognize myself in these flawed characters, wrestling with God. Other participants said the same of themselves. This helps to explain why stories that live, as these do, assume an even fuller life when we come together to talk about them. As one participant suggested, the text is never finished until this moment, until this conversation ends.

Then it starts all over again.

In his *Gates of the Forest*, Elie Wiesel tells how the Baal Shem Tov, sensing misfortune awaiting the Jews, made his way to a certain place in the forest where he lighted a fire and said a special prayer so that the misfortune would be averted. In time his disciple, the Magid of Mezritch, also foresaw calamity threatening his people. He went to the same part of the forest and prayed, ''Master of the Universe, I do not know how to light the fire, but I am still able to say the prayer.'' This disaster, too, was averted. More time passed, and catastrophe loomed again. Now Rabbi Moshe-Leib of Savov made his way into the forest and said, ''I don't know how to light the fire and I don't know the prayer, but I know the place, and this must be sufficient,'' and it was. Then it fell to Rabbi Israel of Rizhyn to overcome misfortune. He said to God, ''I am unable to light the fire, I don't know the prayer, I cannot even find the place in the forest, all I can do is tell the story, and this must suffice.''

And it did.

Welcome to the conversation.

PARTICIPANTS

AZIZAH Y. AL-HIBRI

© Don Perdue

Azizah al-Hibri is an associate professor of law, specializing in securities regulation, corporate finance, and Islamic jurisprudence, at the University of Richmond in Virginia. She received her B.A. from the American University of Beirut in 1966, her M.A. in philosophy from Wayne State University in 1968, and her Ph.D., also in philosophy, and J.D. from the University of Pennsylvania in 1975 and 1985, respectively.

Al-Hibri is the founder and former president of Karamah: Muslim Women Lawyers for Human Rights, and is a founding member of the Muslim American Bar Association. She also serves on the advisory board of the American Muslim Council and the Virginia State Advisory Committee to the U.S. Commission on Civil Rights.

Among her many publications, al-Hibri is the co-editor of *Hypatia Reborn: Essays in Feminist Philosophy* (Indiana Univ. Press, 1990), and editor of *Women and Islam* (Oxford, 1982). She is also currently a member of the editorial board of *The Journal of Law and Religion* and serves as an editor for *The American Journal of Islamic Social Services*.

Azizah al-Hibri has lectured and participated in numerous seminars around the world. She makes her home in Midlothian, Virginia.

ROBERT ALTER

© Don Perdue

Robert Alter is a professor of Hebrew and comparative literature at the University of California at Berkeley, where he has taught since 1967. Born in New York City, Alter received his B.A. in English from Columbia College in 1957 and a Ph.D. in comparative literature from Harvard University in 1962.

He is a member of the American Academy of Arts and Sciences, as well as the Council of Scholars of the Library of Congress. He has been a Guggenheim fellow twice, a senior fellow of the National Endowment for the Humanities, and a fellow of the Institute for Advanced Studies in Jerusalem.

Alter has written and published extensively on the European and American novel from the eighteenth to twentieth century, on the literary art of the Bible, and on modern Hebrew literature. His books include *The Art of Biblical Narrative* (1981), *The World of Biblical Literature* (1992), and *Hebrew and Modernity* (1994). His translation of Genesis, *Genesis: A New Translation with Commentary*, was published by Norton in 1996. His criticism has appeared in *The New Republic*, *The London Review of Books*, *The Times Literary Supplement*, *Commentary*, and *The New York Times*.

KAREN ARMSTRONG

© Don Perdue

Karen Armstrong is a London-based author and professor. From 1962 to 1969, she was a Roman Catholic nun. She later received a B.L. from Oxford.

Armstrong has taught modern literature at the University of London and served as the English department head in a girls' school. In 1982, she embarked on a career as a freelance writer and television broadcaster, and a commentator on religious affairs. In 1983, she wrote and presented a six-part documentary TV series on the life and work of St. Paul. Currently, she teaches part-time at the Leo Baeck College for the Study of Judaism and the Training of Rabbis and Teachers in London.

She has written numerous books, including: *Through the Narrow Gate* (1981); *The Gospel According to Woman* (1986); *Holy War: The Crusades and Their Impact on Today's World* (1988); *Muhammad: A Western Attempt to Understand Islam* (1991); *The English Mystics of the Fourteenth Century* (1991); *The End of Silence: Women and Priesthood* (1993); and *A History of God* (1993), which spent over one year on *The New York Times* bestseller list. Her most recent book is *Jerusalem: One City, Three Faiths* (1996), which traces the history of the city from the Bronze Age to the present.

JOHN BARTH

© Don Perdue

John Barth is a writer and professor in the writing seminars at Johns Hopkins University. He received his B.A. in 1951 and M.A. in 1952, both from the Department of Writing, Speech, and Drama at Johns Hopkins.

He began his teaching career at Johns Hopkins, and soon moved to Pennsylvania State University. He has also taught at SUNY/Buffalo and Boston University. Barth returned to Johns Hopkins in 1973 and was named Professor Emeritus of Creative Writing in 1990.

Barth has written extensively. His books include: *The Floating Opera* (1956) and *Lost in the Funhouse* (1968), both National Book Award finalists in fiction, and *Chimera*, winner of the National Book Award in 1973. Barth is also the author of *The End of the Road* (1958); *The Sot-Weed Factor* (1960); *Giles Goat-Boy* (1966); *Letters* (1979); *Sabbatical: A Romance* (1982); *The Friday Book: Essays and Other Non-Fiction* (1984); *The Tidewater Tales* (1987); *The Last Voyage of Somebody the Sailor* (1991); *Once Upon a Time* (1994); *Further Fridays* (1995); and *On with the Story* (1996).

DIANNE BERGANT

© Don Perdue

Dianne Bergant is a professor of Old Testament studies at the Catholic Theological Union in Chicago. Bergant received her M.A. in sacred scripture and Ph.D. in biblical languages and literature from St. Louis University in 1970 and 1975, respectively.

Bergant is a member of the Catholic Biblical Association and the Society of Biblical Literature. She serves as an associate editor of *The Bible Today* and is a member of the editorial board of *Catholic Biblical Quarterly* and *Biblical Theology Bulletin*. Dr. Bergant is a member of the Chicago Jewish/Catholic Dialogue.

She has written numerous books and articles on the Bible, Christianity, and spirituality. Her books include *The World Is a Prayful Place* (Michael Glazier, 1987) and the *Collegeville Bible Commentary* (Liturgical, 1989). Her articles have appeared in *New Theology Review, The New Dictionary of Catholic Spirituality*, and *The Bible Today.*

WALTER BRUEGGEMANN

© Don Perdue

Walter Brueggemann is a professor of Old Testament at the Columbia Theological Seminary in Decatur, Georgia. Brueggemann graduated with a B.A. from Elmhurst College, a B.D. from Eden Theological Seminary, a Th.D. from Union Theological Seminary in 1961, and a Ph.D. in education from St. Louis University in 1974. He is an ordained minister of the United Church of Christ.

Brueggemann has published numerous works of biblical commentary and analysis, including: *Texts Under Negotiation: The Bible and Postmodern Imagination* (1993); *Old Testament Theology: Essays on Structure, Theme, and Text* (1992); and *Genesis: A Bible Commentary for Teaching and Preaching* (1982). He serves on the editorial council of *Theology Today* and is a contributing editor of *Sojourners*. Among the honors and awards that Brueggemann has received are a Luce theological fellowship, a Rockefeller Foundation doctoral fellowship, and honorary degrees from DePauw University, the Jesuit School of Theology, Berkeley, and Virginia Theological Seminary.

Walter Brueggemann, born in Nebraska in 1933, is married to Mary Bonner Miller, an ordained minister of the United Church of Christ. He and his wife have two sons.

✎ BYRON E. CALAME

© Don Perdue

Byron (Barney) Calame is a deputy managing editor of *The Wall Street Journal*, where he has worked since 1965. He was a reporter in New York, Los Angeles, and Washington, D.C., before becoming a bureau chief in 1974. After serving as bureau chief in Pittsburgh and Los Angeles, he was named an assistant managing editor, responsible for the *Journal*'s West Coast news operations. He returned to New York in 1987, becoming a senior editor. He was named deputy managing editor in 1992.

Calame's father was a Methodist minister in rural Missouri and his mother is a retired schoolteacher. A native of Appleton City, Missouri, he received a B.A. in journalism from the University of Missouri and an M.A. in political science from the University of Maryland. An officer in the U.S. Navy from 1961 to 1965, Calame served on a minesweeper that was one of the first naval units to be sent to South Vietnam.

Calame lives in New York City with his wife, Kathryn, who is a professor of microbiology at the Columbia University Medical School. They have two grown children.

✎ NORMAN J. COHEN

© Don Perdue

Norman J. Cohen is a professor of midrash at the Hebrew Union College–Jewish Institute of Religion in New York City, where he serves as the dean of the New York School and the director of the Rabbinic School in New York. He has been on the faculty at the school since 1975.

Cohen received his B.A. from Columbia College in 1964 and his rabbinic ordination and a Ph.D. in midrash from the Hebrew Union College–Jewish Institute of Religion, in 1971 and 1977, respectively.

Cohen has published numerous articles in such journals as *The Association of Jewish Studies Review, The Jewish Quarterly Review, The Journal for the Study of Judaism, The Journal of Reform Judaism,* and *Thought: A Review of Culture and Ideas.* He is the author of *Self, Struggle, and Change: The Family Conflict Stories in Genesis and Their Healing Insights for Our Lives* (Jewish Lights, 1995), and the editor, with Robert M. Seltzer, of *The Americanization of the Jews* (New York Univ. Press, 1995).

Norman Cohen lives with his wife in Yorktown Heights, New York. They have five grown children in their "blended" family.

ALEXANDER A. DI LELLA

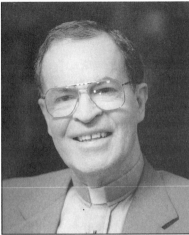

© Don Perdue

Father Di Lella, O.F.M., is the Andrews–Kelly–Ryan Distinguished Professor of Biblical Studies at the Catholic University of America in Washington, D.C., where he has taught and lectured since 1965. Born in Paterson, New Jersey, Di Lella received his B.A. from St. Bonaventure University in 1952, and his S.T.L. and Ph.D. from Catholic University of America in 1959 and 1962, respectively. He received an S.S.L. from the Pontifical Biblical Institute in Rome in 1964.

He entered the Franciscan Order in 1949 and was ordained a priest in 1955. He has been a fellow at the American School of Oriental Research in Jerusalem, as well as a Guggenheim fellow. An active member of both the Catholic Biblical Association and the Society of Biblical Literature, Di Lella has served as a member of the Revised Standard Version Bible Committee since 1982 and as chairman of the board of control of *The New American Bible* since 1988. In April of this year, he was awarded the Benemerenti Medal from Pope John Paul II.

Di Lella has served as editor or associate editor of *Catholic Biblical Quarterly*, *Theology Bulletin*, *Old Testament Abstracts*, and *Studia Biblica*. His books include: *The Wisdom of Ben Sira* (1987); *Proverbs in The Old Testament in Syriac according to the Peshitta Version* (1979); *The Book of Daniel* (1978); and *The Hebrew Text of Sirach: A Text-Critical and Historical Study* (1966). A biblical translator, he has also been editor of *The Holy Bible, New Revised Standard Version: Catholic Edition* (1993).

FRANCISCO O. GARCÍA-TRETO

© Don Perdue

Francisco García-Treto is professor and chair of the department of religion at Trinity University in San Antonio, Texas, and an ordained minister of the Presbyterian Church. He teaches courses in the narratives and poetry of the Hebrew Bible and in biblical Hebrew, as well as introductions to Judaism, Christianity, and Islam.

Born in Cuba, García-Treto received his B.A. in philosophy from Maryville College in Tennessee, and his B.D. and Ph:D. from Princeton Theological Seminary.

García-Treto is the coauthor, with R. Douglas Brackenridge, of *Iglesia Presbiteriana: Presbyterians and Mexican Americans in the Southwest* (Trinity Univ. Press, 1974 and 1987), and has published numerous articles on the literary study of the Bible and other subjects in *Harper's Dictionary of the Bible*, *Lecciones Cristianas*, *Journal of Presbyterian History*, and the *Journal for the Study of the Old Testament*, among other journals.

Francisco García-Treto and his wife, Mary, have two children.

CAROL GILLIGAN

© Don Perdue

Carol Gilligan is a professor, clinical psychologist, and author based in Cambridge, Massachusetts. She is a member of the Human Development and Psychology faculty at the Graduate School of Education at Harvard, where she has taught and lectured since 1967. Born in New York City, she went on to receive a B.A. from Swarthmore College, an M.A. from Radcliffe College, and a Ph.D. from Harvard.

Gilligan is the author of *In a Different Voice: Psychological Theory and Women's Development* (1982), as well as numerous articles and studies on gender differences, feminism, and moral and human development. She is a founding member of the collaborative Harvard Project on Women's Psychology, and with her colleagues has written and edited a series of books, including: *Meeting at the Crossroads: Women's Psychology and Girls' Development* (1992) with Lyn Mikel Brown; *Women, Girls, and Psychotherapy: Reframing Resistance* (1991) with Annie Rogers and Deborah Tolman; and *Between Voice and Silence: Women and Girls, Race and Relationship* (1996) with Jill McLean Taylor and Amy Sullivan.

Gilligan occupied the Laurie Chair in Women's Studies at Rutgers, and was the Pitt Professor of American History and Institutions at Cambridge, England (1992–93). She is a Spencer Foundation senior research scholar and a recipient of the Grawemeyer Award in education. In 1984, Gilligan was named "Woman of the Year" by *MS.* magazine. She has received honorary degrees from Swarthmore College, Haverford College, and Wesleyan University, among others.

Carol Gilligan and her husband, James Gilligan, live with their three sons in Cambridge, Massachusetts.

REBECCA GOLDSTEIN

© Don Perdue

Rebecca Goldstein graduated from Barnard College with a B.A. in philosophy in 1972, and earned her Ph.D. in philosophy from Princeton University in 1976. For ten years she was a professor of philosophy at Barnard College before devoting herself primarily to her fiction. Currently, she teaches writing at Columbia University.

Goldstein is the author of a collection of short stories and four novels: *The Mind-Body Problem* (1983); *The Late-Summer Passion of a Woman of Mind* (1989); *The Dark Sister* (1991); and *Mazel* (1995), which won the National Jewish Book Award for fiction. In 1991, she was the recipient of the Whiting Writers' Award. *Strange Attractors* (1993), her collection of short stories, won the Jewish National Book Award in 1994. Her fiction has also appeared in *Tikkun* and *Commentary*.

Rebecca Goldstein is married and the mother of two daughters. She and her family live in Highland Park, New Jersey.

MARY GORDON

© Don Perdue

Mary Gordon is a writer and professor based in New York. She received a B.A. from Barnard College in 1971 and an M.A. from Syracuse University in 1973. She was born and raised in Valley Stream, Long Island.

Gordon has twice won the Janet Heidinger Kafka Prize. Her first novel, *Final Payments*, won the award in 1979, and *The Company of Women* received the prize in 1982. She has received the Lila Acheson Wallace–Reader's Digest Writer's Award and a Guggenheim fellowship. Her other books include *Men & Angels* (1985); *Temporary Shelter* (1987); *The Other Side* (1989); *Good Boys & Dead Girls: And Other Essays* (1992); *The Rest of Life: Three Novellas* (1993); and *The Shadow Man* (1996). Gordon has contributed numerous short stories for publications such as *Atlantic Monthly*, *Harper's*, *Redbook*, *The New Yorker*, *Virginia Quarterly Review*, and *Salmagundi*. Her stories appeared in the *Best American Short Stories* in 1983, 1989, and 1991.

Currently, Gordon is the Millicent McIntosh Professor of English at Barnard College. She has taught at Amherst College and Dutchess Community College in Poughkeepsie, New York.

Mary Gordon is married to Arthur Cash, an English professor and department chair at SUNY/New Paltz. She has two children.

BLU GREENBERG

© Don Perdue

Blu Greenberg is a writer and poet in Riverdale, New York. She received her B.A. from Brooklyn College in 1957, a B.R.E. from the Yeshiva University Teachers Institute in 1958, an M.A. in clinical psychology from City University in 1967, and an M.S. in Jewish History from Yeshiva University Revel Graduate School of Jewish Studies in 1977.

She has written three books: *Black Bread: Poems After the Holocaust* (1994); *How to Run a Traditional Jewish Household* (1983); and *On Women and Judaism: A View from Tradition* (1982). Greenberg has also been published in many journals and magazines, including: *The New York Times*, *Moment*, *Hadassah*, *Lilith*, *The Jewish Monthly*, *The Ecumenist*, *Jewish Ethics*, and *Jewish Book World*. She serves on the editorial board of *Hadassah* and the advisory board of *Lilith*, and has worked with the (Jewish–Palestinian) Dialogue Project, Women of Faith, Coalition of Soviet Jewry, Jewish Foundation for Christian Rescuers, and the Covenant Foundation. Greenberg taught religious studies at the College of Mount Saint Vincent, and spent a sabbatical year at Pardes Institute in Jerusalem. Her many awards include the B'nai B'rith Distinguished Humanitarian Award, the Myrtle Wreath Achievement Award–Hadassah, and Bronx Woman of the Year.

Blu Greenberg and her husband, Rabbi Irving Greenberg, have five children.

ROBERTA HESTENES

© Don Perdue

Roberta Hestenes is president of Eastern College in St. David's, Pennsylvania, where she is also professor of Christian spirituality. Hestenes also serves as a parish associate at Wayne Presbyterian Church, Wayne, Pennsylvania. From 1975 to 1984 she taught Christian formation and discipleship at Fuller Theological Seminary in Pasadena, California. Hestenes was ordained a minister by the Presbyterian Church, U.S.A., in 1979.

Hestenes received her undergraduate degree from the University of California, Santa Barbara, and an M.Div. and a D.Min. from Fuller Theological Seminary. She has written several books, including: *Women and the Ministries of Christ* (1979); *Using the Bible in Groups* (1985); and *Mastering the Art of Teaching* (1992). Hestenes is also a contributing editor for *Christianity Today, Sojourners,* and *Prism.*

Hestenes has been on the board of directors of World Vision International, an ecumenical Christian international relief organization, since 1980, and served as board chair from 1985 to 1992. She also is a member of the board of directors of the Hispanic Century Fund. Since 1994 she has been a member of the advisory council for the Evangelical Environmental Network.

Roberta Hestenes is married to Dr. John Hestenes, a research scientist, and they have three grown children. They live in Radnor, Pennsylvania.

OSCAR HIJUELOS

© Don Perdue

Oscar Hijuelos is a writer, born, raised, and still residing in New York City. His parents immigrated to America from Cuba in the early 1940's and settled on the Upper West Side in a neighborhood that has greatly influenced and shaped his writing. He attended local Catholic and public schools and Bronx Community College, later receiving a B.A. and M.F.A. from the City College of New York.

After completing his studies, Hijuelos worked for a time at an advertising agency. Before and after hours, he began working on his first novel, *Our House in the Last World* (1983), which received numerous awards, including the American Academy of Arts and Letters Rome Prize and earned the author a fellowship from the National Endowment for the Arts, and an Ingram-Merrill fellowship.

After the success of his first novel, Hijuelos concentrated full-time on writing. His second novel, *The Mambo Kings Play Songs of Love,* won the 1990 Pulitzer Prize for fiction. His third novel, *The Fourteen Sisters of Emilio Montez O'Brien,* was received with wide acclaim. Hijuelos's most recent novel, *Mr. Ives' Christmas,* was published in late 1995.

CHARLES JOHNSON

© Don Perdue

Charles Johnson is the Pollock Professor of English at the University of Washington. Johnson received a B.A. in journalism and an M.A. in philosophy from Southern Illinois University in 1970 and 1973, respectively. His novel *Middle Passage* received the 1990 National Book Award.

Johnson is the author of two other novels, *Faith and the Good Thing* (1974) and *Oxherding Tale* (1982), as well as a collection of short stories, *The Sorcerer's Apprentice* (1986). He has published a work of aesthetics, *Being and Race: Black Writing Since 1970* (1988), and two collections of comic art, *Black Humor* (1970) and *Half-Past Nation Time* (1972). Johnson has served as fiction editor for *The Seattle Review* since 1978.

Johnson has received honorary doctorates from Northwestern University and from Southern Illinois University, which also administers the Charles Johnson Award for Fiction and Poetry, a nationwide competition for college students inaugurated in 1994.

Charles Johnson was born in 1948 in Evanston, Illinois. He and his wife, Joan, have a son and a daughter.

LEON R. KASS

© Don Perdue

Leon R. Kass is the Addie Clark Harding Professor in the College and the Committee on Social Thought at the University of Chicago. Kass graduated with a B.S. in biology and a medical degree from the University of Chicago in 1958 and 1962, respectively. He received a Ph.D. in biochemistry from Harvard University in 1967.

Since the late 1960s, after publishing numerous scientific articles, Kass has written extensively on ethics, science, and human affairs. His books include: *Toward a More Natural Science: Biology and Human Affairs* (1985) and *The Hungry Soul: Eating and the Perfecting of Our Nature* (1994). In recent years, he has published essays on Genesis and biblical themes, including: "Man and Woman: An Old Story" (*First Things*, November 1991); "A Woman for All Seasons" (*Commentary*, September 1994); and "Am I My (Foolish) Brother's Keeper?" (*The American Enterprise*, November/December 1994). His work has been published in a variety of journals, including: *Science, Theology Today, The Public Interest, Journal of the American Medical Association, The American Scholar,* and *Commonweal.*

Kass has held a number of fellowships, including a National Humanities Center fellowship and a Guggenheim fellowship. He has received two teaching awards from the University of Chicago, the Quantrell Award for Excellence in Undergraduate Teaching and the Amoco Foundation Award for Distinguished Contributions to Undergraduate Teaching.

Leon Kass was born in Chicago in 1939. He and his wife, Amy, live in Chicago, and they have two daughters.

FAYE KELLERMAN

© Don Perdue

Faye Kellerman is a Los Angeles-based mystery writer. Born in St. Louis, Missouri, she moved to California and graduated from U.C.L.A., with a B.A. in 1974. In 1978, Kellerman earned a D.D.S. from U.C.L.A., where she also held a research fellowship. After graduation, Kellerman chose to pursue a career in writing rather than practice dentistry.

Kellerman's first novel, *The Ritual Bath*, was published in 1986 and won the Macavity Award for best first novel. Her other novels are: *Sacred and Profane* (1987); *The Quality of Mercy* (1990); *Milk & Honey* (1991); *Day of Atonement* (1992); *False Prophet* (1993); *Grievous Sin* (1993); *Sanctuary* (1994); *Justice* (1995); and *Prayers for the Dead* (1996). Her short stories and essays have appeared in numerous anthologies, nationally and internationally. The two central characters of Kellerman's mystery series are Orthodox Jews.

Faye Kellerman is married to the novelist Jonathan Kellerman. They live in Los Angeles and have four children.

JOHN S. KSELMAN

© Don Perdue

Father John Kselman, S.S., is currently a professor of Old Testament at the Weston School of Theology in Cambridge, Massachusetts, where he has taught since 1987. Kselman has also taught biblical studies and Semitic languages at a number of colleges and universities, including Harvard University, Princeton Theological Seminary, University of Notre Dame, and Catholic University of America.

Kselman received his A.B., S.T.B., and S.T.L. from St. Mary's Seminary in Baltimore in 1961, 1963, and 1967, respectively. He also received a Ph.D. from the Department of Near Eastern Languages and Civilizations at Harvard University in 1971.

Kselman's numerous editorial posts have included general editor for *Catholic Biblical Quarterly*, where he also served as the Old Testament book review editor from 1977 to 1983. He has contributed essays on modern New Testament criticism and the Book of Psalms to *The New Jerome Biblical Commentary*, and written for the *Anchor Bible Dictionary* and the *Encyclopedia of Catholicism*. Kselman also wrote the Genesis section of the *Harper's Bible Commentary*.

John Kselman was born in 1940 and ordained to the priesthood in 1967.

P. K. McCary

© Don Perdue

P. K. McCary is a writer, lecturer, and the author of *Black Bible Chronicles: From Genesis to the Promised Land* (African American Family Press, 1993), a version of the Old Testament aimed at black youth.

McCary has worked as a print and broadcast journalist in New York, Denver, Washington, D.C., and Atlanta. Her articles have appeared in various newspapers and magazines, including *The Atlanta Journal Constitution*, *Black Lawyer*, *The Houston Post*, and *Texas Country Magazine*. Her broadcast reports have appeared on KRIV-TV/Channel 11, Channel 26, and KTSU Radio in Houston.

A member of the Brentwood Baptist Church, Ms. McCary has given motivational lectures to teenagers and adults in a number of cities. She is also the author of *Rappin' with Jesus*, a rendering of the New Testament for youth, and *The Dreamer Awakens*, an anthology of prose and poetry on spiritual themes. Ms. McCary is currently in production with her play, *Straight from the Rib: Dialogues with Biblical Women*, in Houston, where she lives with her three children.

STEPHEN MITCHELL

© Don Perdue

Stephen Mitchell was born in Brooklyn in 1943, attended Amherst, the University of Paris, and Yale, and in 1973 began training in Zen meditation. His books include: *The Gospel According to Jesus: A New Translation and Guide to His Essential Teaching for Believers and Unbelievers*; *Parables and Portraits* (poems); *The Book of Job*; *Tao Te Ching*; *The Enlightened Heart: An Anthology of Sacred Poetry*; *The Enlightened Mind: An Anthology of Sacred Prose*; *A Book of Psalms*; *Ahead of All Parting: The Selected Poetry and Prose of Rainer Maria Rilke*; and *Genesis: A New Translation of the Classical Biblical Stories* (1996).

Stephen Mitchell lives with his wife, Vicki Chang, an acupuncturist, herbalist, and healer, in northern California.

BHARATI MUKHERJEE

© Don Perdue

Bharati Mukherjee is a writer and professor of English at the University of California at Berkeley. Born in Calcutta, India, Mukherjee received her B.A. from the University of Calcutta, an M.A. in English and ancient Indian culture from the University of Baroda, and an M.F.A. in creative writing and a Ph.D. in English and comparative literature from the University of Iowa.

Mukherjee has published several novels and volumes of short stories, including: *The Tiger's Daughter* (1972); *Wife* (1975); *The Middle Man and Other Stories* (1988), which won the National Book Critics' Circle Award for best fiction; *Jasmine* (1989); and *The Holder of the World* (1993). She is also the coauthor, with her husband, Clark Blaise, of two nonfiction works, *Days and Nights in Calcutta* (1977) and *The Sorrow and the Terror: The Haunting Legacy of the Air India Tragedy* (1985). She has also published numerous essays on contemporary Anglophone fiction, American-Asian literature, and diasporic culture.

Mukherjee has received a Guggenheim fellowship and a grant from the National Endowment for the Arts. She currently lives in San Francisco.

SEYYED HOSSEIN NASR

© Don Perdue

Seyyed Hossein Nasr is the university professor of Islamic studies at George Washington University, where he has taught since 1984. He has held teaching and administrative positions at Tehran University, Aryamehr University, Harvard University, the American University in Beirut, Temple University, and the University of Utah.

Nasr studied physics and mathematics at M.I.T., where he received a B.S. with honors in 1954. He received an M.S. from Harvard University in 1956, and a Ph.D. in 1958 in the history of science and philosophy, with special emphasis upon Islamic science.

Nasr has written or edited twenty-nine books, which have been published in many languages. These works include: *Ideals and Realities of Islam; Science and Civilization in Islam;* and *Islamic Life and Thought.* His numerous articles have been published in leading journals throughout the Islamic world, Europe, America, Australia, India, and Japan.

Nasr was born in Tehran, Iran, where he lived until 1979. He now lives in Washington, D.C.

HUGH O'DONNELL

© Don Perdue

Hugh O'Donnell is an internationally recognized artist who lives in Washington, Connecticut. Public venues and collections include the Solomon R. Guggenheim Museum; the Metropolitan Museum in New York; the Museum of Modern Art in New York; the National Gallery of Art in Washington, D.C.; and the Victoria and Albert Museum in London. Additional public exhibitions include the Hirshorn Museum in Washington, D.C.; the Museum of Modern Art in Kyoto, Japan; XLII Venice Biennale, Italy; and IV Medellin Biennal, Colombia.

O'Donnell has a B.A. with honors and M.A. in fine art. Painting fellowships have included Gloucestershire College of Art in England and Kyoto University of Arts in Japan.

O'Donnell has taught art extensively in England and the United States. For ten years he was a senior lecturer in fine art at the University of Brighton in the United Kingdom. He has served as a visiting critic in fine art at most of the major art colleges in England, including the Royal College of Art and the Slade School of Fine Art (London University), and at art institutions in the United States, including Pasadena Art Center, the New York Studio School, Cooper Union in New York, Pratt University, the University of Pennsylvania, Pennsylvania Academy of the Fine Arts, the University of Memphis, and Skidmore College.

Hugh O'Donnell was born in 1950 and has lived in the United States since 1987.

ELAINE H. PAGELS

© Arthur White

Elaine Pagels is the Harrington Spear Paine Foundation Professor of Religion at Princeton University. Pagels received a B.A. and an M.A. in classics from Stanford University in 1964 and 1965, respectively, and a Ph.D. in the study of religion from Harvard in 1970. She taught at Barnard College in New York for twelve years before joining the religion department at Princeton in 1982.

Pagels has written extensively on the Gnostic Gospels and the history of the early Christian Church, publishing over forty-five articles on the subject and serving as a member of the editorial and translation board for *The Nag Hammadi Library in English* (1978). Pagels is also the author of several books, including: *The Gnostic Gospels* (1979); *Adam, Eve, and the Serpent* (1988); and *The Origin of Satan* (1995).

The recipient of a MacArthur Prize fellowship in 1980, Pagels has also held Rockefeller, Guggenheim, and National Endowment for the Humanities fellowships. Pagels received the National Book Critics' Circle Award and the American Book Award for *The Gnostic Gospels*. She is a member of the Society of Biblical Literature and the American Academy of Religion.

She is married to Kent Greenwalt, University Professor at Columbia University, who teaches at the School of Law. They have five children.

SAMUEL D. PROCTOR

© Don Perdue

Samuel Proctor is an ordained Baptist minister, educator, and writer. Born in Norfolk, Virginia, Proctor received his B.A. from Virginia Union University in 1942, a B.D. from Crozer Theological Seminary in 1945, and a Th.D. from Boston University in 1950. He also attended the University of Pennsylvania and Yale University.

Currently, Proctor serves as adjunct professor at the United Theological Seminary in Dayton, Ohio, and as visiting professor at Kean State College of New Jersey. Proctor is Professor Emeritus at Rutgers and Pastor Emeritus of the Abyssinian Baptist Church of New York City. He has served as teacher, dean, and president of Virginia Union University (1955–60) and as president of North Carolina A&T State University (1960–64). He was also a professor at Duke and Vanderbilt University Divinity Schools. In 1990, he was the Lyman Beecher Lecturer at Yale Divinity School.

He has written *The Young Negro in America* (1966); *Sermons from the Black Pulpit* (1984); *Preaching About Crises in the Community* (1988); *My Moral Odyssey* (1989); *How Shall They Hear?* (1992); and *The Certain Sound of the Trumpet* (1994). He has been awarded honorary doctorates from forty-eight colleges and universities, including Columbia, Rutgers, Howard, Morehouse, and the Jewish Theological Seminary of America.

Samuel Proctor and his wife, Bessie Tate Proctor, have four sons.

EUGENE RIVERS III

© Don Perdue

Reverend Eugene Rivers is the director of field operations for the Ten Point Coalition in Boston, Massachusetts, and project director for Boston Freedom Summer. A graduate of Harvard, he has been a fellow at the Center for the Study of Values in Public Life at Harvard Divinity School, and is the pastor and cofounder of the Azusa Christian Community located in the Four Corners area of Dorchester. The community, made up primarily of middle-class professional African Americans, is committed to working in the Four Corners area to combat poverty, violence, and drug use.

Rivers is the executive director of the Dorchester District Youth Advocacy Project—the first church-based initiative of its kind in recent Boston history—which serves gang youth in the Four Corners neighborhood. Rivers also serves as the director of the Seymour Institute for Advanced Christian Studies, which is a research and educational organization focusing on the relationship between Christian faith and social policy.

Born in Boston, Eugene Rivers grew up in Philadelphia. He lives in the Four Corners neighborhood with his wife and two children.

NAOMI H. ROSENBLATT

© Don Perdue

Naomi H. Rosenblatt is a psychotherapist, author, lecturer, and adult Bible class teacher. Her weekly classes include a seminar on Capitol Hill for U.S. senators from both sides of the aisle. Her roundtable discussions in Washington and New York attract a wide spectrum of students from all walks of life.

Born in Haifa, Israel, she majored in biblical studies at the Reali School and served in the Israeli Navy. She earned a B.S. in elementary school education and an M.A. in psychiatric social work from the Catholic University in Washington, D.C.

Rosenblatt recently authored, with Joshua Horwitz, *Wrestling with Angels: What the First Family of Genesis Teaches Us About Our Spiritual Identity, Sexuality, and Personal Relationships* (Delacorte, 1995; selected for Book-of-the-Month Club, Quality Paperback Book Club, Jewish Book Club, and Dell Audio).

Rosenblatt is married to Peter R. Rosenblatt, an attorney and former ambassador. She has three grown children and three small grandsons. She and her husband reside in Washington, D.C.

JEAN-PIERRE M. RUIZ

© Don Perdue

Father Jean-Pierre M. Ruiz, a Roman Catholic priest of the Diocese of Brooklyn, New York, is an assistant professor in the Department of Theology and Religious Studies at St. John's University. Ruiz received his B.A. from Cathedral College of the Immaculate Conception in Douglaston, New York, in 1978, and an S.T.B. in theology, and an S.T.L. and S.T.D. in biblical studies from the Pontifical Gregorian University in Rome in 1981, 1983, and 1989, respectively.

Ruiz has written extensively on theological and pastoral issues. His recent articles include: "Contexts in Conversation: First World and Third World Readings of Job" (*Journal of Hispanic/ Latino Theology*, February 1995); "The Apocalypse of John and Contemporary Roman Catholic Liturgy" (*Worship*, 1994); and "Listening Habits: Teaching, Preaching, Undergraduates and the Bible" (*The Priest*, March 1994). In 1992 and 1993, together with Dr. Leonard Stern, Ruiz organized two Jewish–Christian interfaith symposia entitled "Points of Contact, Lines of Division, Agendas for Dialogue: A Conversation Between Christians and Jews." In 1994 he was appointed to the national Roman Catholic–Southern Baptist Conversations.

Ruiz is the current president of the Academy of Catholic Hispanic Theologians of the United States (ACHTUS). He has served on the ACHTUS board of directors since 1993. He is the associate editor of the *Journal of Hispanic/Latino Theology.*

Jean-Pierre Ruiz makes his home in New York City.

LEWIS B. SMEDES

© Don Perdue

Lewis Smedes is Professor Emeritus of Theology and Ethics at Fuller Theological Seminary in Pasadena, California. Smedes taught Christian ethics at Fuller in what is now the Lewis B. Smedes Chair of Christian Ethics and was the chair of integrative studies from 1990 until 1994.

Raised in Grand Rapids, Michigan, Smedes received his B.A. from Calvin College, his B.D. from Calvin Theological Seminary, and his Ph.D. from the Free University of Amsterdam.

Among Smedes's numerous publications are: *Forgive and Forget* (Harper & Row, 1984); *How Can It Be All Right When Everything Is All Wrong?* (Harper & Row, 1982); *Mere Morality: What God Expects from Ordinary People* (Eerdmans, 1983); *Choices: Making the Right Decision in a Complex World* (Harper & Row, 1984); and *Shame and Grace* (Harper & Row, 1993). Smedes has also translated various scholarly works.

Lewis Smedes is the father of three children. He lives in Sierra Madre, California, with his wife.

ELIZABETH SWADOS

© Don Perdue

Liz Swados is a writer, musician, and artist whose current work concerns characters and themes from biblical narratives. Swados's theater work has appeared on and off Broadway and with the New York Shakespeare Festival, the Manhattan Theater Club, and at La Mama, as well as with other companies in the United States and around the world.

Her theater work includes: *Bible Woman* (1995); *Prince and the Pauper* (1994); *Jerusalem* (Delacorte Theater, 1992); *Trilogy: Medea, Elektra, and Trojan Women*, which won an Obie Award in 1987; and *Runaways* (1976), which was performed throughout the United States and numerous foreign countries.

Swados has created musical scores for several television projects, including *A Year in the Life* and *Seize the Day.* She has also performed with poet Yehudi Amichai, setting his poems to music. Currently, she is working on a chamber opera for the Mark Temper Forum and the Brooklyn Academy of Music entitled *Missionaries on Their Knees.*

Swados received her B.A. from Bennington College in 1972. She makes her home in New York City.

MARIANNE MEYE THOMPSON

© Don Perdue

Marianne Meye Thompson is an associate professor in New Testament interpretation at Fuller Theological Seminary in Pasadena, California. She received a B.A. from Wheaton College in 1975, an M.Div. from Fuller in 1978, and a Ph.D. in New Testament from Duke University in 1985. She joined Fuller's faculty in 1985.

Thompson has written two books: *A Commentary on the Epistles of John* (1991) and *The Humanity of Jesus in the Fourth Gospel* (1988). She is also the author of numerous articles in books, encyclopedias, and scholarly and religious journals, including the *Bulletin for Biblical Research*, *Catalyst*, and *Ex Auditu*.

Thompson is a member of the Society of Biblical Literature and of the International Honorary Society for the Study of the New Testament. She has received a number of academic awards, including a Danforth graduate fellowship, a James B. Duke fellowship, a Pew Evangelical Scholarship Initiative grant, and a Luce theological fellowship. She is currently writing a book on God in the Gospel of John.

Marianne Thompson is married and has two children.

PHYLLIS TRIBLE

© Don Perdue

Phyllis Trible is the Baldwin Professor of Sacred Literature at Union Theological Seminary, where she has taught since 1979. She has also taught at the Andover Newton Theological School in Newton Centre, Massachusetts, and at Wake Forest University in Winston-Salem, North Carolina. She received a B.A. from Meredith College in Raleigh, North Carolina, in 1954, and a Ph.D. from Union Theological Seminary and Columbia University in 1963.

Trible has written extensively in the fields of biblical studies and literary criticism. Her major books are: *God and the Rhetoric of Sexuality* (Fortress, 1978); *Texts of Terror: Literary-Feminist Readings of Biblical Narratives* (Fortress, 1984); and *Rhetorical Criticism: Context, Method, and the Book of Jonah* (Fortress, 1994). Her numerous articles, including "Genesis 22: The Sacrifice of Sarah" and "Eve and Adam: Genesis 2–3 Reread," have been published in the *Journal of the American Academy of Religion*, *Bible Review*, and *Theological Studies*, among other journals. Her criticism has appeared in *The Iowa Review* and *The New York Times*. Her writings have been translated into German, Dutch, Spanish, Korean, and Japanese. Among her awards are a fellowship from the National Endowment for the Humanities and honorary degrees from Franklin College and Lehigh University. She is a past president of the Society of Biblical Literature and a member of the British Society of Old Testament Studies.

Born in Richmond, Virginia, she now resides in New York City.

BURTON L. VISOTZKY

© Don Perdue

Burt Visotzky holds the Nathan and Janet Appleman Chair in Midrash and Interreligious Studies at the Jewish Theological Seminary of America, where he has been a member of the faculty since his ordination as rabbi in 1977. He serves as director of the program in midrash and heads the Louis Finkelstein Institute for Religious and Social Studies.

Visotzky received his B.A. from the University of Illinois (Chicago), an M.A. in Education from Harvard University, and his M.A., rabbinic ordination, and Ph.D. from the Jewish Theological Seminary. He is adjunct professor of biblical studies at Union Theological Seminary in New York. He has also served as visiting professor at Princeton Theological Seminary and the Russian State University of the Humanities in Moscow, as well as visiting scholar at Oxford University and visiting fellow and life member of Clare Hall, University of Cambridge.

His articles and reviews have been published in America, Europe, and Israel. He is the author of four scholarly books and a popular work, *Reading the Book: Making the Bible a Timeless Text* (Doubleday/Anchor, 1991; Schocken, 1996). He recently published *The Genesis of Ethics* (Crown, 1996).

Burt Visotzky makes his home in New York City.

RENITA J. WEEMS

© Arthur White

Renita J. Weems is a writer, minister, professor, and widely acclaimed public speaker. She is currently a professor of Old Testament studies at Vanderbilt University Divinity School in Nashville, Tennessee. An Atlanta native, Weems received her B.A. from Wellesley College in 1976, and her M.Div. and Ph.D. from Princeton Theological Seminary in 1983 and 1989, respectively. She has been an ordained elder in the African Methodist Episcopal Church since 1984.

Weems's articles have appeared in a variety of scholarly and popular journals, including: *Essence*, *Ms.*, *Church and Society*, *Sage*, *The Journal of Feminist Studies in Religion*, and *The New York Times Book Review*. She has published several books, including: *Just a Sister Away: A Womanist Vision of Woman's Relations in the Bible* (1988) and *I Asked for Intimacy: Stories of Blessing, Betrayals, and Birthings* (1982). Weems has recently completed a volume on marriage, sex, and gender imagery in prophetic literature entitled *Battered Love* (Fortress, 1995). She has also contributed commentaries on *The Song of Songs* to *The New Interpreter's Bible* (1995) and *The Women's Bible Commentary*.

Weems, formerly an economist, public accountant, and stockbroker, was an at-large representative to the council of the Society of Biblical Literature from 1990 to 1992, and served on the steering and editorial committees of the African American Biblical Hermeneutics Project.

Renita Weems is married to Rev. Martin L. Espinosa, pastor of Berean Baptist Church in Nashville. They have one daughter.

ROBIN DARLING YOUNG

© Don Perdue

Robin Young is associate professor of theology at the Catholic University of America, where she has taught since 1985. Young received her B.A. from Mary Washington College in 1972, and an M.A. and Ph.D. in the history of Christianity from the University of Chicago Divinity School in 1975 and 1982, respectively. After receiving her Ph.D., Young taught Church history at the Wesley Theological Seminary in Washington, D.C., and was a visiting scholar at Wolfson College, Oxford.

Young has contributed chapters to several books, including *Biblical Interpretation* (1987); *Ascetic Behavior in Greco-Roman Antiquity* (1990); *Spiritual Traditions for the Contemporary Church* (1990); and the *Encyclopedia of Early Christianity* (1990). Her work has appeared in numerous journals, including *Religious Studies Review*, *The Living Light*, *The Thomist*, *Church History*, *Journal of the American Academy of Religion*, and the *Catholic Historical Review*. She is currently preparing a volume on the exegesis of Genesis in early Christian authors.

Young has received research grants from the National Endowment for the Humanities, the American Council of Learned Societies, and the Catholic University Research Fund. She has also held a fellowship from the National Endowment for the Humanities.

Robin Darling Young lives in Bethesda, Maryland, with her husband, Malcolm C. Young. They have five children.

AVIVAH GOTTLIEB ZORNBERG

© Arthur White

Avivah Zornberg is a lecturer in Bible and midrash in Jerusalem. She has also taught in the English department at Hebrew University. Zornberg studied at Gateshead Seminary and received a B.A. and a Ph.D. in nineteenth-century literature from Cambridge University.

Before she began teaching Torah and midrash in 1981, she was a lecturer in the English department at Hebrew University. Since then Zornberg has taught classes on Parshat HaShavua (the weekly Torah reading) to thousands of students in Israel at the MaTaN Women's Institute for Torah Studies, the Jerusalem College for Adults, Midreshet Lindenbaum, and Pardes Institute. She also lectures widely in the United States, Canada, and the United Kingdom.

Zornberg's book, *Genesis: The Beginning of Desire* (Jewish Publication Society, 1995; reprint, Doubleday, 1996) won the National Jewish Book Award (nonfiction) for 1995.

Avivah Zornberg was born in London to a rabbinic family in 1944. She grew up in Glasgow, Scotland, where her father was a rabbi and head of the rabbinical court. In 1969, she moved to Jerusalem, where she currently lives with her husband, Eric, and their three children.

GENESIS

A LIVING CONVERSATION

I

IN GOD'S IMAGE

WALTER BRUEGGEMANN • ROBERTA HESTENES

JOHN S. KSELMAN • HUGH O'DONNELL

BURTON L. VISOTZKY • RENITA J. WEEMS

AVIVAH GOTTLIEB ZORNBERG

I once saw a sculpture in the great cathedral of Chartres so striking it stopped me in my tracks. The artist depicts Adam, the first man, emerging as an idea from the side of God's head; God is *thinking* us into being. With such a beginning we human beings were destined ever after to think upon our existence, to imagine and argue about what it means to be made in God's image. Our participants in this discussion come from different cultures and persuasions, demonstrating once again that being made in the likeness of God does not mean we were made to think alike.

—BILL MOYERS

Genesis (Bere'shit), opening page, *Schocken Bible*, Southern Germany, ca. 1300

God said:

Let us make humankind, in our image, according to our likeness!

*Let them have dominion over the fish of the sea, the fowl of the
    heavens, animals, all the earth, and all crawling things that
    crawl upon the earth!*
    God created humankind in his image,
    in the image of God did he create it,
    male and female did he create them.

God blessed them,

God said to them:

Bear fruit and be many and fill the earth

and subdue it!

Have dominion over the fish of the sea, the fowl of the heavens,
    and all living things that crawl about upon the earth!

God said:

Here, I give you

all plants that bear seeds that are upon the face of all the earth,

and all trees in which there is tree fruit that bears seeds,

for you shall they be, for eating;

and also for all the living things of the earth, for all the fowl of
    the heavens, for all that crawls about upon the earth in which
    there is living being—

all green plants for eating.

It was so.

Now God saw all that he had made,

and here: it was exceedingly good! . . .

and YHWH, *God, formed the human, of dust from the soil,*

he blew into his nostrils the breath of life

and the human became a living being.

YHWH, *God, planted a garden in Eden/Land-of-Pleasure, in the
    east,*

and there he placed the human whom he had formed.

YHWH, *God, caused to spring up from the soil*

every type of tree, desirable to look at and good to eat,

and the Tree of Life in the midst of the garden

and the Tree of the Knowing of Good and Evil . . .

*Y*HWH, *God, took the human and set him in the garden of Eden,*
to work it and to watch it.
*Y*HWH, *God, commanded concerning the human, saying:*
From every (other) tree of the garden you may eat, yes, eat,
but from the Tree of the Knowing of Good and Evil—
you are not to eat from it,
for on the day that you eat from it, you must die, yes, die.
Now Y*HWH, *God, said:*
It is not good for the human to be alone,
I will make him a helper corresponding to him . . .

So Y*HWH, *God, caused a deep slumber to fall upon the human,*
    so that he slept,
he took one of his ribs and closed up the flesh in its place.
Y*HWH, *God, built the rib that he had taken from the human into*
    a woman
and brought her to the human.
The human said:
    This-time, she-is-it!
    Bone from my bones,
    flesh from my flesh!
    She shall be called Woman/Isha,
    for from Man/Ish she was taken!

—excerpts from *The Five Books of Moses*
(*Schocken Bible*, Vol. I), Chapters 1 and 2

BILL: These words are so familiar to us, they are almost a cliché. What do you think they must have sounded like to the first people who heard them?

HUGH: I can't imagine, but I'll tell you that when I read the Bible again recently—and I have to confess, it was after a great lull—it felt very remote, as if the stories were happening on another planet. I found myself thinking, "I don't believe these stories. I'm only interested in these stories insofar as I know these stories."

BURT: What do you mean you don't believe them? You don't believe it happened that way? Or—

HUGH: If I'm asked to believe that in a land beyond time, there occurred this great adventure, the Bible gets put on the shelf along with the other books of fantastic literature. But for me to recognize these stories as something that I can relate to, I need to be able to say, "Yes, this happened then, it happens now, and it will happen again." Then it becomes a continuous revelation about reality. As soon as I can plug into that, I've got it.

BILL: Were you able to?

HUGH: Yes, yes. For example, what does it mean to be made in the image of God? The question of making something in one's likeness is continuously present in the artist's life because one is the author of what one does and yet one doesn't somehow completely own what one does. You make something and it separates from you, as happened to God's creation in the Garden. You can see the same dynamic in art. The *Hamlet* performed on the stage today has very little to do with Shakespeare. Shakespeare's creation is now in the hands of the actors who live in that play and who hold the content of the work, and they, in turn, lend this content to us. As an audience, we recreate this content in ourselves. The play is separate from the creator—but it still praises the creator.

BILL: Are you suggesting that this is going on in the mind of God, as God contemplates this creation?

HUGH: Yes, God projects Himself into a manifestation out in the world, where He can reflect upon Himself and see Himself revealed to Himself. That's the motivation I have when I go into the studio. I want to see myself out there taking up space and looking back at myself.

BILL: What about the notion of creating something from nothing?

HUGH: You have to have nothing in order to really make something. You have to enter yourself in order to find the power—to get the gift of being able to emanate something. You have to create space—or allow space to occur. Rilke once said that in order to know a tree, you have to surround it with inner space—only in your renouncing is it truly there.

BURT: Hugh has just pronounced a principle of sixteenth-century Jewish mysticism. If God fills the universe, how can God create anything? There's no space. So God has to withdraw to create space for the world to exist. But in the Kabala, that gives rise to a terrible flaw because the empty space is then essentially devoid of Divinity. This has cosmic implications. We have to constantly repair that void. Is that something that happens in your art, Hugh?

HUGH: Constantly. Your creation never completely succeeds. And there's a kind of addiction that goes with that because the artist is continuously struggling and failing and struggling again. But it's always a better, richer kind of failure.

BILL: Certainly God's creation in this account is never finished. God can't be free of it. He's always coming back, trying to redeem it.

RENITA: Yes, but what God has created is, at one level, holy space. It bears the mark of God, or the life of God. And the people created by God have a worth and beauty and dignity befitting a holy space. There's a distance between the Creator and creation, but at the same time, there's also a glory that's given to the creation from the Creator. But let me ask Hugh: How do you know when a work is finished? God saw that His creation was good—but how do we know that a piece is good enough to be shown or published or preached?

HUGH: When it is original. When you're astonished by what's happened. To be original, you have to speak for yourself in your own voice. We take inspiration from the past and present and represent this inspiration in our own work.

ROBERTA: Perhaps "good" and "finished" are not the same things. Perhaps "good" is to launch or begin. And it takes the rest of scripture, or the rest of history, to see what that beginning has within it.

RENITA: I've always thought "It was good" meant "It works. It has purpose." If you came to my home, you would find a number of chairs that aren't good. So I would say to you, "Oh, don't sit there, it's not good." I mean by that not that the chair is ugly or not well built, but that it doesn't function the way it was created to function. "Good" is a function. Something that is "good" works. It fulfills the purpose for which it was created.

BURT: What fascinates me about this story is that we're reading about God launching creation and about its being good. But no matter how many times God says, "It's good, it's good, it's very good," not so many chapters go by before God decides, "Well, maybe this isn't so good after all" and destroys it all and starts again. This incredible creation astonishes God. And we are made in God's image, and yet we fail.

BILL: So are we saying that God may have been surprised by what He did? That He is astonished by creation?

HUGH: Well, there are two creation stories here. In one, God creates man and woman as an item. He creates masculine and feminine in one. And then, in the second story, He starts again, but this time He starts doing it in stages. As an artist, you have a conception that starts running around in your brain. You're being driven to do it, and you see the whole thing in wonderful detail. So you roll up your sleeves and get started. But then—bang!—it hits the floor. Something happens you don't expect. And then you know you haven't really got an idea until what you've actually started to build survives.

BILL: As you say, there are two accounts of creation here. In the beginning, God seems to create man and woman in one simultaneous act. But a few verses later, He's taking a rib from Adam and creating woman. What do you make of that inconsistency?

AVIVAH: It's very striking that the word God uses when He looks at Adam is lo tov—He says it's "not good." He takes

creauit d̄s celum ⁊ t̄rram; Terra aūt erat manis
et uacua; ⁊tenebre erant sup facie̅ abyssi ⁊ sp̄s d̄i
ferebatur sup aquas; dixq̄; d̄s; Fiat lux; Et facta e̅
lux; Et uidit deus luce̅ q̄d ee̅t bona ⁊ diuisit luce̅
a tenebris; apellauitq̄; luce̅ diem ⁊ tenebras nocte̅;
Factumq̄; e̅. uespe ⁊ mane; dies unus;   II

Dixit quoq̄; d̄s; Fiat firmam̅tum in medio
aquaru̅; et diuidat aquas ab aquis; Et
fecit d̄s firmamentu̅; diuisitq̄; aquas que erant sub
firmam̅to ab his que erant sup firmam̅tum; Et
factum e̅. ita; Uocauitq̄; d̄s firmam̅tu̅ celu̅; et fac
tum e̅. uespere ⁊ mane dies secundus;   III.

Dixit uero deus; Congregent̄ aque que sub
celo sunt in locu̅ unu̅; et appareat arida;
Factumq̄; e̅. ita; Et uocauit d̄s aridam
t̄rram; congregationesq̄; aquaru̅ appellauit
maria; Et uidit d̄s q̄d ee̅t bonum; et ait; Germi
net t̄ra herbam uirente̅ et faciente̅ se̅m ⁊ lignum
pomiferu̅ faciens fructum iuxta genus suu̅; cui̅
se̅m in semet ipso sit sup t̄ram; Et factu̅ est ita; Et
ptulit t̄ra herbam uirente̅ ⁊ afferente̅ se̅m iuxta
genus suu̅; lignumq̄; faciens fructu̅; et habens unu̅
q̄dq̄; seme̅tem sed̅m specie̅ suam; Et uidit d̄s quod
ee̅t bonu̅; factu̅q̄; est uespe et mane dies t̄tius; IIII

Dix aūt d̄s; Fiant luminaria in firma
mento celi; ut diuidant die̅ ac noctem;
et sint in signa ⁊ tempora ⁊ dies ⁊ annos
⁊ luceant in firmam̅to celi; et illuminent t̄ram;
Et factum e̅. ita; fecitq̄; d̄s duo magna luminaria;
luminare mai̅ ut p̄ ee̅t diei ⁊ luminare min̅ ut p̄
ee̅t nocti; ⁊ stellas; et posuit eas d̄s in firmam̅to
celi ut lucerent sup t̄ram ⁊ p̄ ee̅t diei ac nocti; et
diuiderent luce̅ ac tenebras; Et uidit d̄s q̄d ee̅t
bonu̅; ⁊ factu̅ est uespe ⁊ mane dies quart̄; v

Dixit etiam d̄s; Producant aque reptile
anime uiuentis ⁊ uolatile sup t̄ram; sub
firmam̅to celi; Et creauitq̄; d̄s cete grandia;
⁊ omem anima̅ uiuente̅ atq̄; motabile̅; qua̅ pduxe
rant aque in species suas; ⁊ ome uolatile sed̅m gen̅
suum; Et uidit d̄s q̄d ee̅t bonum; benedixitq̄; eis di
cens; Crescite ⁊ multiplicamini ⁊ replete aquas
maris; a uesq̄; multiplicent̄ sup t̄ram; Et factum
est uespe et mane; dies quintus;   VI.

The Creation of the World, Souvigny Bible, France, late 12th c.

the word "good," which has been the stamp on every aspect of creation until now, and He says, "It is not good that man should be alone." Then, as a kind of secondary rethinking of the situation, God allows man to discover for himself how "not good" it is. Notice that God doesn't create woman until man has started naming the animals. According to Jewish tradition, Adam notices that the animals come two by two, so he begins to ask himself questions about his own life in the world. According to some traditions, he notices that he has "animal potential" in himself. All the symbolic characteristics of all the animals are within himself. So he too looks for a partner. He looks for someone who isn't simply a sexual partner, but someone who can share the totality of his being. And he notices, through his senses, that there is something amiss about the way he's been created. Only when he fails to find any counterpart in the world does God put him to sleep. Before God can create woman, man must realize the divine dissatisfaction in his own experience. God says it's not good for the man to be alone, but doesn't act until the man becomes aware of a dissatisfaction in himself.

BURT: There are really two levels here: God's dissatisfaction—saying it's not good that man be alone—and then Adam's dissatisfaction. The rabbis of old suggested that one of the reasons God does not like man being alone is this problem of monotheism. God worries that if man is all alone, he will begin to think, "Ah, just as God is all alone in the universe, I'm all alone in the universe." And that will give rise to idola-try. God gives man a partner so that everything but God has partners. Only God is uniquely alone. There is no other equal to God.

WALTER: But the history of interpretation enacted the very thing the rabbis were afraid of—male authority, male domination. The image of humanness we get in this story is very male and very alone.

HUGH: Well, it doesn't seem to me that creation really begins until Eve. Otherwise, Adam would have said, "This isn't enough. I need something more." In my mind, he has not developed full consciousness. He's not aware of duality, of opposites.

AVIVAH: But where the story says he didn't find a helpmate, isn't that a way of describing man's sense of quest? His awareness of what is not there? This is the beginning of consciousness, this awareness of being incomplete, unfilled—of needing the other.

BILL: Hold on. You're all passing over that first account of creation, where it appears that God creates man and woman simultaneously—

ROBERTA: —"and in His image," which is expressed in the plurality of language that at least hints at communion within God. "Let us make man in our image." James Weldon Johnson wrote a wonderful poem about creation in which God says, "I'm lonely. I'll make me a man." I found myself asking, "Was God lonely? Is God lonely? Does God need humans? Is the creation of man and woman a response to some need inside of God?'' After wrestling with the text over a number of years, my own answer is ''no.'' I believe the creation is an outflowing of the fullness of God. It's a gift, and a demonstration of the richness and wonder of God. He creates and lets that creation have a separate identity. He doesn't grasp it and hold it and control it in some narrow, constricting way. The relationship between man and woman expresses something of the community within God and the relationship that exists eternally with God.

HUGH: But he doesn't give them freedom. They have to take it.

RENITA: And it's not absolute freedom. It's—

ROBERTA: It's not absolute freedom. The basic mandate is to be fruitful, to have a responsible stewardship over the earth. God doesn't keep all those tasks to Himself. Maybe it's because I'm a college president and into delegation a lot that I notice this. You know, the temptation always with power is to act unilaterally. Sometimes I think we look at God and ask, ''Why isn't God doing this?'' But God delegates, so to speak. He allows man and woman to share. They're co-creators, with a very special opportunity and responsibility.

BILL: What about the interpretation of the second story of creation—where Eve is created from Adam's rib—as suggesting that Eve is subordinate? Is the story implic-itly claiming that Adam is a little more divine than Eve?

ROBERTA: No, I don't think that's what the story says. As a woman, I see these stories getting at some basic questions of my identity: ''Who am I? What am I for?'' This is not just a question of interpretation, it's a question of my living. So I think we read the text wrongly when we read these accounts separately. We have to read the first version and the second version together—the one doesn't contradict the other.

HUGH: Yes, I think of Adam as more of an angel than a man, until Eve brings him to consciousness. I certainly don't see this story of creation as putting woman in any kind of subordinate role. Once we start seeing Eve as a devolution from the divine, then we're in trouble and get it wrong from there on.

ROBERTA: Yes, and you can see Eve's creation exactly the other way, as climax rather than secondary.

WALTER: But, Hugh, you can't really change the text to turn Adam into an angel.

HUGH: Well, Eve is the pinnacle, in one sense. The story starts with light and then goes to higher and higher levels of completion, all the way up to Adam—and there's still Eve to come. The crowning act of creation, one could say. When Adam and Eve are together, they form an integrated whole. I think of Adam on his own as an angel because he feels less corporeal and not fully formed as a human being.

RENITA: I don't think the story says, or even hints at, or is interested in the question of whether Adam is more divine than Eve. What has happened through our interpretation is that, over the centuries, we have developed a theology based upon chronology. That Adam was created first, we think, means he is better, the preferred one. But if we want to follow that chronology all the way through, we should notice that the last child is almost always the preferred one—Jacob, for example, or David. Within that theological tradition, perhaps Eve was the preferred one. If we're going to base our theology on chronology, let's look at the entire Hebrew Bible and not just at this one story.

BILL: In the rest of the Hebrew Bible, there are not many echoes of the Adam and Eve relationship.

ROBERTA: But the New Testament letters of Paul suggest a chain of command that was set up at creation and meant to be that way for everybody. So I think it's very important to go back and wrestle with the creation stories—because they have enormous practical consequences in everyday life.

BILL: Well, let's wrestle with them. I agree with Walter. We have two stories here, and I don't think you can make them one story. Read them in the original—they sound like two accounts, pointing to two different things. Adam and Eve are created simultaneously in the first, and in the second, Eve comes from Adam's rib.

BURT: It's even a little more complicated than that. In one story, humanity is created at one fell swoop, which implies man and woman are equal. And it also suggests something about how we read God—that God can't simply be seen as He. If humanity reflects God, we have to understand that God has both male and female aspects in some miraculous way. But the second story is even more intriguing because not only is woman created from man's rib, but man is created out of dirt. God picks up something and makes it stand and blows life into it. Even then, it's not quite everything that God needs. Both man and woman are much more subordinate to God in that second story. They have a much more complicated relationship with God, as well as with each other.

JOHN: It's further complicated by the trial-and-error approach in these stories and in the stories that follow. God tries something in creating Adam. But it's not quite right, so He tries something else. And later on, He decides it's not good at all, and He's going to destroy the whole thing and start over again. God is experimenting. Some things work. Others don't.

BILL: So what do you make of that?

JOHN: This is a God the narrators thought was very much like us. In the first creation story, God is remote in some sense—transcendent. God is not one of us or intimate with us. But then in the next story, God starts getting related to us in various ways. The trial-and-error method shows that God works at things the way we work at things.

ROBERTA: I think you can make too much of playing one story against the other—unless you're assuming that the person who wove these stories together didn't have any sense of their fundamental unity. The first account gives you not so much trial and error as a summary. When I cook a dinner, at the end I say, "Let's eat. Dinner is served." But I could do it differently. I could tell everyone that I will first show them my recipe and the pots and pans and all the stages of preparing that meal. Now the first story in Genesis gives you the summary: "God created, and it was very good." The second story takes you inside the process, and you get more of the tension, the dynamic, the interaction. The second story is not about man and woman in the image of God, it's about man and woman in relation to each other.

BILL: And what is that second story telling us about the relationship between men and women?

RENITA: That they are connected. The second account is not so much interested in the issue of equality as it is in the fact that they find themselves in one another. At last, she is "bone of my bone, and flesh of my flesh." And he realizes something was missing.

BILL: When you hear that phrase—"bone of my bone, and flesh of my flesh"—what do you think?

RENITA: She is like me. She is like me.

ROBERTA: Finally!

BILL: It is a love poem.

RENITA: Oh, yes, I believe this is the first love song a man ever sang to a woman.

"This is the first love song a man ever sang to a woman."

WALTER: That's a wonderful idea. I must tell you, though, it makes me nervous to say that the editor had some overarching intentionality in putting these stories together. I feel the cutting edge of systematic theology coming in, trying to make all of it fit together. Storytelling communities tend to cluster stories. We say, "Well, you know, whenever we tell this story, we also tell that story." So they begin to seem natural together. But that does not imply any great intentionality about how these stories fit together, except that we always tell both of them together.

HUGH: But they're separate, you're saying?

WALTER: I would say so. I want to resist the kind of reductionism that takes place either in critical studies or in Christian systematic theology to say that these stories are indeed prized, but they are enormously illusive. I don't want to imagine too much that the storyteller had something quite specific in mind by putting them back-to-back. The reading community in every generation, including us, is given a great deal of freedom about the connection we will imagine between the two. But the back-to-backness of the stories doesn't seem intrinsic to the connection.

AVIVAH: I accept that point. The reader or listener has a certain freedom in responding to the story. But at the same time, as soon as you imagine an author, the question of intentionality has to be given a little more serious consideration.

BILL: Okay, granted. So why do you think the author or editor included both stories?

AVIVAH: Something dialectical, I think. Rabbi Soloveichik wrote an important book, *The Lonely Man of Faith*, in which he

Hieronymus Bosch, *Paradise* (left panel from *The Garden of Earthly Delights*), ca. 1510

says the first story expresses the majesty of God, with man dominating earth as a being of majesty and control. But the second story gives us a different human being, one who lives in the world of the senses, where there are weaknesses and deficiencies—and who also reflects God. There's no defeating of one story by another.

WALTER: I'm uneasy about reading across from the first story to the second one. It's much better to celebrate the tension between the stories than to turn them into a sequence wherein the second overcomes some problems for the first one.

BILL: What is the tension?

WALTER: The tension is what we're talking about. In the first account, male and female are created equals; but in the second, there is some hint of Eve's subordination. How to hold these two stories together is a problem of interpretation. With our current awareness of patriarchal ideology, we are drawn to the first story, where male and female are created equal. Day-to-day living in the first story has to do with helping the earth produce and getting food and being sure there's a next generation and celebrating the Sabbath, which comes at the culmination of the story.

HUGH: But isn't the first story the abstract one and the second one the specific?

WALTER: I don't think it's abstract, I think it's symmetrical and grand. I don't see what makes it abstract at all.

HUGH: The first story is grand, but somehow very general to me. When Eve arrives, mankind seems to have a genuine independent will and reflects that will back to God. As a couple, Adam and Eve are living in the world I know. The day-to-day living of life is what we have to be concerned with, how people connect these stories to the real world.

WALTER: But look at the implications for day-to-day living in the first story. Look at the emphasis on producing food and making sure there's a next generation—and celebrating the Sabbath, which comes at the culmination of the first story of creation. You have to do that every week, so you don't forget the kind of world this is. That's a very practical implication of a story you claim to be abstract.

BILL: The creation story says that on the seventh day, God rested, and later we are told to keep the Sabbath. What do you make of the fact that this injunction about the Sabbath is so little honored in the modern world?

WALTER: The Sabbath statement belongs to the whole narrative of creation. When our lives are not lived in that narrative, but are lived in a narrative of production and consumption, then the Sabbath becomes an add-on that has no particular meaning. I like very much the statement of M. Tsevat, who says that the Sabbath is the day in which he hands his life back to God every week to remember that it is not his own. That acknowledgment that we belong to a generous God changes how we live the other six days of our lives. It's necessary to stop producing and to acknowledge that our lives depend on receiving as well as asserting.

BURT: The Sabbath is where you recapture Eden. Heschel says that when God creates the Sabbath, it's not a place, it's a structure, "a cathedral in time." We take a piece of time and set it apart. And in so honoring that moment, we have the Garden of Eden once again. We cease work at that moment and imitate the Creator in recognizing, yes, there is a moment of pure bliss. Of joy. Of receiving, rather than just constantly working and producing.

RENITA: In its most noble moments, religion reminds us that there are festive moments that are different. There's ordinary time, and then there's sacred time. But we've lost our sense of the holiness and sacredness of time.

WALTER: Not entirely. In the Christian tradition, the sacraments are at least a momentary approximation of being in Eden.

ROBERTA: The word the New Testament picks up about the Sabbath is "rest," the cessation of frenzy or activity. You have the words of Jesus that the Sabbath is made for humans.

WALTER: And the creation of the Sabbath also shows that God is not anxious about the world. On the seventh day, He doesn't show up at the office. He lets it be. That shows some confidence on God's part that the world has coherence and vitality.

"The creation of the Sabbath shows that God is not anxious about the world."

The creation of the Sabbath is an antidote to the enormous anxiety we have about the fragility of the world.

JOHN: But both stories show how precarious the world is. The first story begins with a stormy sea, a place in which ancient Israelites felt least at home. The second story begins with a picture of a desert, no land under cultivation, no water, no human beings to cultivate the land. God then makes for us a habitable world. Both stories concern God's gift of food to human beings. That may seem ordinary to us, but not for the ancient world, where producing food and having enough for the long, dry season is so problematic.

ROBERTA: Yes, the gifts of God are glorious. Creation provides for the needs of the human family—but creation is not God. There is distance as well as intimacy between Creator and creation.

HUGH: I just cannot accept that creation is not God. How can this possibly be? Because if God has made something that's supposed to have continued, and God is happy to let it continue, you have to as-

Andrea Pisano, *Creation of Eve*, Campanile, Florence, ca. 1336

sume it has this divine principle as its animating energy—the life force is God's.

ROBERTA: Creation did not make itself.

HUGH: No, but we are working from the divine principle that is alive in everything. That's the only way creation can happen.

BILL: Hugh, as an artist, what goes through your mind when you hear the words "the Lord God formed man of the dust of the ground and breathed into his nostrils the breath of life. And man became a living soul"?

HUGH: I actually try in my own work to do something like that. Of course, breathing life into somebody is God's ability, not mine. But once, when someone I know got very sick, I felt the desperate urge to imagine a way to blow life into him. The idea of creating something that would resuscitate somebody was a direct motivation in a dance production I collaborated on called *Drawn Breath*. The concept for the dance was centered on the idea of resuscitation. Breath in art is the reminder of the soul, the *anima mundi*. It completely changed my life as a painter to be connected with that level of mortality and to confront it directly—not to go into some ideal or fantasy, but to do something specific about life and death. I think I actually started to become an artist at that point. On the other hand, when I created my own daughter, I didn't feel I had much to do with it. I felt separated from the process and slightly outraged that this process had gone on without me. I was just an instrument—it came through me, and it happened. I felt very small. I still find it difficult to deal with that.

BURT: Fathering a child didn't give you the sense of creation you got from creating a work of art?

HUGH: I wasn't aware of it so much. In creating *Drawn Breath*, I felt that I needed to create something that was up to the task of saving my friend. Of course, there is a powerful irony here when one thinks of art and healing. Art has its own immortality, but it does not guarantee the life of the flesh. But in making art, the artist literally gives his body to the world. This is what embodiment means. Our mortality is our biggest inspiration, and making art is an act of remembering. This remembrance helps to lift the fear of living and dying, of isolation, of being a prisoner of the skin. In this particular case, I wanted to make a painting that was larger than me. And I wasn't up to the job.

ROBERTA: You said you felt you didn't have much to do with the creation process that resulted in the birth of your daughter. But surely, this is one of the differences for women—giving birth. It would be very difficult for me, as a mother of three, thinking of the childbirth experience, to feel anything but totally involved in that creative process.

HUGH: For a man there's a helplessness when it comes to the specifics of organic life.

BURT: Yes, I was frustrated as a father, knowing I had so little to do with the birth of my two children. How this relates to the story is perhaps the hint we get from Genesis that God had to let go once He got the process started, like a father does. The rabbis in one marvelous text from the fifth or sixth century imagine that in fact God is talking to Adam and Eve, and God is saying, "Okay, you two, I will create all of this on my own. But from this point onward, we *three* have to be involved in the process." There has to be a woman. There has to be a man. And there has to be a divine spark. All three must be present for there to be any subsequent creation of humanity. So when God says in that enigmatic passage, "Let us create humanity in our image," it means man, woman, God. When you were talking about fathering, Hugh, you made me think about how God must have felt having created Adam and Eve—a kind of wistful "Oh, well, there they are, and they seem so independent. What did I really have to do with it?" That's both good and frustrating to God.

> *"There has to be a woman. There has to be a man. And there has to be a divine spark."*

AVIVAH: Another fascinating rabbinic image that always moves me is the idea that of all the creatures, only man was not created by the word of God, but rather by the hands of God. I find that a very powerful observation.

HUGH: The painter Cézanne says you don't create with your eyes, you create with your hands.

AVIVAH: With your hands, yes. The rabbis say that only man was created as a potter works in clay. If you look at the famous chapter in Jeremiah about the potter and how he works, you might at first imagine that the potter has total control. "I can do what I like because I am the artist—and if I don't like what I've made, I can simply discard it and try again. I make what I want." But if you look more closely at the text, you'll see that the object actually tells the creator what it's going to be. The object dictates to the creator on every level. In a sense, God says, "Can't I do that to you, House of Israel?" In other words, God is saying through this image, "I don't have total control. I respond to the movements under the hands. I respond to how you are to me." That's how it is with artists. Thomas Mann intended the very long novel *Joseph and His Brothers* to be a short story. That was the plan.

BILL: You've just drawn from this text two provocative images of God—God the poet, Who speaks, where the words of God create the image; and God the potter, working not with words, but with the hands.

ROBERTA: There's also God the lover. Because man is placed in a Garden, he is given everything that is needed. But now woman is needed. So God is the giver, the lover, the one who acts for human well-being to provide what we need in our essential natures.

BURT: But the lover par excellence is the one who works with both words and hands.

BILL: God the poet, God the potter, God the giver and lover. If this story were all we had, what would we learn about God from it?

RENITA: That's a good question because I wish creation had stopped there. Then we would not have had all these problems—who's first, who's last, who's subordinate, who has power—all the things that bedevil the human race. Those things only happen after the Fall, as Hugh said. The story we're talking about says, "And they were both naked and not ashamed." A beautiful, beautiful line.

WALTER: I agree with that, but creation didn't stop there, so we have to deal with what we've got.

BILL: Do you see yourself as made in the image of God?

AVIVAH: Exactly in that sense of "image." Even though I sense myself as having tremendous reality, I also sense there is a being of greater reality than myself whom I've very much related to. I have a sense of the Otherness of His face. What this means is that I've been given some-

thing to cultivate, something that is not a fact, but a project. Being in the image of God is a project in the French existentialist sense of "project," where being a human being is the *project of becoming* a human being. One starts off with a human being's idea of the ultimate reality of God, which provokes in one a sense of longing for a potential in oneself that is yet to be developed. If I am in His image, I am splendidly assured; but at the same time, as the great French Jewish philosopher Levinas put it, I am "called into question" by His face. I then respond to that challenge by creating the project of becoming fully human.

RENITA: But that is where our language trips us up continuously, because a man and a woman are both created in the image of God, and yet God is more than male or female. Our language in the text and our language in this circle and our language in this century is of the masculine God—who is *He*? And yet that first story insists that male and female were both created in the image of God. This says there is masculinity or maleness, femininity or femaleness, and that both derive from God. And no doubt God is even more than that. Even femaleness and maleness are shadows of the divine being, the divine presence.

AVIVAH: Man is made in the "image" of God. "Image"—*tselem* in Hebrew—is less than and not identical to the model. At the heart of that word is the word "shadow." When we say "shadowy," there is the sense that the human being is a shadow that God casts in the world. One of the primary functions of shadows is to say something about the reality of what is casting a shadow. Once you have a shadow, then you know that the object that's casting the shadow is substantial, is real. So if the human being is God's shadow, that says something about the reality of God as human beings experience God. We have a reduced reality within the limits of sensual experience that human beings know in their own finite awareness.

ROBERTA: Another thing I get from this story is that life is a gift. I didn't give it to myself. I'm responsible for it, but I receive it, and in receiving it, one of the emotions is gratitude. Several weeks ago, I had a heart attack. I lay in the hospital bed, listening to the doctors come and go, thinking of life and the end of life as we know it—all of those kinds of things. And I experienced a new sense of gratitude for the gift of life.

"Life is a gift. I didn't give it to myself."

BILL: Do you ever feel the contradiction—composed as we are of both the dust of the earth and the breath of God?

ROBERTA: That's the essence of what it means to be human. The dust is so real— the finiteness, the dependence, the fragility, the brokenness, the struggle. And yet there's this longing inside us, this hunger and yearning for joy and a sense of self-

transcendence. All of these other things, someone has said, are rumors of angels. We're not content simply to be dust returning to dust. Because we bear the image of God within us, we long for something more than dust.

HUGH: What about the gift of death? Do you see that as part of what you're thankful for?

ROBERTA: From my recent experience, I would echo the New Testament language which talks about the "sting of death." Sure, death is an enemy. It's a reality, but I don't "go gentle into that good night."

BURT: Roberta, you remind me of the rabbinic story that quotes a line from later in the Bible when Abraham says to God, "I am but dust and ashes." The rabbi suggests that human beings are precisely that, but to keep a balance in our lives, everyone should have two pieces of paper. On one piece of paper is written "I am but dust and ashes." When you need to be reminded of that, you can take it out and read it. But on the other piece of paper, for your low moments, is the reminder "*Bishvili Nivra haslam*"—"For my sake, the universe was created."

BILL: That seems to me both realistic and consistent with the tension in the story of creation itself. In the beginning, there is an affirmative, if not euphoric, description of God creating all this, looking around, and saying, "It is good." Then, a little later, there's an ominous change, when God says, "Now, wait a minute, this is all very good, but there's one tree here that if you eat of it, you will die.'' Suddenly there's a chill cast over the story. What do you make of that?

B URT: God is very much like a parent. At a certain point, parents realize that their job is just to let go. You've done what you can, your children are launched, and you've just got to sit on your hands and see what happens. So, on the one hand, God has confidence creating humanity; but on the other, God is a very nervous Creator. You send these creatures off, and you get a little nervous about what they're going to find out in the world. So God says to his

kids, ''If you're going to do that, you're not coming back.''

RENITA: We're talking about this image of a nervous God, Who sees that creation is good, but then decides later on that perhaps creation is not good, a God Who ''gods'' by trial and error. This sounds very reasonable—so where does the more prevailing notion of a sovereign, infallible God come from? We're making it sound as if God is very much like us.

WALTER: Both of these portrayals occur in the Bible. I imagine ideology and

Gateway to Paradise, tile, Ottoman Syria, 17th c.

interpretive necessity have caused us to lift up the infallible God, at our great cost.

BILL: I'm not really comfortable, Renita, thinking that God is more like me. I'm more comfortable with the notion that God is sovereign, that God is Other. If He's like me, He's deeply flawed.

HUGH: Yes, but is God in control? What about that?

WALTER: I think, in some texts, yes, and, in others, no. All these different texts reflect different experiences we have had through time. In our preaching and teaching, we latch on to the text that resonates to the place in which we find ourselves. Or we reverse it and latch on to the text that counters our present experience.

BILL: When you read these texts, do you see God as remote and omnipotent? Or do you see God as nervous and questioning, unsure of what's going to happen to the creation?

WALTER: No, the categories in which God is understood in the Bible have to do with issues of fidelity and infidelity, so all these mechanistic categories of sovereignty and control are essentially alien. Fidelity and infidelity are issues that come up in a marriage. You count on fidelity, but if it's a real marriage, it's not a closed book. With God, everything is always open for freedom and risk and healing and forgiveness and homecoming. The relationship always has to be renewed and rearticulated be-

cause a gamut of potential infidelities is always available.

HUGH: What do you mean by "infidelity"—breaking your word?

WALTER: Yes, it's clear that Israel acts in unfaithfulness—but there are many texts that the Church doesn't like in which God is also accused of infidelity.

ROBERTA: All this conversation about the nervousness of God makes *me* nervous. I don't believe Genesis 1 and 2 are about God's nervousness. I think they show that God is purposeful. The prohibition against eating the fruit of a particular tree is not an absolute, arbitrary, capricious rule, it's a description of the finiteness and the limited circumstance man is in. Man is not autonomous. There are limits—and that's good.

BILL: Would you concede that even if God is not nervous, when He gives Adam and Eve freedom of choice, He is not certain how they will choose?

ROBERTA: As a modified Calvinist, that language doesn't work for me.

BILL: That's an oxymoron—modified Calvinist.

ROBERTA: Oh, yes!

JOHN: As I read the story, without the larger story, God did not know how it was going to turn out. Now these are stories, these are images that Israel is struggling with to express the immense reality of God.

These authors can talk about the nervousness of God, or they can talk about the limitations of God, they can talk about God not knowing what is to happen.

BURT: Yes, because one of the things about relationship is that there are two parties. However powerful God is, there are still these very frail humans who are part of the relationship, and so, in some way, God relinquishes a certain amount of control to our frailty.

AVIVAH: And our frailty affects God. We are told that "God was sad in His heart." I think that's the most poignant expression in the whole Bible.

BILL: Where does that appear?

AVIVAH: Just before the Flood, it says God was "sad in His heart." That word—*Va-yitatsev*—is one that recurs. That's the word that's used to describe the parent-child relationship that Burt was talking about, with its built-in frustration. In the end, you can't control things.

ROBERTA: It's anguish.

AVIVAH: And that's the word that's used about the relationship with Adam, too.

HUGH: God's own creation gives God the gift of suffering.

BILL: Why couldn't God create a creation that doesn't suffer and save Himself that sadness "in His heart"?

HUGH: Because for it to be whole, it has to have the dynamic of total failure.

BILL: You can't have wholeness without the Holocaust? God's creation has to contain the seeds of genocide?

WALTER: Well, I think some other God could have. But you can't rewrite the Bible about this God. That's Who this God is shown and known and confessed to be. You can't really explain that. All you can do is acknowledge that that's Who we've got.

ROBERTA: But you can't talk about the Holocaust without talking about human freedom. The freedom is genuine. We have the freedom to make choices that have consequences in the real world—the freedom to do evil as well as good.

BURT: That's what it means to be created in God's image—it is to have that freedom. Let's not forget that the Bible itself says that it's God Who creates evil. God makes peace and also creates evil. Evil is a possibility for God. And God does some things in the Bible that are very distressing, by my standard of ethics—binding Isaac, wiping out whole villages, destroying the world. God can do horrific things. I won't judge them. Let's assume there's some justice in what God does. But in creating us in God's image, God has given us the privilege and responsibility of choice. I think it's that choice that makes God so nervous.

RENITA: But those of us who have suffered have a desperate need for a God Who, irrespective of freedom, will step in. We

want to believe that at some point, somewhere, God will intercede on our behalf and
not just let evil play itself out.

HUGH: Has that happened to you?

RENITA: Again and again, yes. I
glimpse the hand of God. Most of the time
it's the back side of God, as Moses talked
about. But I do glimpse the presence of God
intervening on my behalf.

AVIVAH: That's your perception.

RENITA: Oh, absolutely. But what
makes a miracle a miracle is not that you
could not explain how it happened, but
that it happened when it did. It's a miracle
because of its timing—I needed it at that
moment. If you're a student, and you're
trying to get money for school, it doesn't
matter that the check was in the mail, but
that it came the moment the registrar said,
"You're booted out of here." That's the
miracle, even if you can explain that the
money got lost through the U.S. Postal Service. That's not the issue. The issue is that
it came at the time when you were about
to die.

BURT: I agree. As Jews, we are reminded
again and again that in every generation,
we're supposed to see ourselves as though
we have been brought out of Egypt. That's

Creation, Paradise, and Temptation of Eve, Seder
towel, Dreyfus Family, Alsace, 1829

the classic case of God intervening in history. And you're right—sometimes in the most petty circumstances, like walking down the street, something happens in my life, and I'm reminded in the moment that in a very tiny way, I am reliving that redemption. I know that God acts in the world—and that creates a host of other theological questions. "Why me and not the poor person on the street?" What is there, though, is the reality of that relationship with God in the moment.

BILL: Is this what you meant a minute ago, Walter, when you said, "This is the only God we've got"? Are you saying that we just have to make do with what we know, even though we don't know a whole lot?

WALTER: If we're going to live inside the narrative of the Bible, rather than some other narrative, that seems to be what we're either blessed with or stuck with. Yes.

RENITA: And that is a narrative about suffering. Suffering is not something outside us. These are stories of a people trying to explain suffering—to explain not goodness, but evil.

BILL: Is that why you choose to stay within this narrative, even though there are other choices for you?

RENITA: Oh, yes.

BILL: And you do, too?

WALTER: Yes, I certainly do. But I wouldn't say this is a conscious choice—I'm so compelled inside of this story that I couldn't imagine or think myself outside of it. I belong to the world created by this narrative. Critics talk about the world that is generated by the narrative. I have two adult sons who belong to a generation that seems to be tempted to live in the world that is generated by TV consumerism. That is another made-up world.

BILL: Your imagination has been shaped by these biblical stories—but your sons are being shaped by other stories and images from popular culture.

WALTER: Yes, and I believe that the true situation of most of us in the U.S. culture is that we are pulled apart by not wanting to choose between these two narrative worlds because there's so much good stuff in the consumerist world that we don't want to give up. But—and this is rather apocalyptic—I believe the time is coming when the choice between those narrative worlds can be put off no longer.

BURT: Yes—but, Walter, that hasn't changed for millennia.

"If a man deserves it, then he has a wife who is against him in the right ways."

WALTER: I mean only to be describing our situation. I'm not arguing that it's unique or unprecedented.

ROBERTA: That gets back to who we are as humans. Are we primarily economic beings? Are we consumers who define ourselves in terms of getting and spending—or, as the story tells us, are we moral beings? Do we have the capacity and obligation to make the kind of choices that shape the world we're part of?

HUGH: People are not choosing for themselves, they're just being spoon-fed with information. They lose their genius and originality, becoming flat, two-dimensional beings.

BILL: Let me raise another point. Some people interpret this text to suggest that the normal social order in this world of Genesis is a man and woman being fruitful and multiplying.

AVIVAH: Yes—but this is not necessarily a primary, natural idea because to be married is a very complicated business. It's not just relating to my partner, but relating to an adversary as well. The word that's used for the helpmate is "the opposite." If a man deserves it, then he has a wife who is against him in the right ways. If he doesn't deserve it, he has a wife who is always with him in the wrong ways. In Jewish tradition, we refer to being made in the image of God when a couple gets married, not when a baby is born. We celebrate the maturity of a man and woman who have made certain choices and reached a point when they can begin to create their lives and create new human beings. That's what it means to be in the image of God—not the primary natural condition.

> *"Every family in Genesis is a fractured family."*

RENITA: If that is the ideal social norm, and we live in a culture where we make choices, or choices are foisted upon us, what about the woman who cannot have a child? What does it mean, to say she doesn't fit the ideal social norm?

BILL: And what about homosexuals? This leaves them out, too.

BURT: Listen, this is but one story in a very large Bible. It's true that as God creates humanity here, male and female, that's one model. Later on, we get another model, for instance, of Jacob with four wives. We get a commandment that if things don't work well in a couple, you should be divorced. We get stories of all kinds of relationships—childless women, single parents, and so forth. All the models we can find in our current society are there in the Bible—and then some.

JOHN: What do you make of the fact

Angels Bow Before Adam and Eve in Paradise, Falnama (Book of Divination), Iran, ca. 1550

that every family in Genesis is a fractured family—what we would call a "dysfunctional" family? The creation story is almost one of bliss in this relationship—but all the other stories have a dark side.

AVIVAH: It's very painful. But when you say "bliss," I think you're using exactly the wrong word. Bliss is perhaps a theoretical construct of the Garden of Eden, but as soon as you emerge into the real world—

BURT: "Bliss," as in "Ignorance is bliss"—

AVIVAH: Unconsciousness. Unconsciousness is bliss. But then you enter the real world. There's that terrible line in Kafka that always sticks in my mind—"We read stories that wound and stab us. The purpose of a story is to be an axe that breaks up the ice within us." If the Bible were a series of happy stories, what would we read it for? We read stories that remind us of our own moments of fracture, that constantly rub the wound. If we have been lulled into any kind of equanimity, the Bible comes and breaks up that equanimity. It says, "Yes, but remember that things don't go the way you would perhaps like them to go."

WALTER: The other piece of the story line is that the families in Genesis continue to carry the blessing. And I take it that the blessing means something like the capacity to create a future. The amazing thing is that these fractured, dysfunctional families are adequate vehicles for that. This madness about family values in our current political ideology says that you've got to get the family perfectly straightened out morally before it can do anything. Genesis isn't interested in that at all. Just get on with it, in the shape in which you find yourself, and look after what has been entrusted to you.

BILL: Is there moral content in this story we just read? Is there a moral order in this world, as we see it in Genesis?

WALTER: Yes, I think there is, but I don't think that the family stories in the second part of Genesis pay much attention to that, or are very upset about it.

HUGH: For me, the crux of creativity that's going on as a blessing is really crucial to understanding this story and the question: How does one carry on that covenant?

"My father saw my being an artist as about the most dangerous thing I could do."

I know from my own experience that it happens on a metaphysical and a physical level. You literally have to turn your back on God to make your own choices.

BILL: How's that?

HUGH: It happens that sometimes you literally have to turn your back on your own parents. For me to be able to be an artist, I had to get into a physical confrontation with my father. It was forbidden to be an artist. My father saw my being an artist as about the most dangerous thing I could do, and it was something he didn't know how to help me in, so he felt very fearful. The moment when I got "born," you might say, was when I turned around to my father and said, "Shove it, I'm not going to do what you want me to do." The two of us were grappling, rolling in the dirt, kicking and screaming. Finally he got cut all the way down the side of his face, and when he looked and saw blood, he stood up and laughed. And he said, "You're all right." From then on, he never gave me any trouble. He was happy that I had made the physical separation and that his responsibility for me was over. It was like receiving my birthright.

WALTER: Yahweh says, "My people have prevailed over me."

BILL: You exercised your freedom that came with being his son. Do you read something akin to this in the image of God creating Adam and Eve and then saying to them, "You can eat of this Tree of Knowledge, but you will die"?

HUGH: Well, what are they there for?

BILL: To show you how to resist temptation. To build character.

HUGH: No, because He is fearful of the next level of evolution to which His whole work is going. Even God cannot predict his own creation. Otherwise, it wouldn't be creation. Creation evolves. If He could just completely predict the entire thing, what's the point?

BURT: God creates humanity in God's image, and yet when God says not to eat of the fruit, God also says, almost in an aside, "Because if they eat of the fruit, they'll be too much like me." Well, you can't have it both ways. Either we're going to be in God's image, or we're not going to be in God's image. I think this is the ambiguity inherent in God as a parent—God wants us to be independent, yet God is fearful of the consequences of this independence, much as we ourselves are for our own children.

AVIVAH: That reminds me of Levinas's wonderful phrase—"the temptation of temptation"—the problem of Western man, the illusion that the experience of being tempted is what life's all about.

BILL: We'll come to temptation in more detail in our next chapter. For the moment, let's stay with creation. What is the image of paradise that emerges in this story? At least on the surface, there's plenty of food, no one toils or sweats, and there's no violence because they're vegetarians eating the fruits and vegetables in the Garden and not the meat of slaughtered animals.

ROBERTA: But they do work. They are placed in the Garden to work it.

BURT: Roberta is right—they do work.

God sets them in the Garden to work it and preserve it.

ROBERTA: It's only on the other side of Eden that work is a curse, with thorns and thistles. But the work itself is a gift. It's a calling. We live in a culture that says not to work is the big ideal. Retire early. Have a vacation. Figure out energetically how not to work. Here in the Garden we see that work is part of what it means to be human. Work is the co-creation of beauty and order and fruitfulness.

HUGH: But we didn't learn that in Eden—we learned it here.

AVIVAH: In the next verse, God says, "You can eat." Rabbis say that the story teaches that even in Eden, if you don't work, you can't taste the food.

RENITA: Is the objective of the believer to return to the other side of Eden? Are we supposed to aspire to Eden as the ideal? Or are we forever on this side of Eden?

ROBERTA: Eden is closed and guarded. There is no way back. In the Book of Revelation, we are told we can look forward to a new heaven and a new earth. A new paradise is there, so there's a forward movement in the Christian journey. But there are elements in the first two stories that tell us something important about who we are. It tells us that work is not only a curse, but also a blessing, not only something that comes with sweat and toil, but also something that gives meaning and purpose to life. So hedonism isn't necessarily the best

philosophy that I want to adopt as a human on this side of Eden.

JOHN: But even in the Hebrew scriptures, there is a possibility that God can restore something like Eden. There are passages in the prophets where, once again, humans and animals have the harmony that they had before, where the earth is productive—

ROBERTA: —and the lion lies down with the lamb.

JOHN: So, in one sense, Eden is closed, but in another sense, Eden is a possibility, not by our work, but by what God does.

HUGH: Living here—this has to be where we find Eden.

ROBERTA: Are we homesick for Eden? Is that part of the human poignancy, that we are homesick for that impossibility? I do a lot of work with refugees in places of absolute poverty—Mozambique, Bosnia, Rwanda—places that just devastate you and tear you apart. In the midst of that, there's a constant temptation to say, "Look at the human animal. Look at the terrible things we do to each other. Look at the horrible ways that the value and dignity of human beings are degraded." The Genesis stories say to me that no, God meant us for more. What is in us is worth more. We are meant for love. We are meant for relationship. We are meant for community. And this brutality cannot be allowed to stand. Genesis points us that way, even if we can't expect to live in Eden.

RENITA: I believe there's a degree to which we can never return to Eden. The verse that says, "On the day that you shall eat it, you shall surely die"—that verse doesn't necessarily have to do with mortality. Even before God brings up the notion of death, it is looming somewhere in those first creation stories. That statement means that something in you, in humans, shall permanently die. At the point Adam and Eve ate the apple, something in humans died. I don't look at it in terms of obedience, but as having crossed a boundary. Maybe what died in us was our ability not to wound one another—our ability to resist evil permanently. If nothing else, we need community in order to keep us from being continuously evil. I need someone to check me, to tell me, "You've gone too far" or "That was wrong."

HUGH: Has anyone had any experience in their life of actually glimpsing Eden?

ROBERTA: It's really not Eden so much as the promise of covenant and reconciliation. There are those moments when there's been brokenness, and you see healing. When there is hatred, and forgiveness comes. When a country has been torn apart, and people have somehow found their way back together again. There are those moments.

BILL: They come for me, more often than not, in a moment of music. There are moments in Verdi's *Requiem* or in Mozart where you suddenly feel no brokenness whatsoever, no fragmentation. It's nothing

I can explain—just an experience of another reality.

HUGH: So it's out of a human act that you've been given access to something.

BILL: You mean creation? Yes, but where did the music of Mozart come from?

HUGH: Well, of course, straight from God.

BILL: In the original Garden, before the brokenness, God gave human beings a special position. What do you take to be the meaning of human beings having dominion over the earth?

RENITA: I take it as responsibility. I have a two-year-old child—there's the rumor that I have power over her. What I have most is responsibility for her.

BILL: Would you apply that to nature as well?

RENITA: Yes, absolutely. I was in South Carolina during Hurricane Felix, and it's clear we don't have dominion over nature—not all of nature, not all of the time. But we do have responsibility for nature.

BILL: How does the artist see this?

HUGH: When I think of subduing the earth, I take it that the first thing you subdue is your own earth. Yourself. You bring order to yourself. And you learn from nature. You learn from creation. I live in the country because I want to be taught by such things as the trees and the lake, by everything that grows around me. I want to evolve and know myself through a correspondence with the natural world.

BILL: Are you trying to recapture Eden?

HUGH: I don't think of it like that. I think of it as an occasional awareness of something that is veiled most of the time. One is trapped within a sense of one's own finiteness, yet all around us, somehow not in our conscious mind, is this fantastic creation.

BILL: And you're saying creation is here for you to share in as process?

HUGH: Yes. The Taoists say that when government becomes confusing, you have to look back to heaven. We're at a time now when we need to look back at the Garden. Our consciousness is constantly being polluted by advertising. We have to look back at how the earth truly works. As an artist, I'm trying to practice the principles of nature. I'm looking for a sense of "likeness" with the rest of nature. The tree, with its vertical stretching up into space, is a constant motif for me, a lesson in how to grow slowly and patiently. It is also a guide in how to play. Children respond to trees by climbing and swinging on them. They want to know them physically. In this play, a child acquires a body memory of the world. A constant bombardment of media information can cause us to lose our grip on the tangibility of things.

JOHN: One of the ways that people have

traditionally looked at creation is to think of creation as coming out of nothing. There's a sense in which that is true, although not in these stories. In both these stories, the creative act of God brings order out of chaos.

HUGH: As an artist, I have to create chaos before I can create order.

JOHN: I've never found you had to create it—chaos is all around.

HUGH: No, sometimes you go around in a constriction of rules and regulations and mental recipes. You have to shatter that and put it all back together again.

BILL: God reconfigures chaos through His breath. What do you make of the image of God breathing into this dust His own breath and human beings becoming a living soul? What do you make of the term "living soul"?

JOHN: The Hebrew means something like "an animate being." So the text simply means that where there was a sculpted model before, now this model is animated. It has life and therefore possibility. One of the clearest ways the ancient Hebrews spoke of animation was to refer to someone breathing. When people died, they said that God had taken the breath away.

AVIVAH: There's a specific rabbinic translation that identifies "animate being" as the power of speech. This "animate being" is different from the animals. All animals are animate, but when this being

Lawrence Stinson, *Garden of Eden*, American, ca. 1975

becomes animate, it's capable of communication, of language, of disagreement, of relationship.

WALTER: That's very interesting when you think about the incredible zones of repression in our society and how they so often have to do with silencing people. And the kind of rules that you're talking about, Hugh, function primarily in society to silence people.

ROBERTA: This also speaks to the dualism that we tend to fall into, to our own damage and destruction. It's not that human beings are souls that have bodies. The Genesis story tells us that human beings are embodied persons, so there is no dichotomy between body and soul. Those dichotomies or polarizations, between male and female, body and soul, and so forth, are often used in destructive, unhelpful ways.

BILL: You said earlier that both male and female are made in the image of God.

ROBERTA: It's there in the text.

BILL: This means that God would be both male and female. Does it follow, then, that we too contain both male and female?

ROBERTA: I don't think the text conveys that. It stresses that we embody our own distinctive sexuality and are male or female in relation to each other. Perhaps there's some sense that both are one in Adam, in the pre-creation of woman and language. But I don't see that particular concept coming out of the text.

BURT: There is actually a rabbinic reading that is very much in favor of this androgyny. When the rabbis seek to harmonize the two stories of creation, they tell them as though they are one story. When they imagine Eve being separated from Adam, it's not so much from a rib—the Hebrew word can also be read as "side," like the side of a barn or a tabernacle. They imagine the original human being as two-personed. God sawed it in half so that it would be both male and female. The original creature has equal portions of male and female.

AVIVAH: The extraordinary thing, though, is that in the rabbinic tradition, God is also given a female persona. The word *Shekhinah*, for instance, which is a term for God, is a female term.

BURT: It's a term that means "God's presence." When God is really immanent, when God is there with you, that's *Shekhinah*—She is right there with you.

BILL: The living breath?

BURT: Not quite the breath, but the presence, for instance, that's among us now.

AVIVAH: As in the tabernacle, which is the realization of God's presence. *Mishkan*—"tabernacle"—is from the same root as *Shekhinah*.

BILL: The presence of God is feminine?

AVIVAH: It's a feminine word.

BILL: The root meaning of the word *Yahweh*, the Hebrew term for God, is "to be," isn't it? God as Being.

AVIVAH: And *Shekhina* is a state of becoming, or a state of involvement.

BURT: It also means "dwelling."

AVIVAH: And it's feminine. The rabbis are very self-conscious about God having many names. They say, "This is the male persona of God" and "This is the female persona of God."

RENITA: These are delicacies of language that get lost in our English translations. Not only is there the question of how our being is made in the image of God, but also how we image God. Is it possible to imagine God as neither male nor female? If we agree that God, of course, is not male, and God, of course, is not female, why do we continue to use this language?

BURT: We have a long way to go to imagine God at any moment. God is wholly Other. How do we begin to imagine the ineffable? First of all, we are bound to this "he-language." God is male. So the first step we have to take is to imagine God in female terms, also, so that we begin to complement the picture. Eventually we move beyond gender, so that God can really be Other. But that's a long journey and takes many steps. It also takes an enormous amount of imagination, one of the other great gifts that God has given us.

JOHN: And to take that step too soon into a God beyond distinctions would depersonalize God. The very act of speaking of God as male and female reminds us that God is a person like us.

BILL: What, then, do we take away from this story that has meaning for the way we live our lives today?

WALTER: I take away the warning that a great ideological threat in our society is autonomy—that we are self-starters, and that the goal of life is to become self-sufficient. But that goal ends either in destructive pride or destructive despair. It seems to me that these two stories articulate a powerful alternative to autonomy. They tell me that I am rooted in relationship, which gives me my identity. I cannot be human outside of relationship.

AVIVAH: I would see a conflict there, too—or perhaps a dialectic. When I think of what it means to dominate creation, I think of what Gaston Bachelard said about domination meaning the capacity to be on your own, to loom over and see everything, to come to your own notion of order, and not to be related, to be single and alone. At the same time, whenever God says "dominate," He also says shirtzu, to be fruitful and multiply—to "swarm." "Swarm" is a terrible word—used for insects. You can see the terror and destructiveness of that kind of domination on one hand. But, nevertheless, that's what God tells Adam's descendants—that they are to have dominion, and that dominion is part of their greatness. At the same time, they are of the swarming masses. Think of Yeats's poem when he talks about the mackerel-filled seas. That, to me, is a problem. It's not a simple thing at all.

JOHN: I'm struck by the constant repetition that what God creates is good. It's important to me because in the life we live, there's so much world-denying going on. Strands in Christian theology depict the world as evil. But the affirmation in the first chapter of Genesis thrills me with the idea that despite the chaos I see around me, somehow this world is good. That is not only a wonder, but also perhaps a project—that we, as co-creators, have some part in creating the good world that was God's intention.

BILL: Well, yes, but at the same time we have obeyed that imperative to be fruitful and multiply, and we are—to pick up on Avivah's term—"swarming" the earth, overrunning the Garden.

BURT: But when God tells us to be fruitful and multiply, God appends to that "have dominion," which I assume means to have some responsibility. Be fruitful and multiply within limitations. The urge to procreate is the most natural instinct we have, one that we share with all the beasts. And yet, at the same time, it's the first command in the Bible. This command takes the urge, which is animal, and nevertheless reminds us that we have a relationship with the Creator. We are creatures who are under obligation to God, and part of that obligation is the way we behave with the other creatures and with the earth.

RENITA: I agree with that, but there is a degree to which these stories can never answer all the questions we so desperately need them to answer. To me, that is the genius and beauty of them. They aren't doctrinal proclamations, but they are like the answer of a parent to a child who asks, "How did evil come into the world? Why do women hurt when they have children? Why is it so hard to make a living off the land? Why do people suffer?" I love the fact that the serpent doesn't say, "Here, eat." The serpent says, "Come here. Does God really say. . . ." It's as if the serpent is beckoning us to come a little closer and consider things. From the very beginning, there was God, humanity, and suffering.

AVIVAH: In the Jewish tradition, God says, "Where are you?" to get human beings to start telling stories—*le-hikaness immo be-davarim.*

BURT: I would translate your Hebrew a little differently—"to enter into a conversation." These are stories that force us to enter into a conversation with God.

ROBERTA: There's also disclosure in these stories. This is more than storytelling around the campfire. This is God's self-disclosing to the human race. It's, at one level, incomprehensible, a mystery. But there is also truth and knowledge in these stories. We are being allowed to glimpse something—as Moses said, the back side of God.

WALTER: And, in a sense, this isn't just a sequential narrative. It isn't as though Eden simply existed in the past. Eden is an alternative.

BILL: When I was a child in the Central Baptist Church of Marshall, Texas, I thought that faith was a state at which you arrived. But faith is an ongoing conversation between God and me—and among us. Reading from Judaism and other sources, I begin to see the story more whole than I do if I just read my own scripture. I must admit, I learn more from the conversation, from what other people say to me, than I do from any inner voice speaking in mysterious tones.

BURT: In some ways, that is really the grandeur of scripture. That is to say, we can read the Bible all by ourselves. But when we do that, we miss something. We certainly read the Bible within our own faith communities, and that locates us very, very powerfully in a history, a tradition of reading, of understanding the text.

But one of the things this conversation teaches us is that every faith community is also in relation to the others. I don't just read the text as a Jew. I read the text as a Jew who's aware of the fact there are Gentiles on either side of me who read it differently. And, in listening to them, I learn about scripture, and I learn about what it means to be Jewish as well. The conversation is a very complicated one. It mutually illuminates one religion to the other as we all read together.

RENITA: The other part I love about these stories is that when we read scripture, we're also in conversation with those ancient people who experienced God and left us something so that we might also be in conversation with Him. We're in conversation with God. We're in conversation with our neighbors. And we're in conversation with this ancient community who has so lovingly bequeathed to us these stories.

BILL: And when you listen to those ancient ancestors, who say you are made in the image of God, what are they telling you?

RENITA: They're telling me what my potential is—that there's always this potential to be more than what I'm willing to settle for. I need to know that sometimes because it's easy to forget. I need to know that I am made in the image of God. There are things I say now I couldn't say years ago. I hear myself talking about story, and I say, "Is this you, Renita? You grew up in a Pentecostal church in the southern part of Georgia." The hair on my neck rises because I've never really lost that little girl. In fact, she's the girl who brought me here, who brought me to this place.

ROBERTA: I see this process in many ways as a dance in three movements. First, I come to the text, and I ask questions of it: "What is it saying? Why does it repeat? How do these two stories play with each other?" Then, in the second movement, I discover—sometimes to my surprise, because maybe I didn't mean it to happen—the text questions me. The text causes me to self-reflect and rework and wrestle. That movement is from the head to the heart. Then, in the third movement, the text teaches me how to see the world differently. I begin to look at the world of those other faith traditions. I look at pain and suffering and poverty. In this whole moment of the dance, the text is reshaping my faith, my interaction with the world, and the way I live my life within it.

II

TEMPTATION

Leon R. Kass • Stephen Mitchell

Elaine H. Pagels • Naomi H. Rosenblatt

Jean-Pierre M. Ruiz

Marianne Meye Thompson

Robin Darling Young

My mother used to leave her freshly baked sugar cookies right in the middle of the table, warm and inviting but forbidden until supper was over. If she meant the temptation to be a test of discipline, to build character, my brother and I often flunked. I think of this when I hear the story of the Tree of Knowledge in the Garden of Eden. Why didn't God place the forbidden fruit on the very top branch, beyond the reach of innocence? Genesis confronts us with many tempting questions.

— Bill Moyers

Lucas Cranach, *Adam and Eve*, 1526

Y_HWH, *God, took the human and set him in the garden of Eden,*
to work it and to watch it.
Y_HWH, *God, commanded concerning the human, saying:*
From every (other) tree of the garden you may eat, yes, eat,
but from the Tree of the Knowing of Good and Evil—
you are not to eat from it,
for on the day that you eat from it, you must die, yes, die . . .

Now the two of them, the human and his wife, were nude, yet
 they were not ashamed.
Now the snake was more shrewd than all the living-things of the
 field that Y_HWH, *God, had made.*
It said to the woman:
Even though God said: You are not to eat from any of the
 trees in the garden . . . !
The woman said to the snake:
From the fruit of the (other) trees in the garden we may eat,
but from the fruit of the tree that is in the midst of the garden,
God has said:
You are not to eat from it and you are not to touch it,
lest you die.
The snake said to the woman:
Die, you will not die!
Rather, God knows
that on the day that you eat from it, your eyes will be opened
and you will become like gods, knowing good and evil.
The woman saw
that the tree was good for eating
and that it was a delight to the eyes,
and the tree was desirable to contemplate.
She took from its fruit and ate
and gave also to her husband beside her,
and he ate.
The eyes of the two of them were opened
and they knew then
that they were nude.
They sewed fig leaves together and made themselves loincloths.
Now they heard the sound of Y_HWH, *God, (who was) walking*
 about in the garden at the breezy-time of the day.

And the human and his wife hid themselves from the face of
YHWH, *God, amid the trees of the garden.*
YHWH, *God, called to the human and said to him:*
Where are you?
He said:
I heard the sound of you in the garden and I was afraid, because I
am nude,
and so I hid myself.
He said:
Who told you that you are nude?
From the tree about which I command you to eat,
have you eaten?
The human said:
The woman whom you gave to be beside me, she gave me from
*   the tree,*
and so I ate.
YHWH, *God, said to the woman:*
What is this that you have done?
The woman said:
The snake enticed me,
and so I ate.
YHWH, *God, said to the snake:*
Because you have done this,
damned be you from all the animals and from all the living-
*   things of the field;*
upon your belly shall you walk and dust shall you eat, all the days
*   of your life . . .*
To the woman he said:
I will multiply, multiply your pain (from) your pregnancy,
with pains shall you bear children.
Toward your husband will be your lust, yet he will rule over you,
To Adam he said:
Because you have hearkened to the voice of your wife
and have eaten from the tree about which I commanded you,
*   saying:*
You are not to eat from it!
Damned be the soil on your account,

with painstaking-labor shall you eat from it, all the days of your
    life . . .

By the sweat of your brow shall you eat bread,
until you return to the soil,
for from it you were taken.
For you are dust, and to dust shall you return.
The human called his wife's name: Havva/Life-giver!
For she became the mother of all the living.
Now Yhwh, *God, made Adam and his wife coats of skins and*
    clothed them.
Yhwh, *God, said:*
Here, the human has become like one of us, in knowing good
    and evil.
So now, lest he send forth his hand
and take also from the Tree of Life
and eat
and live throughout the ages . . . !
So Yhwh, *God, sent him away from the garden of Eden, to work*
    the soil from which he had been taken.

—excerpts from *The Five Books of Moses*
(*Schocken Bible*, Vol. I), Chapters 2 and 3

BILL: If this story of temptation and the Fall were our only source, what would we know about God?

STEPHEN: Nothing.

BILL: Nothing?

STEPHEN: The god of this story is an all-too-human character in a human story—not the God at the heart of the universe.

JEAN-PIERRE: I think this story tells us quite a lot about God. Up until the events in the story, we have a God Who creates Adam and Eve, but we have no notion of the dimensions of this God—how large this God is, and how complex. We learn that this God is affected by the decisions the creatures in the Garden make. This is not an unchanging God—in fact, the God at the end of the story is much more human than the one at the beginning.

NAOMI: I take the story to be about God's relationship to me, and mine to God. He created humans on the sixth day, at the very end of creation, after He had feathered the nest, like a good parent who fixes the nursery before bringing the baby home. Then, with immense love and generosity, He entrusts us with the greatest gift of all—free will to obey or disobey Him. That's what differentiates us from the giraffe, the lion, and the elephant.

STEPHEN: In this story, a larger sense of God would include God as Adam and as Eve and as the serpent and as the tree and as the whole Garden, not just as the character who walks in the Garden in the cool of the evening.

BILL: But what do you take away from the sound of leaves crunching as God walks through that Garden? This is not a remote Creator. You can hear His footsteps. He asks questions of the other inhabitants of the Garden. This is not the picture of an all-knowing God, but of something much more human.

STEPHEN: But when Adam and Eve eat the fruit, God's reaction toward his children is not what I would wish from any human parent. This is a jealous, bungling, punitive god, not the God we can love with all our heart and all our soul.

NAOMI: Again, this story is not so much intended for us to learn about the nature of God as for us to learn about ourselves. Each woman in this room is an Eve, and each man an Adam. I look at it from

the point of view: "What does the story teach about our lives today?" rather than "What does it tell us about God?" It offers us important insight into the human condition. Adam and Eve respond as so many of us do when confronted with our transgressions: They first deny, then point fingers and assign blame—anything but accept responsibility. This is the first recorded "cover-up" in human history.

BILL: Aren't you a little startled by the picture of a God Who has such changing moods, Who shames His children and then leans over them tenderly, like a mother, and then gets so angry at their disobedience that He closes the playground and sends them out into the streets?

JEAN-PIERRE: The first creation account tells us that human beings are created in the image of God. The second account doesn't tell us that. It shows instead the personality of God. And God seems to have a personality very much like our own. In the comical scene in which God is producing various creatures and bringing them to the man to see which one would be a fit partner, He is like a very indulgent parent who is doting on his child. "Let's see whether this is going to please him. No? Well, let's try again"—and again and again, until God gets it right.

ROBIN: I don't think God seems like a loving parent in this story. He's the Creator, and His motivations are not announced.

NAOMI: Why do we always tend to

bring God down to our human level in order to understand Him? The story of Adam, Eve, and the serpent is an allegory about growing up and leaving Eden— leaving home. It says that when we leave our childhood behind, we who are made in the image of God must learn about the connection between behavior and consequences, between pleasure and responsibility.

LEON: In this story, the human being comes to be Godlike, and only as a result of a transgression. So perhaps this is a story not of the Fall of human beings, but of their rise from animated dust of the ground to being somewhat Godlike.

ELAINE: We often read the story as though it were about the development of human moral insights, which it is, in a way. But, according to the story, that's not what God wants; instead, He prohibits this fruit. Adam and Eve are not supposed to find the knowledge of good and evil.

MARIANNE: Clearly, there is a kind of wisdom that belongs to God alone, and human beings are wrong to try to usurp it. There are boundaries beyond which human beings cannot step—not for some arbitrary reason, but because of the way God created them to be. You can decide the serpent is right, or you can say, "If God really is the Creator, then the serpent has to be wrong in some way, even if it's not obvious in the text."

ROBIN: I once asked a high school religion class what they made of this story.

One kid said, "He was trying to keep us in the dark." I think that's absolutely right.

BILL: Why would God want to keep us in the dark?

STEPHEN: Why would a parent want to keep her four-year-old always a child? There's something so beautiful and precious about early childhood, and part of a parent wants to make that last forever. That part grieves when a child grows up, reaches puberty, and becomes sexually aware. Emotionally, the story is meant to explain how it came about that we left the radiance of childhood, the clouds of glory, how it is that we are so close to God when we're born, and then somehow find ourselves living in a consciousness of separation and loss. But the second stage of awareness, of sexuality and shame, though it is the end of the story in Genesis, isn't the end of *our* story. All genuine spiritual practices are completed in another stage; their intention is to help people reenter the Garden, not only with their adult experience and awareness, but also with a regained innocence. That's what Jesus of Nazareth meant when he said, "You have to become like children to enter the kingdom of God." He knew from his own experience that it is possible for every one of us. The end of the complete story is not exile from the Garden, but reentering it, as if we were coming home.

ELAINE: What strikes me is that God warns that on the very day you eat of this fruit, "you shall surely die." But the serpent speaks more accurately, saying, "You will *not* die"—and, of course, they do not.

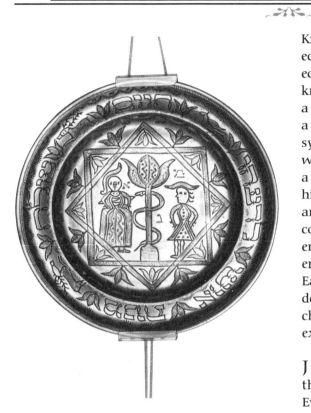

Temptation, Purim plate, 18th c.

S T E P H E N : And indeed, they don't die—but their eyes are opened. The knowledge they gain is a disaster. What they know is that they're naked, and what they feel is shame. If this is what makes them godlike, it's pathetic.

E L A I N E : Yes, there's a strange and powerful juxtaposition of knowledge and sexual awareness in this story.

B I L L : Someone has said that the serpent is the symbol of Eve's awakening sexuality.

N A O M I : I'm intrigued by that. The story, after all, revolves around the Tree of Knowledge. The Hebrew word for knowledge, *da'at*, refers both to general knowledge and to sexual knowledge. We also know that in ancient times, the snake was a symbol of fertility, and we can see it as a phallic symbol. The snake is an external symbol of the sexual stirrings within Eve, which are telling her, ''You know, Adam is a nice boy'' or ''It's okay to reach out to him, to be curious about him.'' What's amazing to me is that in a few spare, laconic lines, Adam and Eve's sexual awakening becomes a direct corollary to their emerging sense of moral accountability. Eating of the fruit of the Tree of Knowledge defines the universal human passage from childhood innocence into the world of adult experience.

J E A N - P I E R R E : But why did God put the tree in the Garden and forbid Adam and Eve to eat the fruit?

N A O M I : Because He wants to teach them that crossing boundaries and overstepping limits carries consequences. Eve tastes the fruit because she wants to be wise. Wanting to be wise is not wrong. It's important to note that ''sin'' is not once mentioned in the Adam and Eve story. Sin is mentioned for the first time when Cain murders Abel.

L E O N : I think there's a more radical reading of the text. God has made a human being who, potentially, has freedom. To live in freedom means to live on the basis of one's autonomous opinions about what's good and bad. To exercise free choice is implicitly to act on some notion of better or worse. That means you can't have a human being without having, at least somewhere in the vicinity, knowledge of good and bad. And yet a benevolent parent knows that the freedom to choose is not the same thing as choosing well. There's a profound warning here that freedom and autonomy, which are expressions of our latent humanity, are fraught with all kinds of dangers to our happiness and well-being. This is a story that says, "Look, the tree of the knowledge of good and bad is just around the corner." A certain kind of benevolence would add, "If you could only avoid this, you could have innocence, contentment, lack of self-division, and lack of corrosive self-consciousness, the kind of self-attention that produces shame."

B I L L : Are you suggesting that within the realm of freedom, Eve is acting in a perfectly reasonable way? She looks at the tree and says, "It's good food. It's a pleasure to eat. It's a delight to the eyes. And I could become wise by eating it." What's wrong with wanting nourishment, pleasure, beauty, and wisdom?

"What's wrong with wanting nourishment, pleasure, beauty, and wisdom?"

L E O N : I take the conversation with the serpent to be not so much about sexual awakening as the awakening of the voice of reason and the fueling of the imagination to consider possibilities other than the merely given ones. The serpent asks the Bible's first question and produces the first conversation. He calls into question the goodness of God: Could God be the kind of being Who could put you amidst all these trees and tell you not to eat from any of them? He calls God a liar—"No, you're not going to die," he tells them. He undermines authority and suggests new and attractive possibilities. Once the authority of command or law or custom or instinct is undermined, the mind is free to imagine new possibilities. When the text says, "She saw that the tree was good for food," we can see that Eve has already made a judgment about the goodness or badness of the tree. In a sense, she's already tasted of the tree, even before reaching for it.

B I L L : Maybe her sin is that she is reinterpreting God's creation for her own ends. She is setting up an alternative ethic by saying, "This is what I want. This is good. I'll decide for myself." She's taking over creation. What do you think is really Eve's sin?

M A R I A N N E : God has made a command that Eve turns into an option. God says, "Don't eat of that tree." It's not hard to figure out how to obey that command. Eating of that tree is a violation of what God has said is good for her. But in becoming autonomous, Eve loses some of her freedom because, as Leon said, freedom to choose does not mean choosing well. Once you choose wrongly, it can become a habit,

"The serpent asks the Bible's first question and produces the first conversation."

an addiction. You lose the freedom of choosing well.

NAOMI: I think God knew what was going to happen. Eve doesn't want to take commands, she wants to understand them. Furthermore, we should remember that God never talks to her directly. He talks to Adam, and she gets the command as a kind of rumor, through another person. Eve exercises her God-given free will to weigh her choice and make a decision, but she isn't impulsive. She doesn't take the fruit, as Adam does, without deliberation. Adam doesn't question her when she offers him the fruit. He's a lot more gullible than she is.

JEAN-PIERRE: Maybe it's not that Adam is gullible—maybe he is simply trusting. He seems to trust her judgment. This is the Bible's first instance of trust— and of misplaced trust.

BILL: The serpent approaches Eve, not Adam. What does that say?

ELAINE: The Church fathers thought they knew what it meant—that she was much more approachable and easier to de-

lude. But you know, even though we talk about autonomy, it strikes me that Adam doesn't have a lot of autonomy. He has a choice—he either obeys God or obeys the woman. One is bad, and one is good. That's how it's set up.

BILL: Adam strikes me as a sort of divine simpleton. Eve is the more interesting of the two. She's proactive, while he's passive. She's curious, while he just accepts it all without any comment. I sometimes find myself cheering Eve on in this story.

STEPHEN: She's the one who makes everything happen, who acts out of love for God, if God is wisdom. It's significant that the god in this story puts the tree right in the middle of the Garden, that he creates the serpent, that he creates Eve with this curiosity—it's a setup for something to happen. God doesn't hide the jar of magic cookies in the attic, He puts it right on the kitchen table. Consciously, He hopes His children will obey, but unconsciously, He is making it very unlikely. The intelligence of the story wants something to happen.

BILL: But what is this tree really offering? What's so bad about distinguishing between good and evil?

LEON: To live one's life in terms of that distinction, while at the same time not possessing the true knowledge of their difference, is to live a life that is troubled, self-divided, painful. When the eyes of Adam and Eve are opened, they don't see that they are like God, as the serpent promised. What they see is that they're naked. Then

Roger Brown, *Adam and Eve (Expulsion from the Garden)*, 1982

the question is: Well, what's wrong with the knowledge of our nakedness? Why is this burdensome? What obtrudes as a result of the transgression, as a result of acquiring the knowledge of good and evil, is a kind of judgment—seeing yourself through the eyes of the other and pronouncing judgment on yourself. In addition to being rational, you see that you're needy and incomplete, and you have rebellious desires within. The other is not your other half. You can't command obedience—the other might not even like you, might even refuse you. All of these things are part of what it means to pass judgment on yourself and to see that you are not a whole and undivided

being, as you had foolishly thought before this enlightenment.

NAOMI: Well, I think that what Adam and Eve discover, with shock, is that we're not all that different from the animals, what with our urges, instincts, and drives. Being human and having free choice means taking responsibility for mediating these drives and instincts.

BILL: So the beginning of knowledge could well be prohibition, boundary, limit.

JEAN-PIERRE: We need to remember, Bill, this story is being told by the descendants of Adam and Eve, who are trying to address, among other things, the dilemma in the fact that people choose evil, or mistake the evil for the good and act toward the evil as if it were the good. This story is a response to the anguished cry—"How can this happen?"—not once, but again and again and again.

BILL: But what did Adam and Eve do wrong in that Garden?

JEAN-PIERRE: I don't know if the story answers that question. Perhaps it just asks the question, because Eve, apparently, does all the right things. She listens, she observes, she seeks knowledge. Somehow that's not enough. She eats the fruit. Adam eats the fruit. And somehow, something has gone awry.

LEON: Why do you call those all the right things? Why aren't they all the wrong things?

JEAN-PIERRE: Because they seem to be the way human beings, ever since, have gone about making prudent decisions—listening, observing, seeking knowledge.

MARIANNE: We said that Adam was the first example of misplaced trust because he trusted Eve. But Eve is really the first example of misplaced trust, in that she trusts the serpent rather than God. You ask what Adam and Eve do wrong in the Garden. They fail to trust in God—that what God says will happen, or that what God prohibits is for their own good.

JEAN-PIERRE: But they're in the perfect Garden. They have no reason to think that anything in this Garden is noxious to them or that anyone in the Garden would lie.

ELAINE: Part of the play of the story involves the question: What is good and evil? The fruit looks good and tastes good, and the story is set up so Adam and Eve have to eat the fruit. And then later, this act is called *felix culpa*—happy guilt. This seems to be a necessary tale about human nature. It becomes a puzzle: Some people say, "Well, you know, it's good that they did eat the fruit" and others say, "No, it was terrible that they did."

MARIANNE: But the story thinks it's bad that they have to leave the Garden. Judgment is passed on what they have done. If it were that good, wouldn't they have been allowed to stay?

NAOMI: Maybe the story is teaching us what it means to be mortal. There is only one God, and everyone else lives and dies. Our goal should not be to escape death, but to embrace life and see it as a blessing. Our only immortality is through our children—

"Once you grow up, you can't get back to the Garden."

and Adam and Eve make children right away after leaving the Garden. Once you grow up, you can't get back to the Garden. Part of being a good parent is teaching your children to leave you, even though it's going to cause you pain.

ROBIN: But there's really no analogy to this story in human life. We can't say God is like the parent, and we are the children, because we're all east of Eden now. We can't assume our reactions are meant to be analogous to those of Adam and Eve, because they were acting in the land of bliss, which we can't know.

STEPHEN: I disagree. Any serious spiritual practice is about Eden and bliss. That's the whole point.

LEON: What do you make of the fact that Adam and Eve are never mentioned again in the Hebrew Bible? Never!

STEPHEN: I think the old writers of the Bible had no concept of a Fall. They felt perfectly secure in the trust that Abraham and others had in God and they would have been appalled at the Christian interpretation of this story—that Adam's sin was an original, blanket sin, and that from then on, all human beings were corrupt and damned to hell unless they believed in Christ.

LEON: We've been talking about the story as if it were history. But what if we said, "Look, we suffer badly in this world. Life is hard. There is loss, there is separation, there is self-division, there is shame, there is guilt. Why is our life like this?"

This story shows us that the seeds of our troubles are within us. If we read the story this way, we can see how the subsequent stories show us how to live, with a wiser knowledge of good and bad, which comes not autonomously, but through God's revelation.

ELAINE: I think that's what the story says, Leon—but that's part of the problem. The creation stories show humankind as if we were quite distinct from nature. Then it blames all of our participation in nature—the suffering, pain, and death—on human fault. That's an amazing claim—that suffering, pain, and death exist because humans have failed morally, not because these conditions are built into the nature of the universe.

BILL: If suffering, pain, and death are built into the nature of the universe, is it not God Who put them there? *He's* at fault!

ELAINE: That's the only other conclusion this story allows. Part of the problem with the story is that it insists that suffering has to be somebody's fault. So, the story says, it's our fault.

STEPHEN: But if you step out of this story, you can see that suffering is woven into the very fabric of life, and that there are wise and sensible ways to deal with it so that you don't cause unnecessary suffering to yourself or others. Shame, guilt, selfishness, and hatred are unnecessary. We're talking within the terms of the story now, and I don't think you can get out of the story once you accept its terms.

ויאכל אדם מפרי אשר נתנה לו חוה ויגלם לא ידעכלם

Evgenii Abezguaz, *Adam Ate and Ate of the Fruit That Eve Gave Him but Knew Nothing*, nonconformist Soviet art, 1975

LEON: The discovery of nakedness is the first fruit of this new knowledge of how far we really are from being God. The serpent had promised that if the eyes of Adam and Eve were opened, they would be as God. The narrator, with wonderful irony, says, "And their eyes were opened, and they saw that they were naked." The response to this not-so-lofty condition of nakedness includes culture—the arts and the attempts through self-help to fix the limitations of nature. But the other effect of this discovery, which is wonderfully powerful, is that "they heard the voice of the Lord God walking in the Garden." That suggests that it's only when we discover our weakness and insufficiency that we're ready to pay attention to something higher in the world. Previously, the narrator tells us, God is present, but there's not much evidence that human beings care terribly much. Now that they see how far they are from being God, there is a kind of relationship to something which, in the long run, might offer redemptive possibility for the ills of human life.

MARIANNE: On the other hand, the text also says, "and they hid themselves, and they were afraid"—which seems to imply that on the previous evenings, when God had walked in the Garden, they hadn't hidden themselves or been afraid. So a new element of distance has crept into the story. Now they clothe themselves, as if to hide from each other. And they also hide from God.

LEON: The Hebrew word for "fear" used here also means "awe." Shame and awe are twins—the apprehension of something higher, before whom we stand as low. This is the germ of God-consciousness in human beings.

JEAN-PIERRE: It's similar to Psalm 8 in which the psalmist observes the order and beauty of creation and very self-consciously recognizes his own insignificance.

"Shame and awe are twins . . ."

In the same psalm, this insignificance is reversed by the psalmist's recognition of his place in that creation and the dignity that is inherent in the precarious and vulnerable position he occupies in the cosmos. He doesn't simply stand in the storm, buffeted by this wind and that, but in His ordered universe, God has granted him a place and a dignity. They're two sides of the same reflection.

BILL: But this story in Genesis suggests the loss of that dignity. Here you have all the pain associated through the centuries with childbirth laid at the feet of Eve for her disobedience. It doesn't seem dignified that women should be so punished for this act of reason, or this act of choice.

NAOMI: I don't see this as a punishment. Yes, childbirth and raising children are accompanied by tremendous pain and anguish. Nobody can give us the kind of pain that our children can. Yet they also give us tremendous joy, satisfaction, love, and a sense of continuity.

ELAINE: You started this, Bill, by asking, "What is the picture of God we would have if we had only this story?" People are speaking very politely about what a good parent He is and what a good provider and how thoughtful and kind. But He's jealous of the species He's made, and He's punitive, and He seems to be deficient in understanding. This isn't a modern characterization. For thousands of years, people reading this story have said, "You can't take it literally. You have to burst through the shell of the story because it's such a strange, provocative story with such limited characterization." Something in us insists that this isn't the picture of God. So Jewish and Christian mystics and others have taken off from this story and opened it up and seen reverse possibilities. Here Eve is punished and suffering—in other stories, she becomes God's wisdom, the manifestation of the divine in the world.

BILL: Are you saying that the story we have here suggests that we suffer because of God?

ELAINE: No, I'm just pointing to the way the first creation story says that God made the world, and it was good. Then why is it so difficult? Why does it hurt so much? Why do we die? Along comes the second story and says, "Well, it's not His fault, it's our fault." It's a powerful rever-

sal of our everyday experience, just as the way Eve is born from the man—another reversal of reality as we know it.

LEON: But the immediate consequence of the transgression doesn't require God's intervention at all. "The eyes of them both were opened, and they saw that they were naked, and they made themselves coverings of fig leaves." God hasn't intruded upon that. There's some kind of sadness and shame in that first discovery. They somehow know how far they are from Godliness. I don't read the rest of the story as punishment—nor do I read the expulsion from the Garden as punishment. We might even argue that mortality is something of a blessing for a creature that lives with this kind of divided consciousness and these sorts of miseries. I would even suggest that the real punishment is God *making known* to this pair what they've just "bought" with the knowledge of good and evil: partial separation from nature, division of labor, rule and authority, civilization and the arts. All that is sorrowful, and especially the consciousness of it.

ELAINE: But, Leon, have we brought upon ourselves pain and death? Does that make any sense to you? Did we invent these? If so, we're not part of nature.

STEPHEN: But death was there from the beginning. After all, they weren't *created* immortal. God even says, "What if they eat from the Tree of Life and live forever?" That's why he banishes them from the Garden, out of jealousy and fear. One point in the story that I'm very interested in is what happens after this "small god" starts quizzing them. Adam points to Eve and says, "It's *her* fault." Eve says, "It's the serpent's fault." I wonder what the serpent's would have been had God asked *him*. I suspect that he would have correctly pointed right back to God and completed the circle.

BILL: Well, I don't see how we can avoid cause and effect. If this world is God's creation, then suffering and death are as much a part of nature as the Garden was. What is the knowledge that God doesn't want Adam and Eve to have? Perhaps the knowledge God wants to withhold from them is the knowledge that they're going to die.

NAOMI: Without death, I don't think we would appreciate life. Death adds an urgency to life. I don't want to think of it as a punishment, because I can't have a relationship with a God who punishes me through death.

STEPHEN: The knowledge of good and evil that you get from eating the fruit of the tree is the acquaintance with opposites and judgments, separation and death. A very poor kind of knowledge—precisely what children don't have. Not-knowing allows the kind of spacious, open mind in which any possibility can happen. That's what the mind of God truly is, the mind that looks at the whole of creation—including suffering and death—and calls it very good. As Isaiah has God say, "I form light and create darkness; I make peace and create evil."

JEAN-PIERRE: The Book of Revelation envisions the culmination of things as a new creation of Eden. And there, not only is the prohibition against eating from the Tree of Life gone, but people are told to enjoy the fruit. That story is told by people who stand in the present, in the ongoing tension between where we've been and where we're going—and hoping that the road that we've been given to follow leads back to Eden.

NAOMI: It does! I must consciously believe that the road leads us forward to where the lamb and the lion will lie down together, and swords will be beaten into plowshares. That's the Eden we'll recreate at the end of days when humans will have learned to use their God-given free will toward good rather than toward evil.

BILL: I have sometimes thought of the curse as the memory of Eden and the awareness that we can never go back.

LEON: Would you really want to go back, to live in ignorance and innocence?

JEAN-PIERRE: In a sense, yes, because it may be the only thing left that I can't have. Knowledge is the source of art, as well as the source of shame. I seem to be both blessed and cursed with this knowledge of something I can't have. It's important to read this story in the context of its subsequent history. The Apocalypse, for example, takes the lion and lamb business very seriously and very paradoxically. The victorious lion of the Apocalypse, Christ, is the dead lamb. We need to take death very seriously here.

BILL: Don't you think we take death seriously enough? We take it so seriously that people make huge efforts trying to deny it. Death is necessary and inevitable.

ELAINE: I don't have much good to say for death.

LEON: But if, as parents, we cling to life, not making room for the next generation,

---

> *"I don't have much good to say for death."*

---

there's something profoundly wrong. There's a case to be made for the blessing of finitude. One of the most beautiful passages in the entire Bible is the speech of Adam after God announces his future to him. He hears this litany of disaster, and he hears one straw of hope in it—that Eve is going to have children. And he renames this woman, this time with no reference to himself, as "mother of all the living" because she has within herself something of the redemptive possibility for a finite and perishable being: procreation. There would be no Godliness in human life were it not for the recognition of our limits. If we had

to make the world over again for ourselves, I, for one, would vote for mortality.

MARIANNE: A few years ago there was an ad campaign—"Your world should know no boundaries." That's not human life. And that's certainly not this story.

NAOMI: I think everything in the Garden of Eden story is a mixed bag. Childbirth is painful, but there is also the joy of rearing children. Adam must work and sweat to till the earth, but there is also the pride of the wheat coming up and pride in his ability to feed the family he's fathering. Like Jacob, we can wrestle with the existential issues of life and prevail—but it will always be a struggle. I don't see any other way.

ELAINE: I didn't assume, as Leon suggested, that we were free to vote about this. My own sense of this comes out of a gnostic gospel that wasn't included in the New Testament, the Gospel of Philip, which says that life and death, good and evil, and light and darkness are brothers to each other. They're all inseparable. There's a remarkable passage in this gospel that says that the paradise you anticipate is the one in which God says, "Eat this" or "Do not eat that—just as you wish."

STEPHEN: I wouldn't want my paradise to have the lion and lamb lying down together. I want my lion to be a lion, not a vegetarian—to love the taste of blood, to be able to use its teeth and claws. When we talk about paradise in the way prophets do—swords into plowshares, lions chummy with lambs—we're talking about a fantasy of safety and tameness, a zoo, not the actual world that God created. The true paradise is *our* world, the world just as it is, with all its suffering, but seen through the eyes that call it "very good."

"The true paradise is our *world, the world just as it is . . ."*

MARIANNE: But don't the prophets and Genesis recognize that somehow, the world is not the way it's supposed to be?

STEPHEN: I think there's a more spiritually mature recognition that if the world isn't right, it's because my own mind and heart aren't right. As soon as I transform myself, I realize that the world is exactly the way it's supposed to be.

BILL: Elaine is raising the question whether the world is the way it is because God made it that way or whether, as Leon argues, it's our choices that make the world the way it is.

LEON: If we wanted to, we could say, "Look, God has made Adam and put him in a lovely place." But the story hints that there are three things that could disturb the happiness of human beings. Two of them are symbolized by the trees. One is the Tree

of Life, which suggests that anxiety about death might be present in a living being. The more serious thing, which God feels the need to prohibit, is the Tree of Knowledge, which we've talked about. But the third thing is that it's not good for man to be alone. The remedy for this is to divide the man into two beings, male and female. And that, as we know, produces other kinds of divisions and conflicts. Most of the troubles of human life are the result of these three flies in the ointment. But you also couldn't have human life without them.

JEAN-PIERRE: I think there's more. There's the curse on the serpent, the mention of the very deep disequilibrium that will exist between human beings and the rest of creation.

LEON: It's true that the earth is somehow cursed, and we will earn our bread only in the sweat of our brow. On the other hand, it's the earth that cries out in violation when Cain sheds Abel's blood. That's a kind of pollution in the normal relation. When God starts over with Noah, once again there's supposed to be a kind of cosmic harmony, in which human beings belong to nature. But we don't simply belong to nature. We are capable of somehow stepping outside nature and influencing it for better and for worse. That's our blessing and our curse.

STEPHEN: That is our nature. And so that, too, is part of nature itself, part of the whole.

BILL: Someone told me that when he

William Blake, *The Angel of the Divine Presence Clothing Adam and Eve with Skins*, 1803

read this story to sixth graders, they always thought God was the bad guy.

STEPHEN: A good friend of mine refused to teach this story to his young daughter because of the harm he felt it would do her as a female. I think he's right. The power of the story makes it very dangerous, and not only to children. For me, it requires midrash—creative transformation—to make it true. Sometimes I like to read it as a story about the consequences of trying to blame someone else. If Adam had said, "Yes, I ate the fruit," then he might still be in paradise. In fact, the story of Judah and Tamar at the end of Genesis echoes this story in a most beautiful way. Judah refuses to give his third son to his daughter-in-law, as he is required to do. She pretends to be a prostitute because she feels wronged, and she deeply wants a child. So she sleeps with Judah, who gives her his staff and seal as a pledge for his payment. Three months later, people come to Judah and say, "Tamar is a whore; she's pregnant." Judah has them bring her out to be burned. But she shows him his pledge and says, "The man who got me pregnant is the owner of this seal and this staff; see if you recognize whose they are." And Judah, in the most dignified way, with the greatest simplicity and integrity, says, "She is in the right, and I am in the wrong." That is the mirror image of the story of Adam. If he could have reacted with that kind of integrity, there would have been no split between his wife and him, and that oneness would have led to forgiveness, which leads to paradise itself.

ROBIN: But there already is a split. Her very creation was a split from him. And the very act of eating the fruit—we don't even know what that fruit is or what it conveys. But somehow it effects an interior change that leaves Adam and Eve different from the way they were before. Not only are relations between Adam and Eve different, relations between Adam and Eve and God are different. It's not just that Adam and Eve are expelled from the Garden, but God is, too. No longer will He be walking among His human beings in the cool of the day.

BILL: There are medieval and Renaissance paintings that depict Adam and Eve with tears in their eyes as they leave the Garden.

ROBIN: The departure is sorrowful—but that's not the end of the story.

JEAN-PIERRE: God chooses to pursue these people. He continues to walk with them wherever they go. If they look over their shoulders, there is God. This God is also preparing a path for them. This is the God who has converted Himself into the Divine Tailor so they could have clothing.

LEON: But He's present more and less and at different times in the story. The immediate sequel to this story is the story of Cain's fratricide—human beings living on the basis of *their* knowledge of good and evil, which isn't a true knowledge. God intrudes and tries to counsel Cain. Eventually, God takes one man, Abraham, by the hand and starts him on a real education. Then God is even more remote from Jacob, and He never speaks to Joseph. So there's a removal of divine presence, and, gradually, things are turned over to human institutions.

MARIANNE: It's not that God disappears, but that you can no longer say that God comes here in the afternoons to walk. You can't hear the leaves crunch as He passes by. As the story plays out, they ask

Expulsion of Adam and Eve in Shame, Church of San Zeno, Verona, 12th c.

not only "Where are you?" but "Who are you?"

STEPHEN: In Genesis, as God becomes less of a character, the humans become more Godlike, until, at the end of the book, in the Joseph story, the character "God" completely disappears, and Joseph emerges as the only spiritually mature character in the entire Hebrew Bible. He is the shaman, the dream reader, the only character who undergoes a profound transformation, from the charming but arrogant brat of the beginning to the wise leader, the insightful student of the Tao at the end. He comes to such a depth of spiritual maturity that he can open his heart and completely forgive the brothers who almost murdered him.

LEON: Elaine, what bothers you about God in this story?

ELAINE: The limitations of His knowledge and the competitiveness with His creatures, and His punitiveness. There's that remarkable statement in which God says, "Behold the man is become as one of us to know good and evil; and now, lest he put forth his hand, and take also of the Tree of Life and eat and live forever—"; and here the sentence abruptly breaks off. Whatever could happen then we cannot know because the statement is stopped, and they are driven from Eden.

LEON: But why assume the reason for that is competitiveness or jealousy? That's an interpretation.

ELAINE: Of course—but it's not a new interpretation. It goes back to ancient times.

ROBIN: What do you mean when you talk about the limit of God's knowledge? What's the problem with God that He's not omniscient?

ELAINE: It's not just that He's not omniscient, it's that He and the serpent give different pictures of what will happen, and both are incomplete.

LEON: What's incomplete about what God says? "On the day that you eat thereof, you will die."

ELAINE: Well, they don't die "in that day," as God specifically says. Instead, they live hundreds of years.

LEON: The question is: What does the remark "you will die" actually mean? Does it mean you will be struck dead? Or does it mean that on that day, you will know that you are mortal?

STEPHEN: But God doesn't say, "On the day"—or, as I translate it, "As soon as"—"you eat from the tree, you'll know that you are mortal." It's a very straightforward statement: "you will die." Not metaphorically—literally.

LEON: The innocent creature does die.

NAOMI: I think we're making a mistake by constantly focusing on God. I'm taught in the Ten Commandments not to mention God's name in vain. I feel that our

Adam and Eve Banished from Paradise, Qisas al-Anbiya (Legends of the Prophets), Iran, 1577

emphasis should be on what the story says about Eden, and Adam and Eve, and you and me today. What is human nature all about? What are the pitfalls? What is it about temptation? What are the consequences of curiosity? Elie Wiesel tells a story about the Holocaust in which, on Yom Kippur, the day of atonement, these skinny old people, with their ribs showing, decide they're going to fast and ask atonement for their sins. There's nothing to eat anyway—but what there is, they're not touching. One of the men complains, saying, ''We have to atone for our sins? What about God, Who allowed us to be in this misery? What about Him asking for forgiveness?'' After a silence, the oldest man in the group says, ''And now let's go and pray.'' So, in turning away from a discussion of the nature of God, I'm not trying to let Him off the hook, but to bring the focus back to our own behavior and accountability.

BILL: One of the seeds that fell from the tree in the Garden of Eden is the Holocaust. God created the world, and He says it is good—and yet, this world has the Holocaust in it. We spend our lives struggling to reconcile this contradiction.

STEPHEN: That's Job's question, too. And it's possible to find the answer.

BILL: What do you make of the fact that after Adam eats the fruit that Eve gives to him, he snitches on her? As a result of snitching on her, he gets to rule over her.

STEPHEN: But there's a beautiful moment in Milton's *Paradise Lost* in which, when Eve hands the apple to Adam, he deeply considers his decision. He knows what's going to happen, and he knows the price of his disobedience, but because he loves her and doesn't want God to create a new wife for him, he fully and consciously bites into the fruit. It's a very moving moment.

ROBIN: It's a little generous to Adam.

ELAINE: Eve is subordinate to Adam—and often enough, that describes the way men and women relate to each other. But the question is: Does the story mean to be prescriptive as well as descriptive? Is this the way it's supposed to be, too?

STEPHEN: It's certainly a story that *has* been read prescriptively for thousands of years. And I think it *wants* to be read that way. That's one reason I find some of the elements in it so repulsive and dangerous.

LEON: I think we're importing too many modern judgments and too little appreciation of what the world might have been like before the morality and teachings of the Bible took hold. Many of the later stories in the Bible correct the dominant and domineering male response to women.

ELAINE: But, Leon, I don't think these are simply modern judgments. What about the ancient rabbinic commentaries that ask, for example, ''Why do women walk at the head of the funeral procession?'' And they answer: "Because woman brought death into the world." And they continue: "Why does a woman menstruate?" "Because she shed the blood of Adam." This is her punishment. That's why it was called "the curse." These commentaries are at least sixteen hundred years old.

ROBIN: But in this story, God doesn't seem to invent the consequences of Adam and Eve's actions but rather to inform Adam and Eve, as if He Himself were somehow not completely in control of the situation.

ELAINE: Are you saying that God doesn't endorse these consequences?

ROBIN: I don't think the story tells us that.

ELAINE: I thought that's what it *does* say. In the beginning God says, "Let us make Adam in our image"—and male and female, He created them. So one thinks of the possibility of a divine being that is dual. Of course, the story doesn't say that, either. It speaks always of the male. But you could playfully think of a preexisting order in which the "us" would be male and female, so that the Deity mirrors the creation.

ROBIN: I think we're meant to keep both creation stories together. God announces things as they are. He doesn't render a value judgment when He tells Adam and Eve and the serpent the way things are going to be.

ELAINE: It's not a judgment to say, "Cursed is the ground because of you"?

ROBIN: No, he doesn't say, "This is good, and I like it." He says, "It's cursed because this has happened."

BILL: Look, perhaps God doesn't ordain the subordination of women to men, but certainly agents invoking His authority have interpreted this text in that way. How many times did I hear it preached that wives should be submissive to their husbands? And the men preaching this followed Paul all the way back to Genesis.

LEON: I understand—but stay in the story, without the help or hindrance of Paul. God tells Eve she will bear children and that her husband will rule over her. Then He turns to Adam and gives him a litany of toil, trouble, and death. But what does the man hear in these two speeches? He hears that the woman is going to bear children. He renames her. He celebrates her. And what's really remarkable is that he accepts responsibility for those children. Now that's not necessarily the way of the world. That's certainly not the way of our primate forbears. The burden of the text is to teach males what it means to live in relation to woman and her generative possibilities.

ELAINE: But this text isn't necessarily about monogamy. Polygamy is certainly an option that is fully available in Genesis. As I see it, this text isn't so much a divine revelation that tells us about God as it is a cultural story that tells us everything about our culture.

Scenes of Adam and Eve, Sarajevo Haggadah, Spain, 14th c.

LEON: Do you think that what we learn from this story is simply the mind of the people that wrote it? Nothing fundamental about men and women?

ELAINE: I didn't say "nothing fundamental." Descriptively, there's a lot in it that any of us could recognize. I study this text out of a religious interest, not just a scholarly one. I'm a scholar because of that interest. But I have to look at some parts and say that this is part of an archaic culture that has a particular style.

LEON: But how do we know which of the things in the story are descriptively true and which are merely the quirks of some old culture that thought this way?

ELAINE: That's the most important question. That's what we're talking about here. That's why we're having such a lively discussion.

LEON: But what's wrong with Robin's suggestion that God is simply describing how things will be?

ELAINE: If I took Robin's suggestion seriously, I'd have to do what Jews and Christians have done for thousands of years—which is to think about what happened before the creation, and why it happened this way.

STEPHEN: But even in these terms, the story is not descriptive of what a marriage can be. Most people have marriages in which that's certainly not the way things are.

ROBIN: In fact, it's not even descriptive of the way future relationships are in Genesis. It's a description of the way it is for Adam and Eve.

NAOMI: In Hebrew, it doesn't say: "You shall be subject to your husband." The word translated "subject" really means you will be yearning, probably sexually, for your husband, even though the sexual contact eventually produces the pain of childbirth. And when it says, "He will rule over you," to me it means that the man is responsible for protecting his wife and children.

ELAINE: Do you think this is an accurate portrait of the relationship between men and women?

NAOMI: I think it's an accurate description of how God intended men to take responsibility for women—particularly in a time when women were totally dependent on men for protection. What's remarkable about Eve is how she takes the initiative in this relationship, how she's the active partner in seeking wisdom. When Eve wants to be wise, to know, I interpret that to mean that she's curious to know about the life force—sexual knowledge. Through the basic universal sexual experience, we gain wisdom about life. This is not the kind of wisdom you get through computers, but the kind you get through the pain and joy of childbirth and bringing up children—the mixed bag of the consequences of sexuality. Adam and Eve have different sexual natures and responses. Sexually, Adam is quicker to respond, less cautious. He simply takes the fruit. Eve deliberates at length before tasting. Men and women are different sexually. But through patience, love, tenderness, and cooperation, through "knowing" each other, we can harmonize the difference between our two natures. I think this is what was intended by the story.

JEAN-PIERRE: I wonder what this story says about the dynamics of human freedom. Are Adam and Eve freer before leaving Eden? Or are they freer later? Are we freer east of Eden than we would have been in the Garden?

ROBIN: In the Garden, Adam and Eve had one kind of freedom—a freedom from time, obligation, division, distortion, and everything else we associate with the passage of time in human life. Afterward, you get the description of human life as it is. Women desire their husbands—true enough. Their husbands push them around—true enough. And the earth does not yield just because we are walking around and blessing it with our presence. It too takes subjugation and domination. This is neither a pretty picture nor a terrible one—it simply describes the way things are in this particular world that produced the story.

ELAINE: As Bill just reminded us, however, Paul draws a very clear conclusion about the subservience of Eve—that woman is made to serve man. This conclusion isn't lost on later generations.

ROBIN: But there was basic equality before the transgression.

LEON: I'm inclined to say that this is not a presentation of an ideal condition but displays the fundamental qualities of human sexuality. First, when the woman is presented to the man, he says, "Now at last, bone of my bone, and flesh of my flesh," and he renames himself a male human being in relation to her as a female. I read this as a speech of possessive sexuality—he exaggerates the degree to which she is his own flesh. Then, after the transgression, both of them are ashamed. They cover themselves, and seem to be interested not just in lustful possession, but also in beautification, adornment, esteem, approval, and so on. That's also an aspect of our sexuality. We want not just the coupling but the willing submission of the other. We want to be esteemed and appreciated, and we hide what we think would give us low esteem. We cover the shameful parts of ourselves. The third aspect of this story, which is profoundly right, is the speech to Eve: "Your desire shall be to your husband." That's connected with the remark about painful childbirth. Pregnancy is long, rearing takes a long time, and before the present age, women had a tough time going it alone. I'm not sure they don't still have trouble going it alone. The woman's desire, which previously was unfocused, such that the serpent could work on it, now is focused on her children. So she really needs the man's support and protection. This was the way of the world, at least until the twentieth century. But how do you get the man to take responsibility for these children that he sires? By giving him *apparent* rule in the household, when he in fact serves the life-giving and child-sustaining potential of woman. Many of the subsequent stories in Genesis show God telling the man, "Listen to your wife." It happens with Sarah and again with Rebekah.

BILL: We know from this story what Eve wants—she wants the fruit of the tree, which was good food, a beautiful sight, and potentially the source of wisdom. Some traditions say that Eve and the snake were the bringers of culture into the world through this desire for something more than sexual satisfaction, more than domination. Eve wanted something spawned by her own curiosity.

STEPHEN: You know what it was? God. In many traditions, the snake is a wisdom figure as well as an image of immortality—it sheds its skin and is born again. It's a figure for the vital energy that can flow through a human body—*kundalini*—and that can be experienced as a great opening into God.

MARIANNE: But the serpent is not a pathway to God, he's a pathway away from God. He's speaking against God. If Eve were seeking or longing for God, which is a genuine human longing, she knows how to find God. Apparently, God has walked in the Garden and spoken to them. This is one of those alternatives she ought not to follow.

STEPHEN: I don't think she's longing for *this* god. I think she's longing for *God*.

BILL: Mark Twain said that Adam wanted the apple not for its own sake but because it was forbidden.

STEPHEN: Yes, and many fairy tales have the one forbidden room—

MARIANNE: —and Pandora's box.

STEPHEN: They know they're not supposed to enter the room, but they always do.

NAOMI: Because curiosity is necessary for getting wisdom.

MARIANNE: But Pandora opened the box and let all that misery—not wisdom—loose.

STEPHEN: It's always a woman, you know.

BILL: And the Fall of Man!

ELAINE: The Christians invented that interpretation. In the rabbinic tradition of midrash, commentators speak of it as a story about the consequences of freedom, as we've said. Following the Fall, you're left with a human nature that has a good impulse and an evil impulse, and the capacity to follow either one. So it's a warning story. The Christian exegetes interpreted this story in the same way until Augustine turned it into a story of moral bondage—of a Fall that has to be undone by a savior.

JEAN-PIERRE: For Christians, the Fall is the answer to the question of why Jesus had to go to the cross.

LEON: But the story itself has God saying, "Now the man has become like one of us." This suggests that we could just as easily say that this story is about the rise of man to a Godlike status—but only in part.

BILL: What does it mean to be like God?

LEON: It means to live in the light of knowing the distinction between good and bad, and being fully conscious of this distinction all the days of one's life. I don't mean to say Adam and Eve have a true knowledge of good and bad—but they now can't live without the distinction.

JEAN-PIERRE: The story doesn't indicate that Adam and Eve are lacking a true knowledge of good and bad.

LEON: I would suggest that the Cain and Abel story is the continuation of this story. There you see what it means to live outside the Garden on the basis of the knowledge of good and bad. God treats Cain as if Cain ought to know what it means to do well.

ROBIN: Cain knows what is good and bad for him.

JEAN-PIERRE: The dilemma is that we know—and choose otherwise.

> "The dilemma is that we know—and choose otherwise."

BILL: Yes. I can identify with Paul's acknowledgment that the good he knew he should do, he didn't do; and the wrong he knew he shouldn't do, he did.

LEON: But once the alternative of evil exists, choosing obedience or Godliness is somehow a fuller embracing of the divine.

MARIANNE: But didn't that alternative exist for Adam and Eve? They had the choice to eat or not to eat, and they chose to eat.

NAOMI: But they didn't understand the moral value of the choice. They just used their ability to disobey, the same way two-year-olds experiment with disobedience without understanding their actions in a moral context. Through their disobedience, Adam and Eve begin to learn about wisdom and the moral choices in life. There's a verse in the Bible that sums it all up: "And in the end, obeying God is the beginning of all wisdom."

ELAINE: One of the major messages I read in the stories of Genesis is that God is God, and human is human, and the two are utterly distinct—or, as Martin Buber said, "wholly other." And when I read mystical interpretations, whether Jewish or Christian, they open up the possibility of the divine and the human as being on a continuum. From that perspective, the question of where the boundary between divine and human is understood to be is a very deep and important one.

BILL: Does this story impede or confirm your faith?

MARIANNE: It confirms it because as it raises questions about the reality of God and what God asks, it presents to us the option and challenge of faith.

NAOMI: This story always reminds me that I am made in the image of God. That means to constantly be walking on a continuum, getting closer and closer to what that potential implies, with all its privileges and obligations. I can never become God. But I can constantly be journeying closer and closer to the potential of being created in the image of God. And because God is not quantifiable, there's no ceiling to God—and there's no glass ceiling for me.

III

THE FIRST MURDER

JOHN BARTH • REBECCA GOLDSTEIN

MARY GORDON • OSCAR HIJUELOS

CHARLES JOHNSON • FAYE KELLERMAN

BURTON L. VISOTZKY

The Bible is the mother of all books to Western culture. Not only are these stories the source of three great religions, they've shaped the imagination and ethics of our culture. When people gather to talk about them, surprising things happen. The Bible is often used as a wedge to drive us apart, but approached in a democratic spirit with respect for the person whose opinion you disagree with, these old stories can point to some common ground for talking about our lives today. This story is one of the most haunting in the Bible; it has challenged the conscience of believers and nonbelievers alike and inspired writers down through the centuries. Nobody gets off easily. Not God, Who plays favorites. Not the hot-headed first son, or his younger brother who does a good deed and suffers for it. And not Adam and Eve, the first parents to learn what it means to "raise Cain."

—BILL MOYERS

Cain Kills Abel, Byzantine mosaic, Monreale Cathedral, Sicily, 12th c.

Now the man knew his wife Eve, and she conceived and bore Cain, saying, "I have produced a man with the help of the LORD." *Next she bore his brother Abel. Now Abel was a keeper of sheep, and Cain a tiller of the ground. In the course of time Cain brought to the* LORD *an offering of the fruit of the ground, and Abel for his part brought of the firstlings of his flock, their fat portions. And the* LORD *had regard for Abel and his offering, but for Cain and his offering he had no regard. So Cain was very angry, and his countenance fell. The* LORD *said to Cain, "Why are you angry, and why has your countenance fallen? If you do well, will you not be accepted? And if you do not do well, sin is lurking at the door; its desire is for you, but you must master it."*

Cain said to his brother Abel, "Let us go out to the field." And when they were in the field, Cain rose up against his brother Abel, and killed him. Then the LORD *said to Cain, "Where is your brother Abel?" He said, "I do not know; am I my brother's keeper?" And the* LORD *said, "What have you done? Listen; your brother's blood is crying out to me from the ground! And now you are cursed from the ground, which has opened its mouth to receive your brother's blood from your hand. When you till the ground, it will no longer yield to you its strength; you will be a fugitive and a wanderer on the earth." Cain said to the* LORD, *"My punishment is greater than I can bear! Today you have driven me away from the soil and I shall be hidden from your face; I shall be a fugitive and a wanderer on the earth, and anyone who meets me may kill me." Then the* LORD *said to him, "Not so! Whoever kills Cain will suffer a sevenfold vengeance." And the* LORD *put a mark on Cain, so that no one who came upon him would kill him. Then Cain went away from the presence of the* LORD, *and settled in the land of Nod, east of Eden . . .*

Adam knew his wife again, and she bore a son and named him Seth, for she said, "God has appointed for me another child instead of Abel, because Cain killed him." To Seth also a son was born, and he named him Enosh. At that time people began to invoke the name of the LORD.

—excerpts from *New Revised Standard Version*
(The Holy Bible), Chapter 4

BILL: Few stories match the longevity and power of the story of Cain and Abel. Augustine, Dante, Shakespeare—this story has fired the imagination of so many. How do you account for it?

OSCAR: The conflict depicted in this story happens in so many families. It's a premise of human experience.

JACK: And we must remember that Cain and Abel are the first fully human beings not made by God but produced by natural parents. The first fully human being is a murderer—and the second is his victim. This first murder is caused by the first religious offering. It's the first fratricide. And there's a whole repertory of human emotions before and after this first murder that Cain is manifesting for the first time, emotions that Adam and Eve didn't display when they were banished from the Garden. So part of the appeal of this story is that it got there first.

REBECCA: The first murder, yes, but also the first death. Death was hanging around as a concept in the first three chapters with the Tree of Knowledge—"Don't eat of this, lest ye die." But now death actually enters the world. And it enters through a murder. The reality of death, with all of its ramifications, is here in this story.

JACK: And still with us.

CHARLES: And there's a sense in which Cain's crime is more of an original sin than the kind of sexual mistake made by Adam and Eve. Murder enters the human experience, and the murderer becomes the first builder of a city. It's almost as if to say that this kind of violence—the elimination of the brother, the other, the double—is foundational for the rise of civilization. You get much the same pattern in the story of Romulus and Remus in the founding of Rome, where Remus is favored in his choice of a site for Rome over Romulus, who slays him. And the victim's blood is in that soil to haunt that civilization. Do we really need an act of violence, the elimination or destruction of our so-called brother, whoever he might be, in order to found a city or a civilization?

"Do we really need an act of violence, the elimination of our so-called brother, to found a city or a civilization?"

FAYE: But the civilization wasn't founded on Cain's seed. It was founded on Seth's bloodline through Noah. Seth was the third son conceived by Adam and Eve after Abel had been murdered.

JACK: The second draft!

FAYE: This is very interesting because in Hebrew, *Abel* means "nothingness" or "futility." So maybe Eve, in naming her son, had a sense that this first pair of sons would not lead to civilization.

BURT: I have to wonder if, when Adam and Eve ate of the fruit, they actually did know the difference between good and evil. If so, then Cain should have known better. He should have understood that if you whop your brother on the side of the head hard enough, he's going to die and that maybe the knowledge of good and evil is knowing you can bring death into the world.

BILL: Is this the first inkling of "survival of the fittest"?

FAYE: I think it's exactly as Jack said—civilization had to go through several drafts before it continued as an entity.

MARY: Certainly, Cain has the impulse to murder. And I'm very interested in the erasure of Abel. One of the reasons the story is so compelling is that it's the erasure of the innocent. The innocent is unable utterly to defend himself. He is left unprotected by God.

BILL: He has done no wrong. He is a just man, apparently living a good life. But goodness and righteousness have nothing to do with his fate.

MARY: Yes, the story is about the absolute necessity for justice—and the impossibility of justice. The blood of Abel, the innocent, cries out from the ground, but it's too late. God doesn't protect him, although God knows that something needs to be done. Morally, I think that's what is so moving about this. God steps in to short-circuit the lust of vengeance. He puts the mark on Cain that protects him. Now, in terms of justice, Cain should be erased because Abel was erased. But what God is saying, simultaneously, is that justice is both necessary and impossible. It's impossible because the quest for vengeance, while motivated by a desire for justice, absolutely obliterates the possibility of a good life.

BURT: Do you think maybe God feels a little squeamish about the lesson that was learned? Cain brings a fruit offering, or vegetables. Abel kills an animal. Abel's offering is preferred, so Cain is inspired to kill, too—except that he happens to kill his brother. Maybe God thinks, "This isn't working out quite like I'd planned. I better put a stop to this measure-for-measure response." So we have to ask, "What is just? What does God want?"

JACK: I've got to put in a good word for Cain here. It seems to me that one of the reasons for the eternal fascination of the story is that it's so full of simple, narrative problems. Poor Cain. Presumably, he has been brought up by his parents, who had eaten the fruit and therefore knew good from evil. Poor Cain invents religion. It's his idea. "Let's make a sacrifice!" Nobody had ever thought of that before. Cain thought of the religious sacrifice. So I'm saying, "Go, Cain." But then his brother ups him. God likes the meat. If I were Cain, my face would fall, too. No wonder Cain is so wrought up.

REBECCA: This is heavy-duty rejection from the Father Who sees you completely.

JACK: Right. This doesn't exculpate the murder, but it certainly is some sort of extenuating circumstance for the puzzlement, disappointment, and wrath.

REBECCA: Yes, this is such a generous impulse on Cain's part. His father and mother have been cast out of Eden, right? They were removed from the presence of God. Cain tries to engage God again through prayer and sacrifice. But it's almost as if he doesn't quite know what he's getting into.

BILL: Think about it. The first murder grows out of a conflict between two worshippers of God.

BURT: I hadn't thought about that. Here's a guy who founds a religion. From him, ultimately, civilization is wrought. And yet, as Charles said, murder is really at the base. But clearly, that's not what God intends.

OSCAR: Listening to all our super-adult interpretations of the story, I'm getting nostalgic about the time I first heard this story as a kid, and what it said to me then. The main thing I heard was, ''It's bad to kill your brother.'' That's what I heard at the Corpus Christi church uptown here in Manhattan. There used to be a priest who always made up stories involving modern kids named ''Jose'' and ''Maria'' and related their lives to tales from the Bible, Cain and Abel being one of the stories he fell back upon. Stories about theft, deception, and violence. It was always about stories telling you what's the right thing to do.

MARY: We weren't allowed to read the Bible. In the fifties, you weren't trusted to be able to interpret it yourself, so I *heard* the stories. But I remember as a child simultaneously identifying with both Cain and Abel. I identified with the helpless position of Abel. As Bill said, he did everything right. He gave completely, from the heart. He was pure and good. But it didn't matter. He did all the right things, and he was destroyed. I think children often feel like that.

BILL: So how did you react?

MARY: Well, it scared me because I thought being good was everything, and yet in this story, it didn't matter. But I also understood Cain's jealousy. Jealousy is an enormously strong passion. Suppose you did your best and gave something to your father, and he liked somebody else's gift better. This story seems to me to be about the breakdown of justice and rationality and the triumph of grace.

FAYE: I don't feel any compassion for Cain whatsoever. It wasn't Cain's idea to bring sacrifices. Oral tradition says that it was his father's idea to tell the brothers to bring sacrifices. Then God took Abel's sacrifice because it was given with a pure heart and didn't take Cain's because it was given begrudgingly. When Cain's face fell, God asked, ''What's the problem?'' and later said, ''Do better, and you'll be forgiven.'' Cain shuns his responsibility and blames Abel. He takes Abel out to the field and starts arguing with him. Then he slays him. Later, when God speaks to him ''in a soft manner,'' trying to get him to repent,

Perle Hessing, *Cane and Abel*, 1985

Cain asks, "Am I my brother's keeper? I don't know where he is." And God says, "Of course you know where he is. You buried him."

CHARLES: Well, remember that God tells him that sin is waiting "outside the door." It's really up to him to make this decision, which he is unable to do. When he kills Abel, it's not really about Abel, not to me. It's about striking back at God. He's motivated by envy—the same emotion that brought down Lucifer many millennia before. And who do you envy? It's someone who must be enough like you, with just a little bit of difference. You don't envy somebody who's totally different. You envy someone with whom you have a relationship. Maybe you're in the same profession. I'm not going to envy a doctor. I'm going to envy Oscar Hijuelos as a novelist. Or John Barth. Why is their offering received so fully and mine not? This is also, basically, the story of Mozart. Mozart has the gift, and his teacher, Salieri, can understand it as others cannot. Talk about envy! It flourishes in this relationship between self and other. It's almost like a doubling, a twin. So all Cain can do is to eliminate him. This idea of the double constantly intrigues writers. For example, look at Conrad's "Secret Sharer." We can accept our heroes having a sidekick or a friend, but not a brother. The brother is the failed possibility of the hero. Why aren't they both heroes? This business with brothers is really interesting. As a writer, I find myself very troubled about the implications of brotherhood. And I'm an only child. I don't have a brother, so this story illuminates something for me about the darker side of brotherhood.

JACK: To pick up on that, Charles—you know, the Greek and other mythologies are full of twin brothers, one of whom is mortal, and one of whom is destined to be immortal. Take Castor and Pollux, for example. It's a recurring motif.

BILL: So what's your explanation for the issue Charles raised—that the hatred is always more furious among intimates? My Greek professor at the University of Texas would always remind us that "the potter envies only another potter."

JACK: It's a little bit like the French proverb that the best swordsman in France will never be killed by the second-best swordsman in France. He will be killed by someone who has never held a sword in his hand before and so doesn't make the right moves. But he will envy the second-best swordsman.

CHARLES: That's intriguing. But this story involving intimates speaks to a deep fracture in our lives. "Same" and "different" are two themes, but no two things are going to be equal. Among twins, this is even more vivid if they are both potters or novelists. There's something asymmetrical and destabilizing about human beings as seen in the story of these two brothers.

BILL: Look. The first human act in Genesis is an act of disobedience. The second human act is an act of murder. Somebody's trying to tell us something here.

MARY: It's a hopeless story in a way—or an impossible one. It says that jealousy and violence are in the heart. I'm awfully interested in our misinterpretation over time of the mark of Cain. We traditionally have thought of it as a mark of opprobrium when it's really a mark of protection.

BILL: Yes. God says, "I will put it on you, and if anyone harms you, you'll be avenged sevenfold."

MARY: But our culture has garbled that message. So when you refer to "the mark of Cain," we assume that that's the mark of the criminal. But it is simultaneously the mark of the criminal and the mark of protection.

JACK: A completely ambivalent mark. Nobody can touch you, but everybody sure does know you're a criminal.

MARY: Which is why I think it's so rich.

BILL: Do you like this story?

MARY: I love this story. But I always worry about Abel.

JACK: Certainly part of the power of the story, whether we like it or find it deeply unsettling, is in the most poignant line thus far in Genesis: "Am I my brother's keeper?" This is one of a series of famously disingenuous questions that run through Genesis—God and others asking questions to which they know the answers.

BURT: Why do you assume God knows the answer?

JACK: Because we assume that the Author of the script knows what is happening. So when God is walking in the Garden, and He asks Adam and Eve, "Why are you naked?", we don't think that's a naive question that He's waiting to hear the answer to, do we? I presume He knows very well why they're naked.

BURT: I'm not so sure that this early on in Genesis, God has the same high qualities that later theologians and later books of the Bible impute to Him.

JACK: So you really believe that when God asks Cain, "Where is your brother?", God doesn't know—

BURT: —God may not know. I'm intrigued about this.

JACK: I'm delighted by this.

REBECCA: In verse seven, you have this cryptic word from God, right before the murder: "Lift up your eyes. Why are you crestfallen? Why is your gaze on the ground?" There's an element of subjectivity in Cain. It's hard to know exactly what's going on inside him. He's made a spiritually expansive gesture, and then he's rejected. He's clearly just cast completely into himself. It's a maelstrom. And then God says something very interesting: "The choice is yours."

BILL: "And if you do not do well, sin is lurking at the door. It's desirous for you. But you must master it."

REBECCA: But there it is. Sin is close enough. God is saying, "The blood is boiling in your veins. But if you get outside it, get over it, look at it, see it, you can master it." It's as if God Himself is not quite sure what man's capacities are yet. Man is something really new in God's experience.

BILL: When I was growing up, we were taught that sin was breaking the rules, especially the Ten Commandments. But here God talks about sin as an aggressive force waiting outside, as an animal yearning for its victim.

REBECCA: In the Jewish tradition, there's a notion of the *yetzer hara*, the evil inclination. It's almost an externalization of your evil inclinations, waiting there to attack you.

CHARLES: There's another interpretation of sin as having "missed the mark"—

Jan van Eyck, *Cain and Abel*
(detail from *Madonna of
Canon van der Paele*),
Bruges, 1436

like a target that you've not struck correctly.

BILL: But here God is talking about sin as something *out there* that's waiting for you.

REBECCA: I hear Spinoza in verse seven. *Spinoza* says that human bondage is a matter of being passive. You simply react. God is saying, "Rise above it." Cain's parents are cast out of the Garden for fear that they're becoming too Godlike in having eaten of the Tree of Knowledge. But here, in contrast, God seems to be saying to their son, "Be a little more Godlike!"

FAYE: Which goes back to what Oscar was saying when he learned the verses as a child. There's a lesson to be learned here: Pick yourself up, do better the next time, and you'll be all right. It's very hard to learn.

BURT: Think of the Hebrew here. What God says is that "Sin is right there at the doorway, and you will lust for it." It's the same term as when Eve is cursed and God says to Eve, "Now your lust will be for your husband." There's something libidinous there, something in our urges that God says we must master.

FAYE: I have more of a problem with the punishment of Abel than I do with the punishment of Cain. Cain failed to master his passion, so I can see where his punishment came from. But what did Abel do?

MARY: —except the best that one can do?

FAYE: Did Abel perhaps gloat? Did he taunt Cain about something? They did go off to the field. They were arguing about something.

CHARLES: This is a parent's nightmare—that at times, you prefer one child over another. And the favored one swells. That does happen, does it not?

BURT: Well, your kids are different ages, so you can do different things with the older than you can with the younger. But I know perfectly well that as the years pass, I'll be able to do the same things when my younger son, when he comes of age. He doesn't know that now, so it makes him itchy.

BILL: A little jealous?

BURT: Yes. I know that these are real issues.

BILL: Are you saying that God does the same? But what if God's choice here is just arbitrary? What if there's no reason for His preference—He just happens to like Abel's sacrifice more than Cain's.

CHARLES: I don't want to believe that. I want to believe that He fully explains to Cain what the problem is, and Cain doesn't respond to the challenge.

REBECCA: It may be arbitrary—or it may not be. The question is: Is it arbitrary from Cain's point of view?

JACK: It's an odd Father Who doesn't

give Cain credit for his good intentions, credit for having, as far as I'm concerned, invented the idea of sacrifice. God doesn't say, as I would have said to my firstborn, "Gee, I understand you were trying to do a good thing. It's a pretty inspired idea you had here, giving up an offering to Dad. I really appreciate that." There's none of that. Some of the commentaries point out that God doesn't exactly reject Cain's sacrifice. He just doesn't have respect or regard for it.

REBECCA: Cain is the firstborn. I was a middle child. Family position seems to me important in understanding these characters.

BILL: As that middle child, were you jealous?

REBECCA: Are you kidding? This is a passion I know intimately. And here Cain's mother, Eve, makes such a big fuss. This is truly the firstborn. Eve even compares herself to God—"*Kaniti ish et hashem*," which means "I have created (or acquired) a child with God." She claims Godlike qualities. In fact, she's more or less crowing.

BURT: And in the Hebrew text, when Eve names Cain, the words "*Kaniti ish et hashem*"—"I've created this person with God"—make it sound as if she and God were in partnership. Then she names her second son Abel, or *Hevel*, which means "futility."

MARY: What a hopeless, hopeless thing, to name your child Futility.

FAYE: Remember, this is a false start for civilization.

BILL: A false start because God made a mistake?

FAYE: I don't know if God made a mistake. Man made a mistake because sin was there, at the doorstep, and he chose to take the sinful path. As the firstborn, Cain could have been greater than Abel. After his sacrifice had been rejected, he could have spent time in penance and self-examination. Instead, he chose to wallow in self-pity and take it out on his brother.

REBECCA: But imagine how it feels to be Cain. You're the firstborn. Your mother makes such a fuss over you. There are all of these expectations. The rejection must have been overwhelming.

BILL: As writers, you must be very familiar with rejection.

REBECCA: This is something we know well!

MARY: But none of us has killed.

BILL: Only in your books.

JACK: I want to go back to something I raised earlier. As with all the great primordial stories, there are moments that have as much psychological poignancy as they would have in contemporary drama. The big one in this story, of course, is Cain's disingenuous answer to what I would still want to believe is God's disingenuous question: "Where is your brother?" At first Cain lies—"I don't know." But then comes the unforgettable line: "Am I my brother's keeper?" That's a remark that has staying power and is morally ambivalent. We all know that yes, you are. But then again, there's an extent beyond which we are not our brother's keeper. That's the thing that makes stories like this, with all their rich incoherences, discrepancies, and problems, just as stinging and relevant today as they must have been the first time anyone heard them.

OSCAR: As I listen to everyone, I keep thinking a cynical person would say that one of the morals of the story is "Don't get caught." What would have happened had Cain come back to the family and said, "Abel and I were in the field, and he disappeared. I don't know where he's gone"? Is this story about being discovered? Is it about guilt? Here we are, talking about God, Who's the Playwright, so to speak, but we're in a world where lots of people assume the absence of any kind of guiding spirit to hold us accountable. Hence, people go around and murder each other. Hence, the endless overload of bad-news headlines.

"We're in a world where lots of people assume the absence of any kind of guiding spirit to hold us accountable."

BURT: The biblical text says, "Your brother's blood calls out from the ground"—as if to say, "Forensic evidence is going to get you." That's our conscience now. That's what we've come to.

MARY: But when you talk about the mythic or narrative power of the story, I remember that the reason this story upset me so much when I was a child is that Abel's fate shows you that being good won't protect you. But I simultaneously identify with Cain as well as Abel. The Romantics liked Cain so much because he is in the grips of passion. We all know that the best thing to do is to master your passions. But we also have experienced the power of passion. Cain is the passionate character who can't get it all together. He can't put things in their correct place. He can't stop himself. He's the character who butts up against desire. That's the secret of the narrative. The story is saying that jealousy, hatred, and the will to do harm are endemic to us. At that moment, you may be able to choose against them. But that's a heroic choice, and not all of us are heroic. It's not surprising that there are more novels focused on Cain than on Abel. It's much easier to get the reader to identify with the one who is in the grips of passion. I also want to say that this is a story that must be read with a post-Holocaust consciousness.

BILL: How's that?

MARY: Abel is the innocent victim, and he's erased. God does not intervene.

BILL: What does this tell you about God? What does it do to your own faith?

MARY: That's the hopeless moment—the realization that goodness and purity of heart do not protect you. It did not protect the Jews. It did not protect the Indians. It did not protect those in Africa who were sold into slavery. It's irrelevant to your fate and your punishment. For me, that's always the moment where doubt enters in. What is it that makes God hard to believe in? That He stands by and allows the innocent to suffer. In the end, Abel is dead. And dead is dead. God doesn't do anything about it. This is the narrative moment when doubt becomes absolutely comprehensible and almost inevitable.

BURT: That message is the message of the canonical text of faith. This is what the book is to religious people who are seeking God. This we make our central text. In the midst of the search for God, the text we read says, "Innocent people die. God stands silent." How do you reconcile that with a belief in the goodness of God?

FAYE: You have faith; that's how you reconcile it. Because if you knew that purity and innocence were always going to win out in the end, where would faith be? We would only do good because of the reward—like some Skinnerian-trained rat.

JACK: It makes the leap of faith more of a leap.

FAYE: But that's what faith is. You have faith even staring at the ovens of Dachau.

MARY: But faith requires that you get out of the story. Faith requires that you say, "There is a larger Story than this

story, and it's not narrative. It's somehow—"

JACK: —Despite the story.

MARY: Precisely. Despite the story.

BURT: I don't understand what you mean.

MARY: Because if you stay in the story of Cain and Abel, the only reasonable position is to say, "How can I align myself with this God Who allows the innocent to be punished"? If you're going to have faith, you have to say, "Outside the boundary of this story, there is a meaning, a plan. There is a God I do not understand." A story assumes understanding. A story says, "I'll tell you this, and you'll get what I mean."

BILL: How do we come to terms with the God Who plays favorites? With the God Whose own preference turns brother against brother, making them enemies? The God Who is silent, as Mary was saying, in the moment of violence? The God Who just doesn't give answers to these deep questions?

CHARLES: I don't see God that way. Look, God explains to Cain what he needs to do and what the dangers are. But he goes ahead and commits murder. I don't make of God quite the heavy that somebody else might.

BILL: But God precipitates the murder by an arbitrary choice of one offering over another.

CHARLES: Is it arbitrary? That's my question.

BILL: There's nothing in the text to indicate that it isn't arbitrary.

BURT: I think God's a tough cookie. I'm thinking here of God playing the role of parent. Sometimes you articulate what you fear most. When God warns Cain, "If you're not careful, this is going to erupt," maybe God's warning God. We know that just a few generations farther down the line, God's going to get so frustrated with humanity that He will wipe humanity out almost entirely.

JACK: And proceed to the third draft.

BURT: Sometimes I imagine that maybe the reason God stays so far back and is so silent is so that God has a moment to compose Himself. You know, when I hear my kids bickering at home, sometimes I think the best thing for me to do is to just go into my bedroom and shut the door for a while so that I don't come out screaming, too.

BILL: Aren't you made uncomfortable by a God Who protects the murderer?

JACK: May I check in as one who is made acutely uncomfortable about these matters? I'm coming from no particular religious background. I have much less trouble, for example, with the God of the Book of Job. There we are told, "Don't try to understand; it's bigger than you are." I may not go along with that, but I can understand it. That's a directly satisfying, though somewhat dismaying, reply. But the God in the episode of Cain and Abel—well, I'm still shaking my head at the end. The mark, as we've agreed, is both an advertisement of Cain's misbehavior and a protection of the most ambiguous kind. Cain is a marked man in both senses.

CHARLES: Well, this is because murder had not existed in the world this way before. Maybe God wants to stop this cycle of one killing another, killing another, killing another. Maybe He doesn't want this bloodletting to go on and on and on.

JACK: But it did. Coming back to what you said earlier, Charles, about civilization—Rome was built on a crime, built on blood. This is where the arts, sciences—all the good stuff—comes from. I'm reminded of Balzac's famous remark that all great fortunes are based on great crimes. We *tsk-tsk* our tongues. But the city has been founded. We've got the arts, sciences, even literature in through the back door. The lesson in all this seems to be, "Start the story over again." God does it with Seth, another of Eve's sons. And when that doesn't work, God starts again with Noah.

MARY: But Noah goes into the Ark with everything that came before him. Even if you're saying it's draft three, as we all know in our revisions, a lot of the original versions are carried over. There's continuity. So Noah goes into the Ark with the legacy of music, metallurgy, and urban life. Knowledge is not wiped out. Yet he also had to go into the Ark with the legacy of murderousness. The ambiguity of being human does not end with the line of Cain.

MARY: The descendants of Cain, the descendants of the murderer, are the inventors of civilization.

FAYE: I have a real problem with saying that creativity comes from violence. It's an apologia for violence—that you are creative and that therefore you're excused from the confines of ethical behavior.

BILL: But some creativity comes from unbridled passion, does it not?

FAYE: Perhaps the same sort of drive. It goes back to what we were talking about—the good within us and the bad within us. You can harness this creativity to do good and to be constructive. Or you can harness this creativity to do evil. Good and evil come from the same drive—but you can lead this energy into two different paths.

"Good and evil come from the same drive—but you can lead this energy into two different paths."

MARY: But let's just look at what this story gives us. In this particular narrative, whatever you want to say are the implications for future ethics, the line that produces civilization is the murderer's line.

REBECCA: But it might not have been

because of the murderousness in him. Remember, part of his punishment is that God hides his presence from Cain. This sits very heavily on Cain. He says, "I can't bear this punishment." He's on the earth alone now. God has withdrawn. Maybe that has something to do with his creativity. He must draw now on his own potential, his own power. Also, death has entered. Now he knows death. Luther said, "You don't know anything until you taste death on your lips." Well, Cain has tasted death. This might have something to do with creativity.

FAYE: You notice he named his city after his son, not himself. He thought he was going to be childless, and here he has this child and builds a city. Perhaps a seed of goodness entered through his heirs.

OSCAR: I don't mean to be rude, but this is getting more abstract as we move along. I grew up working-class—and there were poor people all around us who had it worse. But we all shared the same mutual resentments and prejudices that had nothing to do with morality. I mean, the Bible was about good people—at least I thought so, even though I now realize how it's also about how bad things are brought into the world. In that sense, it's about how people become evil as well. But who were the good people? People like us. I think any discussion of the Bible should address issues like: "Why are people so angry in this day and age? Why do people commit murder? And why do people get away with it?" The Cain and Abel story doesn't seem to address these questions, except in the mythic sense of "Once upon a time there must have

Lorenzo Ghiberti, *Cain and Abel (Gates of Paradise)*, Baptistry, Florence, ca. 1425

been . . ." And I'm very sad to hear that these were not real people. I was convinced they were. I grew up around people like them.

BILL: Where did you grow up?

OSCAR: In Manhattan, on the Upper West Side. It was just working-class.

BILL: Were there more Cains or Abels in it?

OSCAR: We had a mix. I had friends who were notoriously cruel and violent people.

CHARLES: Well, if you're looking for a contemporary connection to this very old story, just think about young gang members. Their badge of honor and courage comes from having killed somebody. I can assure you that a person who has killed another person has a "rep" and a stature. I actually see Cain and Abel in a very archetypal way. This is the first murder. Cities are drenched in violence and criminality. All those characteristics of the city come to mind when I read this story.

BURT: Let me come at this a different way. Cain is the murderer. You almost watch him grapple with what that means. First, when God confronts him, he says, "Am I my brother's keeper?"

BILL: This could be a sarcastic comment.

BURT: It is sarcastic. But, ironically, it turns out to be the seed of all our ethics be-

cause the answer for every reader is: "Yes, of course you're your brother's keeper." Eventually, he learns that his crime is going to haunt him. He says in Hebrew, "*Gadol avoni miniso,*" which is often translated "My punishment is too great to bear." But in fact that's not what the Hebrew says. The Hebrew says, "My sin, my iniquity, is too great to bear." This is a guy with enormous feelings of guilt. He destroys his brother, and as a result, he becomes able to answer his own question: "Yes, I am my brother's keeper." Maybe that's the good side of the foundation of civilization. Once he knows that, he can build a city, despite the criminality and violence.

JACK: That's a pleasing and optimistic thrust—

BURT: —I'm a rabbi—

JACK: —to the story. I have to say that you can, of course, translate this as "My punishment is greater than I can bear." It's refreshing, though, that the Hebrew says, "My iniquity is greater than I can bear." Those are two very different human reactions for this first fully human being. One wants to say that here are the seeds of remorse and repentance: "Oh, my God, look what I've done. Poor Abel is dead. It's more than I can bear." But alas, in his next speech, he's copping a plea: "My punishment is more than I can bear because everywhere I go, people are going to try to kill me."

REBECCA: He really is deserving of death, and knows it.

BILL: There's a moment where I think he shows some courage. In asking the question, "Am I my brother's keeper?"—which I think is sarcastic—he's saying, "You created me. You made me this way. If You don't like the way I'm behaving, You should have stopped me. What is Your responsibility, Lord of the Universe, Creator of all of us? Where is Your responsibility?" And God is silent.

MARY: Interesting. Who's in charge here? Who's the one with the power? If we are contemptuous of Cain for not being his brother's keeper, why should he not then be contemptuous of God for not being the keeper of his sons?

BURT: That's no more acceptable than if your kids were fighting and the kid who started it turned to you and said, "It's not my fault. You should have stopped me."

MARY: No, no. If one of my kids is in a completely horrible, vengeful mood, and I know this kid's nature, and both kids have just made a clay model for me, and I choose one over the other, and then I see the vengeful kid walking around with a big stick, and I say, "Excuse me, I have to go get my hair done"—that is the analogy. God knows the nature of Cain. He knows the nature of Abel. He knows the nature of the situation. There's nothing He does not know. He has given Cain all the equipment and all the ammunition he needs. He's even given him the warning: "Sin is at the door. You can stop it." I think this is the crisis of liberalism. Liberals believe that rationality and virtue will triumph. But, in fact, pas-sion is enormously strong. Jealousy is enormously strong. Rationality and morality in the face of passion and violence are rather weak.

BILL: So God comes offering the moral voice of reason, and it isn't enough?

MARY: No, it's not enough.

JACK: I would go a step farther back than that and say that God almost plants the idea in Cain's head. It's God Who says, "Watch out for sin." It's a little like saying, "Don't eat that fruit over there" or "Don't open the seventh door. You can open the first six. But don't open the seventh." In Chekhovian terms, it's one more pistol hung on the wall, waiting to be fired.

REBECCA: I wonder. You say that God knows it all. I'm not sure that God actually knows what He's wrought here. We all know what it is to create characters and have them take off with a life of their own, and we don't have total control, and they surprise us, right? We've experienced this.

"Here is this new creature of incredible complexity, this embodied consciousness, this animal with a point of view."

God had the angels for company. The animals are pretty simple. But here is this new creature of incredible complexity, this embodied consciousness, this animal with a point of view. Does God really know the implications?

FAYE: We need to ask what the original narrative is trying to say. Isn't it that violence is in all of us, even in God's original creatures?

BILL: It wasn't in Abel, was it?

REBECCA: Well, it could have been. We have no way of knowing because his life was cut short. What I take away from the story is that violence is in all of us. The ability to do bad is in all of us. And we have to confront our own ability to do evil. It lies at the doorstep, just as the text says.

"We have to confront our own ability to do evil. It lies at the doorstep."

CHARLES: I agree with that interpretation. And I like Burt's idea that God may not be omniscient. At this time, maybe he doesn't know. Maybe, like your typical reader, he's held in suspense about how these events are going to unfold. That seems closer to what we have on the page, in the text. We cannot overlook this sense that God takes his child aside and says,

"Look, you do it this way, and it will turn out better. You don't do it this way because there is something outside the door that is really going to cause a great disaster."

REBECCA: Yes, it's after the Flood—which lies ahead—that God gets really precise about the rules. He comes forth with laws. He's not going to leave it to man's inclinations anymore. He's seen what those inclinations are.

CHARLES: So God's on a real learning curve here.

REBECCA: I think so. There's perhaps an indeterminacy in mixing the Godly and the beastly, and God is watching how it unfolds—and then reacting.

BURT: Yes, I think God is learning. God sees the child with the stick. It never dawns on God that this child is going to pick up the stick and clobber his sibling.

MARY: Why not, though?

BURT: Because God has no clue what the experiment of free will is all about. God grants this creature enough Godlike characteristics to do as the creature pleases. And that creature then turns around and does evil. I think God is shocked. The good news of the story is that it teaches us that God is trying to figure out what humanity is all about and what God's relationship to humanity is all about. Eventually, God says, "This isn't working quite as I thought," and starts all over again, like your new draft.

JACK: It's a terribly expensive experiment.

REBECCA: Favoritism really becomes such an important issue throughout Genesis. Now here it's God choosing. But with every generation, someone is chosen. There is Ishmael, firstborn of Abraham, and his brother Isaac. And then Isaac's children, Jacob and Esau. Then Jacob's twelve sons, with Joseph as the favorite. This whole book is very much the story of one being chosen.

FAYE: I see the Cain and Abel chapter as a story that's more about good and evil than chosen versus not chosen.

REBECCA: But sometimes it's pretty arbitrary.

BILL: Oscar, you seem to be wrestling with whether or not this story depicts the world as it is.

OSCAR: I would say so. I don't think human nature has changed much. But the idea behind the story that intrigues me is whether there is a God that's involved. As I get older, I look around and see more, not less, evidence of life's unfairness. Why does a little two-year-old fall out of a crib and that's it for him, whereas a really bad guy like Idi Amin, who committed mass murder—and if that's not outdoing Cain, I don't know what is—is living in luxurious exile in France. Then there's the Holocaust. The question is: Why should you believe in any God or in any principle of morality?

JACK: There's one way of coming at the story that we haven't directly done yet. I'll put it on the table now: If you have the privilege of not having to begin with the premise that this is a divine text and just look at it as a story, not unlike a lot of other stories that other cultures have produced, it could be fit into the category of what folklorists call "the etiological myth." You know, why does the fox have a white tail? How come the snake doesn't have any legs? It strikes me that if one just asks the question: "How come we got these cities with these arts and sciences, where people go around killing each other?"—well, the story of Cain and Abel, like the story of Adam and Eve in the Garden, is one culture's attempt to give an account, not always very satisfactory, of the accidents of history. We're wringing our hearts, souls, and minds to try to make moral or judicial sense out of something that is what Murray Gell-Mann and the particle physicists call "a frozen accident." You have oral traditions that get written down at a certain point, and then they get amended and analyzed in commentary. The "frozen accident" is configured this way, but it could have been configured in many other imaginable ways. But having been configured and then sanctified, not only by religious authority but also by centuries of careful attention on the part of culture, the "frozen accident" takes on a life of its own, even with its discrepancies and problematical aspects. We may do ill with our merely human intelligence to try to iron out the real sense of God's behavior.

OSCAR: But do the stories work? Again,

The First Four Days of Creation, Sarajevo Haggadah, Spain, 14th c.

Adam and Eve in Paradise,
Anthology, Shiraz, Iran, 1410–11

Harriet Powers, *Adam and Eve* (detail),
pictorial quilt, 1895–98

Ellis Ruley, *Adam and Eve,* late 1940s

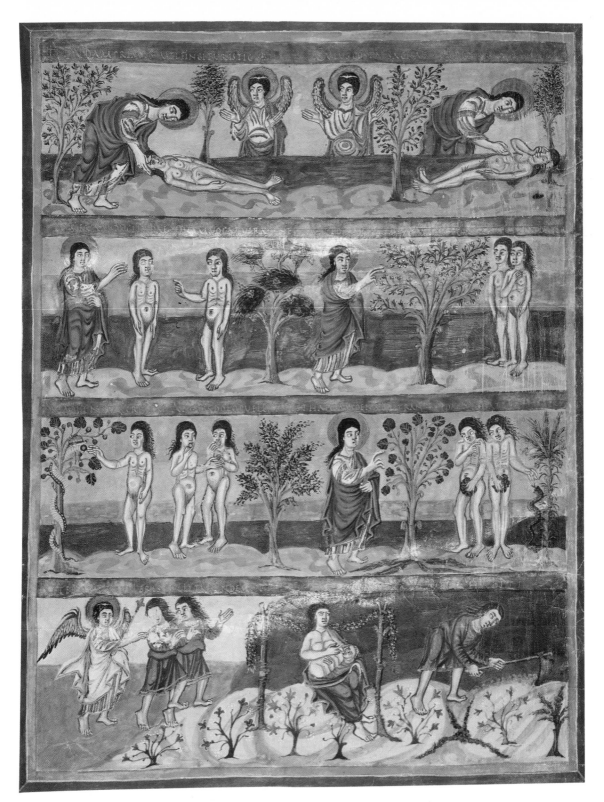

Creation, frontispiece, *Grandval Bible*, Tours, ca. 840

Scherer and Ouporov, *Terra Nullius*, 1994

Cher Shaffer, *The Seduction of Eve*, 1982

Adam and Eve and the Tree of Wisdom (detail), embroidered Bible book binding, England, ca. 1640–50

Herbert Singleton,
Adam and Eve, 1991

Miriam Schapiro, *The Garden of Eden*, 1990

Adam and Eve, The London Miscellany, France,
late 13th c.

Eve, Coptic fresco, Om el Bergat, 11th c.

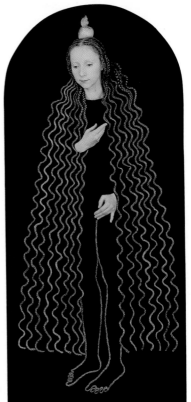

Rimma Gerlovina and
Valeriy Gerlovin, *Eve*, 1993–95

Holly Lane, *She Decided to
Return the Loathsome Gift*,
1992

Cain and Abel, *Naples Bible*, late 14th c.

Alfredo Castañeda, *Our First Parents*, 1986

Masaccio, *Expulsion from Paradise*, Brancacci
Chapel, Maria del Carmine, Florence, Italy,
ca. 1425

Leonora Carrington, *Yaweah*, ca. 1950

Creation, manuscript,
Umbria, 13th c.

Six Days of Creation, from Hildegard of Bingen,
Eibingen Scivias, 12th c.

going back to when I was a kid, when I first heard these stories, I thought they were about real people—although, as you grow up, you come to understand about allegory.

FAYE: You don't think the story is about real people?

OSCAR: I said I think it *is* about real people. I think these stories were supposed to give real people some moral foundation.

BILL: Do you find a moral lesson in this story?

OSCAR: Cynically, "Don't get caught!" But obviously, in the world, you get caught.

BURT: I'm intrigued listening to Oscar. For me, Genesis grapples with issues that virtually every one of you grapples with in your fiction, right? You set the same narrative themes, even though you may work your way to different solutions. And yet almost all of you expect Genesis to offer simpler solutions than anything you would do in your own fictions.

MARY: Wait a minute! I want to speak to the "frozen moment" Jack raised and to this issue of what we expect from Genesis. Look, there's a difference between *War and Peace* and the Book of Genesis. This is not a book like other books. It's not a frozen moment like other frozen moments. It's a frozen moment that's become unthawed and entered into the river or the bloodstream of culture. It's something people

have lived by and been told to live by. Nobody told me to live by *Anna Karenina*. Nobody told me I was going to go to hell if I didn't believe *Madame Bovary*. Nobody really wants to kill anybody for not believing in *Jude the Obscure*. Yes, the Bible is a book—but it's not *just* a book. It has become incorporated into the way people see themselves and the way that they live. Most people, if they had a religious background, heard it at first naively, not as an isolated narrative, but in the context of a whole way of living and a whole belief system.

JACK: You understand that when I spoke of it as a frozen accident, I didn't mean, therefore, that it is without consequences. That a presidential candidate wins by only five hundred votes, let's say, may be a frozen accident, but it has enormous consequences. We get one administration rather than another administration.

BILL: But what is it about Genesis, Mary, that draws us?

MARY: It is the handbook of spiritual authority. It is the handbook of those who say, "You are saved, and you are damned. You are chosen, and you are not." I don't excommunicate, put to death, sit *shiva* for people who don't read my books. People do not come to me at the moment of birth, death, loss, and grievance and say to me, "Make sense of my life." People don't come to my books and say, "By this book I will know who I am and what my place is and what will happen to me after death." Genesis is different.

Francisco de Goya,
Cain and Abel,
ca. 1817–20

JACK: All I was saying is that if we're looking at it from this secular perspective, as a frozen accident, nonetheless it becomes scripture, first for the Jews, and then for the Jews and Christians, and to some extent, for Islam as well. And enormous cultural consequences flow from that. That's one of the reasons we don't live by *Madame Bovary*.

CHARLES: Exactly. And another thing. I write an individual book. You write an individual book. But these stories in Genesis are very much part of our global inheritance. They are very much like coins, two thousand years old. They've been passed around through so many cultures, and they have the sweat and palm oil of so many individuals on them that if we open them up and unpack them, we discover something of our own humanity, something of the possibilities of what we are as a species. There are so many interpretations of these stories and so much is laid upon them and they've been used so often to organize human experience that the problem is not a lack of meaning in these stories—it's too much meaning. There's a surplus of meaning because you're talking about two thousand years' worth of human effort to make sense out of civilization. Brotherhood. Envy.

BILL: It helps us to make sense if we look at Cain and Abel as characters in the story you're writing. What do you think of them as characters?

CHARLES: I think Cain's the most interesting. He's interior, and he has guilt. I think he has subjectivity. He's more like us, in terms of the modern world.

JACK: And he has more time onstage.

MARY: Abel has no dialogue—no lines.

BILL: The victim is silent.

REBECCA: Abel has a transparency as a character. We know all there is to know about him. With Cain, we don't. He has that subjectivity. We know he has passion. We can only guess what it was like to be Cain in that moment.

MARY: I would like to know: What is it like to give with a pure heart? What is it like to give the best and to give without reservation? To me, that's the enormously, humanly interesting thing about Abel. To give without reservation and then—what did Abel experience at that moment when Cain came at him?

BILL: What about the possibility that this fury that Cain feels is directed not at his brother Abel but at God for favoring Abel?

CHARLES: I think that's what he's striking out at. It's not Abel, it's God. Abel just happens to be in between.

BURT: Abel is in God's image.

FAYE: But I think he's striking out at Abel, too. I see Cain as a buck passer, excusing himself because of his own moral limitations. "It's your fault that God didn't accept my sacrifices. It's your fault this is happening."

REBECCA: "If only you didn't exist, God would love me. You are the obstacle between God and me."

FAYE: Isn't there a midrash—an oral tradition—that says that Abel had Cain down, and Cain pleaded for mercy, and Abel let him go?

BURT: That's what midrash does. It gives him some monologue here. The rabbis provide what's between the lines, the interior monologue.

MARY: It's enormously hard to create a good character. Good characters are very few and far between in literature.

BILL: By "good character," do you mean people who are good at heart?

MARY: Yes, morally good, good at heart. Goodness is refraining from being seized by desire.

FAYE: Controlling your violent urges.

MARY: And being seized by desire is really much more fun to write about.

BURT: So none of you would write about a character who is good?

MARY: I've tried. I've really tried. It interests me enormously. And I have been frustrated by the paucity of models. Oscar just did it in his recent novel. He wrote about a really good man who suffers.

OSCAR: I had to wrack my brains for that one, though. My book, *Mr. Ives' Christmas*, is basically about a man who believes in goodness, in God, in work, in religion, and watches his son being killed for no particular reason at all. It's just a pointless death.

BILL: Why that theme?

OSCAR: Because I was thinking about the pointless suffering in this world. How does one stand up against that or preserve one's sense of self? We've mentioned the Holocaust—where was God in all this? I read somewhere that the presence of a moral system in one's life leads to a better death, or to an improvement in the internal circumstances of death. And so for a char-

acter like Ives, who watches his son being killed, it's a horrible situation, but the goodness in his own life leads him to—I wouldn't say an inward comfort—but to an inner sense that the world is still better off because of the belief in goodness.

JACK: I don't see any nuance of that redemptive quality in the Cain and Abel story. It's not as if Cain, when he founds a city, says, "Gee, if only my brother were here to see this!"

OSCAR: But what if after killing his brother, Cain was then tortured for six months and beheaded as they would have done to him in the Middle Ages? How does that make a better world?

BILL: You raise the question in my mind again about Cain's fury. It seems to me that he might be carrying the world's first outrage over injustice—the injustice of God's arbitrary choice of Abel's offering with no explanation. I, myself, have been as angry at God as that.

OSCAR: About the fairness of life or circumstance, sure.

CHARLES: Martin Luther King said, "Unearned suffering may be redemptive." You know, it's purifying in a sense.

JACK: Yes. One wants to say that ire and suffering had *better* be redemptive.

BILL: So is there any redemption in this story?

MARY: There's no redemption for Abel,

certainly, because Abel is dead and has no more possibility. There's no more narrative for Abel. I think the challenge for a moral person is always to be a witness to Abel. That is what it is to be an ethical human being—to say, "I am in the place of that person who is unjustly cut down. I am a witness to that." Now, what happens after that? Do you say, "I then will try to create a world where this won't happen"? Well, there is no moment of ethical progress in this story. It's not a story about ethics or moving forward morally.

OSCAR: So why Cain? Why Abel? What's the difference? What's the guiding principle?

BILL: There's a verse in Exodus where God says, "I will be gracious to whom I will be gracious." This is arbitrary choice. God can bless. God can curse.

OSCAR: So He's temperamental.

BILL: He's arbitrary, at least.

REBECCA: But if the text didn't present the world in this way—as being inexplicably arbitrary—it just wouldn't be true to life as we see it played out before our eyes. Life is arbitrary. That's the great problem, to which one of the possible responses—the one *this* text presupposes—is faith.

BILL: Wouldn't you like a God Who changes the facts?

REBECCA: Yes. But a story like that wouldn't be one that represented our world. Life is arbitrary, and this story shows it that way. The good suffer. There is no explanation for it. We don't get one from God. The world as it's shown in this story corresponds all too well to the world as we know it—which is why the struggle for faith *is* such a struggle. It's a struggle even in a story like this, where God's existence is a given.

JACK: As I mentioned earlier, the God in Job is rather more apprehensible. I don't like the chap, but I find Him at least more apprehensible.

BILL: Oscar, you said you found God more interesting because He exists apart from the world, and that's the only way we can see God.

OSCAR: I think so. Once, in Rome, I had dinner with the papal astronomer. I asked him, "So where's heaven?" He said, "Yes, God is in heaven. But He's not in this universe." So forget it, buddy. He's operating on a totally different plane.

BURT: I grew up with a much more immanent theology. God really does act in history, and God really does act in the universe. This would be my response to your point that there's no redemption for Abel. The fact that four thousand years later, we're still struggling with Abel's death is a redemption for him. The fact that Cain's rejoinder—"Am I my brother's keeper?"—has become a cornerstone of our morality is vindication for Abel. It's the only redemption he's going to get. The study of the narrative is the way in which, all these years later, we can redeem Abel's death and

Max Band, *Am I My Brother's Keeper?*, 1948

make sure that it's not fruitless but meaningful.

JACK: By bearing witness.

BURT: Yes, and that bearing witness is also bearing witness to God's presence because we recognize a moral force in the universe.

MARY: That's where I have a problem. I don't think it's remarkable that human beings would want to personify something in which to deposit their sense of awe. That seems very clear, and God seems like a good candidate for that. I understand the desire to create myths etiologically, to answer questions like "Why are we here?" But what's really mysterious is why anyone would think that the God of the Bible is a moral source—because He really isn't. He is awe-inspiring and a fascinating character. But ethics? I'm talking about the Old Testament God. It seems to me that Jesus does actually give us an example of an ethically lived life.

BURT: But I don't have the advantage of Jesus in my canon, so I have to grapple with the God of the Hebrew Bible. And I think you're right. On the one hand, we're faced with an enormous moral dilemma. In Genesis, in particular, God is very difficult as a character. But we don't just have the God of the Hebrew Bible, we also have the God of the midrash—the interpretation. We have the God of the rabbis. The God of the New Testament—kind of a Hellenistic, nice, good guy. But only to have a good guy isn't going to be helpful. It's not true to reality. To only have this whimsical, arbitrary God isn't going to help us, either. We must have a very, very complicated picture of God. If God is the Creator of the universe, then at least give God credit for being complicated.

FAYE: If life always worked out in a justice pattern, where does the leap of faith fit in?

MARY: But why is one of the first sentences that children say, "It's not fair!"? That's a great mystery.

FAYE: Because you're looking at the here and now. If you believe there's a world outside of our current world right now—

BILL: —you mean like the hereafter?

> "Why is one of the first sentences that children say, 'It's not fair!'? That's a great mystery."

FAYE: The world to come. When I struggle with injustice, which is often in this world, belief in the next life gives me a sense of comfort. There must be a better—

MARY: —but if you gave your five-year-old two cookies, and you gave your three-year-old one and a half, that kid says, "It's not fair." Nothing to do with the hereafter. He wants justice now.

FAYE: But we're talking about adults here.

MARY: I'm saying that before adulthood, there seems to be an innate sense that there is a thing in the world called "justice" about which children are enormously clear.

REBECCA: But noticing when things are not fair is natural for children. What comes much later on is morality, seeing the equal claims that others make. That is not natural, but comes very, very hard. Children are not born with that. We as parents struggle with how to instill this in them. A little kid doesn't start whining because he got *more* than his brother. That would be morality. The task of becoming a moral agent, this distancing yourself from your own desires, is very, very hard. I think that's what we find in this chapter.

JACK: And we have to remember, at least as some of us are reading the text, that the initial unfairness in this story is God's.

MARY: Yes.

JACK: The late Howard Nemerov wrote a little play called *Cain*. In this play, Abel comes in gloating, like, "What, you think God wants to smell these burnt tomatoes? You know, it's *meat* that He wants. It's *blood* that He wants to smell." So Abel's asking for it by taunting.

FAYE: It's blaming the victim?

JACK: It's a little bit of blaming the victim.

BILL: So, Jack, how would you rewrite the end of this story if you could?

JACK: I rather like the way it ends, mysteriously and tidily, from the writer's point of view. To go back to Chekhov again, most of the pistols that get hung on the wall in Act One get fired in Act Three, one way or another. The dice are so loaded already, in the beginning of the story, that any of us who deal in fiction could almost predict what's going to happen. It starts with their names. As soon as they get these two names, we see that one is going to be the victim and the other's going to be some-

thing else. And as soon as they choose their professions, or are assigned to them, we think of that line of Rodgers and Hammerstein's about the cowhand—

REBECCA: —the cowboys and the farmers.

JACK: "The cowboys and the farmers can be friends"—which means, we know, they're not going to be. It's like saying the Montagues and the Capulets can be friends, or the Arabs and the Israelis. It ain't gonna be that easy. And then by the time the sacrifice comes, we're all ready for it. The mainspring of the plot has been cocked already. Then things proceed. At that point, of course, comes the dramaturgically problematical matter not of Cain's motive, but of God's motive in rejecting the sacrifice. No editor would want to let that get by.

BILL: Or the fact that God protects the murderer. Oscar, are you offended that God does this? That Cain doesn't really pay for his sin?

OSCAR: Yes, I'm offended—but what else could you do with this guy? He has to live with his conscience. Does anyone here think that Cain had a conscience?

JACK: If he has a conscience, I don't see it. In the Qur'anic version, he repents, and there's no suggestion of a curse or banishment. But in the Hebrew version, he's sent off. He certainly feels sorry for himself if what he said is, "My punishment is too great to bear." If the Hebrew is "iniquity," as Burt said, then that's the beginning of some kind of repentance. That mark that God puts on him is almost like Hester Prynne wearing her scarlet letter. So while nobody's going to bop him on the head, because that's reserved for God to do, he certainly is carrying the evidence of some sort of crime around with him.

BILL: There's such a fever in America today for an eye for an eye and a tooth for a tooth.

BURT: Let's not forget that an eye for an eye, a tooth for a tooth, is also in the Bible. That is a biblical concept. But the Bible struggles, just as our society does, with these two notions. On one hand, maybe it's not so terrible that God protects the murderer from human vengeance because vengeance just reduplicates murder. There's just more murder in the world. The only one with the right to give life or death should be God. Number two: I think that Cain, in some ways, suffers terribly. This guy's a farmer, and he has the worst of all possible fates for the farmer—he's uprooted from the land and put into exile. He has to wander. It's ironic, of course, because he doesn't seem to wander very far. And he founds a city, the very antithesis of agricultural society.

MARY: To be dead is the worst fate. Abel's fate.

REBECCA: Cain has remorse. The Hebrew, as Burt said, indicates that. And from what I've tasted of remorse, it's very bitter. It embitters life. What Cain has done can never be undone.

MARY: But remorse allows for change. Death does not allow for change. That's why I think the moment in which God protects Cain causes me to love the story. It's so complicated and contradictory—like life. I've known people who have had family members murdered. Whatever punishment is exacted upon the murderer, there's one part of the murdered family that feels it's not enough because he's still alive. "I don't give a damn! He's in prison, making license plates. But he's still alive, and my beloved is not." This is a very deep, human feeling which may have to be overcome. But nothing's more final than death. This is a moment like the moment in *Lear* when Cordelia says, "No cause, no cause." It's the moment at which the terrible machine of vengeance is stopped. And there is a moment of mercy beyond justice that is inexplicable and tremendously beautiful because it's so mysterious.

FAYE: I'm still troubled by the sense of justice—why was Cain spared immediate death? Earlier, Jack spoke about the first murder. Perhaps God showed him leniency because this was the first murder, and Cain didn't know the consequences of what he was doing. So that question—"Am I my brother's keeper?"—is a protest that God had not warned him. God says, "Fair enough." And He gives Cain a mark of protection.

BURT: Are you suggesting that he doesn't ask that question disingenuously? Can we imagine a situation where somebody says, "Am I my brother's keeper?"

and in fact doesn't know the answer to that question?

FAYE: I think it was a rhetorical statement. He's saying to God, "You created this whole world. You created my parents. You created us. Who's the real keeper around here?" Look, if Cain hadn't had God's original warning, it might have been an accurate statement to reflect what was going on at that time. But since he was warned, he can no longer throw it back in God's face. My interpretation of Cain's question is: "You're the guardian of all. You made me as I am. Why are You asking me what happened?"

REBECCA: I also believe that he was asking it genuinely. At this point, it is the voice of utter moral ignorance or moral shutdown. I think that God's warning fell on completely deaf ears. Cain was not in a position to hear any of that wafting, wonderful, rational, get-a-grip-on-yourself advice.

BURT: Is there such a thing as utter moral ignorance in the human condition? Never!

FAYE: Perhaps in the first murder.

REBECCA: We all know that our own desires, for whatever reasons, are poundingly present in our consciousness. And we know people who are shut up in themselves, where their own desires completely determine their world view.

BILL: So what is the sin that is lurking at the door? God warns Cain that sin is lurking at the door if you don't master your passions.

REBECCA: It is the urge to heed your own hurts, pains, passions, and desires, and to let them determine your action completely without any other thought of the claims that other creatures make on your life. That is exactly how Cain behaves.

BILL: And this is inherent in us? It isn't some force from outside that possesses us?

REBECCA: Quite the contrary. It consists by being possessed by oneself. I love the way the Bible externalizes it so that it's almost something outside of oneself that one suffers. But it isn't. It's completely inside.

BURT: Later the Bible refers to it as "in the heart."

FAYE: God says, "This is up to you."

BILL: To do what?

FAYE: Either to do good or to do evil.

BILL: Master your passions?

FAYE: Master your passions. As Rebecca said, in Hebrew, these unmastered passions are an entity, the *yetzer hara*, the "evil inclination." But I think it's clear from God's admonitions that evil is something that exists within us.

CHARLES: Free will—very important.

JACK: I want to rescue Cain's emotional

and psychological complexity by coming down hard in favor of the idea that his question—"Am I my brother's keeper?"—is a disingenuous question. If it's an innocent question, he loses interest for me. He's robbed of a great deal of his psychological complexity. And it's that psychological complexity, carried over in the ambivalence of his being spared as well as stigmatized, that keeps the story interesting.

B I L L : If this were a fiction class, and you were giving the rest of us this plot as an exercise, how would you want us to play with these characters?

J A C K : The first impulse is to straighten out incoherences and discrepancies. The second impulse is to make sure you don't get them *all* straightened out. Kafka has one of his characters say, finally, that this is an unsolved riddle for us to respect. For me, particularly, coming to the Cain and Abel story out of a secular background, the unsolved mystery is of the essence of the story's appeal. This isn't just a straightforward moral parable, even though it has aspects of parable or allegory. But much is dark and unexplained. I like that. So I wouldn't advise my class to do much playing around with these characters.

B I L L : Is there a line you could write that might cause Cain to put down that stone or rod?

O S C A R : I believe the world is divided into two camps—people who are introspec-

Cain Kills Abel, God Banishes Cain, ivory, France, 11th c.

tive and those who aren't. Cain's a hothead, the kind of guy who would shoot you on impulse. I remember a time when West 80th Street had the highest murder rate in New York. A guy was sitting on a garbage can when another fellow came along and said, ''Get off that garbage can! It's mine!'' The first guy said no, and the stranger pulled out a gun and killed him for sitting on a garbage can. If the guy had been more introspective, chances are he wouldn't have shot the guy.

''Cain's a hothead, the kind of guy who would shoot you on impulse.''

FAYE: Introspection is a moral development.

MARY: But why has moral development had such a lousy track record?

OSCAR: Because people tend to confuse physical strength and superiority with the right to do as they please.

MARY: But think of one's own life. I find just trying not to be a murderer completely grueling. It's quite remarkable that I'm not behind bars.

OSCAR: You should see her when she gets angry!

MARY: I feel as if I have enormously selfish and violent impulses. The struggle to be a moral human being is really, really tough. I'm not in jail because I've had family—I've had enormous good fortune.

BILL: You had the Church, did you not?

MARY: Yes.

BURT: Well, that's what I was wondering: Do you identify this idea that people are bad as a fact of human consciousness? Or is this really the Catholic in you?

MARY: I think that if we choose this narrative as a center, it tells us that the murderous impulse is very old to the human story.

BURT: So Augustine was right about original sin—you just want to be violent and disobey?

MARY: Yes, but I disagree with Augustine that baptism takes original sin away. I have a much darker view. But I don't think original sin is the whole story. Call it the tragic flaw—but there really is something wrong with people, or else the world would be a better place. Why is there so much violence?

FAYE: Mary, you personally take your violent urge and channel it into something creative. That's very, very right.

MARY: But why is the violence there in the first place?

"I find just trying not to be a murderer completely grueling. It's quite remarkable that I'm not behind bars."

CHARLES: What I heard you saying is that, to a large extent, Cain's problem is egotism. He's very much anchored in himself. Why do you want to kill somebody? Because there's *this* self and there's that *other* self. In each of us there's tension and conflict. It's all based on dualism.

MARY: But if we believe in corporeal life, and if Abel has a body, and that body suffers, the body of the victim is not a construct of someone else's mind.

BILL: It's a reality.

FAYE: Doesn't Catholicism look forward to another world?

MARY: Well, that's a big problem.

FAYE: But that's a problem that you have with this story—Abel is going from a bad place to a worse place.

MARY: But I don't think that's Catholicism. I think any relationship with a religious tradition that has an afterlife has to have a dual consciousness. If you just believe that everything is going to get all fixed up after death, well, why not act like a complete creep? You have a dual consciousness. Yes, perhaps injustice will be rectified after death—but that does not take away your responsibility not only to fight against injustice, but to bear witness to injustice.

FAYE: But that's also what keeps people in line. If they do good, they will be rewarded.

MARY: It hasn't worked really well.

FAYE: As I said, if everything were made right, and there were a sense of justice in the Bible and in the world, then life would make sense, and there would be no moral attribute to doing good because you'd know you would be rewarded. Doing good when you don't know whether you're going to get rewarded or punished elevates the act.

MARY: That's from the position of the prosperous, the nonvictim. From the position of the witness to the victim, it often seems like a pretty unfair deal.

BURT: I'm just fascinated with your empathy for Abel, your persistence in seeing yourself in Abel's blood. What is it that prompts you to be so closely identified?

MARY: Perhaps it does have its basis in Christianity. Jesus is the victim. The blood of the victim cries.

BILL: I wonder if, because you're Mary Gordon, you wouldn't feel that way if there were no Jesus part of the Genesis story for you. Wouldn't you be concerned for Abel if you were a Buddhist, or Muslim, whatever? There's something in your nature that recognizes sin to be preoccupation with oneself, one's own self, with one's desires and impulses.

MARY: It's an inability to identify with the body of the other, the suffering body. I think that is sin. And what's the source of that? I don't know.

BILL: Faye, do you teach your four children that their incentive for doing good is a reward in heaven?

FAYE: First of all, I have teenagers, so I don't teach them much at all. I do try to instill in them that there is a sense of morality in this world, and doing good should be done for its own sake, not for something tangible. Life isn't fair. Maybe it will get straightened out in an afterlife. I don't know. But doing good is its own reward.

BILL: Abel would tell you, "That's foolish advice to give your children because I was good. I did righteous things. I offered my best offering to God from the purest of hearts, and look what happened to me."

FAYE: Maybe living a righteous life was his own reward. Who's to say what happens in the afterlife? But without even going into an afterlife, there is joy in trying to live a moral life.

JACK: I thought that's what Cain was trying to do when he thought up the idea of bringing an offering to God.

CHARLES: You think he got a bad rap.

JACK: I think he got a bad rap.

BILL: But he did win mercy.

MARY: It's what I began by saying—justice is simultaneously absolutely essential and impossible, and that this moment at which the child, however narcissistically motivated, cries out, "It's not fair" is a very important human moment. And yet, as Hamlet says, if we were all treated after our deserts, who would escape whipping? None of us really wants a world where justice is triumphant over mercy. So I think the great and most beautifully mysterious moment is when God says, "Okay, it's about mercy now." It's not about behavior anymore, it's about something else, and that something else is not in the text. It is very mysterious. It is only that mercy beyond understanding that stops bloodshed.

BILL: So God will not allow an eye for an eye, and a tooth for a tooth?

MARY: Yes.

FAYE: That actually refers to monetary compensation. I've got to say that. It's not, "You take a life, I'll take a life." This sentence and what follows comes in the portion of the Bible that has to do with *tort* law and with *civil* law. It means *monetary* compensation. In other words, if you injure somebody's eye, you pay the difference between a person's work value with two eyes versus the work value with one eye. This method is how personal injury suits are settled today. It is not vengeance. It's not Hammurabi's Code.

JACK: By Burt's earlier reasoning, that's about what happens when Cain gets taken off the land. He can no longer be a farmer.

FAYE: There is a sense in our literature—it's called *mida-kaneged-mida*.

BURT: Yes, "measure for measure." It's found in the Gospels as well. I'm intrigued by this. Mercy is an essential part of the universe, but what do you do when mercy seems to override justice so thoroughly that you're left with the creepy feeling someone's walking scot-free? Maybe Abel's wife is still pretty unhappy about all this.

REBECCA: But the very next chapter is the Flood, right? It all gets destroyed. I mean, this is not mercy. By the next chapter, God has decided to start all over.

MARY: I think it's a mistake to try to make narrative sense of something that is absurd. Somehow, the position of the survivor is an impossible position because you simultaneously want punishment for the murderer. And if the cycle of vengeance goes on, that's hopeless, too. You can only say, "Stop, stop! There's no answer to this, so we'll stop." The moment you say "Stop" is the moment of mercy. "I give up my own desire for bloodshed, vengeance. It is not about me." That's a moment of

grace, a moment of mercy. That's the moment in the story that I love the most and that I find completely inexplicable.

BURT: I'm intrigued with Rebecca's point about how the story unfolds. In the synagogue, we read all five books of Moses in the course of a year, which means, essentially, that it's divided into fifty-four parts. For reasons that are obscure to me, the rabbis chose to have one week's narrative include all the grandeur of creation, the story of Cain and Abel all the way down to the point where God decides to destroy the world. Just one week. It always leaves me kind of breathless. What a depressing end for that week, that you start the reading with the creation of the universe, and you end the reading with the understanding that everything is just going to be thrown away.

FAYE: But it's uplifting in its own way. The next fifty-three parts speak of a better world, one with a developed moral consciousness.

MARY: That hopeful notion is taken from the position of the winners, though—it's not Abel, and it's not those drowned in the Flood.

BILL: Mary, a few minutes ago, you acknowledged your fury—your potential for violence. Everyone else kept silent.

CHARLES: I think I felt it when I was much younger. Twenty years ago, things in the world seemed inexplicable. History seemed like a slaughterhouse. And you do want reasons for that, so you turn to moral philosophy. I don't know if you find a satisfactory answer there. But responding to this rage is what the religious impulse is about. There are no other doors.

OSCAR: You're mellowing it out.

CHARLES: No, not mellowing it out, just recognizing that there are no other doors we can go through. Not science or other secular disciplines. Still, it's hard for me to believe that undeserved suffering is redemptive. If you take a very Buddhist perspective in which there is no self and no soul, then really, nobody's died. But from a Western point of view, that seems a little callous, a little indifferent to suffering. I can't see this great injustice and not feel a certain anger.

FAYE: I think that's what moral education is all about—not necessarily religious education, but moral education. It takes a much higher level of development to delay ego gratification and to empathize with the other.

CHARLES: Which you can find in fiction.

FAYE: Yes, yes! The whole point of the story is to recognize this rage that exists in all of us and to try the best we can, as fallible human beings, to overcome it and rise above it. We've all felt rage.

BURT: If you had a choice, who would you be—Cain or Abel?

MARY: Cain. I'd be alive. And there would be a possibility of rewriting the story. There would be a possibility of remorse, moral education, reformation of life, the beginning of a dynasty.

BURT: But there's no nobility in dying innocent?

MARY: There's no nobility because Abel didn't choose it. Abel's nobility came in the purity of his sacrifice, not in the manner of his death. I think nobility only comes with a moment of choice.

BURT: Are those not the same thing— the purity of his sacrifice and the manner of his death?

MARY: No. He could have made a sacrifice with a pure heart, and that would have been the same moment of purity and giving, whether Cain had killed him or not. Cain's killing him does not retroactively wipe out Abel's purity.

BURT: So Abel's not the blood sacrifice himself.

MARY: No.

BILL: When we asked you to come to this session, did you go back and read the story of Cain and Abel again for the first time in a while? And if you did, did you find something in it that surprised you? That you didn't remember being there?

OSCAR: I didn't remember the whole forgiveness thing. I'm so used to the world as it is that the idea that the mark of Cain would be set out to protect him startled me.

This is a very big question: What do you do with people who've done bad things? I think compassion should be a rule of life. It isn't often, or easily, practiced. I'm interested in knowing if Jack thinks compassion should be part of the picture.

> *"This is a very big question: What do you do with people who've done bad things?"*

JACK: If one's designing a universe? Of if one's writing a novel? God spare us from a universe without compassion. Although God knows, its distribution is unpredictable, even capricious, at least in our eyes, and not to be depended upon.

OSCAR: Like the weather.

JACK: Yes—presumably explainable somewhere, but not to us mere mortals. I had not read the Cain and Abel story since hearing it in Sunday school, many, many eons ago. What surprised me, on going back to reread it, is that it doesn't quite make dramatic sense, or moral sense, until it's leaned on, or until you hear conversations about it like this. Yet that through all of that, and over all those years since Methodist Sunday school, which slipped from me so readily afterward, was the poignancy of "Am I my brother's keeper?"— and the more ambiguous poignancy of

"my sin" or "my punishment is greater than I can bear." These two moments in the history of morality are great dramatic moments, pungent and poignant—yet they don't answer any moral questions.

CHARLES: I was troubled and surprised by this story. It had become remote in my memory since childhood Sunday school classes. I guess what really sticks with me now, and which had me up at four-thirty this morning, is the dilemma of brotherhood, what that means—and how murder is the result of this intimate connection between two people who mirror each other in certain very important ways. I really do believe in the ideal of brotherhood across cultures, and so forth. But to have original sin in the Judeo-Christian tradition is troubling to me. It really is. You go to Rwanda, you go to Bosnia or Northern Ireland or parts of North America, and you find brother killing brother.

BILL: So the author of Genesis is sculpting the material from real clay.

CHARLES: I think so. But there's also something else very interesting between the two characters, Cain and Abel. You go a little bit farther into the Middle Ages, and you see a different interpretation. The one who is the wanderer, the pilgrim, is really Abel. This is not his world. His world is the world to come. And Augustine says that the City of God is that of Abel, and the City of Earth is that of Cain. In the Christian context, that makes you think of shared values and of relinquishing the ego. In the City of Earth, passion leads to bloodshed. Cities are fertilized by the blood of brothers.

Sacrifice of Cain and Abel, Haggadah, Spain,
14th c.

But in the City of God, where you are
among other people who are part of this
community where all of you share the
same values, you can have real brotherhood—not of blood, but of the spirit.

MARY: But most of us live in a largely
secular world. The alternative to a secular
world seems more and more like a kind of
religious tribalism. So what, then, is the
choice for people who cannot find their
home in any religious community? Is there
a choice, other than religious tribalism?

And supposing you say, "I don't believe in
this God. I just don't believe in God. He's
not there. This is an ancient story. It's poetic and tragic and wonderful, but it has
absolutely nothing to do with me." So
many people are like this in developed
countries. A lot of people feel outside the
City of God.

BURT: But that outside feeling is also a
real hunger for community. Ironically, the
thing that drives kids to be in gangs is the
same thing that brings people to religious
communities. In some ways, it's the same
thing that lets us sit here, knee to knee, to
discuss a text that not all of us necessarily
believe is sacred or this or that. But it con-
nects us in some way. In reading and
studying the Bible, whatever your beliefs
are—Jews or Christians, black or white—
you can find some common ground for
discussion. That is the beginning of community—the kind of refuge that we talked
about.

MARY: There are two words that always make me look for the exit—
"community" and "spiritual." America
was based on an enlightenment experiment
that may have been too hopeful and hard
for people. But there has to be a place for
all those human beings who think, "All
there is is what you see. And then you die,
and that's it. There's nothing else to do but
try to be good and make sense of it." There
is a real moral heroism implicit in that. I
admire Martin Luther King, but how do
you become a person of virtue in a world
where values are different? Somehow, I'm
not ready to give up on that experiment.

CHARLES: But let me just interject something here, Mary. I think the founders of this nation—Madison and others—had something in mind with this kind of experience in which people who are given freedom must also possess an internal moral monitor. They didn't think freedom was possible unless people could govern themselves. That's one reason moral education is so incredibly important. Without that moral center, you pull out the foundation for any kind of communal life.

OSCAR: But, Charles, there are a lot of people walking around who could care less about the Bible or any other books for that matter, or things that give moral instruction. That's a cynical view, but it's true.

FAYE: I think we tend to confuse religiosity with moral development.

REBECCA: Whatever moral development we do achieve has to be done in the face of life's unfairness. That is the context in which we have to make progress. We're not in control of our own destiny. Terrible things can happen to us. And we're not necessarily going to be rewarded for goodness, as you say.

FAYE: Unless it's its own reward.

BILL: We're back to Cain and Abel. One of the brothers is an impulsive ruffian, the other a pious victim.

JACK: May I say that the story itself speaks to this question of human consciousness in the face of moral complexity. In a sense, the brain is a story-making mechanism. So, heaven knows, in the face of moral complexity and perplexity and the injustice of it all, one of the things that cultures do, not to mention writers like us, is to make up stories. And these may give small, cold comfort, if any. They may be full of problems and not answer questions, but they are as human a response to moral complexity and difficulty—not to mention the complexity of just keeping your balance and walking down the street—as anything could be. What we've been analyzing, whatever else it is, is one culture's effort to make some kind of sense out of the onstreaming data of injustice—and those fathomless questions of how did we get here, what are we here for, and how come it's such a half-mess—along with life's transcendent moments.

BURT: That's what's great about stories and what's so powerful about Genesis. There's one dilemma after another. There's Cain and Abel. There's Abraham and Sarah. You can go all the way through and be utterly engaged by the text, by grappling with it. And it's in that passionate embrace of the text that we learn to think morally.

JACK: That seems to be more important than any incidental moral preachment, or the dramatizing of moral dilemmas. These stories tell us what it is to be human.

IV

APOCALYPSE

KAREN ARMSTRONG • BYRON E. CALAME

ALEXANDER A. DI LELLA • CAROL GILLIGAN

BLU GREENBERG • SAMUEL D. PROCTOR

BURTON L. VISOTZKY

We have all heard the cry. "Why did I survive the war and my buddy didn't?" "Why was I the only one to walk away from the crash?" "Why did cancer take her and not me?" Surviving a catastrophe is a complex and painful destiny. Just look at Noah. His response to the Great Flood in the Book of Genesis is to build an altar and get drunk. In a way we are all the survivors of that ordeal, and it doesn't make us feel any better knowing that the Author of the Apocalypse was none other than God.

—BILL MOYERS

Noah on the Ark, Qisas al-Anbiya (Legends of the Prophets), Iran, 1577

Now Yhwh *saw*
that great was humankind's evildoing on earth
and every form of their heart's planning was only evil all the day.
Then Yhwh *was sorry*
that he had made humankind on earth,
and it pained his heart.
Yhwh *said:*
I will blot out humankind, whom I have created, from the face of
    the soil,
from man to beast, to crawling thing and to the fowl of the
    heavens,
for I am sorry that I made them.
But Noah found favor in the eyes of Yhwh . . .

Noah was a righteous, wholehearted man in his generation,
in accord with God did Noah walk . . .

God said to Noah:
An end of all flesh has come before me,
for the earth is filled with wrongdoing through them;
here, I am about to bring ruin upon them, along with the earth.
Make yourself an Ark of gofer wood,
with reeds make the Ark,
and cover it within and without with a covering-of-pitch . . .

As for me,
here, I am about to bring on the Deluge, water upon the earth,
to bring ruin upon all flesh that has rush of life in it, from under
    the heavens,
all that is on earth will perish.
But I will establish my covenant with you:
you are to come into the Ark, you and your sons and your wife
    and your sons' wives with you,
and from all living-things, from all flesh, you are to bring two
    from all into the Ark, to remain alive with you.
They are to be a male and a female (each) . . .

They came to Noah, into the Ark, two and two (each) from all
    flesh in which there is the rush of life.

And those that came, male and female from all flesh they came,
as God had commanded him.
Y<small>HWH</small> *closed (the door) upon him.*
The Deluge was forty days upon the earth.
The waters increased and lifted the Ark, so that it was raised
  above the earth;
the waters swelled and increased exceedingly upon the earth, so
  that the Ark floated upon the face of the waters . . .

Then expired all flesh that crawls about upon the earth—fowl,
  herd-animals, wildlife, and all swarming things that swarm
  upon the earth,
and all humans;
all that had the breath of the rush of life in their nostrils,
all that were on firm-ground, died . . .

But God paid mind to Noah and all living-things, all the animals
  that were with him in the Ark,
and God brought a rushing-wind across the earth, so that the
  waters abated . . .

God spoke to Noah, saying:
Go out of the Ark, you and your wife, your sons and your sons'
  wives with you.
All living-things that are with you, all flesh—fowl, animals, and
  all crawling things that crawl about upon the earth,
have them go out with you,
that they may swarm on earth, that they may bear fruit and
  become many upon the earth . . .

Noah built a slaughter-site to Y<small>HWH</small>.
He took from all pure animals and from all pure fowl
and offered up offerings upon the altar.
Now Y<small>HWH</small> *smelled the soothing savor*
and Y<small>HWH</small> *said in his heart:*
I will never curse the soil again on humankind's account, since
  what the human heart forms is evil from its youth;
I will never again strike down all living-things, as I have done . . .

And God said:
This is the sign of the covenant which I set
between me and you and all living beings that are with you, for
    ageless generations:
My bow I set in the clouds,
so that it may serve as a sign of the covenant between me and
    the earth . . .

Now Noah was the first man of the soil; he planted a vineyard.
When he drank from the wine, he became drunk and exposed
    himself in the middle of his tent.
Ham, the father of Canaan, saw his father's nakedness and told
    his two brothers outside.
Then Shem and Yefet took a cloak, they put it on the shoulders
    of the two of them,
and walked backward, to cover their father's nakedness.
—Their faces were turned backward, their father's nakedness
    they did not see.
Now when Noah awoke from his wine, it became known (to
    him) what his littlest son had done to him.
He said:
Damned be Canaan,
servant of servants may he be to his brothers!

                —excerpts from *The Five Books of Moses*
                (*Schocken Bible*, Vol. I), Chapters 6, 7, 8, and 9

BILL: Barney, you're the newspaperman among us. If you were doing this story for the front page of *The Wall Street Journal* tomorrow, what would the headline be?

BARNEY: "God Destroys the World." And the subhead would probably say: "One Family Survives with Many Animals."

BILL: And if you'd been sent out to cover this story, what would be your description of the earth after the waters receded?

BARNEY: It's pretty desolate. If you've been around a flood, you know it leaves muck. There's the stench. A fire consumes, but a flood leaves everything, for the most part, and it can be as awful as almost anything you've seen. Of course, I first heard this story as a child in Sunday school, and then it was all about rainbows and the fun and getting on the Ark and going for a sail with all those animals. It was like your own personal zoo. Coming back to this story as an adult, I'm struck by the awfulness of God destroying the whole earth. The people are evil, with no redeeming social value, but God is very condemning of everything.

ALEX: But aren't you saying this because you're a reporter and writer for a modern newspaper? These events wouldn't strike the original audience the way you've described them. The concern of the biblical writer was not with the devastating effects of the Flood. You're using Western logic.

BILL: What do you think that concern might have been then?

ALEX: Noah plants a vineyard. The Flood fertilized the land, turning it into the most fertile place on earth—"the fertile crescent." I think the point of the story from this ancient writer is not so much from the God perspective as from the human perspective—human beings are responsible and accountable for their actions. God is not the supreme patsy in the sky, the ultimate Rotarian, the supreme good guy. God holds human beings accountable. Why? Because they're made free to obey or disobey God, as is quite clear in Chapter 2 of Genesis. As you know, there are two distinct stories combined in the present Flood narrative. But both contain the same idea—what prompts God to destroy the world is human sin.

KAREN: So where does evil come from? God is the Creator of the world. God is totally good. And yet the people He has created are totally evil. All the imaginations of their hearts are evil. This is one of the problems about monotheism, surely. And I don't agree that the people of the time wouldn't have focused on the destruction. This was a kind of religious nightmare of the ancient world. We hear all the time about creator gods bringing the world out of the chaos of the primal waters. Now you have a creator god using the primal waters to blot out the world. I didn't think about the coziness of the Ark when I was a child. I was thinking about a frightening God. So that when you're told later that "God so loved the world that He sent his only begotten son," you think, "Yes, but what about Noah? What about the Flood?"

BLU: That's exactly why I think the story is not about the accountability of human beings. It's about the transformation of the relationship between God and humanity. In the beginning, God was a perfectionist. In desperation, God would rather destroy His creation than accept it as less than perfect. But then, probably out of love and a sense of loss, God promises to accept human beings the way they are, with all their flaws, and promises never to destroy them again. So the story of Noah is about God growing into the relationship, maturing in it, moving from expectations of perfection in human beings to accepting them as flawed beings. And this paves the way for the covenant. That's what a covenant is—a never-to-be-broken relationship, no matter who falls off the side.

BURT: Blu, when you said that God no longer expects perfection, the first thought that popped into my head was that God actually recognizes humanity is created in God's image. Then God decides: "It's not working! I have to destroy this and start all over."

BILL: Well, why? What happened between the first and the fifth chapter of Genesis? What did human beings do that caused God to reverse His judgment about the goodness of His creation?

CAROL: What's so interesting about the Noah story is that it doesn't really say. I think this is about regret and how destructive regret is. God regrets His creation. It's not clear in the text why He regrets. What is clear is how destructive this regret is because it leads Him to wipe out this creation.

BILL: Look, the first act of Adam and Eve was to disobey the one commandment God gave them. Cain slew his brother Abel after God had said, "Master your passions." The human race turns out to be rebellious and murderous.

CAROL: I think I agree. It's God coming into a relationship with the human whom He has created. It's like moving out of your own fantasy world into a relationship, and the first sense is a desire to move right back and start all over again.

BARNEY: I don't think Alex's accountability works for me because this is a generic destruction. I get no sense that God has gone through and looked up the grade cards. I get the feeling this is the whole human race, and God is saying, "They're all bad." Noah is almost a token.

SAM: You know, my headline would not have been "God Destroys the World" but "God Gives Humans a Second Chance." My emphasis would fall on the rainbow and the cloud and the second chance.

KAREN: This is one of the aspects of religion that I find hardest to take—those of us in the Ark, so to speak, sit cozily inside and forget the people outside. Very often we demonize people on the outside of our faith or our society. Noah does that, too—as soon as he gets out of the Ark, he starts demonizing Canaan. In Poussin's painting, you don't see that Ark, just a waste of waters and a lot of people drowning. But inside the Ark, we're all right. We don't care about the carnage and the pitiable human mess outside.

BILL: We're avoiding the question about God here. Why does God have to destroy everyone just because He's unhappy with the choices we make?

KAREN: In our century, we've had so many examples of purges, where people say, "Let's get rid of all the dross and start again with a chosen few."

BILL: I would suggest that this is why a lot of people today cannot abide the Bible, or the faith, and they can't come to terms with a God Who would do this. We cannot avoid the question of God here because what God has done, so to speak, is to wipe out everybody in New York City—eight million people, except for the eight people sitting in this circle—because God's unhappy with them.

ALEX: Whoa! Let's not forget the kind of literature we're dealing with here. If we fail to understand the literary genre, we will misinterpret the text. We can't read this as if we're reading the second book of Samuel, for example, which is based upon court records. This is not Cecil B. De Mille presenting a colossal Flood, or even a dramatic painting. This is, for want of a better word, a parable of sorts, and therefore it is not addressing the questions that Barney would ask the text. For example, this business that you mentioned earlier, Bill—"God saw how good it was." It's ironic that God says

this seven times and then humans commit seven major sins in Genesis—as if these human sins would negate the goodness of creation! Sin number one is Adam and Eve disobeying God. Sin number two is Cain killing his brother Abel. Sin number three is Lamech boasting about vengeance in Chapter 4. Sin number four occurs when the sons of God admire and marry the daughters of men—a difficult text that probably refers to an abuse of power. Sin number five results in the Flood. Sin number six is Ham doing nothing when he sees his father's nakedness, even though this, too, is a complicated text. And sin number seven is the hubris that results in the Tower of Babel. But no matter how hard humankind tries, it cannot negate the goodness of God. God doesn't give up on human beings.

Building the Ark (detail from Byzantine ivory altar), San Matteo, Salerno, late 11th c.

God is angry because of human sin, but He won't give up. At the end of Chapter 11, we get the call and election of Abraham. So the Flood story is a parable of God's persistence in relating to human beings, in spite of their sins.

CAROL: I think it's a parable, too, but a different one. I think it's a parable about regret. That's where the text starts—God regrets. It's a parable about relationships and families—parents who create children in their own image and then feel regret, which is a terribly destructive feeling that leads you to a sense of anger and betrayal. Who hasn't felt like wiping everything out to start over again? I think this parable teaches us the lesson of the destructiveness of acting on regret in that way. After all, at the end, He's right back where He began. It's a parable of the education of every parent—every god.

BILL: How do you read that line about God's saddened heart?

CAROL: As I said, it's like a parent experiencing the destructive impulse of regret—"I'll just wipe everything out and start again, and this time it will be exactly as I had imagined it." But you can't.

BLU: As a parent, I can't really relate to that. I don't think I've ever had the impulse to wipe out my children and start all over again.

SAM: You haven't? Not for one second?

CAROL: Not one day, one time, thinking, "If I could do it again, I could do it better"?

BLU: I might have thought I would like to jump off the roof or do some other destructive thing. But no, I've never had that feeling. I don't think that's how parents feel—"Just wipe them all out and start over again"—I can't relate to that as a parent. So I think this is a story about God's overreaction. This is a very personal God, with a strong, intimate relationship with human beings. He's not just an uncaring God, you know—"I'll smash 'em all down"—

BILL: —but that's what He does. God destroys everybody except a small handful because He's sad, He's sorry, He's angry. And He wipes them out. That's in the story.

BLU: It's very difficult for a person of faith to accept that action.

BILL: As a person of faith, how do you resolve it?

BLU: First of all, some part of me wants to believe that this is a parable about God *not* destroying every last, living being and every last animal. You can even ask why the animals were destroyed. After all, what evil did they do? What did they have to do with human behavior?

SAM: It never struck me that these stories have to hit on all eight cylinders. It's the nature of these stories to make one or two points—three points at most.

BILL: So what's the point?

SAM: I think the point here is that God made the world, and it was good. Part of that goodness, Bill, was the freedom that humans had to veto God. To say no. Destruction is not the end of the story. It's a part of the story that brings us to the redeeming love of God. That's why I said I would like to alter the headline to read: "God Gives a Second Chance." So instead of resting on the hard-heartedness of God—

KAREN: —but I can't forget about the hard-heartedness of God when I read this. You feel that there is a suffering God, and I think that's interesting. But I can't forget the destructiveness.

BLU: If you stop at the destructiveness, then you have nothing.

KAREN: I'm not suggesting that we stop with the destructiveness, because I think that perhaps the only way of dealing with this story is to say that God can be a shock. The reality we call God can be such a shock that it confounds what we absolutely expect. God is not some nice, cozy daddy in the sky. He—a ridiculous pronoun—He doesn't behave as we would wish. "My thoughts are not your thoughts," says the Lord. "My ways are not your ways." In Hinduism, they say that evil is one of the masks of God. I'm

sorry to say it, but I think that here you see God behaving in an evil way. And where does evil come from?

CAROL: I think it's dangerous at the end of this century to call this kind of destruction "good." Even to rationalize it, to see that it's teaching a lesson—I mean, we have the Holocaust, and we have lived with the specter of nuclear destruction, and to say that some group is going to survive, and it's for a good end, a good purpose—really!

SAM: I'm sorry. I can't leave it at that. I lay that destructiveness on human freedom. The freedom we have is real. We have the freedom to create a Holocaust. We have the freedom to create human slavery. But, at least in Noah's time, we didn't have the freedom to wipe out the world of God. No, we had the freedom to have consummate evil among us. And so God brings the destruction in order to show that God wants a new beginning. My emphasis is on the new beginning.

BILL: So you're reading this metaphorically. You're saying that God didn't really destroy the earth. The storyteller is just telling us these things.

SAM: No, no, no. No, no, no, no. He destroyed the earth in this story, and He renewed things. And I'll show you how consistently this evil goes with the new deal—the first thing Noah does after the Flood is to get drunk and naked!

BILL: No, the first thing he did was to build an altar.

> ## *"God is not some nice, cozy daddy in the sky."*

S A M : Yeah, and then got drunk.

B I L L : What does it do to you as a man of faith to believe in a God Who would wipe out the earth because He's unhappy or angry to save a handful of people He considers righteous?

A L E X : I take the point of the story to say that God is not at all evil, but, as Sam said, that human beings have introduced evil into the world. When we speak about total destruction, we don't mean anything like this ever literally happened. There were floods all over the place.

B I L L : Millions of people believe it did happen.

A L E X : Oh, I know that, Bill. This is one of the problems. We can't take every story in the Bible as historical.

B L U : But can you say that God did something that was not good? Can you say that as a person of faith?

A L E X : Well, I wouldn't say that. I would say that God does things I don't judge to be intelligible.

B U R T : Why won't you say that? The Bible itself says that. The Bible says God *"oseh shalom uvorey ra"*—"God creates peace and creates evil." It's very, very clear. It's in scripture. It's hard for me as a rabbi to say, "Yes, God does evil things." Carol

Herbert Singleton, *The Flood*, 1990

gave me a parable to deal with it—God is blind in this story. God creates humanity in God's own image. You can't have a relationship when you don't really see the other person. All God sees when God looks at humanity initially is God. I would not use the parent-child analogy, though. I would use Hosea's analogy that it's a marriage gone awry. When you look at your marriage partner, and all you see is yourself, you wind up regretting it because you don't really have a relationship.

BILL: And some people wind up murdering.

BURT: Or getting divorced—just ending it. That's what God does. God ends it. The relationship can't continue under those circumstances.

BLU: I'm going to pick up my marbles and walk away.

CAROL: But even in the image of the Ark, this is a book about enclosure. I think that the God of Genesis is such a human god. This is such a psychological story. It's about how people develop and learn. You mention sadness in God's heart. I think it's a story about coming into a relationship. I like what you said, Burt, about it being a marriage story. It's about the education that is involved in any relationship, in a marriage, or in having children. Relationship doesn't come fully formed, and you have to learn. Mistake is built into it. The lesson is: What do you do when you feel you've made a mistake, or when you feel regret? Do you wipe everything out? That impulse is so terrible and destructive. If I take this as a parable, it's a parable about what not to do in the face of a feeling of regret or mistake.

ALEX: But it's more than simply regret. "Regret" is only one of the meanings of the Hebrew verb, which can also mean "to be sorry." In one form of the story, the reason for the Flood is that God felt sorry He had made humankind because the thoughts of the human heart were wicked. In the second form of the story, the reason is lawlessness. What's very clear is that in both forms of the story, the Flood is a parable of divine retribution for human wickedness and lawlessness.

CAROL: But then I have trouble with it.

KAREN: Yes, me too.

CAROL: My sympathetic reading is to read it as a deeply moving story about regret with a terrible human lesson in it. But if I see it as a story that when someone is lawless, you have a license just to wipe them out because they're "other," and they're not holy, or they're not like you and God, then I really have trouble with it. Most of the terrible destruction in the world has been justified that way.

KAREN: And in religion, too. Some of the worst things have happened in religion when people have said, "We have the power to bring goodness out of this by wiping people out"—the Crusades, the Inquisition—

CAROL: —the Holocaust.

KAREN: The Holocaust, which wouldn't have been possible without a thousand years of Christian anti-Semitism in Europe.

CAROL: The wiping out of the Native American population in this country. The enslavement of Africans.

SAM: We tend to assign anthropomorphism to God, to say that God acts like human beings act. Look, God didn't just dictate this story. God doesn't send telegrams. Some human wrote it. And the human who wrote it assigns to God responses that are psychological. To me, it looks like a simple case where the writer is saying that there was a time when God became upset. God regretted that human beings had behaved in such a way, and He wanted to start all over again. It's a very simple kind of thing, but I think that's what the story is saying. My mind is on the bow and the cloud and the new beginning. I don't park myself right there, where, halfway through the story, God is upset.

BILL: That's because you're a man of faith, and you look back through the lens of faith.

SAM: I think the Bible is a book of faith.

BILL: But imagine yourself as somebody trying to get from the other side, who isn't yet a person of faith, who's struggling with this idea of God.

SAM: I would say that if you act ugly, you're going to be held accountable, and God's going to smack you around in ways you'd never believe. And then, after that, God redeems and saves and brings you back.

KAREN: But He doesn't bring back all those people who died in the Flood. They're finished and gone and so are the animals who haven't done anything wrong at all.

SAM: Now you're reading it in the light of twentieth-century ethics. Ugly, mean, and crazy things happened in those days that we could never justify—"God's gonna kill you because you didn't obey God," and God says, "Kill all the babies"—you know. What kind of an ethics is that? We can't live with that today. But I've got to look at these stories in the light of the way people saw ethical issues at that time.

BARNEY: But I'd like to focus on the human side of God. Bill was asking what changed between the creation and God being very unhappy just before the Flood.

SAM: Freedom!

BARNEY: All right. What happened between the Flood and God saying, "Here's the rainbow in the sky"? It does make Him so human. For me, at least, one of the things about Genesis and the Old Testament is that God is so personal. God causes the Flood. There is regret. There's second thought—and, in effect, God brings home some roses, as you would with your spouse.

SAM: That's what life is about—new beginnings.

Hans Baldung Grien, *The Flood*, 1516

BARNEY: Here He comes. And if I see it in a very personal sense, this God is a human being Who gets angry, Who has regret, maybe with some cause, and Who does harsh, sweeping things.

BLU: You mean, God is *like* a human being?

BARNEY: I'm sorry—yes, God is *like* a human being.

KAREN: Perhaps, also, instead of seeing God just as an adult, you can also see God as a child. You know how children are when they've made something and don't like it and just smash it. *Whoomff, whoomff, whoomff!* This is an undeveloped God.

BARNEY: Or a petulant teenager.

CAROL: I think it's all about the education of God.

KAREN: God is growing up in Genesis, and we see Him here—He's inchoate. He doesn't understand what He's doing. He hasn't issued any instructions, as far as I know, to human beings, except "Go forth and multiply." Noah is righteous, but we haven't actually got a clear code as yet. Then God says, "I don't like this." *Wham, wham, wham,* like a child knocking down a sand castle. Gradually, God has got to grow up and learn like the rest of us how to relate to other people.

CAROL: That you can't just wipe them out. The fact is, this story ends with a covenant—God says, "I'm going to stay in this relationship and work it out in this relationship."

BLU: This is the point of the whole story. The truth is that people have always lived with floods and chaos. Here the Bible is telling us that such destruction will never happen again, at least not on a planetary scale, because God really cares. God admits, "I'm never, ever going to do this again. I'm not going to pick up my marbles and walk away when things go bad." That's the beginning of permanent relationship between God and humanity, the covenantal relationship which is about staying together and trying to perfect the world together. It's a process that is still going on because the world is far from perfect, but not altogether hopeless. That's what the religious enterprise is all about.

SAM: I see that part of the story as the writer expressing the writer's understanding of the way God is.

BURT: Sam, why are you so protective of God? Why can't you say that—

SAM: Can we have a moment of silence?

BURT: But our faith is strong enough.

SAM: Some say that the thing you can conceive of is not God.

BURT: No, this is the God of the universe. Can't God endure some criticism here?

SAM: No, not God. Not the God I know.

"This is the God of the universe. Can't God endure some criticism here?"

Not the God of perfection and holiness that I'm talking about. No, no. It's our business to try to comprehend, in the light of argument, what it is that God is doing. And this writer is helping us way back in that ancient day to understand that when we act the fool, God is gonna call it to our attention and in ways we'll never forget. Then God still holds out the new covenant, the promise of renewal.

BILL: I had a professor in seminary who believed that African Americans saved Christianity in America because it would have died under the weight of slavery had they not held on through the long ordeal in their belief in the God who their oppressors were saying condoned their enslavement. That's a belief in renewal.

SAM: Yes. The black folk read the Bible over the white people's shoulders. They saw the Bible itself, and not the way these people were acting out. They read through that Bible and they heard enough to let them know that they could identify with all these stories. So black people identified themselves with Daniel in the lion's den, the Hebrew boys in the furnace, the Israel-ites coming out of the Flood. They saw the Bible in the context of their own experience, and they kept it alive. It is as though they ignored this other. They used to sing, "Some people talkin' 'bout heaven ain't goin' there." You see? They took that whole Old Testament, the Hebrew Bible saga, and made it their own story.

BILL: Why didn't they blame God for their fate?

SAM: Because they believed people were free.

BILL: God made people who were free to hold other people as slaves?

SAM: That's how much freedom you've got. You are free enough to wipe out a whole population. In some of these countries where people are starving, and the rich classes have all the money, rich people are free to hold the money and see their blood starve to death. That's how free people are.

BILL: What kind of God creates that kind of freedom?

SAM: God made people free. God did not make us robots or puppets. We're free. I'm so burdened with my freedom that I'm free to love people who hate me. And, automatically, I know how to hate them back.

BILL: Is this how Jews felt in the Holocaust when—

SAM: Some did. Some survived.

Noah's Ark, The London Miscellany, France, late 13th c.

BLU: I think that reading this story of total destruction at this time in history, after the Holocaust, you come to it with different kinds of questions.

BILL: How has it affected your own faith? What questions are you asking now?

BLU: How could God let this happen? Not necessarily: How could God do this? But how could God let this happen?

ALEX: He had to.

BLU: That's not an answer that satisfies me. I think you're allowed to ask the questions and not necessarily have an answer for every question. You're allowed to ask questions about the Flood, just as you're allowed to ask questions about the Holocaust, and know that there's not going to be a good answer out there for you. And what it means to be a person of faith is sometimes to live with the questions, even as you believe in God and God's goodness and power and omniscience—and hold these things side by side.

BILL: If God is omnipotent, could He not have stopped the Holocaust?

BLU: Certainly.

ALEX: Yes, yes, He could have.

BLU: And yet it comes back to the question of human freedom again because human beings carried out the Holocaust.

BURT: That's why the Flood story is an even better story—because, in a way, you

"What it means to be a person of faith is sometimes to live with the questions, even as you believe in God and God's goodness and power and omniscience—and hold these things side by side."

can't blame humans for opening up the heavens and the depths and flooding the world. It was God. God was completely in control there. I'm with Blu on this. As a Jew, I also happen to read the Hebrew Bible and see it as my people's history, and it makes me furious. I think that one of the great things about God in my life is that because God is God, God can endure my anger.

BILL: Yes, but can we endure God's anger?

SAM: Now, we've got to step back from this. We are humans. We are finite creatures. We are not God. I read in the paper the other day that the spaceship *Galileo* had been traveling for six years. I can't conceive of that—sending back pictures the whole time, going 106,000 miles an hour. I have no conception of anything that's been traveling for six years. What kind of a Creator is it who has space enough out there and unchartered highways that they follow electromagnetically and send pictures back? All of this lets me know that I don't have a clue as to how wise and how great and how well informed God is.

BURT: I'm with you on that. I think God has space enough for my anger.

SAM: I can't be quite so presumptuous as to say, "Why would God do this or do that?" If God gave us the freedom, we're free to do the ugliest and meanest things possible to one another. In my own mother continent, Africa, they've been killing each other, fighting over small turfs. They're free to do these evil things, whether they like it or not. But then there's God, Who calls us back, haunting us like the hound of heaven. With unhurrying pace, God is on our case.

KAREN: Sometimes, though, we have to look at the catastrophic side of things like the Flood or the Holocaust, even if only to shock us out of our sometimes simplistic notions of God that bring Him into our corner of the world and not into other people's corners. For example, we all have a lot of thinking to do after the Holocaust—Christians and Jews from different perspectives. When we do, we find that old ideas of God as being totally omnipotent and benevolent are difficult to sustain. We should take in this difficulty and not jump to a Pollyanna conclusion. I think of that story from Auschwitz, where a group of Jews put God on trial for what was happening and said that they could find no exonerating clause whatsoever. There's no

excuse for this at all, they agreed, and they decided He deserved to die. They sentenced Him to death. When the trial was over, a rabbi said, "The trial has ended. It is time for the evening prayer." You see, the struggle to understand must continue, but to back out of the struggle and say that there is no problem, or that there's just the rainbow, loses the whole—

SAM: —not just a rainbow. Black people could have put God on trial, but instead, we put white supremacy on trial. We didn't put God on trial for slavery. We put those people on trial for slavery who had gone off and colonized other people all over the world. Europe owned the dark and brown and yellow people of the whole world. We didn't blame God for that. People had gunpowder and ships, and they used their freedom and went out and enslaved other people. But then, in time, we can correct these things. I'm living with that bow in the cloud right now. And if I'm the last optimist left, I don't mind that at all.

BILL: Let's come back to Noah. What do you make of the way that Noah is presented in this story as a man "righteous in his generation"?

BARNEY: Well, I come away thinking Noah is a wimp. It seems to me that he's a good man, but we never hear from him. He has to be encouraged to get on the Ark. He has to be nudged along. And he's rather anonymous. It's really different reading the scripture now from my days in Sunday school class, where I can remember very vividly the little cards with the picture on one side and the words on the other. The picture would be of the Ark, with Noah standing very majestically as the animals came in. And the rainbow was in the sky. That was my image of Noah. Even though somewhere in my teenage years I read the whole Bible, it didn't hit me until I came back to this story this time that there was this *other* Noah. To be honest, while my childhood says he's a hero, I don't see it here.

KAREN: My quarrel with Noah is that he doesn't ask God about the other people. God says to him, "Build an Ark and save your family." Unlike Abraham, who argued with God to save the people of Sodom and Gomorrah, Noah doesn't try to save anybody. So what is righteousness? Is righteousness someone who keeps the rules? Or is righteousness something else? *Schindler's List* was originally called *Schindler's Ark*. Oskar Schindler is anything but righteous. He's a playboy—

BILL: —yet saves others.

KAREN: Yes, he sticks his neck out and risks himself.

BILL: Whom do you prefer, Noah or Oskar Schindler?

KAREN: Schindler, any day. He might not be the ideal human being, but I would love to feel that if I were in that position—in Nazi Germany, say—that I would have had the courage to go out and try to save some of the others and not just build an Ark to take me and my own through to safety. It's one of the questions you ask yourself again and again: "Would I have

the courage to do this? Or would I just be a Noah and get into my own Ark, barricade myself in?"

ALEX: What you want to do, though, is rewrite the story. Let's stay with the story, okay?

BLU: Well, the story is, in a way, tacit criticism of Noah as a bystander to other people's suffering, especially so in comparison to Abraham, who pleads and pleads on behalf of the people of Sodom. On the other hand, I also want to take seriously the designation of Noah as a righteous person. The rabbis actually deal with this question: What does "righteous" mean? Why is Noah righteous?

BILL: What's your answer?

BLU: Well, in the first rabbinic interpretation, Noah is "righteous in his generation" because he didn't go along with peer pressure and become lawless, evil, or depraved. That's the implication of the term "his generation." He stands out remarkably because he stands above the depravity of his generation. He follows his own inner gyroscope. The other rabbinic interpretation is that he's righteous *only* in this depraved generation. If he had lived in Abraham's generation, he might not be considered so righteous. I think the comparison to Abraham includes, in part, the idea of speaking up on behalf of his fellow human beings. Noah doesn't protest, argue, or plead on their behalf.

BILL: Alex, is that staying with the story?

ALEX: Well, the Abraham story is a different kind of literature. It's a saga—the heroic tale of a people. When we deal with the Flood story, we're dealing with "*ish tzaddik tamim betorothow*"—"a righteous man, blameless in his generation." The text also says that Noah walked with God.

CAROL: The distinction between walking with God and speaking with God is a very interesting one. The distinction between Noah and Abraham is that Abraham speaks with God. He argues with God.

ALEX: Because the Abraham story is a different kind of literature.

CAROL: Well, let's say a different kind of relationship. But in order to speak, you have to have someone who listens. The God of the Noah story is not listening. So I think "in his generation" is an interesting qualification because in a generation where God is not listening, where people are not speaking with God, Noah is a righteous man because he tends his garden, takes care of his animals and his family, and walks with God. It's a profoundly important story for our time. It's an education of God, an education about coming into a relationship. It's not possible to have a relationship unless both sides listen. Noah, in a way, is innocent. He doesn't know; he just walks with God. And in the course of the story, he loses his righteousness. He becomes, in the end, simply Noah.

ALEX: How does he lose his righteousness?

CAROL: When a person of Noah's goodness is put into a situation of radical discontinuity, he has to turn his back on other people—"I'm different from" or "I'm other." The cost of doing that starts to erode the righteousness of Noah. So often when people are chosen by virtue of their righteousness, the very quality that led them to be chosen is eroded by what happens. If you think about what happens to Noah, closed up in this Ark, you would imagine that at the least, he would have bad dreams.

BLU: That's a fascinating point. I need to think about the implications of that. There are many possibilities. For example, maybe he gets drunk because he suffers from bystander guilt. The enormity of what he has not done begins to sink in. But Noah overreacts in the same way that God overreacts. He curses the child Canaan. Noah too has a perfectionist side, so he too has to learn restraint and how to live with other people's limitations.

BURT: I read him differently. Yes, he's an innocent. But I think his righteousness is indeed that he walks with God. That is to say, Noah continually sees the good in the people around him.

BILL: I don't see that in the text. He doesn't speak up for humanity. He doesn't go around warning any of his neighbors.

BLU: But he takes a long time to build the Ark. The rabbis say he did that so his neighbors would have a chance to look at

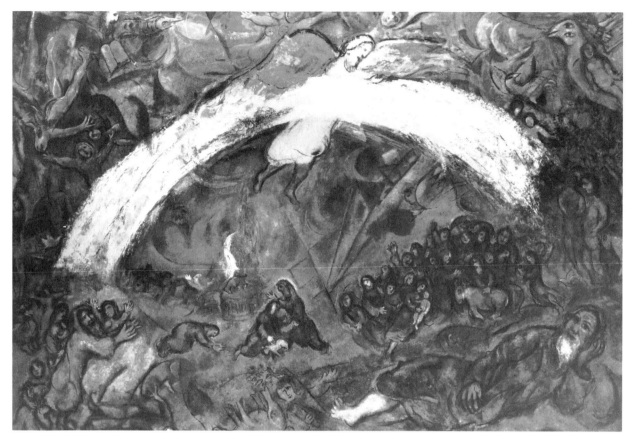

Marc Chagall, *Noah and the Rainbow*, 1961–65

the scene. They had plenty of time to repent.

CAROL: I think it's a mistake to confuse disengagement with righteousness. This is a story about disengagement—God's disengagement from His creation and Noah's disengagement from all the people around him.

BILL: He just goes into his Ark and says, "If I can be saved, that's enough."

CAROL: That's right because God told him to do it.

BARNEY: I think if Noah had been Schindler, he would have been hiding a neighbor between each pair of animals. Some of my friends were in the worst of Vietnam, in units that were terribly decimated. They came back, survivors. I think of people who have been in car accidents where they're the only surviving member of a family. That leaves a burden of guilt. Survivor's syndrome can hurt people's lives. For me, Noah has survivor's syndrome. It's very human, after a crisis, to get drunk. Remember, he planted a vineyard. That's a sign of hope for the future, a belief in the covenant. I want to believe he got drunk because he felt so horrible. It doesn't save him from being a wimp. But that's the place I get his humanity.

BILL: Why do you think he was chosen?

ALEX: Precisely because he is set apart. That's what "chosen" means—to be set apart. He's righteous, he's *tzaddik*, he walks with God. To walk with God means having a relationship with God. See, I don't want to rewrite the story. I'm hearing some of you say that you want to rewrite the story. Well, fine. You rewrite your story. But don't say that's what the Bible says.

BILL: But the Bible leaves us with the question: What is righteousness?

ALEX: Righteousness has a whole gamut of meanings. It means having a right relationship with God, with human beings. It means abiding by God's law.

BILL: But if you're in a right relationship with God, would you be indifferent to all the people around you who were about to die in a deluge?

ALEX: Why do you want to rewrite the story to have Noah contradict the elements of the story that—

BILL: I'm not. Just tell me, in your own judgment, in the biblical sense, what does it mean to be righteous?

ALEX: Doing what needs to be done when it's supposed to be done. When silence is called for, that's when Noah is silent.

BURT: I agree with Alex.

ALEX: He speaks up when something horrible happened—namely when Ham sees his father's nakedness, whatever that means. But don't forget that in terms of the story, Ham represents Canaan, where those terrible pagans indulge in all sorts of orgiastic, sexual aberrations. That's why the Israelites were not supposed to have anything to do with the Canaanites. So the story serves that purpose.

BILL: Ah, so righteousness is serving God's purpose, even though that purpose—

ALEX: —may not be obvious to us.

BLU: I'd like to take a crack at staying with the story and interpreting what righteousness is. When we try to equate Noah simply with righteousness, we're missing something very profound in the text. There's a very important subtext running through this whole story. Righteousness is something about integrity of human relationships—interpersonal relationships, family relationships, sexual relationships. This is politically incorrect, in terms of today's mores. But feeding into the Noah story is the issue of depraved relationships.

"Noah paves the way for all the flawed models that follow in this Book of Genesis."

I think Noah's merit and his righteousness are about understanding and living by rules of integrity—of family life, of marital life—

KAREN: But we don't know any of this.

BLU: Well, we do. I'm saying we can read this subtle tone that is carried throughout the story. Even the notion of going to the Ark—man and wife, male and female, two by two—expresses this theme.

BILL: He was living by these standards, even though the whole society around him was depraved and licentious.

BLU: Right. I think it's one of the reasons he's described as "righteous." I think God chose Noah because God loved him, because the elemental dignity and decency of his life was such a compelling contrast to a world turned to violence and depravity, with everyone guilty of grabbing off whatever they could. Think of the internal compass it takes not to feel that you are missing out on the next orgy. For all these reasons, Noah found special favor in God's eyes.

BARNEY: Did God not love all the other people?

ALEX: Yes.

BLU: Perhaps God did. I think it brings into sharp focus the fact that there's no standard measure of righteousness. There's a wonderful Hasidic story about a man who did not live the examined life and did a lot of dastardly things. At the end of his life, the man comes to the heavenly gates

for judgment. They put his good deeds on one scale and his sins on the other, and, of course, the sin scale is much heavier. The pleader on his behalf says, "Well, try to remember something else you did." The man remembers a time when he was in the

"The Bible does not offer us perfect heroes. They're not so beyond our reach as models."

woods and came upon a family in a wagon that's stuck in the mud. He helped pull out the wagon and the people. So they put that on the scale, and it still tips in the direction of sin. The pleader says, "Try to remember something else." The man then says, "Well, there was mud on the wheels." So they add the mud onto the scales, and that mud finally tips the balance in his favor. We don't always know what will enable a life to be called "righteous." Sometimes it can be one act or one dimension of character that puts you over the top.

KAREN: I think perhaps God changes His notion of righteousness in this story. At first, He wants Noah to be a righteous man like Enoch, who walks with God and then disappears into heaven. But the Buddha says that after enlightenment, a man must come down from the mountaintop and return to the marketplace to engage himself and practice compassion, to involve himself with humanity. That's what Abraham does. He has his visions, and he pleads and struggles, and he is chosen to be the father of his people. Noah, though, is living at a time when humanity is as yet undeveloped in its conception of righteousness. Indeed, God is learning what He wants from the human race.

BLU: You know, that's a difference between perfection and righteousness. Noah paves the way for all the flawed models that follow in this Book of Genesis, because every one of them, whom we call "righteous," is flawed. It's one of the great insights of Judaism. The Bible does not offer us perfect heroes. They're not so beyond our reach as models.

BILL: There's another element here, too, though—in the narrative that runs through Genesis, God is picking His favorites. Righteousness may mean simply that Noah found favor in this God's eyes and became an instrument of this God's purpose. Maybe that's why he's considered righteous.

BLU: That would make God's choice too arbitrary. Besides it ignores the clear counterpoint: Immediately after describing how evil humanity is, the text says, "But Noah found favor . . ." Also, the rabbis comment that there was tremendous suffering and that Noah offered the most tender care. Finally Noah offers a sacrifice. That's the mark of a person who feels gratitude, a person who, even though wounded, isn't broken or destroyed. And when God responds, you get the feeling of how much God loves human beings, with all their flaws.

BILL: That's interesting, Blu, because when I read this story again last night, I was struck that when Noah built the altar, it wasn't the act of homage that God responded to, it was the smell of the meat.

CAROL: I want to come back to the view of the world from the Ark. We have to keep before us that image of bloated bodies floating in the water, and these animals all around, dead. And Noah turns away. At that point, he's not righteous anymore. He's like Aeneas at the end of *The Aeneid*—he is "pious Aeneas" at the beginning of the epic, but by the end, he is "savage Aeneas." The story of Noah is one of the first times you see the costs of the patriarchal model of family life—God the Father—because we're all calling God "He." And, by the way, why are we doing that?

BILL: Yes, why are we?

CAROL: Because if we call God "She," we can't imagine this act.

BILL: So much misunderstanding has come from the use of "He" as the source of authority.

CAROL: Yes. In this context, for example, we have a God whose solution to marriage problems is to wipe out the relationship—to separate and start over again.

BILL: Blu has suggested that one possibility for God's selection of Noah is that Noah was faithful to the idea of family, faithful to his wife, faithful to his children. He was living by some standard God had raised prior to the Ten Commandments. Are you saying that in order to preserve that standard of a traditional family, God destroys everyone else?

CAROL: No, I'm saying that Noah is chosen by a God Who wants him to make such a break with the rest of humanity that it destroys the very righteousness that allowed him to maintain that standard. So that at the end, trouble has come into Noah's family.

BLU: That's very human. His merit and his flaw grow out of the same thing—so much feeling for his family, and so much commitment to them. But, unfortunately, he only looks after his family.

BURT: If you are in a universe where everyone around you is really unredeemably evil—

CAROL: I don't think that's the conclusion of the Noah story. Everyone is unredeemably evil? I don't know what "unredeemably" means—that people are born evil? Are we into original sin now?

BURT: No, it's not original sin. But that is what the Torah says—that God chooses to destroy the world because God regrets that the human beings God has created are *rac mineurav*—they're just unredeemable.

CAROL: Well, then, we come back to God because if God has power to redeem, what does it mean to say people are unredeemable? If we believe in life, if we believe in hope, if we believe in change, if we believe in redemption, then we have to work

out these problems in life itself, not through wiping everybody out.

BILL: Well, clearly, God thought it was an irredeemable race because He wiped out everybody except this—

BURT: Let me just finish this. If it's true that humanity is unredeemable, and Noah chooses to say, "I'm not going to participate in that society; I'm not going to wallow in sin and evil," then it's not so unreasonable that Noah only looked after himself and his family. That's round one. Round two is Noah to God. Noah makes it clear that he will obey God's law to the extent that he gets in a rudderless boat and floats. He puts himself entirely at God's mercy. God closes the door on that Ark. God locks Noah in this floating casket. Now what does he hear around him? The sounds of rain and the sounds of dying. And he comes out very damaged.

CAROL: Yes, but it's a big point that he comes out damaged. Because to survive, he had to cut off the very sensitivity that made him righteous in the first place. I think that happens so often in our contemporary society.

BILL: In this whole record, there isn't one peep from the victims. There is not so much as a cry of mercy left in the biblical record. What do you make of that silence?

BLU: I would say that a cry would be too much, too hard to handle. As it is, it's painful enough. If this was personalized, it would become overwhelming. When you hear about six million people dying in the

Holocaust, you don't have the same wrenching reaction that you have when you hear the story of one survivor.

BILL: The Holocaust was itself blanked out, just as the consequences of the Flood were blanked out, until individual witnesses began to speak.

BLU: Elie Wiesel spoke for twenty years before people began to listen to him. He poured his guts out, day after day, year after year. People were just not ready to hear the story.

BARNEY: I want to say a good word for Noah. It's very interesting to see him quietly obeying. The people who were destroyed were standing on firm ground. Noah has had the faith to get into this little floating box and go on the water. He did have the window. As a newsman, though, I have to wonder why he didn't go up and look out the window as the water really began to rise.

BILL: Because he was not the kind of man who wanted to see this. He saw it coming and turned his face away. He said not a word to a neighbor. They asked, "Why are you building this Ark." "Oh, I'm just going to take a little Sunday sail." He didn't say, "And you'd better go build one, too, because the Deluge is coming."

BLU: We don't know that. He could have said, as rabbinic commentary suggests, "Change your ways and come into the Ark, and you will be saved." He might have said

that, too. And he didn't open the window because water would have come in, and the Ark might have sunk.

SAM: When your father was preaching from this story in the mountains, Barney, I don't think anybody in the whole church believed the story. I don't think anybody believed that the lions and the monkeys and all these people could ever have lived in a boat together. I had a little dog who wouldn't have let any other animal come on the boat with me. Nobody believed that story. But when it was preached and taught, they accepted it just as it was given, looking for the main point. Now, I wish I could have read a story in the Bible with all the nuances that you all are bringing out of this—you know, examining Noah's character and all that stuff. Take righteousness. The writer just meant that according to God, Noah got an A, that's all. You don't need to look so deeply into that. He was a guy who got an A, and everyone else got an F. He got an A—and then the story moves on. But we're looking at it in the light of the twentieth century. Sure, I wish so much that we could have had a story with all this commentary on Noah's motives and why he didn't ask somebody, "Would you like to come in with us and join us?" That's not the point at *all*. The point is that humans can use their freedom in such a way as to make God sick and tired. God said, "It grieves my heart. *Bam!* We're going to start all over again." That's the burden of the story. And if you don't hurry up and get to the bow in the cloud and the new beginning, you've missed the main story of the story.

The Story of Noah, Book of Hours of the Duke of Bedford, Paris, ca. 1420

KAREN: Okay, you have the bow in the cloud—but you also have this extremely depressing story about Noah and Canaan. After he's planted his vineyard, Noah falls into a drunken stupor. Then when he finds out that his son, Ham, has looked upon him without covering his nakedness, Noah curses. He doesn't curse Ham—he curses Ham's son, Canaan.

BILL: His own grandson.

KAREN: He doesn't ask, "Whose fault was it that I was exposed this way? Mine?" No, he's projecting out. He's a damaged survivor who's acting like a mini-god. He curses Canaan, leading the way for the new massacres of Joshua, where the people of Israel will be told to go into the land of Canaan and kill every single human being in the land. So there's going to be a new holocaust. You come out of the Ark, a damaged survivor, for all the reasons we've talked about, and what do you do? You lay the seeds for a new catastrophe, a new massacre, a new holocaust.

BURT: So Noah learned nothing from the whole thing.

KAREN: No.

CAROL: But God does. God learns that you can't just turn your back on your creation and say, "I'm sorry I ever made this, and I'm going to start all over again." You're in life, you're in time, you're in relationship, and you just have to work out the problems. So God makes a covenant.

SAM: He'll never do it again!

CAROL: Difficult problems in marriage, in families, with God—these things work out slowly, through many different events. You can't just undo what you've done; you have to stay with the implications of what you've done. Noah was righteous in his generation, and it came at such human cost. Think about the people from Vietnam or people who have survived the Holocaust. We want these survivors to be totally good because we are so sympathetic with what they went through. But we see what happens to good people when they go through these kinds of experiences—their sensitivity, their humanness can be blunted. This story of Noah is a terrible one—but it's also extremely important. We live in a culture that says, "If you don't like it, leave. Separate. Become independent. Build a little Ark and take care of yourself." That's why I think the story of Noah is so important—it shows the cost of doing that.

ALEX: But it's part of a story that we should remember without rewriting it. As you know from the prophetic literature, walking with God is the way of the Lord, not an incidental detail. It tells us something about Noah. You talk about Noah as a flawed character because he plants that vineyard and gets drunk. But he's an innocent. He doesn't know the power of wine. Psalm 104 speaks about the heart being warmed by wine. Well, his heart was warmed by wine. And the little business of cursing Canaan—that serves the literary purpose of showing the hateful characteristics of the Canaanites. So I don't see—

KAREN: Excuse me, but when we look historically at the Canaanites, we know perfectly well they were not evil people. Yet one of the first things that happens after this huge catastrophe is that these people are cursed and in the biblical account, at least, destined for another holocaust, another massacre. I'm distressed to hear anyone support this idea that the Canaanites are irredeemably evil.

ALEX: No, I'm talking about it from the biblical perspective. I'm not justifying anything any more than I'm justifying the so-called "wars of the Lord" in the Old Testament, where the Lord is said to justify wars. No, quite the contrary. As a believer today—and I believe in the inspiration of scripture and all the rest—I don't think many of those stories make any claim on my religious belief right now except for what is, in a sense, the theological freight of the story. The cursing of Noah is a paradigm of the attitude one should have toward sexual irresponsibility in the name of religion. Don't forget that what's condemned in the Bible is not *Playboy* or *Playgirl* or the kind of irresponsible sexuality that comes with so-called sexual liberation, but a form of idolatry.

KAREN: A religion.

ALEX: Exactly. They thought that the Canaanite god Baal and the goddess Ashirah were the givers of fertility. The Lord has to remind His people repeatedly, through the prophets, that "No, it is I Who am in charge." So I'm not saying that it's a good idea to write off people or kill them off. The Bible seems to indicate that, but the truth for me is the attitude one should have

toward the evil represented by those people.

KAREN: But that has all kinds of political implications today. There are people in Israel who say that this biblical attitude toward the Canaanites justifies certain aggressive attitudes toward the Palestinians.

ALEX: Indeed.

BURT: We said that in Vietnam, too—"They're the enemy, the other."

KAREN: The nonhuman. When we demonize others and fail to see their humanity, we are simply laying the seeds for a new holocaust in the next generation. We pass the burden of our pain onto others, projecting our misery and suffering onto others, in a vicious cycle. As the poet Philip Larkin says, "Man hands on misery to man, it deepens like a coastal shelf . . ."

CAROL: I want to say that God wasn't innocent here. You can't ignore the fact that God's back is turned on most of humanity that He has created. I think the power of Genesis is the point that people live in time and relationship, and therefore, change is always possible, for better or for worse. The story of Noah is about change for the worse.

ALEX: I don't see how Noah changes for the worse. Don't forget that right after this episode, the business of the covenant comes in. Yahweh blesses Noah, which means fertility. He and his children people the earth. Even the one who's cursed is also in covenant with God, which means the possibility of redemption. The rainbow is a very physical image of the covenant. It reminds God—"I will see the rainbow, and I will remember my covenant with Noah and his children." That means *all* of his children. Everybody has hope. I see this as a tremendously optimistic view of the Flood story.

BLU: I agreed with everything you said, Carol, except your last point about this being a change for the worse. The Noah story has a good deal of tragedy in it— flawed overreaction, God's mistakes, human lack of caring, and so forth. But I come out of the story thinking that this is a change for the better, not only in terms of the history of humanity in relationship to God, but also in terms of my own relationship with God.

BILL: Why?

BLU: Because it paves the way for an ongoing relationship. God doesn't expect perfection. God expects goodness in human beings and holds them accountable. But never again will God destroy them for falling off the path or destroy them for acts of evil. And that sustains the relationship. How can you have a relationship if you feel you're going to get *whammed* every time you step out of line? That's number one. Number two—as the covenant with all humanity, this covenant paves the way for all other particularist covenants and is the sustaining covenant that is replayed in all future covenants. There's self-restraint on each side in the covenant, self-limitation, but also a great sense of interdependence. I read into the feeling of the text that God loves humanity and that God regretted God's acts of destruction. God remembers how much God loves humanity, is dependent on humans, and needs the relationship with them. That's something I have to keep in my own life for a relationship with God.

CAROL: I see this story as the education or development of God.

BLU: The maturation of God.

CAROL: Yes, God learned, in a sense, from His creation, which is to really be in relationship. But for Noah, it is a bad end. He was a righteous man in the beginning, but the word "righteous" disappears from this text.

BILL: Could this be because he is a survivor, and the pathology of a survivor is very profound? Elie Wiesel talks of survivors being haunted by a sense of guilt. "Why was I spared?" He says of Noah that when he comes out of the Ark, he is the new Adam, the potential founder of a new dynasty. He builds his little altar, prays to his God, then goes off and gets drunk. Something's happened to this man.

BLU: But as Burt said before, Noah went in as a man of total faith. How does he manage to come out with this faith intact? Maybe that's the first question.

CAROL: This is the way I think of all survivors, whether of Auschwitz or of family incest—that their very righteousness or goodness was so stained by this experience that they've almost had to close themselves off because it's so overwhelming to take in what's happened. I see it not as their pathology but what happens when you assault a human being in the way that the Flood assaults Noah.

BURT: I think you're giving us a very profound reading of this story. On one hand, there's terrible pessimism that in the end, humanity is no better off. They really haven't learned the lessons they're supposed to have learned. But at least God has learned some lessons from all of this. If we learn to follow God's model, we might also learn how to be in relationship, to build covenant, and to have new beginnings.

ALEX: Well, it's sad that we don't follow the injunction right there in the Old Testament, in Deuteronomy, "Love God above all," and in Leviticus, "Love your neighbor as yourself." Believers—Christians, Jews, Muslims—don't think that applies to the political process. But it does.

BILL: Sam, you were nodding yes when Burt talked about new beginnings.

SAM: The bow in the cloud, Bill.

BILL: An original member of the Rainbow Coalition!

SAM: I think that's why the story's there.

BILL: And, Blu, I know you've been struggling with the whole question of the Holocaust. You're an Orthodox Jew, right?

What kind of assault do stories as horrific as the Flood and the Holocaust make on your belief? Or do they assault your belief?

BLU: They do. It's a powerful assault, and it would certainly be easier to hold a whole faith without these catastrophes, and without asking questions about where was God. But it doesn't mean that one has to abandon faith or a personal relationship with God. Somehow a human being has that capacity to hold faith and doubt—or perhaps not to hold faith and doubt simultaneously, but to shuttle back and forth in your mind, or in your heart, between moments of faith and moments of doubt.

BILL: Let me read this description by Elie Wiesel, a survivor. "April 11th, 1945. Buchenwald. Hungry, emaciated, sick, and weakened by fear and terror, Jewish inmates welcome their sudden freedom in a strange manner. They do not grab the food offered by the American liberators. Instead, they gather in circles and pray. Their first act as free human beings was to say Kaddish, thus glorifying and sanctifying God's name." I thought of Noah, coming off that Ark. Forget about everything else we've said about Noah for the moment—but when he gets off the Ark, the first thing he does is an act of worship.

BLU: He does. It's just incredible. I'm blessed with knowing many survivors in my own community, through my work and my husband's work. I'm amazed at the capacity of human beings to build second lives and to go on—not to give up all hope and faith, but to still believe in humanity.

B I L L: Do you still believe in humanity?

B L U: Yes, I believe in humanity.

A L E X: Because God does.

B L U: And because you can see the good in humanity. You know, I could never understand the lushness of genealogy at the end of the story of Noah. It almost seems inappropriate. And yet, as I look at Jewish life after the Holocaust, I understand it.

B I L L: What do you mean?

B L U: The amazing assertion of life forces. Life affirmation. The highest birthrate in Jewish history was in the DP camps after the Holocaust. To me, that's an incredible statement about human beings choosing life and loving life and wanting to go on with a relationship with other human beings, and wanting to continue the personal relationship with God.

B I L L: But it doesn't answer the question: Where was God? Does anyone answer that question?

K A R E N: When Noah got out of the Ark and saw these bloated bodies, this absolutely catastrophically damaged universe, perhaps there should have been a certain silence. It's different with the Holocaust because it was Hitler, not God, who put the people into the camps. Now for Noah to walk out of the Ark and immediately offer a sacrifice in a sort of knee-jerk way in the midst of this carnage, this slaughter, this absolute catastrophe of a total holocaust

which had been caused by God—this was not the moment to offer a sacrifice of praise. I don't like the image of God sniffing the sweet smell of meat. It reminds me too much of those pagan deities in Lucretius, snuffing up the smell of people's sacrifices and utterly indifferent to human suffering and pain.

B I L L: You were a nun, were you not?

K A R E N: Yes, I began life as a nun with very simplistic beliefs about God, but not much faith in God. That is, the opinions I held about God did not actually yield any

"How does a survivor wake up in the morning, in sanity, and get through the day in decency and goodness How did Noah get up in the morning every day thereafter?"

sense of life's ultimate meaning and value. I found I was haunted by stories like Noah, in which God would look at a certain sector of humanity and wipe them out forever, and put them into hell. Hell was very much part of my religious worldview in childhood. And God was a terrifying God for me.

Whatever they said about God loving the world and dying for us on the cross, God was terrible. I get all this back when I contemplate the Flood story. Now, there's more to it—and more to the whole religious quest—than that. But after what we've seen in this century, instead of returning mindlessly to the old beliefs and rituals and sacrifices of praise, perhaps there should be just a moment of silence—what the spiritual writers used to call "going into a cloud of unknowing." Going into the dark night of the soul. Going up the mountain, Mount Sinai, and entering the cloud where God is, but you can't see anything. Perhaps we should pause before we instantly just carry on with the old worship, the old style of religion.

BILL: This whole century has been a Deluge, hasn't it?

KAREN: Yes, so I don't want to just offer a mindless sacrifice to God. I think there should be a period of silence.

BLU: After any destruction or mass evil, you can't just go on with business as usual. You can lose hope, or you can intensify life. There are ways you commit yourself to renew life. I see them in my community, helping to rebuild Jewish life and learning and the family—all the things that were destroyed in the Holocaust. It's not simply to ask, "Where was God?" but to ask, "Now what can I do as part of this people to help restore, renew, refresh?" I think that the point Burt made really speaks to the question for me—that there's enough room in the relationship with God to find

moments of rage. But there are still deep wells of love in the relationship—and that is an amazing capacity of human beings.

KAREN: Some people don't make it, though—think of Primo Levi, for example.

BILL: He was the Jewish writer who took his own life not so long ago.

KAREN: Yes—he found the burden of survival beyond his powers.

BLU: That reminds me of the daily heroism of survivors. How does a survivor wake up in the morning, in sanity, and get through the day in decency and goodness? How did Noah get up in the morning every day thereafter? And his children and his sons and daughters-in-law?

BURT: I'm not so sure Noah was mindless when he offered the sacrifice. But I think we may be in error if we think the sacrifice was offered in love and praise. Noah had just witnessed, in the most awesome of ways, how terrifying God can be. I think that as soon as he got off that boat, the first thing he did was to propitiate God in the best way possible.

BLU: You think he's just trying to cover his back?

BURT: "Let God be happy—let Him smell barbecue—anything! I don't want this to happen again." There's real terror. That terror of God is something we don't often contend with. There's more than one way to approach God. Yes, we can approach God with love. But awe, trembling, fear—those are real ways of dealing with something wholly other, something terrifying.

BILL: In Genesis, doesn't God ask less for love than He does for obedience? That He wants awe from us, not necessarily affection?

SAM: One of the most troubling aspects of being at the end of this century and of this millennium is that people are turning back to religion in ways that are so anti-intellectual, so mean-spirited, so closely allied to some of the worst forces. I'm afraid that people are rushing toward God, but in a perverted way—

KAREN: —trampling other human beings.

SAM: Yes. I was teaching a class down at Duke, and one of the students was talking about God this and God that. I said, "You know, you sound like you're not aware that there was a God before there was a Bible." He said, "Run that past me one more time?" And I said, "You're equating God with your literal interpretation of every line in the Bible. I want you to know that God was here a long time before the Bible. That gives you some running room. That gives you an opportunity to examine the God-human encounter all through the Bible." And that's my contention right here in this discussion, too. In the legends and narratives of the God-human encounter that we have in our Bible, we get some very crude ideas of the Deity. When we read these stories too literally, we lose the fact that we have matured in our understanding. If God is God, and God is Creator, we ought to learn something about God in the light of what we've learned about the cosmos and about the long drifts we see in history. Our God idea ought to cause us to meditate deeply and sort out all of the other distractions. We called a lot of things demons then that we have other names for now. If we could go back over the whole demon world, we could put names and labels on those things. So I'd like to see the century close with a return to beautiful religious expression, not go backward to some primitive views. We have a God idea that's big enough to get us beyond some of the primitive notions that are now being revived or that are haunting us now.

CAROL: It's hard for me, at the end of the most violent century in human history, to think that we have learned so much or matured so much. We've learned some psychology and gained some understanding of certain patterns in the human world. I think the psychology in the story of Noah is a very profound psychology. God's discovery in the story of Noah is that if you assault people, you destroy the very humanness of humans. I don't like the word "primitive" because the eye-opening lesson of this century is that it was in the middle of the "civilized" world that the Holocaust happened. Many of the assumptions about civilization, education, and culture were shattered by the fact that the Holocaust occurred in Germany, in Europe. So I go back to the story of Noah. The lesson of the story and the kind of faith I can hold after reading it is that seeing what happens to people when you assault them the way God assaulted them, you learn that this kind of assault destroys the capacity of people to love and be good. So the faith I have is that we can learn not to assault one another.

KAREN: If I can just come back to you, Burt, for a moment. Yes, Noah comes out of the Ark, and maybe he does offer sacrifice to God out of craven terror. But that's been Noah's problem all along, as far as I'm concerned! God says, "I'm going to wipe out the earth. Make an Ark." Noah scurries off and does that. He hasn't learned a thing. It's precisely this kind of craven terror of God that leads him then to wage war against Canaan and that leads to the demonization of other people. Noah can't deal with the tragedies within himself. He has been assaulted by the whole ghastly experience of the Deluge. And he offers a sacrifice to a murderous God. And then, instead of giving all his hatred and anger to God, he projects them onto the people of Canaan.

CAROL: Then he gets drunk and exposes himself. We live in a world now where we're looking at these as very problematic human behaviors. So let's not just have an old boys' club view of this. These are behaviors of somebody who has been pushed beyond the limits of his humanness. I think of Noah at the beginning as someone who is a man, who is taking care of his animals, feeding his flock, living under the terror of God. In his generation, righteousness means being obedient in the

face of that kind of terror. But the consequences of it are really devastating at the end.

BURT: So do you think there's progress then? Ten generations after Noah, Abraham is willing to argue with God.

CAROL: That's the progress.

BURT: And there can be a whole different kind of covenant, a mutual set of expectations.

KAREN: That's progress. Discussion with God and no demonization of others—that's progress. Abraham goes around the land of Canaan and offers a sacrifice to Melchizekek's God. He doesn't bring his own God with him into the land of Canaan. He worships El, the god of the local people. He and his sons wait for the land to open itself up to them. He does have a few problems with Isaac, I'll give you that.

BILL: Does it concern you that the women in the story of Noah have no names? We never hear their voices. We don't know anything about Ms. Noah. They are just simply there as passengers on the ship.

SAM: Somebody has to clean up the Ark.

CAROL: Of course it concerns me. In fact, it's the signature of the tradition in which women have no names, and their voices are often muted, if they're heard at all. If Mrs. Noah had a voice, she would ask, "What about our daughters?" We are told it is Noah and his wife and their sons who go on the Ark, and nobody asks about the daughters. Do they have daughters? Are they leaving their daughters behind? That would explain why Noah's wife has no voice—because if she were willing to leave her daughters, at some point, she has left herself out. This tradition depends on a woman leaving herself to go with a man and live with him in a man-woman couple, in a patriarchal, heterosexual culture in which it is as if women and girls are not really there.

KAREN: In the Middle Ages one of the very first dramas created in Europe was the mystery play of the Flood, the Deluge. There Mrs. Noah is a comic figure. She is a truly ill-minded woman who refuses to get into the Ark. She's busy gossiping. They have to drag her on by force. So one of the first appearances of a woman in history is as a figure of fun. The serious people are men.

BLU: All of this is true. There's a real problem not just for women today, but for everybody who reads the Bible. This was all grounded in a patriarchal context. But we will never be able to rewrite history. These are our sacred texts. Our task is to find ways to right the balance or to rebalance the inequity between genders—to listen to women's different voices and to search for equality in all the ways that we can in real life today, given what we know about how words and images so powerfully affect the psyche. Even though God has no gender, using the pronoun "He" exclusively still has a very powerful effect, maybe even

more powerful because it's so subtle. The psyche is altered by language.

KAREN: Because of this, people in my country are still arguing about the ridiculous question of whether women can be priests or not. Still!

BILL: Barney, where are you in your faith at the moment? Is there any residue of the "faith of our fathers"?

BARNEY: There's a lot of residue, and sometimes the residue seems to be the problem. It won't go away. It hangs in very close. You can't sweep it out the door. I think that from my very early years, whether women were movers in the biblical story was not a big concern. It's understandable because this was a God who would destroy you with hellfire and damnation—that was a very big part of the theology. I can remember hearing about Jonathan Edwards's sermon *Sinners in the Hands of an Angry God.* That sermon could make grown men weep. At that time, hell was very real to me. I've moved away from that feeling that God could do this, so I must say, coming back to the Noah story reminds me of the very stern God Who was part of my youth. But it leaves me reaching for the idea that humans have been put here by God and left free.

BILL: But do you think God expected that when we exercised that freedom, we would do so with such injustice and cruelty?

BARNEY: I have trouble giving God the

credit for everything when I don't feel I can give God the blame for bad things happening to good people. When it comes to car accidents, plane crashes, tornadoes, that sort of thing, I simply believe that certain laws are in effect and that we as human beings are groping our way through this world.

BURT: I'm intrigued, Barney. Did your Vietnam experience shift your perception of God? You went through your own Flood. You saw the bloated bodies. You were there. Did that change your theology?

BARNEY: Well, I was there very early, and there was some shooting, but not the kind of awful experience people had later. I think the feelings of awfulness that I'm more concerned with have to do with events like the Holocaust. You know, I grew up not seeing black people or Jews. The first time I met a Jewish person was when I went to the state university. For some years, I lived in a county where black people were not permitted to stay after sundown. It was called a "sundown law." So to come out of that existence and be exposed to the Holocaust—which I don't fully understand, even today—things like that have depressed me in more ways than Vietnam.

BILL: But when you asked the question "Where was God?" from your own perspective as a Christian Pilgrim, where was God? We keep dancing away from that question.

BARNEY: Maybe we're obliged to keep dancing. I don't want to face the awfulness of some of the pictures of God that we see created at various times.

BILL: What I meant, Barney, is that if God chose Noah to survive what was to be a carnage, God must have had some purpose beyond our knowing. Maybe He didn't care about the Holocaust and what happened to the six million because He has some other inexplicable purpose. We may not like it. We certainly don't understand it. But there's something at work in the Deity, the Reality beyond our reality, that isn't as intimate with us as most people around this circle would like to imagine.

BARNEY: I'll buy that.

KAREN: But that's thinking about God too much as though He were a human being like us with a personality, writ large, and with likes and dislikes similar to our own.

BILL: I thought I was saying just the opposite—that God may *not* be like us. God may not be moved by Auschwitz.

KAREN: No, you're still talking about God as though He were somebody with a plan for the future. It's still anthropomorphic. We need to walk away a little bit from this personalized view of God. In the Noah story, for example, we've got a very personalized God, a God Who starts off by saying He's fed up, He regrets, He's sad in His heart, He wants to change His mind—all the things that God is not supposed to do or be in classical theism. He behaves just like an inadequate human being. The result is that when Noah comes out of his holocaust, he has the blueprint to imitate God and to say he's going to wipe out the people of Canaan. And that continues. So, as I said, perhaps we need to go into the silence for a while. If you look at religious history, you see that in all three of the main traditions of monotheism, monotheists have insisted you have to walk away sometimes from the idea of God as a personality. That's why the Greeks created the doctrine of the Trinity—to remind us that we can't think about God in simple, personal terms.

BLU: What else must go into the silence? Can you explain that a little more?

KAREN: When we think about God, we're at the end of what words and thoughts can do. Science is helping us do that by opening up such huge, cosmic vistas that simplistic ideas of a God Who created the world, rather as you or I might make something, are just shot to pieces. So science is opening us up to the fact that we've come to the end of what we can think and know. Holocausts can do this, too. When we look at a catastrophe of that magnitude and try to measure it with our little theologies, we can be in the silence, that state of awe and amazement. I think that religion is at its best when it asks questions and at its worst when it seeks to answer them.

BLU: Well, I could go into the silence with you in that way, but not to find other answers as substitutes. I think going into the silence doesn't mean you have to sus-pend the idea of a God as a powerful God and Creator, or that you have to suspend your relationship with God.

CAROL: No, but it may require a change in the religious dialogue. Barney, you referred to the physical laws in the universe—I think there are psychological laws as well. That's why the story of Noah has a ring of truth in today's world. We can all talk about regret and sadness. But if we want to change the voice, we have to bring in voices that haven't yet been heard—women's voices, for one. And if we absorbed some of the things there are to learn from this text, maybe we could speak in a new voice about ourselves and our human world.

ALEX: In parts of the Old Testament, though, women's voices are very clear, as Sam brought out—the Book of Ruth, for example.

CAROL: But that's a big exception. And the Book of Ruth is a different book. That's the point where Sam starts referring to God as "She," because the Book of Ruth is how the world sounds when you suddenly bring out into the text the voice of the women who are in the world. I'm not saying that Mrs. Noah—look, even the fact that that's our name for her—

KAREN: Yes, yes, right.

CAROL: Let's give her a name.

BURT: Miriam?

CAROL: Yes, let's call her Miriam or Rachel or Sarah. She had a voice. She spoke. But it wasn't a voice that was seen as worthy of being carried forward. The fact that Mrs. Noah has no name and Noah has no daughters says something about the story itself.

ALEX: What does that have to say for the story, though—if we can return to the story? I'm talking about the story as we have it. It's the only thing we have.

CAROL: But Genesis is so powerful because when women enter, things change—when Rebekah enters, she changes the course of history.

ALEX: Indeed. And Sarah.

CAROL: Ruth and Naomi.

BLU: Surely there's a loss in the Bible when women's voices aren't heard. If they had been allowed more of a role, the story would have been different. We just don't know *how* it would have been different.

ALEX: I'd rather just take the story as it is.

CAROL: But this is a lesson that's in Genesis, which is fascinating. It's not something that arose at the end of the twentieth century. It's there for us to see if we want to see it.

Matteo de' Raverti, *The Drunken Noah and His Sons*, Ducal Palace, Venice, early 15th c.

ALEX: Right. But I don't like to make absolute any elements in that story that demonize what God does by wiping out people.

CAROL: But that's not where I want to go. Suppose I say that the story of Noah shows you what happens in a world where women don't speak—that in such a world, things go to extremes, and it is really dangerous. In a world where women aren't speaking, we might be in danger of a catastrophe like this.

ALEX: That's fine for you as a twentieth-century person. But—

CAROL: No, I'm taking the text literally. Men's issues are the issues that are going to replicate.

ALEX: When we try to reach some understanding of that text, with all the intelli-

gence that we have, through textual criticism and study of the ancient languages and cultures and all the rest, we've got to compare that text with other similar texts. For example, there's a Babylonian flood story in which the gods decide to wipe out human beings because they were staying up too late at night having raucous parties. Therefore, the gods destroy them. No moral dimension at all. Now, the author of this story in Genesis comes along and puts it into a moral perspective.

SAM: That's what I was talking about.

ALEX: Exactly. We see that there is a moral dimension to human waywardness, that humans are accountable to God. That's why the rainbow and the covenant at the end of this story are so hopeful. We shouldn't miss the subtle irony in these stories, which is that God doesn't give up on human beings. He makes a covenant with them. Remember their fertility after the colossal destruction of the Flood. Remember the new creation, when God's breath blows over the waters and dries them up—an exact reflection of the first chapter in Genesis where God's breath and word create this marvelous universe that we now have. Now, the other point with regard to the nature of God—it's very important to have God talk, otherwise we wouldn't have any theology, and some of us would probably be out of a job. But we have to be careful because faith is not necessarily God-talk. Faith means belief in a transcendent Being. We get indications of that transcendence and that Being in different parts of the Bible, not just in this one

> "If we looked at various affirmations about God in the Old Testament, we would see that there is a God Who often decides to relate to us in silence—but that does not mean absence."

part. We see that God is essentially mysterious. He says to one of His chosen ones, "My name is mysterious"—meaning His very essence is mysterious. God is unspeakable. But that doesn't mean God can't relate to people. The great prophet Jeremiah shouts at God, "Why do you treat me like this? You've abused me." He uses words almost bordering on blasphemy. But that's prayer. Jeremiah takes God seriously because God's taking him seriously, essentially to do a thankless job—to try to bring back a jaded people to authentic religion. Karen, you talked earlier about what people said about God when you were growing up. The way we talk about God gives Him an awfully bad name. God doesn't need friends like us to talk like that. If we looked at various affirmations about God in the Old Testament, we would see that there is a God Who often decides to relate to us in silence—but that does not mean absence.

KAREN: The trouble is, though, that the stories we hear when we are very, very young are formative. Whatever we say afterward and however we try to qualify them with nice, uplifting theology or subtle ideas, the hideous story of Noah, with God wiping out humanity, remains in many people's minds. And many people like that kind of God.

BURT: Blu, you said we can't rewrite the story, and you're absolutely right. But we can reread the story. And, Alex, you're right in saying that one of our tasks in reading the story is to capture it in its ancient background of the other literature of its time. But the fact is that we're here in the twentieth century, and we have no other glasses but these. We must approach these stories as late-twentieth-century readers and try to hear women's voices—because they're here to stay. They were here in biblical times, too, but they weren't listened to. We've learned to listen. So I think that we're obligated to read the story as children and to read it year in and year out, always hearing something anew. It's an ongoing process.

BILL: I'd like to go around the circle and have each of you say what lesson you draw from this. What do you think the Bible is trying to teach us in the Noah story?

BARNEY: It says to me that God has promised not to take any broad swipes. It doesn't mean that He won't be examining each of us individually as to how we live our lives and develop our faith. That is a hopeful sign to me. I want to keep that rainbow in my head. I'm human.

KAREN: I'm sorry. I can't see the rainbow without also seeing the bloated bodies and the animals and the mud. I take away from the story the idea of a developing God. We start off with an infantile God, knocking down His sand castles—a regretful God Who learns maturity and in the process brutalizes humanity—which then passes on the burden of suffering to other people.

BURT: If I identify with Noah, you're right—I see the bloated bodies. If I identify with God, though, I learn that no matter how terribly I fail at something, even something as important as creating the universe, there's another chance. We can start over. There is a possibility of a rainbow at the end.

ALEX: To me, the essential aspect of the story has to be seen in relation to other stories. Despite the dreadful waywardness and lawlessness of human beings, God still has faith in human beings. Above all, we relate to God in covenant. We are meant to stand in relationship to each other. At the end of these eleven chapters at the beginning of Genesis, God chooses a specific group of people to carry on His message with the idea that it would become universal. This business of God's choices is beyond human scrutiny. There's a lovely little poem by William Norman Ever—"How Odd/Of God/To Choose/The Jews!" It's odd, perhaps, from a non-Jewish point of view.

BURT: It's odd from a Jewish point of view, too.

ALEX: But it's a profoundly theological thing that God did—God's freedom to choose, even though we don't understand.

BILL: So the lesson that you draw from the story of Noah?

ALEX: I can't figure out everything—there's mystery, but my faith is not contingent upon the doubts I have about the affirmations I make about God. Some of the images of God I grew up with I don't subscribe to. Those images are horrendous. Why do parents subject children to such hideous things? Why did I even read some of these stories without a great deal of ex-

planation? In other words, I think the failure is not on the part of the Bible, but on the part of well-meaning people who read

---

> *"I can't turn loose this story of Noah and the Flood because after all of the devastation and the bloated bodies, there's the rainbow and the cloud."*

---

these stories or other stories from the Bible that are horrendous in some of their implications. But they make no claim on my allegiance. I see this as an ongoing revelation that God deals with people as they are.

BLU: What I take away from this story is that there is life after destruction and that there is a chance to rebuild. You don't have to abandon a vision of perfection of the universe, or of humanity, or of relationships, but sometimes you have to accept flaws and accept the imperfect partner in getting there. It also teaches me that there is an ongoing relationship between God and humanity that will never be broken; that human beings have responsibility for each other; and that the covenantal relationship between God and humanity is a paradigm for relationship between human beings.

SAM: My father, who was a Sunday school teacher, taught me this story. Sometimes we laughed at the ridiculous aspects of it, but we didn't talk about the history behind it, and we didn't try to rewrite it. We drew from it what it said right then to the people and went on. Every Wednesday, though, my daddy would press his trousers and go down to the Philharmonic Glee Club rehearsal. These sixty black guys—table waiters, coal trimmers, truck drivers— would give one big concert a year to the white population. When we kids went to hear it, we couldn't sit where we wanted to, even though our daddy was singing—we had to sit in the back. But in the midst of all that rejection, hate, and spite, they sang. And do you know the song they sang at the close of the concert? They sang, "Dawn is breaking, and a new day is born/ The world is singing the song of the dawn/ Yesterday the skies were gray/but look, this morning they are blue." *Noah!* "The smiling sun tells everyone come/Let's start life anew/Let's sing"—and *bam!* they'd knock the top off—"Let's all sing, hallelujah/for a new day is born/The world is singing the song of the dawn." Sixty black guys in tuxedos in the 1920s, with lynching everywhere and hatred—"nigger" this and "nigger" that. But they had something we need to recover right now. I can't turn loose this story of Noah and the Flood because after all of the devastation and the bloated bodies, there's the rainbow and the cloud. And I can't take that bow and the cloud out of my universe. I'm not going to live without that kind of hope, you see? That's what that story means to me.

CAROL: I also thought of the song "We Shall Overcome"—that sense of not being passive in the face of this kind of tradition, and not feeling that it's the only tradition or that it's the way it is or the way it has to be. Because I think the profound lesson for me is that, first of all, God learns. What God learns is that terror and destruction don't change things and that the very evil in the story of Noah that God wanted to eradicate comes back. So God then makes a covenant to stay in relationship with us, and that creates the possibility of change. But this is an imperfect God because God makes the same mistakes, again and again, like people do. What God learns about humans in the story of Noah is that people are vulnerable. If you assault that vulnerability, or force humans to cover their vulnerability, to close themselves off, or, as with the image of the Ark, to put themselves into a box and not see or care what happens to their neighbors, then you destroy the humanness of humans. At the end of the story, Noah curses his son into slavery, saying "slave of slaves shall he be to his brothers." It doesn't go away. The dove comes back with a fresh olive leaf, signifying the renewal of life, a new generation— but there is a history. And like the mud from the Flood and the bodies, this history leaves its traces. There is a physical residue of the Flood, and there is also a psychological residue. The covenant goes two ways. The creation of the human world has the potential to reveal things to God, too. By the end of the story of Noah, it is a two-way relationship.

V

CALL AND PROMISE

AZIZAH Y. AL-HIBRI • ROBERT ALTER

BHARATI MUKHERJEE • EUGENE RIVERS III

LEWIS B. SMEDES • ELIZABETH SWADOS

BURTON L. VISOTZKY

John Gardner tells us that history never looks like history when you are living through it. It looks confusing and messy, and always feels uncomfortable. You can certainly say that about history as we find it in the Book of Genesis. God is founding a dynasty, the beginnings of Judaism, Christianity, and Islam. One might expect the storyteller to paint the First Family ten feet tall with several coats of whitewash. But the picture we get of these men and women is uncomfortably human. There is so much marital conflict and sibling intrigue they almost forfeit the call and fumble the promise. Yet the storyteller refuses to clean up their act. This is the amazing thing about the people of Genesis. The more we talk about them, the more they look like people we know—faces in the mirror.

—BILL MOYERS

Abraham Receives the Promise [?], Dura Europos Synagogue, Syria, 245

Now the L<small>ORD</small> *said to Abram, "Go from your country and your kindred and your father's house to the land that I will show you. I will make of you a great nation, and I will bless you, and make your name great, so that you will be a blessing . . ."*

So Abram went, as the L<small>ORD</small> *had told him; and Lot went with him . . . Abram took his wife Sarai and his brother's son Lot, and all the possessions that they had gathered . . . and they set forth to go to the land of Canaan . . . Then the* L<small>ORD</small> *appeared to Abram, and said, "To your offspring I will give this land." So he built there an altar to the* L<small>ORD</small>*, who had appeared to him . . . And Abram journeyed on by stages toward the Negeb.*

Now there was a famine in the land. So Abram went down to Egypt to reside there . . . When he was about to enter Egypt, he said to his wife Sarai, "I know well that you are a woman beautiful in appearance; and when the Egyptians see you, they will say, 'This is his wife'; then they will kill me, but they will let you live. Say you are my sister, so that it may go well with me because of you, and that my life may be spared on your account . . ." The Egyptians saw that the woman was very beautiful. When the officials of Pharaoh saw her, they praised her to Pharaoh. And the woman was taken into Pharaoh's house. And for her sake he dealt well with Abram; and he had sheep, oxen, male donkeys, male and female slaves, female donkeys, and camels.

But the L<small>ORD</small> *afflicted Pharaoh and his house with great plagues because of Sarai, Abram's wife. So Pharaoh called Abram, and said, "What is this you have done to me? Why did you not tell me that she was your wife? Why did you say, 'She is my sister,' so that I took her for my wife? Now then, here is your wife, take her, and be gone." And Pharaoh gave his men orders concerning him; and they set him on the way, with his wife and all that he had.*

So Abram went up from Egypt, he and his wife, and all that he had, and Lot with him, into the Negeb. Now Abram was very rich in livestock, in silver, and in gold. He journeyed on by stages from the Negeb as far as Beth-el, to the place where his tent had been at the beginning, between Beth-el and Ai, to the place where he had made an altar at the first; and there Abram called on the name of the L<small>ORD</small>*.*

—excerpts from *New Revised Standard Version*
(*The Holy Bible*), Chapters 12 and 13

BILL: What's the moral of this story?

BOB: I wish there were a simple moral. Like a lot of stories in the Bible, it sets your mind going a lot of different ways. For example, what does it mean for a human being to be chosen by God? Does it elevate you to a different status? Does it put you into a different moral category? I think it doesn't.

BURT: I disagree. Abraham *does* seem to be put into a different moral category, which lets him get away with things that don't belong in everyday morality. This is a fellow who pulls a scam on Pharaoh, one that involves selling his wife—not nice. By the end of the story, he's very wealthy, mainly because God has acted as his protector. God then comes in later and says to Pharaoh, "Don't touch da lady." It's a horrifying story. God's choice of Abraham allows him to be metaethical—he can do anything and get away with it.

GENE: Abraham's moral ambiguity is an argument for the position that you don't have to be a goody-goody to function as an instrument of God. Like all of us, Abraham is a flawed human being. But he receives a call from God, and he responds to that call, even though the response is imperfect.

LIZ: As I was listening to the story, I was reminded of the theater. When you're casting a play, you choose actors for what you need them to be at the moment, in a particular role. Sometimes people get the idea that to be chosen is to be zapped, when the truth is that you're being chosen for the moment to further a certain story. You're chosen to act out a particular story, not to be the representative of God.

BILL: Would you have chosen Abraham as a leading man?

LIZ: For that moment in the story, he seems to be well cast because he's a go-ahead person who's morally ambiguous. Abraham is perfect for the role of Abraham. You know, he's not that special—he's simply doing Abraham's story.

AZIZAH: Let me tell you, I'm a little troubled by the negative image of Abraham coming out here. I don't think this story should be abstracted from the rest of Abraham's life. In the Qur'an, we see why God might have chosen Abraham—because even as a child, he spoke out against his own people, who were worshipping idols. He said, "I believe in the one true God," even though speaking out this way endangered his life. He had to leave his own land, not just because God said, "Leave," but because he stood up for God and truth in his society. Before Abraham came to the idea of the one true God, he tested a whole series of ideas—he considered worshipping the sun, the moon, and a lot of other things first. He came to the idea of the one true God through his reason, even though he was imperfect. So Abraham was on his own journey before God ever talked to him. If you are in a society, and you have different moral values from that society, either you try to establish your point of view or, if it becomes impossible for you, then you pack up and leave. Abraham did. He wanted to go wherever he could worship the one true God.

BILL: Adin Steinsalz, the great Israeli Talmudic scholar, says that although we think of Abraham as having brought monotheism into the world, he actually retrieved this notion from an earlier time. In the cities of Abraham's day, monotheism had been lost.

AZIZAH: And for bringing back that idea, Abraham was blessed. Now, let me tell you, his wife Sarah, according to the stories I've read, was never touched by Pharaoh. She never became his wife. When Pharaoh reached out to touch her, his hand froze—and that was how Pharaoh found out about this one God.

BURT: In rabbinic midrash, when Pharaoh is smitten by the plague, the rabbis say, with a twinkle in their eye, "Yeah, and the plague was impotence"—thus saving Sarah.

LEW: Abraham is not given a task to do other than listen and go. He's not given a job or told that he has to be a model of anything. God simply says, "I'm God, and I want you to go where I want you to go, and I'll show you where it is when you get there. If you do that, I'll see to it that you're a blessing to the nations." All he's told is "Follow me, and through you something is going to happen."

BOB: He was simply called to be an immigrant.

AZIZAH: What Abraham showed was his ability to yield to God. Whatever God told him to do, he did it, and he took the risks because he knew God would be there for him.

BHARATI: He needed to hear God. I think God communicates with everyone. Those of us who need Him, or are ready to listen, do hear and see God. So we should really begin the story right before Abraham's father dies. If you do that, you can see Abraham as a cult leader. He's got a following, but when the patriarch dies, his people don't want to move on. The new patriarch has to establish his authority. In the Fox translation, the Lord doesn't appear to Abraham—Abraham is described as seeing God. This distinction is quite interesting because we have only Abraham's word that the Lord appeared. He needs to publicize the fact that God has provided this instruction in order to get his troops to go on a rather difficult journey. Abraham, in a sense, is the prototypical American. He's got hustle. It's like a guy saying, "Look, I need to inspire my followers to take this arduous journey, so I'd better have God come on. I'd better bring on the voices, bring on the vision." This is different from the Lord appearing, which is how the rest of you read the story. In your version, the Lord treats Abraham as a kind of passive subject and says, "Go, baby, do your thing, but I'm not gonna tell you how to do it."

LIZ: Passive subject? That's a stretch. You don't get passivity from this story. The individual can always make a decision. My understanding of this reality is that God

God's Promise to Abraham, Vienna Genesis, early Christian, 6th c.

has spoken to me, and I can decide either to obey or disobey.

L E W : Yes, but what if Abraham were the only one to hear the call? Somebody else might have said, "You think God came to you in a dream. I think you just dreamed that God came to you." There's a big difference.

L I Z : I wonder: Is "call" the same thing as "chosen"? What is the literal translation of "call"? In musical terms, call and response is something that comes from within the person. You hear it within yourself, and you externalize it. Maybe the call does come from an external God—but maybe

the call is influenced by Abraham's own music. If he's looking for God, maybe the call is initiated within himself, like a piece of music. In religious music, often the call is a long, sustained note. The shofar on Rosh Hashanah plays a long, sustained note.

B U R T : You have this long note, the call—but what is the response? What does the other voice say?

L I Z : Both voices come from the imagination.

B U R T : So "it's all in his head," right?

LEW: No, Liz isn't denying the call, she's just locating it in a different place.

BILL: But what does it mean to hear God speak to you? Is Abraham hallucinating?

LEW: Well, if he were my neighbor, and he said, "God came to me last night and told me to go to the Los Angeles airport and that He would tell me which airline to go on and which destination to go to, and I'm never coming back," I would say to him, "Either you're crazy, or God is doing something very peculiar."

BHARATI: I come from a culture where people being visited by God in dreams is perfectly natural. Miracles are part of the ordinary life cycle for me. So I don't see any problem with God speaking to Abraham.

GENE: And if we went to any Pentecostal church in Harlem on a Friday night, we'd find people who would resonate and say, "I heard the voice of God. I spoke to the Divine, and the Divine spoke to me." For a substantial number of people in this country who are not particularly theologically sophisticated, that's a very vivid reality.

BILL: You're theologically sophisticated—is it a reality for you?

GENE: Yes, the notion of a call shapes my entire life.

LIZ: But it shapes mine, too. As a composer, I never write serious music without hearing it. Where does that come from? That is a voice.

GENE: When I use the term "call," I mean something different. I used to be a painter, but when I refer to "call," I'm talking about the sense of God's calling on my life. That's very different from an aesthetic impulse.

LIZ: Excuse me, but I feel that God has made an extreme demand on my life to write music forever. The Hebrew Bible is sung from its beginning all the way through. I don't feel I'm here just for the aesthetics.

GENE: No, but I was distinguishing between experiencing divinity within an aesthetic context and actually having a theological encounter where I intuit a demand on my life to do a particular thing.

AZIZAH: There are many ways God gives us the call. The way God gives you a sign or message might be very different from the way God would give me or Abraham or the Prophet Muhammad a call. It might depend on our readiness—how much we can take. If we're really ready, we'll probably get the message in a more direct way than if we are not ready. But God is always in communication with people. According to the Qur'an, there are signs for us to see. Do we see them? That's the question.

LIZ: I work with gang kids. They told me a beautiful story about how break dancing began. One time, during some gang wars, a Rastafarian came out of the ghetto and said to the gangs, "Make your movements dance." So when they dove for each other, they dove on the ground. I thought that this Rastafarian must have had a call to stop gang wars and invent break dancing.

BHARATI: You know, God talks to me all the time, and ghosts visit me even in my San Francisco bedroom.

BILL: Are you equating the two?

BHARATI: Not at all. I'm saying that a complete, invisible world surrounds me. When the lights go off, this world is far more real to me than intellect and reason. I can't imagine writing anything without being aware of the moral implications—every little act of daily life has a moral context.

LEW: This conversation is very interesting because we're asking how our experience is like Abraham's. But I don't read the story as a model of how God comes. This story isn't teaching us the religious dynamic of being in touch with the eternal. This is a particular guy, and God comes to him with a particular mission, one that Abraham didn't even envision. God, who is very different from Abraham, comes and says, "I've got something I want to do, and you're going to be my instrument." If Abraham had had a tape recorder, would he have picked up the voice of God? I'm sure if I heard God, I wouldn't pick it up on the tape recorder. I have a hard time making Abraham's call a model for mine because I don't hear God.

BURT: I share your dilemma. I'm actually surprised to be sitting here surrounded by people who so readily hear voices. I'm a praying Jew, so I talk to God all the time. But I don't usually hear answers. It's a much more subtle process. Abraham's process is very radical. A voice comes to him and says, "Get up and go. Change your life. Change everything about it." Nobody ever says that to me. Everything is in very slow increments. If I hear God at all, it's somewhere between the lines of a page I've been studying for hours. And what I hear is maybe just "Well, it's time to turn the page."

BOB: You know, every time I hear this story, there's one little voice in my head that wants to yell out to Abraham, "Don't do it! Look at all the trouble you're going to be getting yourself into!" And then I think: "What is he asked to do? He's asked to go to a land of unspecified identity." And God says, "I'm going to give you this land. I'm going to make you a blessing. And you're going to have this multitudinous seed." At this point, of course, he doesn't have any children. But there's something else here I immediately identify with. Nationalism is a hot potato in our world, and you might say this is a nationalist fable. God says, "Your descendants will dominate this land." But then Abraham goes in the opposite direction. You have this swing between a nationalist and a rootless cosmopolitan who goes from one end of the civilized world to the other, from Mesopotamia to Egypt.

BURT: He's called to go to Canaan, but he doesn't have the land. It says explicitly that the Canaanites are still in the land.

God sends him to the land and says, ''I'm going to give it to you,'' but when he gets there, it's not quite his. And God says, ''I'm going to give you offspring,'' but he's got a barren wife.

GENE: That's the life of faith. If you believe in the call or that the promise has been made, you see the situation through the eyes of faith. I identify with the call. And I identify with the nationalism in the context of the black community, a community completely coming apart in every way. Disarray, confusion, nihilism, and decay—

that's what I see. Using Abraham as a case study, I could say of the black community: ''There's no land, and there's no people. But there is a call and a promise.'' So I have a decision to make: ''Will I obey as a person of faith?'' Because it's on that basis that a people will come into existence.

LEW: Yes. I can imagine Sarah waking up about four in the morning, hearing the bustling noises of Abraham packing. And Sarah says, ''What are you doing, Abe?'' ''Packing.'' ''What for?'' ''Well, we're leaving.'' ''Where are we going?'' ''I don't

Giovanni Benedetto Castiglione, *Departure of Abraham*, ca. 1650

know." "Why are we going?" "Because He told me to." "Who's 'He'?" "He didn't tell me." And then I could imagine Sarah calling her father: "What am I going to do?" Her father says, "I knew you shouldn't have married this nut."

AZIZAH: But in my tradition, Sarah is presented as somebody who taught religion to the women, as Abraham did to the men. She's not disconnected from what Abraham is doing.

BURT: That's different from what we have in the Bible. All we have is Abraham saying to Sarah, "Tell them you're my sister so I'll make some profit."

BILL: Does it trouble you that God chooses a man like Abraham? As Burt says, Abraham hides behind his wife's skirts and resorts to trickery and cunning.

LEW: I'm not happy that Abraham was not more perfect. But I'm very happy that his imperfections are part of this story. That's the best part of the story to me. And we don't have to make him out to be a monster.

LIZ: Yes, we can say Abraham is this or that—I can say "this macho pig," but that's me, whereas you're more sympathetic toward him. But that's the beauty of a great story.

AZIZAH: We should not be sitting here in judgment over Abraham, because we didn't go through what he went through. He had to go through all these difficulties

and find ways to protect himself both in his own tribe and later, in Egypt. I could imagine someone facing a difficulty that might lead him to say, "This is not my wife, this is my sister." And then you would hope that God would come through and help you.

LEW: Abraham was not just trying to save his own skin—God's promise was at stake.

"Abraham was not just trying to save his own skin—God's promise was at stake."

LIZ: We can look at the story and say, "Okay, yes, I understand, I care." But I still don't have to say that it's fine to put your wife into a harem and pretend she's your sister. You don't have to let this story be an excuse to treat women today in a certain way.

BILL: But isn't this a classic theme of stories through the ages—the woman making a sacrifice for the success of her husband?

LIZ: Yes, unfortunately.

GENE: We're viewing this story through a twentieth-century lens and then superimposing our context on a very complex historical, cultural, and political context that we don't fully appreciate.

BURT: We don't have a lot of choice—the twentieth-century lens is the only one we have. I study how the Church fathers and rabbis read this story, but even as I do that, I'm keenly aware that I'm reading the Church fathers and rabbis through my twentieth-century lens. Azizah reads this story as a Muslim, in the Qur'anic tradition—so she reads it in a very sympathetic way. And Lew reads it as a Christian theologian. If I limited myself to a purely rabbinic reading, I would also read Abraham in a very sympathetic way. But the rabbis knew there were two kinds of reading. There is the rabbinic reading, the midrash. But there is also what the story says. In the story, I see Abraham much more the way Liz does. He says, "Say you're my sister so I may live." And I'd say: "Yes, he was worried about saving his life and preserving the promise." But then Abraham adds, "so that it may go well with me on your account." That means "I'm going to profit." And the proof of that comes just three verses later—sheep, oxen, donkeys, servants, maids, she-asses, camels. This guy made a fortune off that transaction. There's something not happy there. It's not good.

AZIZAH: Well, I can see one reason I'm more sympathetic than you are. I don't have that story to deal with—it's not in the Qur'an.

GENE: So how do you respond to this version?

AZIZAH: It does appear in our version of midrash. The story came to the Muslims via the Jews. Some of our writers say that when Abraham said, "She is my sister," he was not lying—she was his sister in faith. So there it is again—this attempt to say that Abraham was a good guy. He was in a difficult spot, and this was the best way he knew to get out of it. But God helped him because he had yielded all his destiny to God. Now what Prophet Muhammad said is that a free-spirited woman, regardless of the hardship she is in, would never use herself as a commodity. Here I see Sarah being used as a commodity, and that troubles me. But again, you know, this story is not part of my tradition.

BURT: It's not clear to me that the whole history of Abraham, at least as it's told in the Hebrew Bible, is inconsistent with this story. Abraham does a lot of things that leave us to wonder about his moral judgment. Abraham and Sarah do this again. And they even have a son who, with his wife, does it again. It clearly works.

BILL: So if Abraham does a lot of morally questionable things, what's the Bible trying to tell us here?

BURT: Well, one lesson Abraham seems to have learned is: If you sell your wife, you make a lot of profit!

LEW: Bill, I think the answer to your first question: "What's the moral of this story?" is that there is no moral. This is not a story with a moral but a story that explains the origin of three great religions. It's about the Maker of the Universe coming into an encounter with a human being—not as a divinity rising out of the human being and not as a droplet coming out of some divine faucet, but as another saying, "I'm going to do something with you."

> "This is not a story with a moral but a story that explains the origin of three great religions."

LIZ: But why aren't we looking at this from Sarah's point of view? She's taken into a land, she's given over to a Pharaoh, she's told to do whatever—so what's Sarah thinking during all of this? I think Sarah is gaining patience and wisdom.

BURT: Rabbis don't normally ask questions about women, but I think it's within rabbinic tradition for us to have to ask: "Where is Sarah in this story?" So let me give you one read of Sarah. Sarah is an equal partner in faith. She also hears the promise, and she knows that she is childless. She's really agonizing, "How do I provide Abraham with the seed God promises?" Maybe Egypt provides her an opportunity. Maybe in her passion, or in her neurosis, whatever it is, she thinks, "Maybe I'm meant to be with Pharaoh. Maybe that's how I get with seed. After all,

he is a prince. He's King of Egypt. Maybe I should be bearing that seed." So she goes willingly, as a partner to Abraham, to try and fulfill that promise. That could be one reading.

BILL: But what do you make of Sarah's silence? I find Abraham's behavior more understandable than Sarah's. Either she's playing along with the deception willingly or she feels she has to do it. She's cast into Pharaoh's harem. She's passed off as something she isn't. Her husband is hiding behind her skirts. And yet, in this brief account, we have no indication what is going through her mind.

LIZ: Maybe there's a conspiracy between the two of them. Maybe, like Esther later, she's planning to become Queen.

BURT: It's a wild thing to imagine that had Abraham kept his mouth shut, Sarah would have been Queen of Egypt. We would have had a very different Bible if it had worked out that way.

BHARATI: I think Sarah is actually exercising power in other ways—she's consolidating her superiority over Abraham. She's been humiliated. Now she can say, "You owe me one. When we get out of this situation, I'm going to cash in the chips."

LIZ: But real power is a roof over the head, goods, money. That's what the men are given in the Bible. Throughout, they get it first.

BHARATI: Sarah knows that God can

fructify her if He wants to. But He's with-holding that fructification until the right time. She knows that she's participating in this scheme, which is part of a divine plan.

AZIZAH: I think we find some support for this in a later incident when Hagar is left in the desert. She asks Abraham, "Why are you leaving me here?" And he says, "That's what I was asked by God to do." One could say that Sarah knew that God was always furthering the promise.

BURT: I studied this narrative with a group of bankers, lawyers, and business executives. One of the lawyers said, "Wait, let's look at the beginning of the story. God takes this shepherd, and he's got nothing, right? Morality aside, look what happens. By the end of the chapter, Abraham is talk-ing one on one with a head of state. Leave aside how he sold Sarah. Well, here he is, talking with Pharaoh. He's supposed to be-come the head of a great nation. He's earned start-up costs. Let's face it—nobody likes the fact that he sold his wife, but hey, it worked."

LIZ: And it continued to work until somebody said, "Up against the wall, Abraham."

GENE: My sense is that there's a more complicated dynamic in this story. I don't know of any relationships that are so abso-lute there's no power on the part of the per-son in the subordinate position. It's like a young black teenager—after he's gotten his butt beat by a racist cop, he knows how to retell the story in such a way that he un-dermines the cop's power. Remember, Abraham's a guy who starts out with nothing. When I had a conversation about this story with some of the young guys I work with on the street, one of them said, "Well, man, with the Egyptians coming down on him, what would have happened to Abraham had he not lied about what his relationship was to the woman?" Listen, I can imagine lying. I can see that. Here's a black dude in the inner city. He's got a white wife. A couple of Egyptian brothers roll up on the brother with the white wife. Now this guy's not a complete fool. "Yo, baby, we work together. Right? Pretend you're my boss. You're not my wife, right, because if you're my wife, you may be a widow by the end of this evening."

LIZ: I know it's unfashionable to be lib-eral, but I have to say: Even if a victim is manipulative, even if a victim is snobby, even if a victim happens to have money or go to Radcliffe, a victim is a victim. And the patriarchy, as set up in the Western Bible, oppresses women like Sarah. There is no denying it. Sarah is the matriarch. She is my mother because she is the one who had to endure. She is the first one. With Eve, it's a different story because she was kind of lusty—she went for the apple. But Sarah had to endure what a woman has to endure when her husband becomes a patriarch. She was the first woman to really be the watcher as the society went into patriar-chy. And I have to say that no matter what class, no matter what hypocrisies she may have displayed, she was still the second-class citizen in the relationship. Her silence might very well be the beginning of that.

BURT: Who's the victim in this story? Victims are real victims, but even Sarah, a victim, turns out to be quite oppressive in another part of the story.

LIZ: Yes, of course. I don't say victims are good. I say they're victims.

LEW: I don't think the story is about gender relationships or the patriarchal oppression of women. I don't even think it's about the character of Abraham. I think it's about a being called Yahweh, coming out of the blue, with a peremptory demand for obedience and faith, Who says, "I'm going to start a new movement in this human family, and you've got to come along."

BURT: But it's interesting how Abraham sees himself as a victim, too. He thinks if the Egyptians see Sarah and think she's his wife, they'll kill him. He's going into a strange land. He's a shepherd, and he's going into an urban society that's very civilized. He's very nervous. He immediately sees the Egyptians as the enemy and thinks they're going to kill him. Yet later, Pharaoh says, "Why didn't you say she's your wife?" Out of all people, Pharaoh is morally outraged. In other words, he's saying, "We Egyptians are not like that. We don't do that." This is the problem with white and black, and men and women—

BHARATI: —and colonialism.

BURT: We see them as the other, and the other is always evil.

BHARATI: We need to see the other as evil in order to justify our own campaign for betterment.

BURT: But if we saw the other as us, might we not do better?

BILL: Folks, there's just no room in this story for idealism.

GENE: That's right. This is Abraham being human. He is not God.

LEW: And he's not a model human being.

GENE: He is broken creation, as we all are. I identify with Abraham. I used to be a hustler on the street, victimizing and being victimized, and trying to negotiate all these difficult relationships. All of us have a side of ourselves that uses people, or has the potential to use people.

AZIZAH: Moses killed somebody. And if God could choose such people as prophets, we have a chance of being saved, of God blessing us despite our mistakes.

BHARATI: In the Hindu gospel *Bhagavad Gita*, God gives a sermon on the battlefield urging Arjuna to go kill the enemy, and saying that violence is necessary at times. So I don't see a problem, especially in the context of ethnic rivalries.

BURT: But this is the same Bible that reminds us that we're all created in the image of God. What if Abraham had gone to Egypt and instead of saying, "They're going to kill me," he had said, "Pharaoh is my brother. Pharaoh was created in the image and likeness of God, as were you, as was I. Let's go in faith and see whether God protects us, rather than go through this whole scam." What might have happened then?

BHARATI: It may have worked. It may not have worked.

LEW: That would have made Abraham come off better, and we would have liked him more.

LIZ: Pharaoh reminds me of a Hollywood executive. I have the feeling he's playing along with whatever happens in the moment. When Sarah turns out to be Abraham's wife, and he goes, "Oh, what? I didn't know," it's so phony.

BILL: For me that moment had just the opposite impact. Obviously, you don't get to be a pharaoh by being a paragon of virtue, but I had the sense that this guy gets chastised by God for acting in what he thought was an honorable way. The moment he finds out Sarah is not Abraham's sister but is instead Abraham's wife, he says, "I don't want anything to do with it."

BURT: Yes, but he finds out by virtue of a plague. I'm a little suspicious, too.

BOB: I think we have to read this story alongside the replay of it with Abimelech, because that story functions as a kind of critical revision of the first. In the second version, there are no plagues, but God grants a night vision to Abimelech, who says, "Oh, I didn't touch her." And God says, "Because I didn't *let* you touch her." This king is really a good guy. He says, "I have done this with the purity of my hands and the innocence of my heart." And in the Hebrew dialogue, he actually almost stammers. He says something like, "And—and she—she also said that—that she was his sister." When Abraham talks, at first he has no answer for Abimelech. He talks in a kind of lawyerly circumlocution, saying, "Well, in fact, she is, after all, from a certain point of view, my sister, because she's my half-sister" and so forth. So the father of Israel looks not so good, and the other turns out to be the moral exemplar.

BURT: We Jews call Abraham our father. And here is the father with this very tainted history. I think one of the things we can learn from this is that if we can't look back on our ancestor as being morally upright, the least we can do to redeem him is to hope that he listened and learned from people whom we normally think to be the enemy. We redeem him by learning that lesson.

BHARATI: Even for someone outside the Judeo-Christian axis, this is a story to learn from because it raises difficult questions and doesn't provide any answers. I don't want to know exactly what the moral is. I want to discover the questions.

BOB: That's why I resisted Bill's initial question: "What is the moral of this story?" The fascinating thing about the Bible is that millions of people have looked to it as a source of moral guidance and in-

The Catapulting of Abraham into the Fire, Hadiqat al-Su'ada' (Garden of the Blessed), Turkey, ca. 1600

spiration, but really, it's not a didactic book. It doesn't have simple, unambiguous lessons.

AZIZAH: I'd like to say a word to my cousin—because, you know, Abraham is my ancestor, too. And maybe I don't feel at all ambiguous about Abraham. Just let me quickly tell you the stories about him in the Qur'an, so that you can see where I'm coming from. There is the story about Hagar and Ishmael. There is the story of Abraham building the Ka'ba in Mecca with Ishmael. And there's the story of Abraham talking with a mighty king, identified by some commentators as Nimrod, the King of Babylon. That's the story you referred to as the second example where Abraham introduced Sarah as his sister. The Qur'an doesn't speak about that at all but says that Abraham actually stood up to the King and said, "My God is stronger than your god. He is the real God." And Nimrod said, "You know, I am the most powerful. I can put people to death or grant them life." And Abraham said, "God brings the sun from the east. Can you bring it from the west?" Through all these stories, Abraham is willing to suffer. He gives himself up to God, and God takes care of him.

LEW: I think in the Qur'an, we do have Abraham as a more powerful exemplar, just as we do in the midrash. But Bob's point was that for generations people have been looking at this as a story that teaches morality. But it's not that simple. The process that produces the Christian tradition or the rabbinic tradition is a process like this conversation. The point of the story is to have this conversation. It's in talking like this, in banging our heads together, that we can find some moral ground. This terrible, difficult narrative is the perfect springboard for groups to be able to learn what is important for them. For us Christians, Abraham is our father, not because he's a good guy, but because he is the reminder that our relationship with the Almighty is a relationship defined by grace. What really matters is not whether Abraham is good or bad or cowardly or heroic, but that God pursues His design for the welfare of the human family with people like that—in other words, people like us.

> *"What really matters is not whether Abraham is good or bad or cowardly or heroic, but that God pursues His design for the welfare of the human family with people like that—in other words, people like us."*

BILL: Do you see Abraham's faith as a model for your life?

LEW: In a way I do, but in a way I don't.

I haven't been called to be the father of a race or a blessing to mankind, at least not in the sense Abraham was. But his faith is a model to me because if I want to know whether I am at peace with my Maker, the answer has to be found in the grace of the Maker, not in the quality of the person.

AZIZAH: I totally agree. That idea is in the Qur'an, too. God can extend His grace to whomever He wishes, even to the most sinful.

LIZ: But you know, something else is going on here. When I work with young people in the theater, I find that it's very difficult to get them to commit to the moment, to be absolutely present so that you're so alive on the stage that people can't help but be drawn to your energy. Every gesture embodies the whole self, including the history of that self. Everything you have ever learned becomes available to you. It's a state of grace. Suddenly you're so open and ready, you could do anything. In order to get them to understand that kind of commitment, I make a space, a circle, on the carpet, and I say, "From the moment you step into that space, everything else is gone away." This act is as much about belief as about anything else. You create a little world, right there in that space. When you feel that committed to a piece of text, you become the characters. Abraham and Sarah are inside for all of us. Abraham's faults are in us. Sarah's silence is in us. We can bring up in ourselves the selling out of someone, and we can bring up a pious Abraham deciding that God is one, and that no matter what, he will fight

for that. These different aspects can exist simultaneously in us.

LEW: What you say about commitment in the moment in the theater is also true of preaching a sermon. On Friday night, I can wrestle with my doubts—"Is this really true?" On Sunday morning, I can preach on the same subject, and I am so committed to that moment that I believe what I am saying intensely and completely and undoubtedly. On Monday, I might be wrestling with doubts again. But on Sunday, my belief is not feigned.

BURT: Abraham is on that circle of carpet, and he never gets off it. He's God-obsessed. Whatever it is he does with Sarah, he does not have good relations with her. In fact, he doesn't have good relations with either of his long-awaited sons. The only one that Abraham has any kind of consistent relationship with is God.

GENE: In the Christian tradition, Abraham serves as a model because of the singular focus on that relationship.

LEW: You know, if I thought God was telling me to sell off my pension and leave all my friends and everything in my past that has identified me as who I am and start all over in another place with another people and a totally different situation I can't even imagine, I'd have a hard time.

BHARATI: That's what happens with an immigrant. Abraham's faith is not disinterested. God says, "I'm going to reward you if you do things my way. The pastures are greener where I'm going to lead you." In a sense, he's going for a prize. And he'll use any wiles necessary in order to get to the promised land.

LEW: There's one critical difference. My parents were immigrants—but when they came, they had seen pictures of America, they had gotten letters from America, they knew something of what they were doing. Abraham had none of this.

AZIZAH: It wasn't as if Abraham thought, "I'll submit to God and then I'll get this prize." It's rather that he understood a very basic truth in my religion and, I think, in yours, which is that in the final analysis, all there is, is God. All we have is transitory. It comes and goes because of God.

BURT: That relationship with God is like the relationship between the actor on that circle of carpet and the director. Their relationship with you and their perception of you is what makes them in the moment.

LIZ: That underestimates the actors. As a director, I really am not God. The role of director is to make the actor a more powerful and independent person.

GENE: In this story, you cannot get away from the director. We can talk about Abraham, or we can talk about Sarah, but the bottom line to the story is Abraham's relationship to his God.

BILL: What's the picture of God we get here?

LEW: He's a powerful character. When you get right down to it, God is all—but He has created somebody who can argue with Him, who can say, "Look, You promised. When are You going to deliver?" As flawed as Abraham is, he has the courage to argue with the Maker of the Universe.

AZIZAH: That's also true in the Qur'an. In a couple of places, Abraham asks God for an explanation, and God says, "But don't you believe?" Abraham answers, "Yes, but I need tranquillity in my heart."

BURT: I used to have a teacher, Professor Lieberman—may he rest in peace—who was in his eighties when I studied with him. He had grown up in the Talmudic academies of Europe and was one of the great Talmudists in the world—a really Old World Jew, and a man of great piety and learning. He once asked one of my colleagues, "Who is the most tragic character in the Bible?" The colleague thought for a while, and then said, "Ezekiel." Lieberman said, "No, no, no." My colleague thought again and then said, "Jeremiah." Lieberman said, "No, no, no," and then he just couldn't wait. "No, the most tragic character in the Bible is God." This is a God Who

" 'The most tragic character in the Bible is God'."

creates a universe, and behold, it is very good. Within a chapter He decides He has to destroy it because it's not so good after all. This is a God Who sends Abraham on a journey, and the journey perhaps turns out far different from what God had intended. As long as humanity has free will, God has to learn again and again how to relate to His creatures.

AZIZAH: There's another story in the Qur'an that does not show up in the Bible, and that is the challenge of Satan to God. When God orders Satan to do a certain thing, and Satan says, "No," God asks, "Why?" We know that God is all-powerful and all-knowing and that He could have zapped Satan, but didn't. There is a moral in the fact that throughout the Qur'an and the Bible, God allows people to talk to Him and to challenge Him. Part of that moral is about how we relate. The relationship with God is not a relationship with an all-powerful patriarch, but with Someone Who loves us and has mercy upon us and talks to us.

LEW: God is strange for all kinds of reasons. For example, why in the world did God take so long to fulfill His promises? He promised, so why did He play around with Sarah? Why not just give her the child instead of leaving her dangling for so long?

BOB: —while the promise gets more and more incredible.

LEW: And the promise itself is not all that clear. The promise of land is clear and the promise of many children. But what's this

Miriam Schapiro, *Four Matriarchs: Sarah*, Temple Sholom, Chicago, 1983

"blessing"? I can't even sense that Abraham is preoccupied with being a blessing. He wants kids and a place. Abraham isn't God. And God isn't a human being. There's a polarity and an encounter, a confrontation, a dialogue.

BILL: Do you like this God?

LEW: I have a very hard time thinking of God as someone I like. Somebody asked me not long ago, "What are you going to do when you retire?" I said, facetiously but seriously, "I'm going to work on my friendship with God." It's hard for me to be a friend of God's because friends have to be equal—or at least not too disparate. God is somebody for me to be in awe of, to worship, adore, and obey. But, in my experience, He's not very friendly. He doesn't talk to me very much.

GENE: I have a different experience. I have a very intense sense of God's immediate presence. My mother passed last year, and it was a very difficult process. She was diagnosed with pancreatic carcinoma, and all the odyssey questions emerged: "Why is she suffering?" As I prayed, through the eyes of faith, my mother was communicating to me: "I'm going home. I'm going home to rest. I've run the race, and I'm ready to go home." I sensed God's presence—real tranquillity. You know, because of my work in poor neighborhoods, my home has been shot into twice over the last six years. When this last happened, a church van that was parked in front of our building was shot twenty times. One of the bullets landed within twelve inches of my son's head. My wife and I asked ourselves whether we should leave the neighborhood. The issue of the call came up—and it was our personal relationship with a personal God that determined the choice that we made. I told my wife, "Sweetheart, you decide." And she said, "I believe that God has called us to this place to do this thing for this season." Now this is really difficult for my wife, who came from the Jamaican middle class and went to a Swiss prep school and was a Harvard Phi Beta Kappa.

BURT: But what if she had said to you, "Look, you're the minister, I'm not. And I don't want any part of this. We've got to get out of here." And what if you still felt the call to stay?

GENE: We would have left because she and I went into a covenantal relationship as husband and wife. We responded to this call together.

BURT: Do you think that's what Abraham is doing? Is this parallel? When Abraham answers the call, he endangers Sarah. When they go to Canaan, they experience famine, and when they go to Egypt, she goes into Pharaoh's harem. The question is: Does Sarah hear this call, too?

LIZ: For Sarah, the call does not come all at once. It's not a revelation. But there is a sense of waiting. She waits ninety years to have a child. She has to wait in relation to the Pharaoh, wondering if Abraham will be called. Things come in increments to her. Just as Abraham is the father, Sarah is in some ways the mother, waiting.

BOB: Yes, and the waiting is rooted in her bodily experience as a woman. We finally get a brief insight into her viewpoint when she says, "After being shriveled, will I bear children?" And then she adds another little clause: "And my husband is an *old* man." It's hard not to see some kind of conjugal accusation in these last words.

BURT: Sarah's relationship with God, Who spoke to Abraham and not to her, is even more interesting than her relationship with Abraham. God came to Abraham with a promise. On the basis of that promise, Sarah agrees to go with him to God only knows where. And God doesn't come across. She's getting old. Waiting with hope is probably the hardest kind of waiting because you need or want something you don't have. When she's told she's going to have a son, she's incredulous. She actually has a rather snide remark to say about her husband, which God has the good sense not to repeat. But in time she gains a voice. Maybe it's because she's a little older, or maybe it happens because she becomes a mother and so has quite a ferocious voice when she needs to protect her son. This woman, who starts out absolutely silent, who goes, apparently without demurral, into Pharaoh's harem, becomes very powerful and speaks as a prophet. And God verifies her work.

BILL: But she has to wait and wait. Liz, if you were writing music for the waiting of Sarah, what kind of music would we hear?

LIZ: I wouldn't want to hear real tones.

It's like a heartbeat . . . and tears dropping. You have the sense of a pulse, but an unpredictable one. It doesn't build, and you don't know how it will end. It just keeps going. In that softness, it's very determined. Do you know the poem about Sarah by Delmore Schwartz? It begins: "The Angel said to me, 'Why are you laughing?' / Laughing! Not me! Who was laughing? I did not laugh. It was / A cough. I was coughing. Only hyenas laugh. / The second verse begins, "It was the cold I caught nine minutes after / Abraham married me when I saw that I was slender and beautiful, more and more / Slender and beautiful. / I was also / Clearing my throat." Schwartz was writing about his mother, but he was also writing about the waiting.

LEW: But in her waiting, isn't there anxiety? Isn't Sarah nervous and anxious?

LIZ: Not after ninety years!

BURT: As long as she's waiting, isn't she also doubting whether it's actually going to happen?

LIZ: As a young woman, she would have experienced more tension. But after a cer-

---

"After a certain time, waiting becomes a kind of wisdom in itself."

tain time, waiting becomes a kind of wisdom in itself.

BURT: She says, in effect, "I can take it or leave it. I want it, but I can take it or leave it."

LIZ: I don't think it's anything like that. I think it's hope. Her distress is not anxiety. She's beyond that.

LEW: There is a deep serenity and peace and acceptance, even though she's still waiting.

LIZ: It's neither acceptance or serenity. It's an irony. And that irony, strangely enough, is why I love the Bible. You can have an irony that's almost bitter, but there's hope.

BOB: "Irony" is a beautiful word for Sarah. After she gives birth to Isaac, she proclaims a kind of triumphant thanksgiving poem, which begins with "Laughter God has made me, all who hear will laugh." (I'm translating very literally.) We don't know what the preposition that follows "laugh" means in Hebrew—it could be "laugh with me" or "laugh at me" or "laugh for me." I think all three meanings are present.

LEW: So it could mean "laugh" in the sense both of ridiculing and of celebrating.

BOB: Exactly. It's a great moment of triumph and exultation for her. But she probably also has this ironic sense of the absurdity of the whole thing.

AZIZAH: In the Qur'an, two angels come to Abraham, and in Sarah's presence, let him know that he's going to have a child. Sarah says exactly the same thing you quoted—but in the Qur'an, her laughter comes before the tidings, so it's a whole different idea. But as I sit here, trying to give you my rational interpretation of things, that's not where I'm coming from. I start with a personal relationship with God. When I'm in trouble, I leave it to God. I ask God to help me understand, if possible. God knows what we do not know. We do not know God's logic. He will allow us to understand only what He wants us to understand. But He gave us a lot of equipment to deal with the world—a lot of logic, a lot of heart. And we have to do the best we can with that. God can choose to give His grace to us or not to give it to us. I count on His justice and His mercy. Every single chapter in the Qur'an begins with the words: "God is all-merciful." That for me is God—not the patriarch, not the scary God, not the God Who punishes, but the merciful God Who loves me and Who will help me along, if I only submit.

BURT: But there are two sides to God. On one side, there's the God of mercy Who bestows grace. As creatures, we really have no choice in the matter, except that we either receive the grace, or we're ungrateful. We don't know that we've received it. But on the other side, there's a God of justice Who demands things of us. I worry that if we just submit utterly, we no longer have any responsibility for our lives. This may be a way in which Judaism differs from both Islam and Christianity. Judaism de-

Abraham and the Three Angels, early Christian mosaic, Church of Santa Maria Maggiore, Rome, 432–440

mands that we be responsible as well. That's why there's law in Judaism. God expects things of us. Sometimes we stray from that path, and then we hope God is merciful, and we hope for God's grace. But even a person who willingly disobeys can be forgiven by God because that's God.

AZIZAH: Yes, but don't think that submitting to God is abdicating responsibility. We have the concept of *ijtihad*, which

means you read the Qur'an and you do all your homework to prepare yourself for understanding the Qur'an, and then you interpret it for yourself. We don't have clergy.

BILL: You mean the ayatollahs are not clergy?

AZIZAH: They have a moral position in that they are learned—they spend many years reading the Qur'an and the surrounding literature. They might come up with a judgment on a certain issue, and others, who don't have the time or capability to study the Qur'an as carefully, might choose to be guided by their views.

BILL: Burt referred to grace. Is it grace to be chosen?

BOB: Grace is almost an alien concept in this story. The Hebrew word that is often translated as "grace" has more to do with fidelity in relationships, or loyalty. The Jewish tradition tends to view the relations both of humans with each other and of humans with the divine in contractual terms.

LEW: You know, I had an experience with my family last Christmas Eve that was a parable of grace. I was sitting around with my wife and adopted children in a mobile home at the beach, and it suddenly dawned on me that none of us in this family is blood-related. There is nothing that holds us together except grace. Then it struck me that there are three dimensions to that relationship. The primary dimension was that no matter what—ugly, beautiful, failing, achieving—they were my children, forever and ever. That's the grace of acceptance. There is also a grace of pardon. When they have done things that are wrong, especially if I think they are wrong in relation to me, I act in grace by forgiving them. But grace has another dimension to it. Not only is it accepting and pardoning, but it is also empowering. When my kids are absolutely sure of my loyalty to them, that is power. That frees them.

BILL: That relates to the notion of being chosen—when you adopted these children, you chose them.

LEW: No, absolutely not. That was the myth we bought into years ago. In the nice books about adoption, the parents say to the adopted child, "You're special because you're chosen." No, we took what we were given. There was no thought like "No, I don't like his looks. I'll wait for another." We chose to adopt, but we didn't choose those particular children. But after we adopted them, it was as if we had chosen them.

BILL: You said that you don't imagine yourself like Abraham, as the father of a nation. And yet, in choosing to adopt, you were choosing offspring, continuity.

GENE: But the responsibility for a nuclear family is very different from the responsibility to bring a people into existence. It's like the difference between being called to be a shepherd and being called to be a prophet. Playing the prophetic role, speaking truth to power, is a very different vocation from shepherding.

BHARATI: Which brings us back to the subject of nationalism. This is a patriarch who isn't doing what he's doing simply for his family.

BURT: And to the extent that Abraham sees himself as the father of a nation, he may make choices that do his family a disservice.

AZIZAH: I don't see this as a story about nationalism because God made promises to Abraham concerning both Isaac and Ishmael. God was giving a promise to the whole world, or at least to those who have the faith and who are just.

GENE: But that's a false dichotomy between the particular and the universal. In other words, nationalism doesn't mean that you refrain from speaking to the larger human experience. Most people live their lives through the lens of a very particular national, ethnic, geopolitical, or geo-religious reality.

AZIZAH: That's the nationalism of the nineteenth century.

GENE: No, I'm not talking about the nineteenth-century essentialist concept of nationalism that led to what happened in Nazi Germany. Nationalism can be defined as the recognition of a call to be a people, which is related to history, tradition, place. We're not making a genetic argument.

BILL: Well, in this story, it's Abraham who is chosen. And here's the problem with chosenness: It's great if you're chosen, but hell if you're not. Take Pharaoh. He's tricked by Abraham into taking Sarah into his harem. Abraham deceives him—and it's Pharaoh who gets punished! God sends a plague on the deceived. In God's script, the unchosen people become the victims.

AZIZAH: But you can choose to be chosen. If you choose to believe in God, you can be one of the circle.

> *"In this story, it's Abraham who is chosen. And here's the problem with chosenness: It's great if you're chosen, but hell if you're not."*

BHARATI: But surely Pharaoh thought of himself as part of a chosen group, too. And if there are many chosen groups, how do they cooperate?

AZIZAH: If it's hard not to be chosen, it's harder to be chosen. Look at the suffering Abraham went through, just to defend his faith.

BILL: But, in this story, Abraham prospers. It's the Egyptians who suffer the plague.

GENE: But that's taking the story out of context. Take slavery, for example. The influence that African Americans have been able to have in civilizing the culture suggests that while we were brought here as slaves, we've been able to impact the culture. We are more than the sum total of our violations.

BOB: As someone whose people have often been victims, I'm not buying into the ennoblement of victimization. To be victimized is not noble.

"If it's hard not to be chosen, it's harder to be chosen. Look at the suffering Abraham went through, just to defend his faith."

GENE: No, I'm not suggesting that at all. The enslaved individual resists and struggles. There is a national liberation movement. The critical factor is our growing realization of God's presence. This is the ideological impetus for why I resist oppression. The nobility is not in being a slave; the nobility is in the realization of God's presence, which becomes the impetus for my resistance and struggle against my violation as a people.

BHARATI: But why did God choose one group as the master, and the other group as the slave?

BILL: In this story, it seems that God is really playing favorites.

LEW: He's also imposing a terrible burden.

BHARATI: But the burden of the master is much easier to bear than the burden of the underdog.

LIZ: I don't think we're always going to know why certain people are victimized. But in reaching to know, we find God. When Job suffers and asks God why, God basically says it's because He's the Creator. I would never say that oppression is right—but what I would say is that I don't know what God is up to.

BILL: Is it reasonable to conclude that God is above it all? That the character and plight of human beings are not the subject of the story? That what is more important to God is His purpose in history, whatever happens to people?

LEW: But the goal in the call to Abraham is to bless all nations. There is a happy ending for everybody who is willing to be chosen.

BHARATI: But what about the non-chosen, the deselected?

BILL: Bharati, I recall your writing that because Abraham is a revered figure, nothing can turn out tragically for himself or for his people.

BHARATI: Yes, which means that there's a kind of justification for the oppression of the rest of us.

BURT: No, that can't be—because if Pharaoh is a genuinely nice guy, and God comes in and beats him up, then we can have no way of knowing God's will. But if Abraham is right in thinking that he would be killed in order for Pharaoh to take his wife, then God favors Abraham and punishes Pharaoh because Pharaoh acts immorally. Abraham is simply acting to save himself and his wife.

BOB: In the larger context, this story foreshadows the sojourn in Egypt. Even the language is echoed later. For example, Abraham says, "Me they will kill and you they will let live." At the beginning of Exodus, you read, "Every male born will be thrown into the Nile. And every female child will be allowed to live." So the oppressors and oppressed are reversed in the Exodus story. Nobody in history is ever always the oppressor or always the oppressed.

LEW: Don't forget that the chosen become the poor.

BHARATI: But that's a rather comfortable way of being poor and oppressed. I would rather vote that all persons are created equal, and that everyone—no matter what class, gender, or race—is chosen. I see Genesis as a way of metaphorizing the idea of cooperation with God. It's not a matter of submitting to the will of a God that is absolutely, intractably visualized, but to cooperate when you hear the call. And then to make sure that you see yourself as someone who is chosen rather than simply as a second-class citizen.

BURT: We have to be careful about our chosenness. As Bob said, we have to understand that if we're the oppressor now, we may be the oppressed generations later. It says explicitly in Deuteronomy, "Don't oppress the stranger, because you are strangers in the land of Egypt."

GENE: The biblical literature suggests that connected to the concept of chosenness is an equally intense notion of accountability.

BILL: Chosen not for privilege, but for service.

BHARATI: But that's like the white man's burden.

GENE: No, the white man's burden was not driven by anything theological.

BHARATI: They certainly gave it a theological twist.

BILL: Yes, many of the pioneers of the West felt they were fulfilling a divine destiny.

GENE: That's an ad hoc rationalization, like the theological arguments that were spun out to defend slavery.

BHARATI: But how do we know Abraham wasn't always rationalizing in the same way?

BILL: Abraham Joshua Heschel once said, "All human history as described in the Bible can be summarized as God in search of man." What does this story lead you to see about the character of God?

BOB: I have a little difficulty in thinking about God as a character. He partly is and He partly isn't. Nevertheless, there are moments that are revelatory about His character. Maybe the crucial one is when the

Aaron of Gewitsch, title page with scenes from the life of Abraham, *Book of Laws and Prayers for Circumcision*, Vienna, 1728

man to man, as it were, and to see what Abraham's moral instinct is. Does this man care about the survival of humanity—those to whom he is not related by blood? For me, in this moment, God becomes a great character.

LEW: This story shows that the Maker of the Universe is not content to simply watch people in their evil and suffering. God takes the initiative and says, ''However long it takes or whoever will be my servant, I will bless the people.'' Through Abraham, God began His movement of blessing. I think we all ask ourselves, ''But if He wants to bless us, why does He allow these terrible things to happen?'' There's a lot of ambiguity because God plays around with Sarah. I have all this anxiety waiting for God to finally bring His blessing—but that's what the story is about to me. The character of God is initiative for blessing. And for Christians, the cross is the answer as to whether the character of God is benevolent. He becomes not only the God of the suffering, but the suffering God.

BHARATI: I think of God as a geophysical, large force, which in Hinduism would be called *Brahman*. You can metaphorize this force and worship it in any image you want. My personal visualization is of a God who loves me. Reincarnation is a form of recycling, where the dust or ashes merge with the rest of the universe. And salvation is understanding that this isn't the only world, and this isn't the only life one has. Abraham as a chosen person is not the only person whose life matters. There are all

three strangers show up at Abraham's tent—two of them are angels and one is God. After the promise is made, the angels head toward Sodom, but God remains, and we are given an interior monologue in which He asks Himself, ''Shall I conceal from Abraham what I intend to do? No, I cannot because I've made this covenant with him so that his progeny will perform justice and righteousness.'' Then he gets into the debate with Abraham about the survival of Sodom. All of a sudden we have a God Who is willing to face His creature, these other people with whom he must relate and whose welfare he'll have to think of.

BURT: In the Genesis story, there is a very clear notion of a transcendent God, a God Who is beyond the human norms of ethics. God comes in and blows away Pharaoh because God has chosen Abraham, and, as with Job, it may be beyond our understanding. On the other hand, this is a God Who desperately wants relationship with humanity, with God's own creatures. Every human created in God's image is a little different, and God has to learn all over how to have this relationship. God has to grow in this love relationship. And God does that with Abraham and Sarah. We just looked at the very beginning of their relationship, where God's relationship to Abraham is crude, and God's relationship to Sarah is not verbalized at all. As the story unfolds, all the characters grow, God among them.

BILL: God keeps trying, doesn't He? He creates this paradise and Adam and Eve deceive Him. Cain commits fratricide. Then God decides to wipe the whole thing out and start over again. To me, God is a changing character in the play, not the director.

LEW: But there is constancy, too. One constant is "I want to bless my creatures." Another is "I want justice and mercy upon them."

BILL: Someone told me that one of the words that recurs most often in the Bible is "remember."

AZIZAH: In Arabic, the word "human" comes from the same root as "to forget."

BURT: That's a very different world—you assume forgetfulness, and Jews assume memory.

GENE: But you're a community of memory because you're both included in these stories. I resonate with Abraham, and I identify with his frailty and humanity. I love the fact that from this story I know that an eternal God will be in conversation with the most broken, mischievous, pragmatic, and self-centered individual. Then, on other occasions, that same individual, inspired by God, can be elevated to heights of heroism.

"I love the fact that from this story I know that an eternal God will be in conversation with the most broken, mischievous, pragmatic, and self-centered individual."

INCIPIT LIBER DABREIA IN
ID EST VERBA DIERUM
Q D EST PARALIPOMENON

DAM
SED h
ENOS
CAI
NAN
D A
LEDEL

iareth. enoch. matusale. lamech. noe. sem. cham.1 iafeth;

VI

A FAMILY AFFAIR

Azizah Y. al-Hibri • Robert Alter

Bharati Mukherjee • Eugene Rivers III

Lewis B. Smedes • Elizabeth Swados

Burton L. Visotzky

Sometimes the details of the stories we are discussing from Genesis sound like pulp fiction. In this one we come to the first triangle: Two women share the bed of the same man. The squabbling gets mean. Everybody gets hurt. The stuff of a cheap novel and a fast read. But peel back the layers and the Bible is Tolstoy, Shakespeare, and Faulkner. The themes in this story are deep and painful—a woman's infertility, surrogate motherhood, class differences, and the price human beings pay for God's will to be done. And something else: This triangle does set off fireworks, and by the dawn's early light Judaism and Islam go their separate ways.

—Bill Moyers

Muslims, Christians, and Jews in Abraham's Lap, Souvigny Bible, France, late 12th c.

Now Sarai, Abram's wife, bore him no children. She had an Egyptian slave-girl whose name was Hagar, and Sarai said to Abram, "You see that the LORD has prevented me from bearing children; go in to my slave-girl; it may be that I shall obtain children by her." And Abram listened to the voice of Sarai.

So, after Abram had lived ten years in the land of Canaan, Sarai, Abram's wife, took Hagar the Egyptian, her slave-girl, and gave her to her husband Abram as a wife. He went in to Hagar, and she conceived, and when she saw that she had conceived, she looked with contempt on her mistress. Then Sarai said to Abram, "May the wrong done to me be on you! I gave my slave-girl to your embrace, and when she saw that she had conceived, she looked on me with contempt. May the LORD judge between you and me!"

But Abram said to Sarai, "Your slave-girl is in your power; do to her as you please." Then Sarai dealt harshly with her, and she ran away from her. The angel of the LORD found her by a spring of water in the wilderness, the spring on the way to Shur. And he said . . . "Return to your mistress, and submit to her." The angel of the LORD also said to her, "I will so greatly multiply your offspring that they cannot be counted for multitude . . . Now you have conceived and shall bear a son; you shall call him Ishmael, for the LORD has given heed to your affliction. He shall be a wild ass of a man, with his hand against everyone, and everyone's hand against him; and he shall live at odds with all his kin." So she named the LORD who spoke to her, "You are El-roi"; for she said, "Have I really seen God and remained alive after seeing him . . . ?"

Hagar bore Abram a son; and Abram named his son, whom Hagar bore, Ishmael . . . God said to Abraham, "As for Sarah your wife . . . I will bless her, and moreover I will give you a son by her . . ." Then Abraham fell on his face and laughed, and said to himself, "Can a child be born to a man, who is a hundred years old? Can Sarah, who is ninety years old, bear a child?" And Abraham said to God, "O that Ishmael might live in your sight!" God said, "No, but your wife Sarah shall bear you a son, and you shall name him Isaac. I will establish my covenant with him as an everlasting covenant for his offspring after him. As for Ishmael, I have heard you; I will bless him and make him fruitful and exceedingly numerous; he shall be the father of twelve princes, and I will make him a great nation. . . ."

The LORD *dealt with Sarah as he had said . . . Sarah conceived and bore Abraham a son in his old age . . . Abraham gave the name Isaac to his son whom Sarah bore him . . . But Sarah saw the son of Hagar the Egyptian, whom she had borne to Abraham, playing with her son Isaac. So she said to Abraham, "Cast out this slave woman with her son; for the son of this slave woman shall not inherit along with my son Isaac."*

The matter was very distressing to Abraham on account of his son. But God said to Abraham . . . "Whatever Sarah says to you, do as she tells you . . ." So Abraham rose early in the morning, and took bread and a skin of water and gave it to Hagar . . . And she departed, and wandered about in the wilderness of Beer-sheba. When the water in the skin was gone, she cast the child under one of the bushes. Then she went and sat down opposite him a good way off . . . for she said, "Do not let me look on the death of the child . . ." She lifted up her voice and wept. And God heard the voice of the boy; and the angel of God called to Hagar from heaven, and said to her . . . "Do not be afraid; for God has heard the voice of the boy where he is. Come, lift up the boy and hold him fast with your hand, for I will make a great nation of him." Then God opened her eyes and she saw a well of water . . . God was with the boy, and he grew up . . . in the wilderness of Paran; and his mother got a wife for him from the land of Egypt.

—excerpts from *New Revised Standard Version* (*The Holy Bible*),
Chapters 16, 17, and 21

BILL: Are you struck, as I am, by how this three-thousand-year-old story sounds as if it came right out of yesterday's newspaper?

BURT: Yes—the story of this family is so distressing. In the synagogue, we read the Five Books of Moses, the Torah, every year. When we come to this story, I find myself holding on to my chair, trying not to flee. It is so immediate, partly because I have this sinking feeling that it's not just about my ancestors, but about the mixed family so many of us experience now—first wife, second wife, surrogate parenthood, children, conflict. Everybody in this room knows someone who's gone through something like this. I just find it terribly wrenching. When I was young and happily married, this was a much easier story to hear. Now I'm older, fatter, and divorced, and my own life intrudes into my listening of the story.

BOB: I agree that there's something compelling in this story, something that touches the lives we're living now. But

"When I was young and happily married, this was a much easier story to hear."

equally compelling is the way the Bible treats the distinctive social institutions of its world. Here we have three institutions that the Bible doesn't seem to question: slavery, polygamy, and surrogate parenthood, although a different kind of surrogate parenthood from the contemporary sense. Take slavery. Hagar, to put it brutally, is a piece of property. Most of the English translations fudge this by talking about her as Sarah's "maiden," which makes you think of a European courtly situation. But the two Hebrew words for her, *Shifhah* and *Amah*, both mean "a slave woman." In my translation, I decided to call it "slave girl" to make it as demeaning as possible because, face it, she's a piece of human property, owned by Abraham and apparently acquired in Egypt. And Sarah, following a fairly well-known path in the ancient Near East for barren women, says, "I'm not able to have children, so you, Hagar, will bear a child. And so, in a fashion, I will have a child, although not my own." Then the text tells us that Abraham took Hagar as a wife. Again, many translations fudge this by saying "concubine." But the word that's used means "wife." It's the same term that's used for someone in a legitimate conjugal relationship.

BURT: Yes, it's the same noun that's used for Sarah.

BOB: So here are these three institutions—slavery, surrogate parenthood, and polygamy—and they don't really function well together. The woman, who is both a slave girl and a co-wife, conceives, and when her pregnancy becomes visible, she immediately senses herself to be Sarah's superior. Sarah cannot tolerate this. The squabbling begins. The institutions are not rejected in the story, but they don't work, creating all kinds of human problems.

LIZ: Well, Sarah, as a woman, is supposed to be in charge of the future. She is the mother, but she's barren. So she brings in Hagar. But at a certain moment, Hagar gives Sarah a look, a kind of smirk, and Sarah goes ballistic. It seems like a little thing—but I can understand it. I don't have children, and I have no intention of having any, which is not easy. It's a choice. But I've worked with kids ever since I was twenty-six. Every now and then I get the illusion one of them is mine, especially when I've been working with them for ten or fifteen years. Then their real mother comes into the picture. And that's a kind of smirk, right? That look. I also think this story shows the beginning of class and cultural identity and false pride—in a sense, racism. Sarah suddenly thinks, "It must be our destiny, our people, not the offspring of Abraham and Hagar."

BHARATI: But let's just come back to the storytelling for a second. As a writer, I've learned so much about narrative strategy from this story. It's so passionate and concentrated. And the repetitions are what we do in contemporary American writing. We work in sets of three. If you have one event, then it's just one event that could go either way. If you have two or three, you have either contrast or reinforcement. It's never an either/or situation. In the same way, whoever put the Genesis story together has made me sympathize with all the characters. In the move from the original land to Canaan, my sympathies are mostly with Abraham. But here they are with Hagar. As an Asian woman of an elite class, who became part of a despised minority in a white society, I understand Hagar's position. But I understand Sarah's, too. It's not so much that Hagar smirked, but that here is an older woman who feels that her sexuality is nil. And here's Abraham with his nice trophy mistress, who probably has great muscle tone—

B O B : —the famous Egyptian build.

B H A R A T I : Right! So something happens in bed between Abraham and Hagar, which is not about sex. Sarah could have accepted a mixed-race child if she hadn't felt jealous of an emotional connection between the two.

B U R T : This is a complicated business because, as you say, it's not about sex. You just said Hagar is Egyptian—and in saying that, you've duplicated the rabbinic comment, because, while it's not in the text, Hagar must be part of the property that Abraham and Sarah got from Pharaoh. She's an Egyptian, their property. Remember that Abraham basically sold his wife to Pharaoh to save his skin and then in the end got even richer. Now look at the turnabout. Sarah, having been used that way, and perhaps feeling a lot of anger at Abraham, now turns the tables on him. She puts an Egyptian in his bed. But I think it's even more complicated than that. When the angels tell Sarah she's going to have a child, she laughs and says, "Look, first of all, I'm an old lady. I'm postmenopausal. Forget it." And then she adds the kicker line: "And my husband's an old man." In those words, in Hebrew, you get a glimpse of a really dysfunctional marriage. And I get a sense of Abraham's impotence there, too. They haven't had sex in a long time. So here is Sarah, faced with no children, and with an Egyptian who reminds her of her own misadventure. Abraham is always saying, "Yeah, we would have offspring and fulfill God's promise if only you weren't barren, dear. Right?" And she's thinking, "Me barren? He's impotent! I'll call his bluff." And she gives him Hagar.

L I Z : I think that demeans Sarah, because I think that her character, which we don't know and so can only imagine here, is somewhat steadfast. She's a matriarch, a strong lady. She's been through a lot. She's been waiting. She's still waiting, and she believes in the future, but—

B U R T : —but I'm trying to understand why she goes ballistic.

L I Z : Because she's ready to do what an ancient Jewish woman is supposed to do—to take charge of the future. The key moment in the story is when Sarah sees another woman who is about to succeed in taking charge of the future by having a child.

AZIZAH: It's more fundamental than that. In a broader, metaphysical sense, Sarah sees Hagar as an alien "other." It is the "otherness" of Hagar that threatens Sarah beyond her own expectations. The promise is becoming fulfilled through the line of an alien "other."

BOB: Sarah sees herself as a failure.

GENE: Well, that's a fairly common human emotion.

BHARATI: That's why it's an archetypal story.

GENE: I mean, this doesn't have to be rocket science. You've got a very basic situation. As I'm reading this story, it's basic, funky, real-life. Sarah says, "I've failed as a wife."

BHARATI: Hey, in real life, failed wives don't hand over their husbands to the maid.

BILL: We all know friends and relatives who have turned to surrogacy.

BHARATI: Yes, but that's contractual.

This arrangement may have started out as contract, but then it became a matter of jealousy.

GENE: That's my point—old-fashioned jealousy. That's what's great about this at the level of just regular human beings. Folks can resonate to the basic funkiness of a human relationship like this. "I'm a failure as a mother" or "I'm a failure as a wife, and there's this younger thing that's going to upstage me." Sarah's response—

Adriaen van der Werff, *Aged Sarah Offers Her Egyptian Servant Hagar to Abraham*, ca. 1680.

BURT: Sarah's response is violent. She physically abuses this woman.

GENE: Does that surprise you? Here's this woman who upstages me and upsets my home. Sure I'm going to be pissed. Why is that surprising?

BURT: I'll tell you why it's surprising. When Abraham gives Sarah over to Pharaoh back in Egypt, she doesn't say a word. Now she gets ferocious and immediately turns to physical abuse. The Hebrew term used for her abuse of Hagar is exactly the same term used later in the Book of Exodus when the Egyptians abuse the Hebrew slaves.

LIZ: This is where the story becomes somewhat political and about class.

BOB: And gender.

LIZ: Hagar is a slave, right? There's an unspoken assumption—"I can abuse you because I own you."

BOB: You make me think of one very puzzling term, which I would like to talk about for a second. Sometime after the birth of Isaac, when Ishmael, presumably, is still no more than a toddler, Sarah is said to see Ishmael "laughing." Now, that word, which I've translated as "laughing," can also mean "mocking." Remember, the Hebrew word for Isaac, *Yitzhak*, means "he who laughs." So I think Sarah sees Ishmael, this child of the slave girl, *presuming to be Isaac*. Here you seem to get the class thing. That is, Sarah now at last has a son.

This son is everything she's invested in. All of a sudden, here comes Ishmael, "*Yitzhaking*" it, imitating or mocking Isaac. And then the fascinating thing—as Bharati said earlier, you learn so much about storytelling because the stories are so compact, so explosively compact—Sarah never refers to Ishmael or to Hagar by name. She says, "Banish, drive out, expel the son of this slave girl." She refers both to Ishmael and to Hagar only by social status.

BILL: This is the child she wanted.

BURT: And when she gives Hagar to Abraham as a wife, she also doesn't mention Hagar's name.

BOB: Right.

BURT: She just can't get the name out of her mouth. She'll call her a "wife," but she won't call her by name.

BILL: What's the storyteller trying to tell us there?

LEW: She couldn't imagine what she would feel like if she did get what she wanted when she put Hagar in Abraham's bed.

BHARATI: I think she could imagine what Abraham would feel like. To me, a lot of the story is told through omissions. So while we're getting either a real or a fantasized description of the smirk of the slave woman, what we're not getting is the spring in the step of Abraham. Really, the story is about the marriage. In this crisis,

Sarah calls on God to be a kind of marriage counselor. In effect, she's saying to Abraham, "If you don't shape up, I'm going to make sure God punishes—"

BURT: And what's the storyteller trying to tell us? I think the fact that Sarah can't speak the name of Hagar or Ishmael tells us why everything goes awry. Sarah never actually looks on Hagar as another person.

BOB: Right. Because names are so important in their world. Not to call their names is to deny their individual uniqueness.

BURT: And had she thought about Hagar as a human being with a name, she might have realized that it was all going to fall apart because if you put your husband in bed with a real person, something's going to happen. And poor Abraham! I feel terribly sympathetic to Abraham. He's in the classic position of damned if you do, damned if you don't. Sarah says, "Go sleep with the cleaning girl." He says, "Okay" and then he does. She says, "You slept with the cleaning girl!" He's real smart about it, though. He says, "She's yours. You take care of it. I'm out of here. I will not deal with this." But Sarah doesn't let it go. She says, "No, God has to judge between you and me." Abraham is to blame here. Something happened between Hagar and him. Sarah won't let go of that.

BHARATI: And Abraham is reducing it to a catfight between his wife and his concubine.

BILL: This is not the first time that people have been ignorant of the consequences of their passion. Remember Adam and Eve and their aspiration for the fruit on that tree?

BOB: Actually, one of the profound aspects of the moral realism of all these Genesis stories is that many of the characters do get what they wish for, and it turns out not to bring them happiness.

LEW: Be careful what you pray for—your prayers might be answered.

BILL: The Bible doesn't make any effort to whitewash these characters.

LEW: No, never. And there's another dimension of the story that gives it universal

R. B. Kitaj, *Sarah Laughing*, 1992

"The Bible doesn't make any effort to whitewash these characters."

appeal, and that is the absolute necessity of living by hope. Everybody has to hope. Sarah and Abraham were given a promise. Everything was in the future—the land wasn't theirs, the people weren't theirs, and apparently the blessing wasn't theirs. So all they had was hope. Hope always has anxiety attached to it, and a sense of discontent. There's nothing more cruel than hope given and taken away. That helps me understand Sarah, even though it doesn't excuse her. Sarah hopes for a child. The promise has been given, but it hasn't been fulfilled, and time is running out. She's got to do something, but she does something wrong and dumb. It's a mess.

BURT: Do you think what she did wrong was that she lacked faith? That if she had just held out a little longer, God would have helped her get pregnant?

AZIZAH: It's the opposite, I think. Sarah is a very possessive, exclusive person. At that time, it was not unusual for a man to take many wives. Here's Abraham, who's busy with his God. He has no children. For most of his life, despite the promise, he has no urge to marry another woman. We don't hear him complaining in the Bible, "Let me marry another woman.

Let me have a child. God promised certain things for my offspring." Neither does Sarah give him her slave until she's hopeless both about herself and him. That is an example of her possessiveness. She wants Abraham for herself, and she wants the promise for herself, and if she can't get it through herself, he won't get it at all. But then at a certain moment, she says, "No, maybe I should let go a little bit." When she lets go, when she lets Abraham have a child with Hagar, then God rewards her by giving her Isaac.

BILL: Do you see her ten-year wait eliciting sympathy from God?

AZIZAH: No, I see it bringing Sarah to the point where she realizes, "I should share. I should give. I should not be so jealous and exclusive."

BURT: Then she has to wait another thirteen years to have Isaac.

AZIZAH: Yes, and that's another test.

LEW: Are you saying that God rewarded Sarah for giving Hagar to Abraham?

AZIZAH: For being willing to consider the possibility that Abraham might have a child with someone else. When you love, you can give sometimes and not just go on taking. But later, she reverts. When Ishmael and Isaac are old enough to play together, Sarah drives Hagar and Ishmael out. You were talking about racism and classism—they both come from a very basic idea: exclusivity, that "I am better,

> *"There's nothing more cruel than hope given and taken away. That helps me understand Sarah, even though it doesn't excuse her."*

and I deserve this." Maybe it goes back to what happened in Egypt, when Abraham sent her to the Pharaoh. Now she says, "I've worked for this. I've sacrificed. Now I am entitled to what I want."

LEW: I'm troubled here. Whether it was customary in those days or not, it was wrong and dumb to have Hagar sleep with Abraham and have a son and have them all live in the same house.

BILL: And what about the little bit of scripture we have on it, which says that once Hagar learned she was pregnant, "Sarah was lowered in her esteem"?

LEW: It was perfectly natural for Hagar to feel resentment. "This man's child is in my womb. I'm bearing this man's child, so why shouldn't I be treated as his wife?" I admire Hagar for this. I don't read her as an upstart slave who is claiming something that is not hers. I would expect her to act this way. Sarah was obtuse and unimaginative not to suppose that she might be that way.

BILL: As a writer, Bharati, what do you learn about the character of Sarah and Hagar?

BHARATI: Well, there would be no story if poor Sarah didn't provide all of us and herself with another obstacle. You need conflict, conflict, conflict. I hope that Hagar smirked. I'm not sure that Sarah didn't imagine the smirk, but if Hagar did smirk, then I read it as guerrilla warfare. The smirk is the only way of dissenting that is allowed a woman from a despised class and ethnicity.

BURT: But where do you get the despised ethnicity part of that?

BHARATI: I come from reasonably close to that part of the world. Ethnic hostilities have been in the blood for thousands of years. Today you have Hindus versus Muslims and Aryans versus non-Aryans. In India, your last name—Mukherjee, in my case—indicates not you as an individual, but your caste and class. I'm talking about as late as 1995. In India, you would know right away that someone with the name Bharati Mukherjee belongs to such-and-such caste and is therefore entirely defined by caste and class.

GENE: But we don't have to be that elaborate. There are some very basic emotions here. Here's a wife, and here's another woman who has given birth to a child by the wife's husband. That's explosive.

BHARATI: But that's what's great about good storytelling, that it suggests all sorts of complications.

Nicolas of Verdun, *Isaac Is Born to Abraham and Sarah* (detail from Klosterneuburg altarpiece), late 12th c.

BURT: Yes, you can't read the Bible and see a Jew and an Egyptian together, or an Israelite and an Egyptian, and not know there's going to be some sort of tension. That's a definite part of it.

GENE: Understood. But that's the easy part.

LEW: There's tension because there's a slave and a master.

GENE: Okay, so what we've got in one case is a master-slave relationship. Now I must resist the temptation to superimpose the North American version of slavery, the black-white stuff, with all of its complexity and nuance and subliminal—

BHARATI: Hey! Come on! Chattel slavery is part of every kind of slavery.

AZIZAH: But Gene is bringing up

something very important here—to understand slavery, we have to understand it in its historical, social context.

GENE: Thank you. Absolutely. That's very basic.

AZIZAH: If we were talking about a present-day situation, probably Sarah would not tell Abraham, "Marry my friend." She would say, "Let's dissolve the marriage," or "Let's have surrogate motherhood." But in that ancient society, it was appropriate for her to consider the alternative of Hagar conceiving by Abraham. It was even appropriate for Abraham to consider it much sooner, especially if we're thinking of a patriarchal culture where offspring was very important, and where God had made a promise to Abraham. But Abraham, as I would claim, was too busy being obedient to God, and he let God take care of his offspring. It was Sarah who was really busy trying to make sure that the offspring was hers.

LIZ: We are in Genesis, right? As an artist, I look at Genesis as a beginning. Nobody's advanced, and everybody's learning. Everything's happening for the first time. In this story, we're a little bit closer to the basics. We're more in touch with the music of life, the impulse, the immediacy. So instead of property, I think of territorial possessiveness. Something happens to Sarah when her territory, Abraham, is encroached upon and when it looks as if the promise might be fulfilled through another woman. Suddenly the animal in her is not just betrayed, but freaked.

BURT: You know, nobody actually asked Hagar whether she was happy with any of this. Abraham is an old man, and she's a young woman.

BOB: It's a great career move.

AZIZAH: May I shed some light on Hagar? First of all, you'll be surprised to know that this story is not in the Qur'an. Yet it's a very important story for us because it affects what we do as Muslims when we go to the pilgrimage. For example, we have to travel seven times between two hills, Safa and Marwah, because when Abraham took Hagar away, he left her in Mecca. She looked at him and said, "You're leaving me in a land with no water or food? Who are you leaving me to? Who are you depending on to take care of the child and me? Is it God?" Abraham said, "Yes." And then she said, "Well, if it is God, He will not let us down." Hagar is shown to be a very religious person who is willing to take serious chances because she is also part of what Abraham stands for. She's willing to do this for God. Even back in the experience with Sarah, Hagar was a believer. And that coincides with the commentaries. Again, this material is not in the Qur'an, but certain Jewish commentaries say that Pharaoh gives Hagar to Abraham because he is afraid of the plague that has befallen him. If that is the case, she would have had good reason to be sympathetic to Abraham's God and to learn from Sarah, who taught religion to the women.

BURT: Azizah, in the Hebrew Bible, Hagar enters into conversation with God well before Sarah does. She has a long conversation with God that is on a par with Abraham's conversations with God, and she gets a series of promises from God, much as Abraham does. It's Sarah who's out of the loop.

BILL: And the powerful aspect of the story to me is that Abraham must share equally with Sarah. God talks directly to Sarah and makes her the mother of a great nation. Hagar too will be the mother of a great nation. Both of these women deal directly with God or God's messengers.

LEW: Don't you wonder what Genesis would have looked like if it had been filtered through the Church mothers instead of the Church fathers?

BHARATI: But Hagar is being treated like a second-class citizen, even by God. She's first visited by the messenger, rather than directly by God. And what is it that she's promised when she is pregnant and totally stressed out? "You will have a son, Ishmael, but he's going to be a wild ass of a man and he's going to be a brawler. Everyone's going to hate him."

BURT: But she's also promised that she'll be as fruitful as the stars. She's promised twelve tribes. She becomes a matriarch like Sarah.

AZIZAH: Yes, it was part of the promise.

LEW: One thing I've found fascinating in this discussion is that we've been talking for some time, and only now has the main character come up.

BOB: Ishmael?

LEW: No.

AZIZAH: God.

LEW: Right. We're talking about the Book of Genesis, and the wonderful storytelling, and the conniving woman, and the humble and believing Hagar. But the main character is God, Who is making the new start and doing what He promised, in spite of the conniving woman and what, in my judgment, is a very wimpish patriarch. I don't find much sympathy for Abraham. And I'm not all that sympathetic with Sarah. But I think the relationship between God and Hagar is magnificent. Just because Abraham and Sarah are chosen doesn't mean that they're the only ones who are chosen.

BURT: There's a very clear message in the Torah itself that Ishmael and Isaac are genuinely brothers. They share a father, and God gives a promise to both.

BOB: They bury Abraham together.

BURT: That's a very powerful message. They both have a relationship to God.

BILL: One important difference: The covenant goes to Isaac.

LEW: Yes, but God still says to Hagar that not only will Ishmael be a fighting man, but "I will be with him." Isn't that the essence of the blessings of the covenant?

BHARATI: I don't need a rebel who's going to be a loser in the long run, just because it's been programmed that way.

Hagar and Ishmael Expelled by Abraham, Cloister of Santa Maria Novella, Florence, 14th c.

AZIZAH: Ishmael is not a loser.

BHARATI: Apparently, God as author, as opposed to God as distributor of morality, needs a guy with a black hat and a guy with a white hat. If you don't have a Cain, you can't have an Abel. If you don't have an Ishmael, you can't have an Isaac.

AZIZAH: But here's the story. God is showing that the promise is not only through Sarah's line but also through another line that isn't even from the tribe of Abraham. Remember, Hagar is an Egyptian. Her son by Abraham is of mixed blood. And Ishmael marries someone from the land where he and Hagar were left by Abraham.

LEW: Egypt?

AZIZAH: Not Egypt. Saudi Arabia today.

BILL: With all that oil, he came out all right.

AZIZAH: So the blessing grows more diverse. In other words, the "chosenness" by God goes to all people. You know, I mentioned that we Muslims on pilgrimage go back and forth seven times between two hills, as Hagar did when she could not find water or food for her son. And then she said, "Please, God, let me turn my face. I don't want to see him die." And Ishmael kicked and where his foot struck, water came out. To this day, on that spot in Mecca, there is the Spring of Zamzam. When people drink from it, they say, "Here is the water that came from the foot of Ishmael when he kicked."

LIZ: But, you know, I find this to be a very sad story from a woman's point of view. Sarah was supposed to be a seer, and Hagar was supposed to start a whole new people. And yet, one woman goes childless for ninety years, and then when she finally has a child, it's after giving another woman the right to have a child that she wanted. Another woman, who's a slave, gets beaten up for doing what she's told to do and is sent out into the desert by the father of her child. Everybody can say, ''Oh, poor Abraham.'' But where's his humanity?

AZIZAH: It's very clear, at least in the Qur'an. In the Qur'an, when Abraham takes Ishmael out to the desert, he says, ''God, You made me leave them in a barren land. Please take care of them. I want my offspring not to worship idols. I leave them in Your hands.'' And God says, ''I bless your children, those who are just.'' So Abraham is torn apart by what happens. But he is enough of a faithful believer to say, ''I will submerge myself and rely on God. And God will take care of me.''

LEW: I want to believe that, but I have a hard time being sympathetic to a man who was given gold and silver in Egypt for having used his wife in a sordid way. Then he sends his own son away into the desert with a skin of water and a hunk of bread.

BURT: This is a complicated story, and, obviously, Abraham is a problematic figure. To whatever extent Abraham submerges his own sadness, that repressed sadness comes out later. And he acts out against both his sons. But we have to remember that Abraham also has a brother, Haran. And when Haran dies, his son, Lot—Abraham's nephew—becomes Abraham's favorite. Lot is always with him.

BILL: Yes, but would he have been satisfied to have a nephew instead of a son to carry forward the covenant with God?

LIZ: Let me just ask a question while we're talking about all of this. We talk a lot about the covenant. What is the covenant? A lot of stuff happens because there's this covenant. It goes beyond God saying, ''I'm going to give you riches, you're going to have a son.'' There's something else implied.

BHARATI: It means the chosen.

LIZ: The chosen. But what does Abraham have to do? What does Sarah have to do to keep the covenant? Tell me what the whole deal is. Because people get hurt as a result of this covenant. Tell me.

LEW: I think we have to remember that the Bible isn't a collection of short stories. This is a chapter in a big story whose author is also the chief character in the story. The picture I get is of the Creator saying, ''I want to get involved. I want to make a new start for those creatures of mine. This is how I'm going to do it. I'm going to come to one of them and make a deal with him.'' It doesn't seem to matter much who. But He chooses Abraham and says, ''I make a commitment to you. From now on I am, as it were, stuck with my commitment to you.'' He doesn't say, ''I'll make this commitment on the proviso that you do likewise.'' He just says, ''It's going to be yours.'' It's only later on that He requires something of Abraham.

LIZ: I still want to know: What's the deal? What do I get in this covenant?

LEW: You get God.

BOB: There's more to it. In one way, the covenant is a contract in the sense of being a political treaty. For example, when Abraham goes out against the confederation of eastern kings, he takes his allies with him. The Hebrew word for allies is "members of the covenant of Abraham." So there it clearly has a specifically political meaning. Then you get the concrete sense of the covenant in one of the most haunting and mystifying moments in all of Genesis, the so-called "covenant of the cloven animal parts." God and Abraham are sitting opposite each other as the sun is setting, and they've cut up animals in two. What the experts on these things tell us is that throughout the ancient Near East and also in Greece, you enacted treaties and mutual pacts this way with the notion that if you violated the treaty, then what happened to these animals would happen to you.

LEW: And yet, there are times when Israel in the sight of God has broken the covenant—

BOB: —again and again—

LEW: —and then God comes back and says, "But that is not going to make me abandon my program."

LIZ: But I still don't know what I get when I get the covenant.

BOB: Okay. A hundred words or less. Look, the terms unfold progressively. To begin with, you're going to become lots and lots of people—like the stars in heaven, like the sands on the shore.

LIZ: Lots of people like me? What's so good about lots of people?

BOB: Lots of people will need plenty of land. That's part of the deal. And then the next crucial element is that this people is going to be a blessing for itself and for all the peoples of the earth. So you really begin to have the seeds of Isaiah's vision in that promise—that this people will have dominion over all the peoples of the earth.

BILL: Sovereignty? Power?

BOB: Yes, except that this people will be a blessing—it is moral as well as political ascendancy.

LIZ: To have a child is a big part of a covenant with God, right?

AZIZAH: That's the way people thought at the time. You have to look at it in the context of the times. The Qur'an speaks of blessings and promises, but only to the just among us. In the Qur'an, under most interpretations, it is Ishmael, not Isaac, who is offered as a sacrifice. Ishmael says very clearly to Abraham, "Father, do it, because we're doing it for God." Sarah, Hagar, Abraham, Ishmael—they all have special relationships with God. They're all pious. But each is on a different level of consciousness and therefore displays a different level of piety. God does not penalize them for that. He accepts all of them and blesses all of them. And He teaches them

Guercino, *Abraham Expelling Hagar and Ishmael*, 1657

through events. Sarah is taught through her life journey with Abraham, Ishmael through the acts of sacrifice and exile, and Hagar through her life journey with Abraham and Sarah and subsequent exile. That's God's way of teaching us how to rise to a higher level of spirituality.

BURT: Let's come back to the covenant. There are two partners in this covenant. God promises to give offspring, land, and blessing. But the people have to give something back to God. In the initial stage, with Abraham, what God asks back is circumcision. Circumcision physically marks your body, indicating that you are in relationship with God.

BHARATI: It's like a gang tattoo.

AZIZAH: Muslims circumcise, too.

BURT: Yes, when God commands that the household be circumcised, Ishmael, then thirteen, is circumcised. But then God makes the command specific, that from this point on, all should be circumcised on the eighth day, as Isaac is. Later, when they come out of Egypt, the covenant gets a little more complicated. God has brought His people out of Egypt, and it's almost as if there were a debt to pay—"We were enslaved, and You freed us. What do You want us to do?" Answer: the Ten Commandments, or, in Jewish theology, 613 commandments—a whole complex of commands that we are obligated to do for God.

LIZ: It's the males who get circumcised. And the one thing about this story that sets off a really bad train of thought all through the rest of the Bible is this thing about sons. You know, everybody has to have sons. Sons are the most important things in the world. Isaac, Ishmael—I mean, what is that?

GENE: Well, this business about sons is interesting to me because it's played out in the black community. When you look at the first chapter of Exodus, you see that the Pharaoh says, "The Israelites are getting too strong. Kill the male child." On the one hand, there's an emphasis on sons, but that has to be balanced against the fact that in certain contexts, the male child is the most vulnerable.

BHARATI: Wait a minute. It's much simpler than that. In these cultures, land is not simply about real estate, it's about ancestry. If I'm asked what is my home, I'm supposed to give the name of the village in what is now Bangladesh, which I have never seen, because that is the ancestral soil. And the land is passed on only to sons. You will sacrifice everything to hang on to *bhumi*—the land.

BOB: But in the Bible, if there are no sons, the land passes to daughters.

GENE: When I read these passages with their emphasis on sons, I see something completely different, because I'm in a community where the sons are biologically the most vulnerable. There are no patriarchs. The mothers give the sons a privileged place because the male child is the most threatened. In Exodus, Egyptian social policy for an oppressed minority is "Kill the sons." For me, there's a parallel between that and the United States regarding black males. So this son business is more complicated than simply patriarchy and misogyny gone mad, or giving privileged status to males because you hate women.

LIZ: I'm still just asking why.

BILL: Maybe it's because the winners write history. Remember that Hagar and Sarah are daughters before they become mothers. God deals with them the same way He deals with Abraham, saying to both of them, "You will be the mother of a great nation." Then this business of circumcision comes in. By the physical act of circumcision, the power is shifted to the male, and the people who write the history are males. So the role of the daughter, without whom there would not have been an Ishmael or an Isaac, is diminished in the telling of the story.

AZIZAH: One commentary says that Sarah was so mad at Hagar because of Abraham's attention that she decided to mutilate her in some way to make her less interesting. And that's how female circumcision started.

BOB: That's a frightening story.

LEW: Even if the cultural conditions had been totally different, and there had been a matriarchy, the basic problem and drama of the story would be the same. This story does not depend on the cultural situation of the males.

BURT: Even so, this story has a bit of matriarchy in it. The blessing comes from Abraham, but it has to follow through Sarah's lineage. God is quite explicit about that.

BILL: God's playing favorites here because He's passing the lineage through Isaac?

BHARATI: The promise God is making reduces a woman to a womb.

AZIZAH: I see an interpretation here that is very narrow—because even when God says, "Through your line, Sarah, your offspring will do this, and I will give you this promised land," it doesn't mean exclusivity. He didn't say "through Sarah only."

BURT: I certainly don't mean that. Women do have some role here. God makes Sarah's status clear, and later on in Genesis, there are stories in which the mother has the power to determine which of the children will get the blessing. In the story of Jacob and Esau, for example, the mother in some very powerful way controls the plot.

LEW: I need to say: Remember the Christian story of Mary and Joseph. Joseph becomes a figure almost forgotten in the background. Mary is exalted as the most blessed of women.

BURT: Yes, but Mary also gives birth to a boy.

GENE: That's okay.

AZIZAH: Can I tell you something from my family's point of view? When I was studying the Qur'an as a child, I asked my teacher if there was ever a chance for a woman to be a prophet. "Why are all the prophets men?" He said, "Well, there have been many prophets we don't know about. The Qur'an says that 'Every nation has a prophet in its past.' " My teacher added, "Some of them might have been women." Now when I think about it today, I have to deal with it as a feminist. This leads me to a philosophy of religion. How does God relate to us? How does God change our consciousness? From my Qur'an, I see it very clearly. There is a whole notion of gradualism, teaching us throughout the process of history. At the time these stories occurred, people lived in a patriarchal society. And from the time of the stories until today, we have been living in a patriarchal society. God talks to people who are active in the society in order to get the message out. If Sarah or Hagar tried to spread the message, they would not have been able to go very far. At the same time, the message itself contains elements that deconstruct patriarchal society. That's where the progress in history becomes promising.

BURT: In the Hebrew Bible, remember, women do have status as prophets. When Sarah wants to throw Hagar out, and Abraham is worried about it, God says quite explicitly, "What she says, listen to." Later, Miriam is explicitly identified as a prophet. This comes back to a point you made, Bill—that the victors write history. But even though men wrote this book, they gave women an enormous role. In the same way, although this is an Israelite story, Ishmael has a very powerful role. Ishmael is not depicted as a bad guy—

BILL: —just a wild ass of a kid.

BURT: Ishmael can't be edited out or marginalized.

AZIZAH: Let me tell you why Ishmael is not only not a bad guy, but a blessed guy. In the Qur'an, after Ishmael has grown up a bit, Abraham comes back to him, and together they build the first house for God on earth, the Ka'ba. And that is in Mecca. They build it together. And Ishmael has been pious all this time.

BHARATI: But I would sue Abraham for nonpayment of child support. He has abandoned Ishmael.

BOB: I want to follow up on that. To put it in contemporary terms, the biblical writers worked both sides of the street. That's part of the greatness of the Bible. As Burt said, it's an Israelite document. One of the vehicles for the covenant is a national community—Israel, in this account. So here you have a tract for Jewish nationalism.

BILL: Jewish scripture. The Jewish story.

BOB: But looking at what goes on in the story itself, which, as a literary critic, I try to do all the time, you see a flip side. Ishmael is also a blessing, and he is also the father of twelve tribes, and he's going to become the progenitor of a great people.

LEW: And God is with him.

BOB: And God is with him. On the other hand, even if the image of the "wild ass of a man" in biblical poetry is probably a positive image, there's a sense that his nation will exist only through constant martial effort, with "the hand of all against him and his hand against all." There's even a kind of game the narrator plays. Just as Sarah can't bring herself to mention Ishmael's name, neither can the narrator in Chapter twenty-one—and neither does the angel, who refers to him as "the lad." But the ghost of Ishmael's name hovers over the story because the divine messenger says, "God has heard the voice of the lad where he is." And that's what *Ishmael* means— "God has heard." This kind of narrative game suggests that Ishmael's heirs will be a great people, legitimate in every way.

LEW: I love that part of it. But I read it just a little differently. I see Sarah as using Hagar and Ishmael for nationalistic or family purposes, as you said, Bob. And Hagar and Ishmael are of use to Sarah only in her purview. But when Isaac is born, Ishmael is the utterly marginalized person. And then Yahweh comes in and says, "Not quite." He says, "I have a covenant with you, Sarah and Abraham. I'm not going back on that. But just because I have a covenant with you does not mean that I marginalize Ishmael. I choose him, too."

BILL: True. In Bob's translation, God hears the cry of the child under the bush. God hears the abandoned Ishmael and responds.

BURT: It's exactly the phrase we get in Exodus, when the Jews are enslaved. God hears their cry.

BHARATI: But does that mean that even God is surprised—that like Sarah, who didn't anticipate her emotional reactions to Hagar being pregnant, God didn't know He would respond this way to the child?

LEW: That's a very interesting question.

BILL: Are these unintended consequences for God? Or is it that maybe our lives are just stories that were mostly written before we were born? And that we are playing out the plot, and the only real choice we have in the middle of the story is

Jean Baptiste Camille Corot, *Hagar in the Wilderness*, 1835 whether or not we're going to fully live or resist the plot. That's the choice Abraham, Sarah, and Hagar made that I really appreciate. They didn't resist the plot, but went with the story and lived fully in response to whatever card they were dealt.

AZIZAH: That's why I say God gives us a realm of responsibility and moral freedom. We must make our choices and live with the consequences. That's how God teaches.

LEW: And that is the essence of building character. The only way you can live a life is to take whatever raw material or destiny God has given you, and ask yourself, "What am I going to do with that?" I have a son, who was not only given away by his natural parents but also inherited from them a very serious blood disease. He didn't choose that. And he didn't choose to be adopted. But those were his raw materials, and he can't change that. He must build a life out of those raw materials.

BILL: And Abraham, Sarah, and Hagar were the raw material God had to work with. As a novelist, Bharati, would you tell the story differently?

BHARATI: Yes. I'd do something with the scenes that are left out. I'd like to see a big conflict scene between Sarah and Hagar, for example.

BURT: What? You don't think Sarah beating her up is enough?

BHARATI: No, I want Hagar's response

to it. What if, at the end, Hagar says, "Enough is enough. I'm out of here!"

AZIZAH: She does just that in one commentary.

BURT: That's why there's commentary.

LIZ: What I'd like to see is the two of them singing. Not the catfight, not just the two women after each other. I want the unspoken moments where the disparate kinds of music, the Egyptian music and the Hebraic music, would be heard together—where one woman who can bear a child looks at the woman who is childless and isn't just smirking at her—and where the upper-class woman looks at the slave and realizes she is a real woman. Those moments are all made up without the text. But it's all potentially there. The two of them see in each other what could possibly be the future of their relationship.

BURT: I'm taken with Liz's suggestion because it's implicit within the text. Hagar is Sarah's servant, who, I don't know, maybe dresses her in the morning. There's this intimacy between them. Hagar grows up in that household, knowing all about Sarah's anguish and her troubles with Abraham and probably being sympathetic to her. It's only when she becomes pregnant that there's a rift between them. Up until that point, they're singing the same tune.

BILL: Yes, there is a rabbinic story that when Sarah left Pharaoh, he offered her any slave she wanted, and she chose Hagar.

She has an attraction to Hagar, a sense of kinship.

LIZ: If only Sarah could look at Hagar and say, "You are a woman, too. You have imagination. You have sexuality. You are the same as me." If only she could see her as not "the other."

BURT: Through Hagar's physical being, there is real memory for Sarah of that sojourn in Egypt and her fling, or whatever it was, with Pharaoh. In some very powerful way, Hagar represents Sarah's sexuality.

LEW: Right. That's beautiful.

GENE: I love this story—and I identify with all three of the characters because they're so human. When I tell it to the young people I work with on the streets, I say that there are one or two ways to respond to the injustice of life. You can whine and complain about the injustice of it all, the fact that I wasn't the privileged one. Or you can see through the eyes of faith that every adverse circumstance is an opportunity to see God work out his ultimate desire for wholeness and reconciliation in your life.

BILL: You've been working with difficult kids, real castoffs—

GENE: And that's precisely my point. See, the funny thing about this is that most poor people don't need any of our liberal clichés about the unfairness of it all because they know that infinitely better than we do. So much of what salon intellectuals do

in the academy, where we go through a kind of hand-wringing routine about the injustice of life, really has no bearing out there in the streets. This is why the scriptures are so important for people. The adversity, the unfairness, the injustice are all there. So on the streets, these kids can do one of two things. They can just commit suicide. Or they can seize this as an opportunity to exercise faith in God and have a tragedy transform into an opportunity for triumph. That's what poor people have to see, or there's no point.

BHARATI: But listen, as someone whose skin color caused me to be spat upon, to be sent to the back of the bus and refused service in hotels—

BOB: Where?

BHARATI: In North America, during my fourteen years in Canada. I don't want to see what is the lesson in adversity, I want to see empowerment. I want to be the Hagar who then takes action and says, "This is not right! I will change it."

GENE: It's not either/or. What I tell the young people is: "Look, here you are in the wilderness of North America. It's a bad break, okay? You know you're gonna catch hell from 'can't see' in the morning till 'can't see' at night. That's the card, the material you have to work with. You can do one of two things. You can just be a victim; or you can use these crises as opportunities to transcend both the oppressor and the oppression. Through the eyes of faith, the impossible is transformed into the possible." I teach that. But then I say, "Look here, brother. In the Christian tradition, faith without works is dead. Faith disconnected from action, struggle, a real fight is meaningless." I want to empower individuals in groups and communities by saying, "Here's adversity. God has a lesson for us as to how we can transcend and transform tragedies into victories."

AZIZAH: Isn't that what Malcolm X did?

GENE: Thank you. Listen. The most important dimension of the Malcolm X story, which for me is a great parable for all of black America, is the conversion experience. The most politically important chapter in the entire autobiography is the one entitled "Saved."

AZIZAH: He went on the pilgrimage and saw everybody of all colors sitting together, eating from the same plate.

GENE: That's right.

AZIZAH: Because God has blessings for all of us who have faith.

GENE: There you go.

BHARATI: Well, it's also Mahatma Gandhi who used religion for political consolidation and to resist colonialism. So it's the word "transcend" I have trouble with. If "transcend" means submission—

GENE: Of course not. Biblically, theologically, and politically, transcendence means that when I'm confronted with oppression, I'm going to embrace a vision of myself that says that I am more than the sum total of the brutal acts committed against me. I am more than all the attempts to denigrate my being and to suggest that I am anything less than a child of God. So I transcend—it's an act of epistemological repudiation.

LEW: Can you translate that word "transcend" as "hope"? Nobody changes unless they have hope that the change they want is possible.

GENE: The biblical story provides the ideological and moral basis for resurrecting hope. See, in the black community, faith and hope have died, and as a result, nihilism and decay prevail. The scriptures function as an emancipatory mechanism to resurrect faith and hope so that a person who is oppressed can transcend the whining, can transcend the limousine liberalism where you're just whining about rights. Now it's not easy to sit down with a group of young drug dealers, and try to demonstrate the relevance of the biblical scriptures for governing their lives. They ask some very basic questions. We can talk about hope. But they'll say, "Look, Minister, let's make sure we get this story straight. You're telling us we should play by the rules of the game. That's part of the moral prescription of the book—that we'll do well if we do right. Okay, we're willing to do right—but where do we see the 'do well' part of it? This is just more drugs—you're trying to give us your version of narcotics." They say, "Look, we don't wanna hear the clichés of the flat-earth fundamentalists, who are basically Afrikaaners. Because what happens is that they give us the Bible, and they take the money. They have all the resources, while we starve and sing good jubilee songs to entertain them. We're not going to play that game.''

B U R T : Gene, this brings us right back to the text we were reading. The blessing given to Ishmael includes that he'll be successful, but it is also very clear that he will be a wild ass of a man with everyone's hand against him. But that too is presented as a blessing that speaks very directly. The question is how you transform being a wild ass of a man into those riches.

B H A R A T I : Political action.

B I L L : Well, it's not only political action. Abraham does it by trickery and cunning in the first story. They do it here by a little sexual activity.

A Z I Z A H : Malcolm X did it by refining his understanding. He grew with Islam, understanding what it is to have justice. It is justice for all. That means action, but not the kind of action he engaged in early on. And let me say that whatever we say about African Americans is also true of so-called ''Third World'' countries. They are resorting to religion because they have finally rejected the view of themselves that the West exported to them.

B H A R A T I : They should be demanding their rights. That's why I want to be an Ishmael who works for civil rights and then the enforcement of those rights. I don't want to wait for some good to trickle down to me. I'm sure Abraham is great, and I'm sure God is great, but whether I am Isaac or Ishmael, I want to think of destiny as cooperating with God.

G E N E : You're absolutely right. Religion is not about waiting for the mother ship to come down. It's not about postponing the realization of the good. Spiritual transformation and a power politics of justice are indivisible. When Malcolm X is spiritually transformed, he is introduced to a new politics of justice. And what we're going to come back to in term of the black community is that spiritual transformation leads to political and economic justice. You will not have political freedom or justice separated from spiritual transformation at the individual, personal, and corporate level.

> ''Religion is not about waiting for the mother ship to come down.''

B H A R A T I : Would you be willing to substitute the word ''moral'' for ''spiritual''?

G E N E : No, because while they are related, they are also distinct. Somebody can be spiritual and not necessarily be moral.

BOB: And vice versa.

AZIZAH: I once heard Malcolm X talking to an audience at the American University of Beirut. The audience responded to him as if he were their leader and they were his people. Once you have a universal concept of justice, and once you know what are the ills in society you have to change, then you can become a world leader. That's what he did.

LEW: What did a spiritual transformation do for Malcolm X?

GENE: The conversion experience radically transformed his hierarchy of values and completely reconstructed his concept of identity. Here was an individual who was blinded by the gods of this world—materialism, white supremacy—which he had internalized. As a result of his conversion, the shackles fell off, and the blinders fell from his eyes. And then we see him on a spiritual journey because the conversion experience, the transformation, is a process, not an event. Part of what happens with this fundamentalist stuff is that the conversion experience is reduced to an event—TV, you know, *Alacazam*! That chapter called "Saved" in Malcolm's autobiography is probably one of the most powerful documents we have in American literature.

BURT: In a way, Hagar goes through this kind of transformation. It is a long process. Having been physically abused, she is told by the angel to go back and endure some more. Now "go back and endure" is not a message anyone likes to hear. But through her endurance, she merits blessing and becomes someone who speaks with God. She is transformed. This is a very powerful message.

BHARATI: But I see that same theme in the text as being an instrument for reinforcing the patriarchal order. It's to the advantage of Sarah and Abraham if Hagar comes back and is their slave again. Hagar hasn't gone through sufficient consciousness-raising.

BOB: The divine messenger said that the child to be born wouldn't really be Abraham's son, except in a technical, biological sense, unless she goes back and puts up with all that nonsense from Sarah.

LEW: It is only when Hagar is dismissed by Abraham, with God's encouragement and at Sarah's insistence, that the way is open for God to say, "Now, we're really going to begin, Hagar. We're going to make Ishmael great." And Ishmael does become great.

BILL: I like something that was said earlier about seeing in this story an unflinching moral realism. There's no whitewashing here. But are we sure that was the reality of three thousand years ago?

BOB: Well, I think it was. On the one hand, lots of things change. We don't have polygamy. And I'm not quite sure whether our modern notion of a conversion experience is quite applicable to the Bible. On the other hand, many of my academic colleagues hold the position that there's no such thing as human nature, and that everything is a social construction. Male, female, individual identity—it's all a reflex of a particular ideology, and a particular set of social institutions. My resistance to that idea is not a dogmatic one. But based on the empirical facts of three thousand or more years of literature and, above all, the biblical literature, we know that some things don't change. We're all born out of a female body, and most of us have a mother. Most of us have lived with siblings and have struggled with the pecking order for siblings. Certain things may change between a man and a woman in a conjugal relationship as the concept of marriage evolves. But other things remain constant. That's precisely why we could all identify with Sarah's outburst of fury. So we have to beware of turning everything into this year's point of view. In fact, there are some things that speak to us not because we're seeing visions in our head, but because they're really there in the text.

B I L L : One is the affirmation of childbearing. But you can't read the scriptures of three thousand years ago in the light of modern women, can you?

B O B : Well, you can and you can't. It's clear that some things have shifted. A woman can make a conscious decision, as I gather Liz has, not to have children. Or a woman might not be able to have children and be perfectly at peace with that. Yet I think we all know women who may have great personal fulfillment, who may be distinguished professors or lawyers or CEOs

or what have you, but who have a kind of private sadness in their lives because they don't have children. Or women who have been on the career track and then at the age of thirty-five discover that it has become desperately important for them to have children.

B H A R A T I : Men need children more than women do because it's the ultimate expression of virility.

B O B : I don't buy that.

B I L L : I need children to love, to allow for tenderness and nurturing. I would feel like Sarah if I had not had three children.

B U R T : I think there's a little bit of truth in Bharati's point. I'm a divorced parent with a son and daughter, and I share my children fifty-fifty, which means I spend a lot of time with them. Part of me is just proud about having them. And part of me is proud that I'm a capable parent, that I can make breakfast and get them dressed and get them out of the house in the morning, which is a minor miracle. I'm very tied up in that identity. Part of it is virility, and part of it is the way I construct myself.

B I L L : We haven't heard from the two women who have not borne children.

A Z I Z A H : As a Muslim, I look at the life of the Prophet Muhammad. He had no sons that survived him. His line comes from his daughter. When I think about these things, I see that God is teaching me a lesson. Throughout the Qur'an, God dismantles the institutions of slavery, of patriarchy, of economic classism—all these things—but only in a gradual form, which we can comprehend and then catch up with. That is why the Qur'an is a Qur'an for all times and ages. Every day I understand it differently as my consciousness rises.

LIZ: I have a particular love for this story. In fact, I have set Sarah to music and am progressing my way, musically, through this story. The sadness I feel in relation to the story is also very beautiful to me because I can see it from both sides. I committed myself to the arts as a young child and decided for that reason not to have children because I know what it means to give psychically to a child. I'm in a generation of women who are in conflict, even the ones who have children. When I was in my early twenties, I lost my mother very violently, and the mother who adopted me, even at the age I was, was black. She introduced me to world music and made it possible for me to go to Africa. She is the person who said, "You have a gift." So I see Hagar, and I see Sarah. And I want to write a piece of music where they come together.

LEW: What you say is important because while it's good to have children, it can also be a situation in which you become nested and snug and forget about the rest of the world. Does Mother Teresa have children? In a way, she has. Jesus never had a child. There is a wonderful scene in the Gospels where somebody says to Jesus, "Your family's out there. Your mother and brothers and sisters are looking for you." He looks beyond and says, "I have many more brothers and sisters than those."

AZIZAH: The way Bill articulated his desire for children was different from the yielding to God that the story speaks about. Male progeny is the way to propagate the person who dies. It's a way of gaining immortality. The story of Adam and Eve in the Qur'an interests me because it says that they ate from the Tree of Immortality. That has been a quest of human beings for a long time. If you want children because they make you feel warm and you love to hug them, that's one thing. But seeking immortality is wrong because only God is immortal. You can have a tribe, or twelve tribes—but if God zaps them, they're gone in a moment.

BILL: Well, I didn't mean to suggest that I've enjoyed my children because they make me feel warm and fuzzy. Sometimes they have been wild asses.

AZIZAH: That's a positive statement, though.

BILL: What I'm trying to say is that I continue to fight against absorption with myself, and children are a way of linking me with another.

BURT: It's true that you can't have that high a view of yourself in the middle of changing a diaper.

AZIZAH: Why couldn't that link be made with someone other than children?

BHARATI: If you have children, you

just don't have time to think about whether you have self-esteem because you're so busy.

LEW: My wife and I had an interesting conversation after seeing a play recently about a young couple trying to have a child. The man had been dispossessed by his family, and the wife eventually had to have a hysterectomy. At the end of the play, the man says, ''I have no past, and now I have no future.'' I asked my wife if she had that feeling, because I understood the passions of this guy who had to have offspring. I said I could feel for him. My wife said she had no feelings for him at all.

BILL: Why does just simply talking about these biblical stories spark such wide-ranging discussions that often stray very far from the text?

BHARATI: That's what great stories are all about—to make you think about the big issues and to make you go through experiences you have not been destined to have in this life.

LIZ: I find that all these conversations are in the Bible. This book might be great literature, it might be great music, or it might be God. But it contains all these conversations.

AZIZAH: And every time you open and read the Qur'an, for example, depending on the dialectic of your own life, the dynamics of what's happening to you, your consciousness, you see a whole new reality. Whole new issues come before you that you never thought about.

Scenes from the Life of Abraham, Haggadah, Venice, 1609

BURT: Azizah's point of view is a very rabbinic one.

AZIZAH: Yes, because we share the concept of *ijtihad*, which, for Muslim scholars, means to read the Qur'an and interpret it in light of the sayings of the prophet as well as other criteria.

BURT: And we read the Torah every year in the synagogue—all five books. By the time you're twenty or thirty, you've heard the stories a lot of times already. But the fact is: Every time you hear a story, you're older, which means you're a little different, which means you hear a different story. The rabbis have a marvelous notion of the revelatory power of scripture. They say, "What was given to Moses at Sinai?" What was given was not just the written words but what many generations in the future will offer as interpretation. That, too, was in Sinai. In other words, it's all there in the text. We build a community, and as a community we consent to make this book sacred. The minute we do that, in reading together, we knit ourselves together.

"We build a community, and as a community we consent to make this book sacred."

BHARATI: Into the community, yes.

BURT: That's what's happening here, too. We're building this little community.

We're not just sharing our reading of the words, we're sharing our lives with one another. That's what Bible study is meant to do. And that's why the Bible is such a powerful book.

BHARATI: Yes, and it encourages reading and listening and love of God through story.

BURT: And love of one another.

LEW: Would you not agree, though, Burt, that as fascinating as these stories are, and as economically as they are told, there are many important stories in other books and traditions? But what makes these biblical stories important and the reason they are preserved is that they are about people establishing themselves as a community in response to a divine initiative.

BURT: Yes, I would. Certainly there is enormous power to Torah, to the New Testament, to the Qur'an because the readers firmly believe that God's word is somehow implicit in that narrative.

BILL: Or explicit.

BURT: Or explicit in the narrative. But the fact of reading communally is equally powerful. God doesn't speak in a vacuum. This book only says something when we open it and read it together. That's when we hear the voice of God.

LEW: Absolutely, but in community formation, I can also read great literature—

"God doesn't speak in a vacuum."

Dostoyevsky, for instance. In a secondary sense, great literature offers significant revelations, too. But the Bible is different because of what has happened as a result of its being. The trail begins there at Genesis, with God coming out of the blue, not being ordered by anybody, not being prodded by anybody, not following a scheme or a script. He just comes and says, "I'm going to begin something new here." The drama of the Bible is always a drama of where we are with respect to God.

BOB: I'd like to propose a less theological view of this. I make my living as a teacher of literature and a literary critic. I wouldn't deny that this book is very concerned with God. But as a reader over the years, I've come to the conclusion that there are two kinds of texts: brilliant literary texts that are exhaustible, and others that are inexhaustible. It may have to do with the quality of imagination, the way they're articulated. For example, I love Henry Fielding's *Tom Jones*. Fielding is a witty, subtle, ingenious writer who plays with all kinds of ironies and who is delightful to read. But by the fourth time I read *Tom Jones* very carefully, I decided that I wouldn't read it again. I still think it's a great novel, but I've seen everything I as a person or a reader am capable of seeing in *Tom Jones*. But I've never felt this about the

Bible. Even apart from theological considerations, something about the awesome compactness, the ability to fuse multiple perspectives into a few words—all make this an inexhaustible text.

LEW: I think it's also important to remember that the Old Testament isn't only a text of stories but includes Proverbs and Psalms as well. In my tradition, the Psalms are our songbook. We are as deeply rooted in the Psalms as any Jew could possibly be. I've told my family that if I'm ever in deep trouble to whip out Psalm 139: "If you make your bed in hell, I'll be there to hold you. If you fall off the edge of the world, I'll hold you. If you walk in darkness, I will be your light."

BILL: Well, that certainly raises the question: Have any of you felt like Hagar and Ishmael must have felt when they were abandoned in the desert?

AZIZAH: They didn't feel abandoned. They knew God was with them. Still, there have been many times when I felt abandoned in the desert, especially as an immigrant of Arab descent in the United States. But I always knew in my heart that God was with me.

GENE: You can feel abandoned while at the same time believing that God is there. At the level of psychology and emotion, I can feel great pain—but I believe God is with me as I go through the valley of the shadow of death.

AZIZAH: Like Abraham.

BILL: Like Hagar and Ishmael. The young people you work with in the streets must feel abandoned.

GENE: Yes, and part of the antisocial behavior that they're playing out is to say, "Look, the society has rejected me, so I reject the society." There's a logic to that. Society has rendered a verdict on them, so they return the compliment. Consequently,

> "You can feel abandoned while at the same time believing that God is there."

for these young people, the Bible is more than simply great literature. This is a word from God. They want to know what the Lord says.

BURT: Bill, you asked if we ever feel abandoned. And Lew was talking about the Psalms. As soon as he mentioned the Psalms, a verse from Psalms popped into my head. It's exactly at this point of the year that I'm midway between the anniversaries of the death of my father and mother. So they're very much on my mind, and my loss of them is very much on my mind. Sure I feel abandoned. But my response, as a Jew and a rabbi, as a believer, is a verse of Psalms: "*Ki avi veemi azavuni, vaadonai yaasefayni*"—"My father and my

mother have left me, but God gathers me in."

LEW: You don't have to be in the ghetto to feel abandoned. You can feel abandoned in Bel Air. There I was a few years ago, undergoing a pretty tough experience of depression. That's a feeling of abandonment. I went to an island in Puget Sound alone for three weeks—no newspapers, no books, no telephone, no TV, no radio. Nothing. About a week and a half later, I had an experience, as real as being with you here. I was feeling the deepest sense of abandonment when I heard my mother say, "I can't help you." I heard good friends say, "I can't help you." I felt utterly lost. But then at some miraculous moment, I felt a powerful sense: "No, you're not lost. I'm here, underneath you. I'm holding you up." I arose, and I thought for the first time in my life, "I know the meaning of joy." It felt so marvelous. I said to myself, "Now I know what the Psalmist means"—that "Even when you make your bed in hell, I'll be there, and I'll hold you up."

BILL: Before we leave our story: Can you imagine that scene when Ishmael and Isaac actually meet at their father's tomb?

BOB: Isn't that amazing? And they bury him together.

BURT: In the Hebrew Bible, after Ishmael is sent out, he never has a recorded conversation with Abraham again. And after Isaac and Abraham go through the binding of Isaac, and Abraham puts the knife to his throat, they never have conversation again. But Isaac and Ishmael do meet again at their father's funeral. I can only imagine what they must have been like. What a conversation!

BILL: I wonder if Hagar and Sarah get together again?

BOB: I don't think so.

LEW: I've never read a Bible story yet without wondering what happened to some of these people.

BURT: But remember, there's an ironic footnote to this story—that after Hagar and Sarah, Abraham has yet a third wife and six more kids.

AZIZAH: And one wonders: Were they blessed, too?

BURT: It's reported so matter-of-factly. Abraham takes this woman, Keturah, who the rabbis immediately identify with Hagar, as if, Sarah being dead, Abraham goes back to Hagar. But assuming it's a third wife, it would be as if after all the family dysfunction for all those years, Abraham, now in old age, finally settles down and has a normal family. At this point, God's out of the picture. Abraham doesn't have a relationship with God anymore. But he has a normal life.

BHARATI: But is his perspective changed as a result of this harrowing and joyous journey? Or is he now just a middle-class householder?

LEW: We don't know. But what we do know from this story is that being chosen can be a burden and a pain in the neck.

GENE: Yes, there's an image that as a chosen one, you're privileged. Folks don't know that's just a small part of the story.

BILL: "Let this cup pass from me."

GENE: That's exactly right.

VII

THE TEST

DIANNE BERGANT • NORMAN J. COHEN

FRANCISCO O. GARCÍA-TRETO • P. K. McCARY

SEYYED HOSSEIN NASR • PHYLLIS TRIBLE

BURTON L. VISOTZKY

No story in Genesis asks harder questions. Would God make an unethical demand? Should we consider pious or crazy or both the father who puts a knife to the throat of his son because he's heard the voice of God telling him to do so? And why would the mother who waited so long and fought so fiercely for this child now fall silent as his life is threatened? Jews, Christians, and Muslims wrestle with these questions, because each of the great religions finds revelation for itself in the story of Abraham and the sacrifice.

—BILL MOYERS

Binding of Isaac, embroidered Torah mantle, Pfaffenhofen, Alsace, 1876

Now after these events it was
that God tested Avraham
and said to him:
Avraham!
He said:
Here I am
He said:
Pray take your son,
your only-one,
whom you love,
Yitzhak,
and go-you-forth to the land of Moriyya/Seeing,
and offer him up there as an offering-up
upon one of the mountains
that I will tell you of.
Avraham started-early in the morning,
he saddled his donkey,
he took his two serving-lads with him and Yitzhak his son,
he split wood for the offering-up
and arose and went to the place that God had told him of.
On the third day Avraham lifted up his eyes
and saw the place from afar.
Avraham said to his lads:
You stay here with the donkey,
and I and the lad will go yonder,
we will bow down and then return to you.
Avraham took the wood for the offering-up,
he placed them upon Yitzhak his son,
in his hand he took the fire and the knife.
Thus the two of them went together.
Yitzhak said to Avraham his father, he said:
Father!
He said:
Here I am, my son.
He said:
Here are the fire and the wood,
but where is the lamb for the offering-up?

Avraham said:
God will see-for-himself to the lamb for the offering-up,
my son.
Thus the two of them went together.
They came to the place that God had told him of;
there Avraham built the slaughter-site
and arranged the wood
and bound Yitzhak his son
and placed him on the slaughter-site atop the wood.
Avraham stretched out his hand,
he took the knife to slay his son.
But YHWH'*s messenger called to him from heaven*
and said:
Avraham! Avraham!
He said:
Here I am.
He said:
Do not stretch out your hand against the lad,
do not do anything to him!
For now I know
that you are in awe of God—
you have not withheld your son, your only-one, from me.
Avraham lifted up his eyes and saw:
there, a ram caught behind in the thicket by its horns!
Avraham went,
he took the ram
and offered it up as an offering-up in place of his son.
Avraham called the name of that place: YHWH *Sees.*
As the saying is today: On YHWH'*s mountain (it) is seen.*
Now YHWH'*s messenger called to Avraham a second time from*
*   heaven*
and said:
By myself I swear
*—*YHWH'*s utterance—*
indeed, because you have done this thing, have not withheld your
*   son, your only-one,*
indeed, I will bless you, bless you,

I will make your seed many, yes, many,
like the stars of the heavens and like the sand that is on the shore
of the sea . . .

Avraham returned to his lads,
they arose and went together to Be'er-Sheva.
And Avraham stayed in Be'er-Sheva.

Now Sara's life was one hundred years and twenty years and
*   seven years, (thus) the years of Sara's life.*
Sara died in Arba-Town, that is now Hevron, in the land of
*   Canaan.*

—excerpts from *The Five Books of Moses*
(Schocken Bible, Vol. I), Chapters 22 and 23

BILL: I'm intrigued by the structure of the story. It begins and ends with Abraham. Isaac appears, but dimly and passively. What's the narrator telling us?

DIANNE: There's another structure, too, that begins and ends not with Abraham, but with God. The story begins with God testing Abraham and ends with God blessing Abraham. Within that structure, we could ask, is this a story about Isaac? Is this a story about Abraham? Or is it a story about God?

NORMAN: When Abraham responds, "Here I am" to both God and Isaac, he uses the Hebrew word *hineini*, which is the word of response in relationship. Just the mere fact that Abraham uses the same word of response to the divine as he does to his son teaches us that when we respond to our child or husband or wife or parent, it's tantamount to responding to the divine in the world.

BILL: I'm struck in one translation by the repetition of that most poignant line: "And so the two of them walked on together."

NORMAN: The irony, of course, is that at the end of the story, when Abraham returns to Beersheba, the line is repeated—but in relation to his servants. Isaac is no longer there, and Abraham is walking together with the two servants. That's all he's left with at the end of the journey.

BURT: Not only does Isaac not come down the mountain with Abraham, but we're never shown another conversation between them. The next time you see them together, Isaac is burying his father—which, in some way, speaks of the horror the son has undergone at the hands of his father. When Abraham says, "Here I am" to his son, it means "Here I am with a knife in my hand, about to put it to your throat."

NORMAN: The rabbis say that at the climax of this story, as Abraham raises the knife and is about to take his son's life, tears drip from his eyes into Isaac's eyes, and Isaac's vision is impaired for the rest of his life. We know from the Jacob and Esau story that when Isaac is old, he has difficulty seeing. It's as if to say that the impact of the near-sacrifice on Isaac is so devastating that the way he sees the world is changed at that moment.

BILL: Later in the Bible there's a reference to "the God of Abraham and the terror of Isaac."

NORMAN: If we could only invite Isaac into our group and hear his voice! How would he recall the events on Moriah?

BURT: In one ninth-century commentary, the rabbis do give voice to Isaac. They show him as being much more involved in the binding itself, saying, "Now, be sure to tie me up tight because I'm really nervous, and if I tremble, and the knife slips, then the sacrifice will be improper. So tie me well." The rabbis also make Isaac much older than what I imagine from reading the story in the Torah. So he becomes a willing partner to the binding.

HOSSEIN: The Qur'an does not men-

tion the name of the son of Abraham offered for sacrifice, so early in Islamic history there was debate as to whether the son was Isaac or Ishmael. Later, Qur'anic commentators and religious authorities in general gravitated toward Ishmael. Putting that question aside, though, we have to remember that Isaac and Ishmael were prophets, and, as prophets, they did not have our ordinary human consciousness. To read our own reactions into what Isaac or Ishmael experienced would be to misunderstand what the heart of the story is. Isaac's or Ishmael's surrender to the will of God is no less than that of Abraham. Islam sees Isaac and Ishmael as being mature enough to understand that they have been brought into this world in a special manner to fulfill God's purpose. So, whichever son it was, he was willing to give himself in sacrifice.

BURT: The Hebrew term for prophet, *navi*, has the connotation or nuance of "madness." Sometimes you're imbued with God's spirit. But sometimes you're just insane. Every now and then someone comes along with a glint of madness in their eyes, and they wind up being great leaders. But most of the time, they lead us astray.

"As a parent . . . I'm horrified by this story."

BILL: This is such a short story. Most of what we want to know isn't there.

BURT: But we have the opportunity to flesh out the story. One way to flesh it out is to use the biblical record. For example, Isaac is a long-awaited son, born when Sarah is ninety and Abraham is one hundred. After waiting all that time to have a child, Abraham gets the command: "Kill your son." And then there's oral tradition. And then there's the modern filling in of the story. For example, we have this incredible story with the fierce mother, Sarah, absolutely silent. It's unbelievable that she could be silent, so we want to hear her voice, too. But it took us many years of telling this story until Sarah got a voice, which now modern readers are able to hear.

DIANNE: But is it Sarah's voice or the voice of the modern reader? If it's not someplace in the story, it's a kind of ventriloquism. To talk about the reader's interpretation is to talk about the world in front of the text. But we could also look at the world of the ancient writer, the world behind the text. The world within the text is the fictive world. This matter of interpretation is what makes an African American reading or a South African reading or a Hispanic reading all such different kinds of reading. Readers bring different concerns to the text.

P.K.: Isn't that the beauty of the scriptures—that we're all on a personal journey, with our own interpretations? As a parent, for example, I'm horrified by this story.

Since my parents were strict disciplinarians, I understand why Isaac didn't resist. But, as a parent, I don't think I could have done what Abraham did.

BILL: Just taking the story as it appears

"If this were my test, I'd flunk it."

---

in the text, let me ask whether any of you have any problems with it.

FRANCISCO: I do because I think this is a terrifying story. As P.K. said, this is a God who, even if in the end He's not going to let you kill your child, is willing to put you and your child through this kind of trauma. When we pray in the Lord's Prayer, "Lead us not into temptation," this literally means, in Greek, "Do not bring us to the test." At the heart of my faith is the conviction that God would never put me in this situation. If this were my test, I'd flunk it. Besides, why does God need to test Abraham? In effect, Abraham's life is close to the end, and the promise has been set in motion with the birth of Isaac.

NORMAN: The question is: Who is testing whom here? As I read the account, it seems to me that the voice Abraham hears commanding him to sacrifice his own son is perhaps Abraham's own voice. It's Abraham's ego that needs to prove his fidelity and his faith to himself and the world. Maybe the point of the story is how Abraham comes to understand what God really wants. God doesn't *want* human sacrifice. Here we have Abraham, who's gone through trial after trial, the last of which has been the banishment of his son Ishmael. In every previous test, there's been some kind of promise from God that things would work out. But here, in contrast to all the other trials, there is no guarantee. In fact, the test is one that undermines the entire promise about the future because it involves the sacrifice of Abraham's son. How could this possibly be what God wants?

D I A N N E : The text points to two gods. For the first part of the story, the word used is *Elohim*. As soon as there is the intervention, the divine name is used.

B I L L : Are you suggesting that perhaps it wasn't God Who commanded that Isaac be sacrificed?

Sacrifice of Isaac (detail from Sarcophagus of Consular Junius Bassus), St. Peter's Basilica, Rome, 359

PHYLLIS: No, this story is terrifying precisely because it is God Who sets up the test.

HOSSEIN: A verse in the Qur'an says that God puts you in this world in order to test you. The whole of life is a test. The test that Abraham is put through is the supreme test. The question is: How can we attain the faith of Abraham that we do not possess? Today most people would not associate the death of a child by cancer with the trial of Abraham. But if we understand a premodern cosmology, according to which God acts in human life, then this story serves to enable us to face the most difficult tasks of life, which are like losing one's own son.

BILL: But this is God once again directly putting Abraham through the test. Every time Abraham has been tested, he passes the test. Surely, by now, God knows that Abraham is steadfast in his faith. Why keep testing him?

HOSSEIN: But the test is not the only issue. Abraham must act as a perfect exemplar for all the problems monotheists face. The question is not whether Abraham is perfect in the eyes of God, but how God creates a perfect exemplar for us.

BURT: Throughout the Middle Ages, persecuted Jewish communities found a great deal of solace in this story. As their children were slaughtered, they imagined themselves as Abraham's descendants. They knew this was the way it was to be, and if they could submit to God with Abraham's perfect will, they were okay, and the tragedy of their life was redeemed. I was in college during the Vietnam War, and, as a result, grew up with a very deep resentment of fathers sending their sons off to be killed. Virtually all of us in rabbinical school reacted the same way to the story of the binding of Isaac—that if this was a test of Abraham, Abraham failed the test. One fellow, a poet named Danny Siegel, wrote a poem that ended, ''I liked it better thinking Father Abraham had said, 'Forget it, Isaac, let's go home.' '' If the story taught us anything, it was not the power to submit, but the power to resist that voice. Notice that in the chapters after the binding of Isaac, Abraham doesn't speak to God. We have a very different Abraham, one who is almost the archetypal family person, who mourns for Sarah, who tries to find a wife for Isaac, and who remarries and has six more children.

''I was in college during the Vietnam War, and . . . grew up with a very deep resentment of fathers sending their sons off to be killed.''

BILL: Why does God put these three people through all this torture?

PHYLLIS: It's not just that Abraham has to learn something, but God has to learn something, too. At the end, God says, "Now I know that."

BILL: God says, "Now I know that you fear God." But don't you think God knew that already?

PHYLLIS: The Bible carries this terrifying note about God as a tester. But the God Who tests is, at the same time, the God Who provides. God will provide the burnt offering. When God calls Abraham at the beginning of the story, God says, "Break with your past," which is something you don't ask of people in ancient cultures. Now, in this story, God says, "Break with your future." Break with your future by sacrificing Isaac, who is the future.

BURT: So what does God learn? What does God need to know?

PHYLLIS: My understanding is that the story has to do with idolatry—the idolatry of the son. Once God has given the gift of Isaac to Abraham, does Abraham focus on Isaac and forget the Giver? The climactic line is "Now I know that you worship God," with the implied "and that you do not worship your son." If we borrow categories from Zen Buddhism, we can see how the story moves through three levels: attachment, detachment, and nonattachment. Abraham is so attached to this child that the issue of idolatry becomes acute for God.

BURT: So is God jealous?

PHYLLIS: It's not a matter of God's jealousy; it's a matter of what is the nature of faith.

NORMAN: I don't think the biblical text tells us how Abraham feels about Isaac at all. In fact, attachment is more apparent in Abraham's relationship with Ishmael, with whom he's lived for at least a score of years. For example, when Abraham banishes Ishmael and Hagar, the text states, "This was terrible in Abraham's eyes because of his son." The rabbis stress that this was the most difficult moment in Abraham's life.

PHYLLIS: But the text says, "Your son, whom you love"—so it does tell us. He loves Isaac.

NORMAN: One could say Abraham loves Ishmael as well. I think, though, idolatry has more to do with Abraham himself and with the promise of future greatness. Abraham has a sense of self from which he has to learn to detach. It's the ego of Abraham that has to be sacrificed on that mountain so that Abraham can come back to the reality of who he is in relationship to God.

"It's the ego of Abraham that has to be sacrificed on that mountain."

Sacrifice of Isaac, Coptic textile, 7th c.

P . K . : When I look at Abraham, I see a man who lies because he is afraid that someone will take his wife away from him and he might lose his life. He seems to be fearful in a lot of ways. When Sarah tells him to sleep with her maid, he says, "Okay, I'll do that." Then when Sarah says, "Now you favor my maid too much," he says, "Do what you want to with her." He is so detached from emotional involvement in other people's feelings that he seems self-centered.

H OSSEIN : I don't think detachment is necessarily identified with selfishness. From a spiritual point of view, detachment precisely goes against selfishness. God is the sacred, and the sacred has the right to ask of us all that we are. This is something that modern people have forgotten. We give ourselves only partially to the sacred. We don't want to give our whole being. One way of giving oneself totally to the sacred, to God, is to be detached from everything. One of the most important aspects of the story is God's demand that Abraham practice supreme detachment.

P HYLLIS : No, the model I'm presenting here is not detachment but nonattachment. Detachment—the opposite of attachment—is just the other side of the same problem. Detachment is the negative form of attachment. Nonattachment is what the sages called "the third eye" of nondualistic thinking. It is the relinquishing of both attachment and detachment. It is a transcendent mode of being in the world.

N ORMAN : From a Jewish perspective, it's specifically the attachment to human beings that is called for—living out our sense of God's presence in the world through our relationships with others. When Abraham is walking on the road to Moriah, he is a self-involved human being who has to prove his faith to God. Then he hears his son Isaac call him: "Father." That's the situation of every person on life's journey. Each of us has our own sense of destiny and universal purpose and profession. Then we hear the singular voice of our child or another loved one. That call is the call of God directing us back to the reality of relationship and what's important to the world.

HOSSEIN: But nonattachment doesn't rule out having mercy or generosity or love for others.

BURT: Aren't you distressed at the notion of a God Who would ask for something that is essentially a suspension of the ethical? Abraham has enough trouble with ethics from the beginning—we don't need God coming into the scene to say, "And while we're at it, go one step further and kill your son." Let's not forget that God worried about destroying Sodom and Gomorrah—and had to tell Abraham about it, in effect saying, "Argue with me about this."

BILL: Abraham did argue with God about Sodom and Gomorrah—but when God asks him to kill his own son, he's silent.

P.K.: Yes, he argued with God about something that doesn't seem to matter as much as his child. It's as if the intimate relationships he has aren't as important as the people in the rest of the world. Maybe it's a male-female thing. I don't think God would have asked the same of Sarah, knowing what her answer would be.

FRANCISCO: When we get to the point where we feel that God is calling us to give somebody else's life up, we're in bad trouble. There's no such thing as a theological suspension of the ethical. This is at the root of the worst things that religions have done.

"There's no such thing as a theological suspension of the ethical."

BILL: And many people who claim to hear a call from God sacrifice their families to their sense of mission.

FRANCISCO: Yes, and that's the ugly side of it.

HOSSEIN: But isn't there a difference between a God-centered and a human-centered view of reality? At the moment, because our civilization is very human-centered, we confuse ethics, as we usually understand ethics, with the whole of religion. We have a lot of trouble with those aspects of the Bible that are not human-centered, or that are against our humanistic sensibilities. In Islam, one of the names of God is "the person who uses ruses" to bring about certain situations in the world. God is the best of those who can trick you. Now, if we just use a purely human-based understanding of morality, we're left with a horrible view of the divine nature. But if we understand, metaphysically, that only God is real, we are already aware that we are living in a world woven with elements of trickery, of illusion.

BURT: Theologically, there's a lot to be said for your point of view. But we have to live our lives every day, and how we live is often divorced from our experience of the divine—I think in healthy ways. An agreed-upon ethical system that works for the betterment of the community, almost independent of God, may promote better community than an exclusivist or aggressive notion of a trickster God Who commands you to kill your children. You know, as a rabbi, I'm very visible in a Jewish community. It means one thing to me—but it means something entirely different to my children. It's not fun for my kids to be "preacher's kids." It puts difficult burdens on them. In some ways, the Abraham–Isaac story exemplifies this situation. My personal relationship with God—my career path with God, if you will—makes demands on my family that may be very unreasonable.

PHYLLIS: That's one reason this story is so terrifying to all of us—because at some level, we all suspect that we've been sacrificed by our parents. And if we're parents, we fear that we'll do the same thing to our children. Parents are always sacrificing their children. Burt, you say you're sacrificing your children to your status as a rabbi. Other parents sacrifice their children to other ambitions, to success, to their pride, to whatever. That's one reason a lot of people hate this story.

NORMAN: The text says that Abraham lays the wood upon Isaac. I'm always caught by that image of Isaac himself bearing the burden of the journey up the mountain. Yes, our own children bear our burdens, too. I can just picture the time when our kids were little, and I would come home from a long day at the office, walking in at seven-thirty at night, and seeing our youngest son standing by the door, just waiting for me to come home. He would say, "Daddy, do you have fifteen minutes to watch the basketball game with me?" He was really saying, "When all is said and done, where are you for me? Am I not important in your life?"

BILL: I spent the first seven years of the lives of my three children caught up in the vortex of Washington. I thought that was the way it was and so paid very little attention to the needs of those children. Much later, I saw what a hole that lack of attention had left in our relationship. But, having said that, aren't we a long way from what Hossein was saying—that we're concerned with ourselves and our children and our needs and careers and passions, when God is concerned only with whatever God is concerned with. And if it takes this sacrifice to achieve God's mission, so be it.

HOSSEIN: Yes, because from a religious point of view, what is our purpose in

"The purpose of human life is the life beyond this world—to return to God."

this world? So what if we have forty-five thousand more generations and they are very happy people who live and die and are buried, and then one day the earth collapses or is hit by a meteor? The purpose of human life is the life beyond this world—to return to God. The life of this world has value only to the extent that it points us to God. Otherwise, I cannot understand the logic of religion at all.

BILL: What I hear God telling Abraham is "Only I deserve your love. Show me you love me more than you love your son." Is this story telling us that when a command comes from God, we do it, no matter what? Isn't that simply blind faith?

DIANNE: Yes, that's one thing the story tells us. In many ways, the story of the binding of Isaac is similar to the Book of Job—both are tests of faith. But it's interesting that whenever the biblical storyteller wants to show human beings rising to almost superhuman dimensions, God does not look good in the story.

BURT: When I read this story, I'm reminded of something Groucho Marx once said about not wanting to be a member of any club who would have people like him as members. I'm not sure I want to be involved with a God Who makes these kinds of demands on me. That's very different from what Hossein would say, I think. The Muslim submits—but I resist. If faith is being tested here, it's a kind of faith I don't want to subscribe to. I prefer to think that God demands a faith that calls for the intellect to be engaged rather than one that just says, "Yes, Sir."

FRANCISCO: Isn't the real question here not whether you would do something if God asked, but how do you know it's God? One of the few tests as to whether or not this is God is whether the command makes sense in ethical terms. I think this story fails that test. What kind of God would ask me to kill my son?

"What kind of God would ask me to kill my son?"

BILL: The story is very clear—this is God speaking.

FRANCISCO: But imagine someone today killing a child and then saying, "God told me to do it."

BURT: People do it all the time.

FRANCISCO: But what do we do with those people?

BURT: We lock them up.

DIANNE: But the child is not killed here. The test is "Jump and trust that I will catch you."

FRANCISCO: No, the test is "Throw Isaac and trust—" That's a very different command.

Abraham's Sacrifice of Ishmael, from Timurid ms., Herat, Islamic, 1410–11

BURT: Isaac may not be killed in this story, but he is very profoundly abused. This is a child whose father has taken a knife to his throat. If this is a test of Abraham's faith, what does it say about the next generation? What kind of faith must Isaac have as a result of this experience? What kind of relationship could Isaac have with God, let alone with his father?

HOSSEIN: It's really remarkable how different the Islamic understanding of this story is from what I'm hearing right now. Isaac—or Ishmael—is seen as a prophet who participates in this sacrifice of his own free will, not as an abused child. In Arabic, the most important title of Abraham is *Al-halil*, which means "the friend." Abraham is the supreme friend of God. Where he is buried today is called *Halil*, which to Islamic mystics not only implies friendship but also means "to be impregnated by the presence of Allah." When we ask, "How can we believe in a God who asks us to do something that is unethical?" we also have to ask, "Where do we get our ethical norms?" If we have a source of ethical knowledge that is independent of God, then we're not living in the biblical or Qur'anic world. Every day, after the evening prayer, Sunni Muslims say the prayer of Abraham. This whole event of the binding of Isaac—or Ishmael, in the Islamic world— has to do with the intimacy of one of God's creatures with God.

NORMAN: If religion leads to human suffering and self-denial, then it's not a religion of which I want to be a part. The feeling of being impregnated with God's spirit can lead to the Jonestown massacre, the Inquisition, the Holocaust—you name it. The result is human misery. Ultimately, religion has to lead us to life-enhancing relationships with human beings through our relationship with God.

BILL: Maybe Abraham has just resigned himself to the test. Maybe he's learned that no matter what our response, God will have His way.

BURT: That's a real issue. For example, when God tells Abraham that Sodom and Gomorrah will be destroyed, Abraham says, "Here I am, dust and ashes, but I can't let this happen. You can't destroy a city if there are fifty righteous people in it." And then slowly, he bargains God down. But in the end, God still nukes the city. Maybe a very sad aftermath to the story of Sodom and Gomorrah is that Abraham learns that it's fruitless to argue with God's will. God's will be done. End of story. So why argue? Just submit.

BILL: In these stories, God tests His people over and over again. He never seems satisfied.

HOSSEIN: Yes, and the Qur'an says explicitly that the purpose of human life is to have the faith God has given us be tested through the free will we have.

BILL: How much free will do you think God recognizes?

HOSSEIN: That's a very theological question. Free will is not partial, just as you can't be partly pregnant. You're either pregnant or not. You're either free or not free. The sage Ibn 'Arabi says that Abraham did not say no to God because he was God's real friend, and he would never say no to a friend.

BILL: If you say that this story brings the whole saga of Abraham to a climax around the question of faith, what, then, is faith?

P.K.: There's an old Baptist hymn that says, "God may not come when we want Him to, but He always comes on time." Faith is knowing that even though we may not see it, it will happen. Somebody asked me, "How do you teach a child to have faith, or teach a child that God will work in his life?"—which is what I think faith is. To teach faith is not to teach some far-off, down-the-road lottery kind of thing about what God will do. It's to get to know that child and find out where God has already worked in its life. Most people don't know God because they think God is far off. Abraham was a man who talked with God. Unless we're quiet about it, if we talk to God, other than in prayer, people think we're crazy.

PHYLLIS: There's another old Baptist hymn that talks about "standing on the promises of God." That's often presented as a model of faith. I juxtapose this hymn with my understanding of the Isaac story because I think the Isaac story is about letting go of the promises of God. That is the radicality of the faith in that story. It is ironic that we should think about this story in terms of blind faith. Putting that adjective "blind" in front of faith demeans faith. Faith is not blindness, faith is sight. Faith is insight. Throughout this story we find the Hebrew verb "to see." In one of the climactic lines of Abraham, translated "God will provide," the Hebrew original says, "God will see." So it is not a blind faith, even though it is a radical one.

BILL: If Abraham's faith is radical rather than blind, in what sense is it radical?

PHYLLIS: What's radical is the willingness to give up even the promises of God—which is a testing of God.

BURT: Phyllis, I couldn't disagree more about this because when all is said and done, somebody comes out of this test blind—Isaac. There's really a victim here.

BILL: You're saying he's literally blinded?

BURT: Yes, the son ends up blind. But let me sympathize with Abraham for a minute. Here is a man who has gone through an enormous disruption in his life. He's moved from his homeland. He's survived two famines. He's had all this trouble with his wife having children, even though God has promised him offspring—as many as the sands of the seas, the stars in the sky. He had one son, but God sent that one away. Now he's got this one son, Isaac, and God says, "Kill him." There's something unconscionable about the way God toys with Abraham. This is something far beyond just a test of faith.

DIANNE: Not every historical narrative is really about the past. Sometimes the story is told in such a way precisely to emphasize something of the present. I think biblical stories should be read with more attention given to those hearing or reading the story than to characters within the story itself, whether those hearers or readers are the audience of the biblical author or a contemporary audience. Historical information is important in order to understand, as best we can, the point being made. But if we believe that the Bible is scripture or revelatory for us, we must be attentive to what it is saying to us today. What an ancient world heard as "good news" might sound like "bad news" to modern ears.

NORMAN: Although the story is shaped to speak to its time and place, it also speaks to us. We are forced to ask, "Who is Abraham at this moment, and what is God

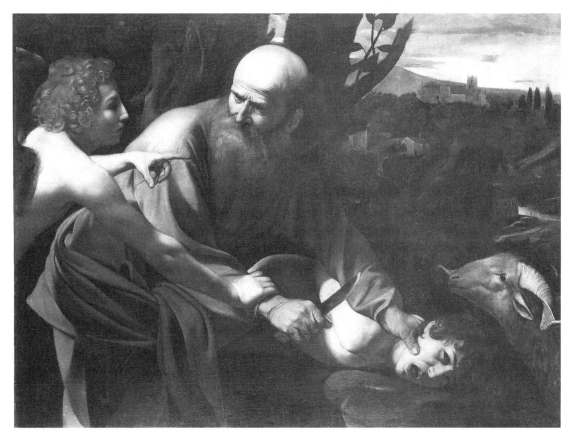

Caravaggio, *Sacrifice of Isaac*, 1603

demanding of him?'' This test is set apart from all the others that Abraham faced. In all the others, there was a guarantee that the promise God had made to Abraham and the future would be upheld. But this is the last test because if Isaac's life is lost, life has lost its value.

FRANCISCO: The only way I can see religious meaning in this story is to look at it from God's point of view. From this perspective, the story has to do with that moment where you approach the mystery, where you as a human being lose yourself to become impregnated by God. However, when we look at this story ethically, it becomes very troubling because it does have to do with the theological suspension of the ethical. It does indeed say to a father, ''Kill your son.'' It does indeed say to a believer, ''Be ready to cause the death of another human being for God.'' The main problem is that this is one of those stories that is meant to be used not religiously, but mystically. Mystics have a tendency to use outrageous symbols. For example, drunkenness is forbidden in Islam. But it is the major symbol that the mystical tradition in Islam uses for becoming one with God.

BILL: But if you take this as a religious story, as I do, it says something that modern American Christians are loathe to say— that love and devotion to God bring with it terror and trauma.

PHYLLIS: The cruelty of God is something from which the Bible does not flinch, whether it's Genesis or Job or Jeremiah—

> ''The cruelty of God is something from which the Bible does not flinch.''

BILL: —or Jesus, where God actually put His son on the cross to bleed in agony for other people. This is a God Who would save us by doing that to a human being?

PHYLLIS: As we've said, it's not a good idea to make this into an ethical story, a ''should'' story. But it is very much alive as a descriptive story. This is the human predicament, and this is how God is perceived. There is a terror in God's mysteriousness and inscrutability.

BILL: Crucifixion, Holocaust, suffering, loss, pain—are all of these at the heart of religion and revelation?

HOSSEIN: They are at the heart of human existence. You cannot exist in this world without these tragedies. Religion tries to make sense of them, but making sense is not always at a single level. But while this is not a ''should'' story on the level of external ethics, it is one on the level of mystical understanding. On the mystical level, Isaac—or Ishmael—is really our carnal, passionate soul, that must be sacrificed before the altar of divine reality in order for us to really be a friend of God. (And this interpretation does not contradict the understanding of Isaac and Ishmael as prophets.) Our passionate soul is that which disperses, that which separates, that which fights against the truth. It is the source of all evil toward other human beings. Once you offer to sacrifice that soul to God, without flinching, God always gives you something better. He will not really kill you, but will transform your soul into that which is luminous—full of charity and love, and close to Him.

P . K . : In college we used to say, "If you let it go, and it comes back to you, it's yours. If it doesn't come back to you, it was never yours to begin with." One minister told me, "If you give with an open hand, you can receive and take out. But if your fists are clenched, nothing can get in or out."

D I A N N E : I think something happens in the story to cause Abraham to realize that what he thought was God's will was not God's will. Our theology shifts, and as we mature and our religious traditions mature, we change. For example, we discover that God does not want child sacrifices. We know Israel was involved in child sacrifice. We find evidence in the foundation of the city of Jericho, for example. It was the firstborn that was sacrificed. What we have here is a move from child sacrifice to substitutionary sacrifice. You don't sacrifice your child, you sacrifice an animal in place of the child.

P H Y L L I S : It has always tantalized people that Isaac does not return with Abraham. The fact that Abraham returns alone

has led to all kinds of rabbinic interpretations of what happened to Isaac. Was he, in fact, sacrificed? I think the absence of Isaac at the end is a way of saying that if Abraham is willing to sacrifice the child, that does not give Abraham a license to reattach himself to that child. Later he establishes a new relationship to that child, treating him as an adult and finding the right wife for him.

B I L L : Why is Sarah missing from this story?

P H Y L L I S : Some years ago, when I began looking at this story from a feminist perspective, I asked myself, "What evidence do we have that Abraham really loved Isaac that much?" I went back and looked at the chapters that preceded this story and saw no evidence of Abraham's attachment to Isaac. In fact, the evidence is that he had the attachment to Ishmael, not to Isaac. So then I asked myself, "Who has the attachment to Isaac?" And the answer is clear. It's Sarah. In the preceding stories, it's Sarah who says, "My son, Isaac." Abraham never says, "My son, Isaac." But he does refer to Ishmael as his son. God sides with Sarah, telling Abraham, "Do what Sarah tells you." The last words we hear from Sarah's lips are "Cast out this slave woman and her son. For the son of this slave woman will not be heir with my son, with Isaac." Once the future is secured through Isaac, there's no more need for Sarah. She dies, without being healed of *her* attachment to Isaac, which has led her to be tyrannical, malicious, and mean-spirited. But let me also put in a good word for Sarah. Both Hagar and Sarah are trapped in patriarchy. And patriarchy has only two places for women. One is the pedestal, and the other is the doormat or gutter. Hagar occupies one of those two places, and Sarah occupies the other. As the woman on the pedestal, Sarah has certain privileges and rights, which allow her to lord it over the woman in the gutter. Now if, instead of Abraham, Sarah had been the chief character, she would have been healed of this attachment to Isaac. By offering to sacrifice him, she would have become capable of nonattachment, and God would have said, "Now I know you fear God." This healing would then have opened up the possibility of a healing between Sarah and Hagar. Now, P.K., you know better than I—but don't African American women see themselves as daughters of Hagar?

P.K.: Right, absolutely.

PHYLLIS: And they see Sarah as the model for the white woman who has abused them. And we know that Arab women identify with Hagar, too, while Jewish women identify with Sarah. Through the ages, this tension has never been resolved. Now here is a story that has the potential to begin a healing process if we, the readers, make the proper appropriation. We don't simply decide from the outside to appropriate the story that way—the story itself gives us permission to do so by saying from the beginning that Sarah, not Abraham, has the attachment to Isaac.

NORMAN: Yet the moment Isaac calls out, "Father," and Abraham answers,

"Here I am, my son," the relationship between the two changes. There begins a bonding of Abraham with Isaac. The irony is, of course, that they never speak again. When Sarah dies, she too is removed from Abraham. When she dies, what I hear her saying is "If this God of Abraham is a God that requires the death of Isaac, I want out."

BILL: Maybe she's the one who says, "Enough. You ask too much."

NORMAN: Her death is a commentary on the sense of powerlessness that we ourselves feel in the presence of a God who demands the taking of life and human suffering.

BURT: Preachers in the fourth and fifth centuries actually gave Sarah a voice in verse homilies. The voice they gave her is not of a woman who says, "I opt out." Quite the contrary. It's a voice neither of the pedestal nor of the gutter. It's a voice that has Sarah take her place as the mother of faith, as an equal to Abraham. In these verse homilies, Sarah finds out that Abraham is about to go off to sacrifice Isaac. She knows immediately what's going on. She says, "I know you. You're drunk with God. And if you're going to do this, I'm going to be an equal partner. I'll dig up the dirt and make the altar. Let my hair be the binding to tie up Isaac." She recognizes her own attachment to Isaac and recognizes that it is a disservice to her relationship to God.

PHYLLIS: We have one more detail about the attachment of mother and son.

Sacrifice of Isaac, copper circumcision plate, Western Europe, 1653

When Isaac marries Rebekah, we have the words "And Isaac was comforted with Rebekah for the death of his mother, Sarah."

BURT: And when Isaac marries, he moves not into his father's tent, but into his mother's tent.

DIANNE: Sarah is really the prime example of how women are victimized in the patriarchy. First, she is barren, which automatically makes her pointless in that kind of society. Then she gets a son through a maidservant, but when she has her own son, she can't afford to have a rival to her son, not only for his sake, but for her own social security. Her son must care for her if her husband dies.

BURT: The Bible tells us that yes, there is patriarchy, but there are also strong women who, despite patriarchy, serve as instruments of God's will.

DIANNE: Yes, but even though they're strong, they serve patriarchal ends.

P.K.: I always got the impression from the story that Sarah was left out of the plans for Isaac's sacrifice and that Abraham just sneaked out early one morning.

BILL: Maybe he left early because Mount Moriah was a long way away—or maybe because he knew what would happen if Sarah caught up with him.

NORMAN: Perhaps by evading Sarah, he's evading the parent in himself who loves this child.

FRANCISCO: Yes, because don't you think that if God said, "Sacrifice your son" to a mother, the mother would say, "Get lost!"? I think that's what Sarah would have said.

P.K.: I was always taught that the story of Abraham and Isaac was really the story of God's ultimate sacrifice for us as Christians, when God sacrificed His only son, and that it was intended to help us understand just how big and meaningful God's sacrifice really is. Even so, I think that the taking of human life is probably the biggest problem we have with this story. War, for example, involves the sacrifice not only of soldiers, but of children and other innocent people. And wars are created by one or two or a group of men who have nothing to do with the rest of us. That seems like what God is doing in this story. What God is doing really has nothing to do with us—it's simply God's own ego.

BURT: In the New Testament, Isaac bound on the altar is quite explicitly seen as a type of Christ.

BILL: "As Abraham did not withhold his son, Isaac, so God did not withhold His son."

BURT: The Jews, of course, see themselves as Isaac bound upon the altar. In one medieval midrash, the rabbis actually have Isaac die and be resurrected because they understood this was the way of the Jewish community. It was literally under the knife, caught between Christianity and Islam. But the Jews had faith that God would not abandon them. And here we are, a thousand years later, still talking about this story. In Islam, there is confusion about who the son is—but it almost doesn't make a difference whether it's Isaac or Ishmael. That fact is that Muslims imagine themselves to be the son of Abraham, who was bound on the altar, just as the Jews do.

BILL: Elie Wiesel says that it's ironic that this most tragic of Jewish ancestors has a name that in Hebrew means "laughing," and that God would use as an instrument of His purpose someone who is able, in the face of this horror, to laugh and to go on laughing.

NORMAN: There are two instances in the text where laughter is mentioned. When Abraham and Sarah are told of the impending birth of Isaac, they both laugh. It's a derisive, perhaps a mocking laughter. How is it possible, given their ages? And then, when Isaac is born, Sarah says, "You made laughter for me. Everyone who hears will laugh not at me, but with me." This is an affirming laughter, a rejoicing laughter. On one level, the two laughters describe the test of the Jewish people. In the face of despair, downtroddenness, and persecution, is it possible to master the art of laughter, to have hope and affirm the goodness of life? Then, on a personal level, when our faith is tested, and we despair because the future seems to be lost, is it possible to be optimistic?

BILL: But life is absurd enough without God making it more absurd.

DIANNE: *Israel* means "I have struggled with the Lord."

BILL: What do you make of the fact that from the beginning, it's not just a struggle with God, but a conflict among the human beings in the story, and within the families in particular?—Adam and Eve disagree, Cain slays Abel, Sarah casts out Hagar,

Isaac blesses the wrong son, Jacob plays favorites among his sons.

NORMAN: The modern reader of the text should be able to see human beings struggling for self-definition and, in the context of family life, trying to come to grips with who they are and what they can possibly become. At the end of the Abraham story, what's become of his family? Sarah is about to die. Hagar is gone. Ishmael has been banished and never sees his father again. Isaac could have been killed. At that point, Abraham comes down from that mountain, and the rest of his life is lived within the context of family.

BILL: But that's a new family, a third family.

Sacrifice of Isaac, mosaic floor, Beth Alpha Synagogue, Heftsibah, Israel, 6th c.

BURT: That's what's scary to me. Is this story suggesting that only after Abraham stops having a relationship with God, only after God stops talking to him and testing him, only then can he settle into a normal family life?

NORMAN: I would translate it differently—Abraham finally understands that his relationship with God is prismed through the relationship he has with human beings.

BILL: Maybe he just says, "Enough, God. Look, You've played me like an organ long enough. I just want a quiet, peaceful old age." And he goes off and marries again and has a pleasant, uneventful life with his new family.

NORMAN: But there's more than that. When Sarah dies, the text says, "Abraham came to mourn for her and to cry for her." It seems redundant to mourn and to cry because if he's mourning, isn't he crying? In fact, if you look at the Hebrew text, one of the letters in the word "to cry for her" is written in miniature, as if it's asterisked. This is the first time Abraham has shown any kind of emotion for another human being.

BURT: Is this what the trial's about, then? Is God simply pushing Abraham to actually care for his family?

P.K.: Yes, it does seem as if Abraham could be pushed by fear or incensed about what's going to happen to people he didn't know personally, but that other than that, no one really touched him.

FRANCISCO: We've been talking about the Abrahamic family, which I think of as Judaism, Christianity, and Islam. One thing that's unique about these three religions is that their mythology is not about gods. Gods are predictable to a fault. You know what they're going to do—that's why people talk about the god of thunder, the god of fertility, or whatever. In these stories, God, the only God, has no other gods to play with, and so has to play with human beings. We humans are devilishly unpredictable and imperfect. Sometimes we rise to the occasion, and sometimes we don't, just like the people in these stories. That's why I think they're such terrible stories to use as religious myth—but at the same time, why they touch us so deeply and why they really hold truth for us.

BILL: You use the word "myth" in relation to these stories. A "myth," unlike a lie, which is untrue, can be true in very deep ways.

DIANNE: Yes, myth is not scientific and historical, but is a story that expresses truth in such a way that people from different points of view can recognize or identify with that truth.

BILL: It's another way of knowing.

HOSSEIN: *Mythos* complements our *logos*, our analytical, rational knowing.

PHYLLIS: We talk about how terrible this story is and how cruel God seems to be in it, and then we acknowledge that it comes out okay in the end because Isaac is not sacrificed. But there's another biblical story that we don't talk about. It too is a sacrifice story, but one in which the victim isn't saved. So this story of Isaac should be juxtaposed with the story of Jephtha's unnamed daughter. You tell me which is the more terrifying story. In the Jephtha story, Jephtha makes a vow, which is not required of him, and which God has nothing to do with, that if he wins a particular battle, he will sacrifice the first person who comes forth—and that happens to be his daughter. She is then sacrificed. God does not appear in that story. Does that make the story less terrible, or more terrible? In the Western tradition, we never take that story into the same account in which we hold the story of Abraham and Isaac. In the Orthodox Church, the two stories have been juxtaposed. For example, the paintings in St. Catherine's Monastery in Sinai juxtapose these two stories.

BURT: But the fact that God isn't there in the story of Jephtha's daughter has led commentators to conclude that this was no test whatsoever. Jephtha's vow was just incredibly stupid, and then, having made it, Jephtha was even more foolish to follow through and actually kill the girl.

P.K.: The sacrifice of Jephtha's daughter and the possible killing of Isaac are tragic to us— but maybe God doesn't look at death the same way we do.

DIANNE: But it isn't just the death of these individuals that's important, but the cutting off of the next generation. If Isaac is killed, so is the promise. And what does

"Maybe God doesn't look at death the same way we do."

Jephtha's daughter do when she hears she is to be sacrificed? She goes out to mourn her virginity—that she will have no progeny.

BURT: The ninth-century rabbis said in no uncertain terms that the story of Isaac teaches resurrection of the dead—that there's never a loss of progeny. Even when it seems that all future generations are cut off, God is with you, and there will be future progeny.

BILL: How does this story resonate in the Islamic tradition?

HOSSEIN: In the Qur'an, Abraham says explicitly that he has taken Ishmael to Mecca, near the house of the Lord. This is a house that is not mentioned in the Torah—the primordial house built by Adam, which Abraham rebuilds. In the creation of this new community, which is foundational to Islam, the role of Hagar is very central. So this is not a patriarchal story at all. To this day, half the rites performed each year by two million people in Mecca are based on what Abraham did. The other half are based on what Hagar did. It is she who ran from one hill to the other, looking for water for Ishmael, which is now emulated by what is called *sa'y* in Arabic, that is, a kind of hopping along between these two hills as part of the rite in Mecca. It is she who was looking for water for Ishmael when the angels came, and the water that gushed forth is now the Zamzam, the sacred water underneath the Ka'ba in Mecca, which all Muslims try to drink. But this whole episode, as many other episodes in the Qur'an, must be seen much more as the history of the soul than as only an external, sacred history. For example, why do we emulate the way Hagar ran between the two hills? Because that is not simply a historical event, but something that must be relived now within ourselves.

NORMAN: I agree that you can read the story on two levels, but it's really the human aspect of it that speaks to modern human beings. For example, when Isaac and Ishmael bury their father, we cannot help but ask, what do they feel about each other? They've shared a common experience of being outcast, banished, and nearly killed by their father. At that moment, we are Isaac and Ishmael, standing at that cave with our brother or sister, whom we haven't seen for twenty years—what do we say to each other? What do we feel about our parents? What life experiences have we shared that ultimately we can learn from? Somehow this is the crux of it for the modern person struggling to find out what it is to be a family member.

BURT: What look passes between Ishmael and Isaac as they bury their father? And it shouldn't be lost on us that Abraham's tomb is in Hebron. What must it be like now in Hebron, with Jews and Muslims looking at one another over literally thousands of graves? How many looks must pass between them before we realize that we are brothers? We have the same father, and we've got to get past a lot of bad history to get on with our faith together.

PHYLLIS: The crux of the problem is not the father but the mother—the conflict between Sarah and Hagar.

FRANCISCO: The first time I went to the mosque in Hebron, something happened that really gave me hope. Even though there were armed guards there all the time, there were both Jews and Muslims worshipping in the same building, the only place in the world where that was happening. Then, of course, the Hebron massacre happened.

BILL: So wouldn't you say that this is not yet a story with a redemptive end?

HOSSEIN: It might be—the end hasn't come yet.

BILL: How is it possible for Isaac to have faith after his experience on the mountain?

BURT: There's an Isaac in every family—it might be our child, or our own spouse.

BILL: Yes, but what happens to their faith?

NORMAN: Let me give you an example of testing and faith. Four years ago, our fifteen-year-old son was diagnosed with lymphocytic leukemia. I will remember, as long as I live, the first conversation I had with him in the pediatric oncology ward at Yale University Hospital. We were sitting on his bed after his testing, and he said, "Dad, they tell me there's an eighty percent cure rate for lymphocytic leukemia in children my age. But what if I'm in the other twenty percent?" Whatever faith he had was being tested in terms of the rationality of the world. How could he summon the strength to know that the world is not all bad, that there are forces for goodness and wholeness that are in him and that can be brought to the surface? Faith is the realization of this goodness that we can draw on so that we can continue living, even when faced with the greatest incoherence, the greatest despair.

"There's an Isaac in every family."

PHYLLIS: I have problems with the phrase "to have faith." Faith is not a possession to have but a mode of being in the world that is the realization that God provides. The story itself has an unresolved tension between the God Who tests and the God Who provides. We want it this way or that way, but the story doesn't allow that.

Donatello, *The Sacrifice of Isaac*, Campanile, Florence, 1420–21

FRANCISCO: Faith is more than a realization because sometimes it's hard to realize that God provides. Faith is a commitment you make.

DIANNE: When Job is struggling with God, he says at one point, "I knew of You in hearing of the word," which means, "I used to know *about* You, but now I know *You*." How did he come to know God? It was through struggling with disappointments, tragedy, violence, suffering, including the suffering of others. When I was little, I had an autograph book that my father signed with a poem that I know by heart: "It's easy enough to be happy/ when life flows along like a song/ but the one worthwhile is the one who can smile/ when everything goes dead wrong." In a sense, it's not just that faith is tested, but that it comes alive after the challenge.

FRANCISCO: One of my professors used to say, "The answer to the theodicy problem is not to think that God put us here to be happy. God put us here to make us good."

HOSSEIN: It's an interesting fact that until now, there's never been another civilization in which so many people have left religion because they see evil in the world. The traditional religions remember the word of Christ—that only God the One is good. Therefore, this world, not being God, cannot be good. The imperfection of the world was accepted as part of human existence. Then in the eighteenth and nineteenth centuries, with Marx, Hegel, and others, this idea of progress began to take hold. People began to think that this world was meant for happiness and goodness, and if there was not sufficient happiness or goodness in life, then there must be something wrong with God rather than with the nature of the world.

NORMAN: There's a rabbinic tradition that the ram Abraham sacrificed in place of Isaac had been there from the sixth day of creation. The vehicle for survival and redemption, in a sense, was programmed in from the very beginning. All Abraham had to do was to raise his eyes from the mundane and see it.

BILL: But, Norman, even that story presupposes that the nature of God requires something to suffer in order for God to be satisfied.

NORMAN: I don't read the story as God wanting humans to suffer. It's Abraham who has to give up his own ego needs so that ultimately he can come to his higher self, which is what God really wants, after all.

FRANCISCO: We have to live in an imperfect world. But within that world, we can appeal to a higher ethical or natural law, even against God, as Abraham did in the case of Sodom. I love the Jewish concept of *tikkun*, of correcting, perfecting, improving this imperfect world. In that process, we become human. In that process, we're faithful to God.

BURT: One of the ways Isaac finds his way back to faith is through realizing that his brother Ishmael has been through a similar experience. He finds faith only in re-building a community. I'm keenly sensitive to the fact that most of the time I study this story, I study it only with Jews. And here I am studying it with Christians and Mus-lims. You can't exist in a vacuum. You can't just be yourself and God. When you do that, you wind up like Abraham, a little crazy. You have to build a community. And as you build a community, all the members of the community get different aspects of revelation.

VIII

BLESSED DECEPTION

LEON R. KASS • STEPHEN MITCHELL

ELAINE H. PAGELS • NAOMI H. ROSENBLATT

JEAN-PIERRE M. RUIZ • MARIANNE MEYE

THOMPSON • ROBIN DARLING YOUNG

A willful mother plots with her favorite son to cheat his twin brother out of his inheritance by deceiving their blind father. It could be a Greek tragedy, or it could be a prime-time soap opera. But this story is from a text sacred to great religions and the deceit means that one son instead of the other becomes the founder of a great nation. The mother justifies the trickery because she has learned from a prophecy that her favorite son is the favorite of God, too, and she's determined to be the instrument by which the divine plan unfolds, no matter what it means to her husband, her other son, or their family values. The further we go into Genesis in this series of conversations, the closer we get to home.
Here now a Blessed Deception.

—BILL MOYERS

Bonifacio Bembo, *Rebecca Dressing Jacob*, San Agostino, Cremona, ca. 1450

Isaac prayed to the LORD *for his wife, because she was barren; and the* LORD *granted his prayer, and his wife Rebekah conceived. The children struggled together within her; and she said, "If it is to be this way, why do I live?" So she went to inquire of the* LORD. *And the* LORD *said to her, "Two nations are in your womb, and two peoples born of you shall be divided; the one shall be stronger than the other, the elder shall serve the younger."*

When her time to give birth was at hand, there were twins in her womb. The first came out red, all his body like a hairy mantle; so they named him Esau. Afterward his brother came out, with his hand gripping Esau's heel; so he was named Jacob. Isaac was sixty years old when she bore them. When the boys grew up, Esau was a skillful hunter, a man of the field, while Jacob was a quiet man, living in tents. Isaac loved Esau, because he was fond of game; but Rebekah loved Jacob . . .

When Isaac was old and his eyes were dim so that he could not see, he called his elder son Esau and said to him, "My son"; and he answered, "Here I am." He said, "See, I am old; I do not know the day of my death. Now then, take your weapons, your quiver and your bow, and go out to the field, and hunt game for me. Then prepare for me savory food, such as I like, and bring it to me to eat, so that I may bless you before I die."

Now Rebekah was listening when Isaac spoke to his son Esau. So when Esau went to the field to hunt for game and bring it, Rebekah said to her son Jacob, "I heard your father say to your brother Esau, 'Bring me game, and prepare for me savory food to eat, that I may bless you before the LORD *before I die.' Now therefore, my son, obey my word as I command you. Go to the flock, and get me two choice kids, so that I may prepare from them savory food for your father, such as he likes; and you shall take it to your father to eat, so that he may bless you before he dies." But Jacob said to his mother Rebekah, "Look, my brother Esau is a hairy man, and I am a man of smooth skin. Perhaps my father will feel me, and I shall seem to be mocking him, and bring a curse on myself and not a blessing." His mother said to him, "Let your curse be on me, my son; only obey my word, and go, get them for me." So he went and got them and brought them to his mother; and his mother prepared savory food, such as his father loved. Then Rebekah took the best garments of her elder son Esau, which were with her in the house, and put them on her younger son Jacob; and she put the skins of the kids on his hands and the smooth part of his neck. Then she handed the savory food, and the bread that she had prepared to her son Jacob . . .*

Abraham and Sarah, Russian icon, 17th c.

Elijah Pierce, *Sacrifice of Isaac*, 1952

Ibrahim About to Sacrifice His Son Ismail, Qisas al-Anbiya (Legends of the Prophets), Iran, 1577

The Sacrifice of Isaac, Gutenberg Bible, 1450–55

The Binding of Isaac, Torah mantle, Germany or Austria, 18th c.

Abraham, Catacomb of Priscilla, Rome, early Christian, 3rd c.

Braunschweiger Monogrammist,
Abraham's Sacrifice,
German, 16th c.

Charles McGee, *Noah's Ark: Genesis*, 1984

Noah's Ark, from *Histoire Universelle de la Création du Monde Jusqu'à César*, Kingdom of Jerusalem, 1260–70

Noah's Sons Covering His Nakedness,
Golden Haggadah, Spain, 14th c.

The Story of Noah, Morgan Old Testament, France, ca. 1250

Hugo Sperger, *Noah's Ark*, 1987

Emeterius and Ende, *The Ark Floats on a Rising Flood*, Beatus'
commentary on the Apocalypse, Spain, 970–75

Attributed to
Miskin, *Noah's Ark*,
India, Mughal,
ca. 1590

*But Isaac said to his son, "How is it that you have found it so quickly, my son?"
He answered, "Because the LORD your God granted me success . . ." Then he said,
"Bring it to me, that I may eat of my son's game and bless you." So he brought it
to him, and he ate; and he brought him wine, and he drank. Then his father Isaac
said to him, "Come near and kiss me, my son." So he came near and kissed him;
and he smelled the smell of his garments, and blessed him, and said, "Ah, the
smell of my son is like the smell of a field that the LORD has blessed . . ." As soon
as Isaac had finished blessing Jacob, when Jacob had scarcely gone out from the
presence of his father Isaac, his brother Esau came in from his hunting . . . His
father Isaac said to him, "Who are you?" He answered, "I am your firstborn son,
Esau." Then Isaac trembled violently, and said, "Who was it then that hunted
game and brought it to me, and I ate it all before you came, and I have blessed
him?—yes, and blessed he shall be!" When Esau heard his father's words, he cried
out with an exceedingly great and bitter cry, and said to his father, "Bless me, me
also, father . . . !"*

*Now Esau hated Jacob because of the blessing with which his father had blessed
him, and Esau said to himself, "The days of mourning for my father are ap-
proaching; then I will kill my brother Jacob." But the words of her elder son Esau
were told to Rebekah; so she sent and called her younger son Jacob and said to
him, "Your brother Esau is consoling himself by planning to kill you. Now therefore, my son, obey my voice; flee at once to my brother Laban in Haran, and stay
with him a while, until your brother's fury turns away—until your brother's
anger against you turns away, and he forgets what you have done to him; then I
will send, and bring you back from there. Why should I lose both of you in one
day?"*

—excerpts from *New Revised Standard Version*
(*The Holy Bible*), Chapters 25 and 27

BILL: This seems to be a story of a mother-and-son team of con artists, who connive through trickery and deceit to cheat a blind man and his oldest son out of the family blessing. Does this story make you queasy?

MARIANNE: Yes, because even though God told Rebekah that the younger son, rather than the older son, would be the heir, making this happen through deceiving an old, infirm man and cheating the older brother is puzzling. You can't help being moved by Esau's cry of grief when he learns that he has been disenfranchised from the blessing. But when I look at the entire narrative, I'm not so much bothered as intrigued by the way God's purpose is hinted at, both in the selection of Rebekah as the wife of Isaac and in the somewhat mysterious oracle to Rebekah during her very difficult pregnancy. The characters who are most responsive to God's somewhat obscure promises are the ones who advance His purpose—and they advance it by the only ways open to them as human beings, which sometimes involves stratagems that might make us a little queasy.

STEPHEN: The story must have made very early readers queasy, too, because the section about the oracle is an insertion, added by the redactor. You can see how upset that secondary writer must have been—he authorizes Rebekah's choice by putting God on her side. Without the oracle, it's a story of how Rebekah loved Jacob, and Isaac loved Esau—the God character isn't even involved. Originally, it's a much clearer, more powerful story. That's why, in my translation of Genesis, I leave out the inserted section. I stick it at the end, in the notes.

MARIANNE: But if the section were really added later, why didn't the writer simply leave the story out or clean it up in a way that makes Jacob or Rebekah look better? There's an acceptance of these characters, warts and all, and God chooses and works through and with them. That seems to be the writer's point. He doesn't need to make the characters look better.

BILL: Why not? This is a story about the founding of a people. When I was growing up, all the stories about George Washington stressed his confession about cutting down the cherry tree, but never mentioned that he owned slaves. If Jacob and Esau had been in American folklore, they would have been six feet tall with heroic virtues and an aura all around them. But that's not what we have in this story.

JEAN-PIERRE: The story raises a very hard question: How can this kind of behavior fit into the plan of God for a people?

NAOMI: God has a vision of what He wants, but He doesn't tell Rebekah how to carry it out. Maybe Rebekah could have brought about God's vision in a different way.

BILL: Do you think it matters to God that the blessing was passed on through deception?

LEON: There's no alternative at this point. Isaac, for whatever reason, prefers Esau. Esau is a man's man, a knowing hunter, a man of the field. He has a kind of immediacy and strength. Jacob is a quiet boy, hanging around his mother and the house. Esau goes off and finds two wives. Jacob is not even interested in women, as far as we know. But Esau is the wrong son for perpetuating the covenant, as is shown by a number of indications in the story. What is Rebekah to do? She's not going to say to Isaac, "Let's go see the marriage counselor." She uses the only means at her disposal, which is a kind of guile. At the start, Isaac says, "Bring me food so that *I* may eat and *my soul* may bless you before I die." He speaks as if something is working through him, unbeknownst to himself. By the end of the story, Isaac himself understands the rightness of what has happened and freely blesses Jacob (again) as his rightful heir.

ROBIN: Sometimes God's plot seems to be advanced by deception, by stepping outside the apparent borders of what is acceptable so that life may go on.

> *"Sometimes God's plot seems to be advanced by deception, by stepping outside the apparent borders of what is acceptable so that life may go on."*

STEPHEN: But what would you do if your children came to you and said, "What does this story teach us? Is it okay to be deceitful?"

MARIANNE: It's okay in some situations. Wouldn't you lie to protect someone you know? Many Christians hid Jews during the Holocaust and then lied, saying there was no one else in the house.

STEPHEN: That's different! Here it's for personal gain.

ELAINE: Abraham and Isaac both lie about their wives. The stories suggest that since they are in a less powerful position than the neighboring rulers, their deception is a matter of survival.

LEON: If this were a story by Machiavelli, we would think nothing of the deception because necessity requires it. But the Bible tells you by subsequent stories that even if the deception is necessary, it's unsavory, and you pay for it. Rebekah figures out a way through a very bad situation in a male-dominated world. Sometimes harsh confrontation is not the most loving way. I would even argue that Rebekah gives Isaac a gift in this deception, in that she enables him to see. He's been blind a long time—not just dim of sight, but blind to the question of his own sons and what it is only his place to transmit. Thanks to this deception, he now behaves in the last scene like a true patriarch.

JEAN-PIERRE: Yet I wonder whether, in fact, Rebekah doesn't lead the situation closer to the brink of the Cain and Abel disaster through her deception.

LEON: But the situation as it is, with Esau about to receive the blessing, has to be fixed.

STEPHEN: The desire to fix things causes huge problems. The wiser way is to trust the intelligence of this universe and the justice of God—to trust that things as they are, are very good, and it's possible to make things right by letting them happen in their own way. The problems that are caused by rushing in and fixing things go down from generation to generation. This is a very honest story about how people cause one another great pain.

> *"The problems that are caused by rushing in and fixing things go down from generation to generation."*

BILL: Do you think you would ever overstep boundaries to get what you want?

STEPHEN: No.

BILL: So you couldn't be standing beside Rebekah.

STEPHEN: Well, she might have tried speaking honestly to her husband. But deceit? I would never do that, no.

NAOMI: I'm overcome with compassion for her. I really love Rebekah for the struggles and suffering she went through.

STEPHEN: What moves me about Rebekah is her response to Jacob's statement:

"What if my father touches me and discovers the trick? I will bring a curse on myself, not a blessing." And she says, "Let the curse be on me, my son."

BILL: Why is Rebekah chosen? What's singular about her?

NAOMI: By marrying into the family, Rebekah takes on the responsibility of making sure that the covenant that was struck between God and Abraham and Sarah keeps its vitality and goes on to the next generation. It's a very fragile, new idea that she has to transmit, and she has to decide between these two boys, neither of whom is a saint or a sinner.

BILL: These boys are the grandsons of Abraham, the founding patriarch, so at this point in Genesis, we are still in the early stage of the story of the people of Israel.

JEAN-PIERRE: Yes, and we're teetering on the brink of disaster here. Rebekah has been blessed with the words "May you, our sister, become thousands of myriads. May your offspring gain possession of the gates of their foes." But up until this surprising pregnancy, the blessing has not had any effect, and she's had no children.

MARIANNE: And when she does get pregnant, she discovers that her children clash. They're already fighting with each other in the womb.

BILL: What about the question Rebekah asks when she feels the strife in her womb?

Birth of Jacob and Esau (left); *Esau Brings Rabbit to Isaac and Rebecca*, A Book of Hours, Moravia, 13th c. (right)

She says, "If this is how it is with me, what does it mean?"

JEAN-PIERRE: It's a difficult sentence, translated in very different ways. She's asking about her place, and she's asking about a struggle that's taking place within her and that she's going to have to shape in relation to the future. She asks, "Why is this happening to me? How do I fit in?"

ROBIN: In many ways, Rebekah is an echo of Eve, particularly in enduring the fratricidal rage of her two children. In effect, too, she is the mother of all the living, although she is the mother of the living of the nation. If we leave out the oracle, the divine part, we might miss some of the connections. For example, it's quite significant that Rebekah is the one who puts the skins on Jacob's hands and neck so that he can pass for Esau. And certainly, when he gives the meal to Isaac, there's a connection to the story of the sacrifice of Abel and its being acceptable to a father.

STEPHEN: There's another connection between this story and the story of Cain and Abel. Much of the suffering in families from one generation to the next is caused by the preference of the parents for one child over another. You could say that the cause of the first murder was that God preferred Abel and didn't accept Cain's sacrifice.

ELAINE: What strikes me is the way that Rebekah seizes the initiative and engages in deceit, as though God could not effect this transfer of the covenant. We have the sense that without her, things would have happened very differently. Like Abraham, Rebekah is the kind of person who makes things happen. She too leaves her family and goes out to an unknown place to meet a stranger to marry.

BILL: Leon once said that we refer to the God of Abraham, the God of Isaac, and the God of Jacob, when we really should be referring to the God of Abraham, the God of Rebekah, and the God of Jacob. Why?

LEON: In this generation, Rebekah is in the place of Abraham. Her brother still has idols, and his daughter carries them off when she goes with Jacob later. But Rebekah somehow comes to embrace this God Whom she didn't know. When she feels the struggling inside her, she goes voluntarily to ask of the Lord. Thanks to her and her perspicacity and courage and prudence, this fragile way, barely begun, survives in this generation, despite the weakness and blindness of her husband. It's not a perfect solution, but she didn't inherit a perfect situation.

BILL: And it's never for her own status that she acts, but for the covenant. So what is Rebekah's ultimate accomplishment?

NAOMI: That the covenant is safely transmitted to the next generation. She sees to it before she dies.

BILL: What is the covenant to you?

LEON: At its foundation, it's a certain kind of orientation in the world, a certain disposition of soul to live righteously and to sanctify this life as much as possible. Rebekah sends forth Jacob on life's journey with the father's blessing, and the voice of Abraham and God ringing in his ear. That's our task. We don't rear our children for ourselves. We try to dedicate them to something noble and fine. I'm terribly moved by this story. And I love this woman.

NAOMI: The prophecy is an important part of the story, because it raises a question that runs throughout the Hebrew Bible: Is Rebekah fulfilling the will of God, or her own free will? There is always a tension between the biblical characters fulfilling the will of God and what they *think* is the will of God.

JEAN-PIERRE: I hear echoes of Rebekah in the story of the Virgin Mary. Gabriel appears to Mary and says, "Listen, there's

---

"There is always a tension between the biblical characters fulfilling the will of God and what they think *is the will of God."*

a plan for you. Are you going to cooperate?'' If the oracle in Genesis is secondary, it becomes much more difficult for Rebekah to discern the will of God—what she must do for the people.

BILL: If you lose the oracle, you lose the fact that this is the first woman in Genesis to whom God has spoken directly, except in response to a question from Him. The people of Israel lose something if God has not chosen this woman.

MARIANNE: Wouldn't the person who added the oracle story have thought that God's will was implicit in the story as a whole? This covenant could not have gone on through Rebekah and her son Jacob unless God had been instrumental in bringing it about. You could argue that within this story, you have the word of God to Rebekah and Rebekah's subsequent action. Was she right in acting? The story doesn't tell us. And what does she actually fix? She doesn't fix the word of God, she acts in a way that put His word into effect. The story poses the question: Who really is the worthy heir here? Who's the person who can found a nation? Clearly, it's not Esau because Esau has already sold his birthright to Jacob for a ''mess of pottage.''

LEON: In the previous generation, it was a tremendous struggle to get the right son, Isaac, born to the right woman, Sarah, and to have that son reverentially accepted by the father, who, in fact, preferred Ishmael, whom he had to send away. One generation of founding has barely been achieved, and the question for this generation is: Can

the new way that was begun with Abraham survive another generation, especially when the father of the second generation is not even half the man his father was? There are all kinds of indications of the weakness of Isaac before this story. But in this story, Isaac appears to have a dubious reason for preferring his firstborn son. He loves Esau because he loves the game Esau provides for him to eat.

BILL: I have sympathy for Isaac because he is old and blind and can't hunt for himself. In addition, he still lives under the trauma of the knife of his father raised above him in the sacrifice. He must be a man who is nervous in the world as a result of it. His son Esau goes out into the world and does the hunting to bring back the game that Isaac likes. I think there's a reason for this affinity.

LEON: Oh, yes, Esau is a man's man, and he has something of what his father is lacking. But Isaac is described as preferring Esau, even before he becomes old and infirm. Earlier in the story, when Abraham sends the servant to find a wife for Isaac, the servant says, ''What if the woman won't come? Shall I take Isaac to the woman?'' Abraham answers, ''Under no circumstances do you take him there.'' He fears that Isaac is the sort of man who could be lost to this new way, both physically and spiritually. God has led the servant to find Rebekah. But Rebekah is going to lead Isaac to Jacob. That's her achievement. In the story in which Esau sells his birthright for a ''mess of pottage,'' you get a naked presentation of both Jacob and

Esau. Whatever you want to say about the questionable character of Jacob's intention, he at least cares about the birthright. Esau says, "I'm going to die. What do I need a birthright for?" It's perfectly clear that Esau's not the right one. You could say that Rebekah is a shrewd woman who really knows her boys. But she has this problem: How do you reverse the order of nature? Nature has put Esau first. How do you reverse the order without fratricide? How do you avoid having the Cain and Abel story all over again?

NAOMI: The hardest decisions in life are in the gray areas. For example, neither Esau nor Jacob are morally perfect people. So Rebekah has to look carefully at the character traits of both boys with the long view of history in mind. Esau gives in to immediate gratification and "spurns his birthright" for a bowl of soup. Jacob, on the other hand, is self-disciplined, tenacious, and resilient, with a strong introspective streak nurtured by many hours in his mother's tent. Rebekah's daring choice in selecting which of her two sons she would transmit the covenant to is the reason we're sitting here, thousands of years later, discussing that very same covenant.

BILL: Jacob seems to be someone who can think and talk himself out of predicaments. He's the wily one, the one with his mother's traits. Someone has said, "Esau is a simple man, and God doesn't favor simple people."

ROBIN: What God seems to want is the person best suited to the task of extending

"Rebekah's daring choice in selecting which of her two sons she would transmit the covenant to is the reason we're sitting here, thousands of years later, discussing that very same covenant."

the nation and the covenant. Esau is clearly not that man.

BILL: Yes, Elie Wiesel says that Esau is a pitiful figure. His own mother seems to resent him, his younger brother is more clever, and when he comes back to his sad, old father with a humble request—"Father, just give me a blessing, too"—his father, whom he loves, rejects him. He's pitiable.

STEPHEN: No, Esau is the opposite of pitiable. And maybe Isaac was right in his preference. God does, in fact, favor simple people. "Blessed are the pure in heart." In the finale of this drama of the brothers, after Jacob has been away for twenty years, the two meet. Esau is the one who opens his arms and his heart and embraces his brother and cries and forgives him. But Jacob is still shifty and deceitful; he doesn't really accept his brother's love. Esau is

The Beguiling of Isaac by Jacob and Rebecca (detail), *Morgan Old Testamant*, France, ca. 1250

much more a representative of the values that good people respect than anyone else in this story. What is openness of heart but being filled by God? Esau's forgiveness of Jacob is parallel to the story at the end of Genesis in which Joseph forgives his brothers and thus closes the circle of pain that was begun by God in the Cain and Abel story.

ROBIN: Although his final gesture is magnanimous, Esau is not enlightened—he doesn't have the capacity. He himself participates in the squandering of himself, first by giving up the birthright and second by

going out on a long hunt and not having the smarts to be aware of a plot going on behind his back.

LEON: And when Jacob meets Esau at the end of the story, Jacob brings lots of gifts, as if to confess that he had gotten all this improperly. Jacob has changed by the end of the story. When he wrestles with the angel, he finally gets a blessing not by guile, but by tenacity and the willingness to confront whoever that being is. In some way, Jacob has earned this reconciliation.

MARIANNE: We've talked about this story in terms of Jacob and Esau. But I wonder how many of us might identify with Isaac? Isaac is known as the son of Abraham and the father of Jacob. But on his own, he's always struggling to find his own role. In some ways, he's just a transition figure. But who is he on his own? He's blind. Rebekah has the word from God, but we don't know whether Isaac has ever been told how it will turn out. He almost gets lost in the shuffle. He's the son of a famous man and the father of a famous son.

JEAN-PIERRE: Looking at Isaac in this story brings us back to the binding of Isaac, when he imagined that he was about to die. And he goes on living. Perhaps at that moment, the exclamation that Rebekah has—"Why am I alive?"—becomes Isaac's question.

ELAINE: One passage of midrash says that the angels watching this terrible scene wept into Isaac's eyes and that's how he was blinded.

NAOMI: In the story, Isaac is shown as being deceived by Jacob and Rebekah. But I'm a little suspicious that Isaac is really fooled. He asks too many questions of Jacob: "Are you really my son? Let me touch you. Let me smell you. How come you got the game so fast?" He and Rebekah have been married a long time by now, and the roles have shifted a bit now that Isaac is infirm and blind. Who knows, maybe he defers to Rebekah, or maybe he's playing along with her and is happy to have her do all the dirty work, so to speak. Rebekah shields her husband from the painful task of demoting his firstborn son to a subordinate status.

LEON: No, I think Isaac really is fooled.

NAOMI: If Isaac is really fooled, then why does he keep asking so many questions?

LEON: He has some doubts. He has only one sense that's really functioning properly—his hearing. He says the voice he hears is the voice of Jacob. But he doesn't trust his hearing. His eyes are gone, so he relies on scent—on smell, taste, and touch—and these senses are fooled. By contrast, Rebekah says to Jacob, "Hearken to my voice, my son." When he discovers that he has been deceived, Isaac doesn't get angry, he trembles—perhaps an experience of awe that somehow, unbeknownst to himself, something working through him has given the blessing to the right son, even though that son is not Esau. Later, Esau marries two Hittite women, and the text says, "And they were a bitterness of spirit to Rebekah and to Isaac." Esau has a certain waywardness. But in the immediate sequel to the story of Isaac's deception, when Jacob is about to flee his brother, Rebekah tells Isaac that she doesn't want Jacob to marry a Canaanite. Isaac then summons Jacob and gives him the full Abrahamic blessing. It seems to me that Rebekah's deception of her husband, cruel as it might seem to us, brings Isaac to his senses so that he finally becomes the son of Abraham and discharges his responsibility, handing on the lineage in the right way. From this point of view, the crux of the

Rebecca with Her Two Sons, Second Nürnberg Haggadah, Southern Germany, 15th c.

story is the trembling of Isaac. At that moment, he could be realizing that he has sacrificed his son Esau, as his father was prepared to do on Mount Moriah. But even so, something profound happens to him in that moment that enables him to step forward. When he gives Jacob that final goodbye blessing, the last word we hear from his mouth is "Abraham." That's the last thing Isaac says in the whole book, as a kind of coming back to taking his father's place. I think it's glorious.

ELAINE: How is this glorious? Look at the discomfort of midrashic readers, who all say that Esau was murderous, idolatrous, evil—they come up with innumerable reasons to explain that he was totally unworthy, none of which is in the text. Jacob is presented as morally superior, in spite of having deceived his father.

JEAN-PIERRE: Yes, it's strange that when Isaac asks Jacob how he could have found the game so quickly, Jacob says, "It's your God Who has granted me success"—almost disdainfully.

MARIANNE: In a way, we know his action really is carrying out the work of the promise. But when Jacob says this, you almost have to gasp a little because it comes close to impiety. God didn't grant him success at all. He's lying to get the blessing.

NAOMI: At this stage in his young life, Jacob feels insecure and inadequate in the face of God and the demands of His covenant. He does not feel entitled to be close to God after what he's just done. He's got another twenty years of struggle ahead of him before he wrestles with the angel and feels that he's earned the blessing rightfully.

LEON: Yes, at this point in the story, Jacob is not a pious fellow. At first he thinks he can fix the birth order problem all by himself, without his father's blessing. But Rebekah understands that you can't aspire to be in your father's place and not care about what he thinks. Rebekah teaches Jacob that he needs his father's blessing. She also sends him off to a place where he will get the right kind of wife. She knows Esau will come back and discover the deception, but she manages to avoid fratricide. And she sends Jacob off with the blessing of his father and the name of Abraham and some intimation of God in his ears, about which he's going to have to learn on the road. Rebekah uses the only means at her disposal to bring her husband to his senses. And at the end of the story, Isaac is not angry but behaves as a patriarch for the first time.

NAOMI: But Rebekah pays a heavy price for her actions. Her life is miserable from this time forward. She tells her beloved younger son to run away to her family in far-off Mesopotamia and puts on a brave face, saying it's just "for a few days." But she knows in her heart that she'll never see Jacob again. And Jacob pays a heavy price, too. He finds no peace until he wrestles with the angel twenty years later—and then there's the painful sequel with his son Joseph.

JEAN-PIERRE: Yes, Jacob's deception comes back to haunt him in ironic ways. For example, in the Joseph story, the sons of Jacob deceive their old dad by bringing back Jacob's coat drenched in the blood of a kid, and Jacob thinks that his beloved son is dead. And why does that happen? Because he loves Joseph the best. And earlier, his father-in-law deceives him when he loves Rachel the best.

BILL: Does it occur to you that Rebekah's sacrifice of Jacob is analogous to Abraham's sacrifice of Isaac?

NAOMI: They're both prepared to make sacrifices for a larger cause. What am I or any of us here today ready to do for a country or cause we love? How would we respond if our faith were truly tested? This story also shows us that conflicts are inevitably built into the family structure. No matter how much we love each child, there's always more to give, and every child yearns for more. Throughout the generations of this family, we learn that family harmony isn't offered to us ready-made, that the complexities of sibling relationships are fraught with conflict.

MARIANNE: This story also points out that you don't have to get rid of family conflicts before God's purposes can be worked out. It is precisely in and through these conflicts that the promise of God is carried out. And because of this belief, the writer of the story doesn't have to make the characters look better. We can identify with this because it is precisely in and through the sometimes messy parts of our lives that God's purposes are worked out.

ELAINE: But this story can't be a win-win situation. Only the older brother is supposed to get the blessing. The story is, of course, about two nations and the preference of Israel over other nations and the validation of that preference by divine covenant. According to this story, that preference is not on the basis of moral superiority.

LEON: Yes, God tells Rebekah not "Two children are in your womb," but "Two nations are in your womb." That means that only one of these children is going to be in the covenant with God. But why, then, were there two heirs? Why does Jacob have to struggle so long with Esau and go the long way around in order to finally be renamed? Why can't it be smooth? Why does the story suggest that the transmission into the next generation requires this opposition? Jacob begins with confidence that his smarts can handle things. But in a way, he's more like the Greek hero Odysseus, who wanders for twenty years, suffering much, before he comes to learn the limitations of cleverness. Jacob has to wander in order to learn what it means to have a brother, and what it means to be in relation with your family of origin, what it means to really be in relation to God.

JEAN-PIERRE: A lot of people these days appeal to the Bible for a very simple set of uncomplicated family values. Well, this is a very complicated family indeed. And the story involves some very difficult decisions about who will be the recipients of blessing.

BILL: You're talking about the social realm of families, and Leon is talking about the story of the people of Israel—

MARIANNE: And these levels are intertwined. What happens at the national level is played out in real human lives.

BILL: This whole story revolves around the blessing. What is the blessing?

STEPHEN: It's the right of the eldest to have the land and to father the people who will be the inhabitants of the land.

MARIANNE: Isn't the blessing also a promise of God's presence with Jacob?

STEPHEN: But in reality, God's presence is not a thing. It can't be given by one person to another. It's always available to us all.

MARIANNE: But don't we experience the presence of God in life in very particu-

Isaac Blessing Jacob, Byzantine mosaic, Palatine Chapel, Palermo, 12th c.

lar, concrete ways? This is the way that God is present with Jacob.

BILL: Doesn't this blessing also determine who will carry on as the next head of the new religion? This family is trying to carry on Abraham's monotheism.

JEAN-PIERRE: It raises the question of whether we are spectators or participants in what's going on outside us. What's the burden of the blessing on us as individuals and communities and nations?

MARIANNE: You said "the burden of the blessing." Jacob learns through suffering and there's always a mystery about it. Even when he meets Esau at the end of the story, he's still wondering what's going to happen. He is somewhat at Esau's mercy. Being chosen doesn't necessarily mean having the dominant position.

NAOMI: That's right. And being chosen means being given a particular responsibility, a task. Even when Jacob prevails over the angel, he walks away limping. Unlike the famous painting of St. George slaying the dragon, where the handsome young knight emerges victorious and unscathed, Jacob limps away. This is my favorite part of the story. In life, there's no such thing as absolute victory. Even though Jacob has been chosen, he will be a bit of a cripple for the rest of his life.

BILL: And the people of Israel are never allowed to forget that the struggle with the angel led to a permanent wound. You were born in Israel—do you feel chosen?

NAOMI: Chosen for a responsibility, not better than anybody else in this room. I remember as a child, standing in the schoolyard in my starched uniform with the sun beating down, and being told that a whole people relies on my shoulders to survive, and that I must put the good of my people in front of my own needs. This was the end of the Second World War, when immigrants were coming in, dragged, psychologically, out of the camps, children who lay under the beds, not on them, for fear of what might happen to them. We were sent to help them. It was our responsibility as teenagers to redeem them, to take them in and make them whole. It was endless responsibility. But the flip side is: The more responsibility you get, the stronger you get. President Kennedy's mother, Rose, said, "God only gives you the cross that you can carry." Those are Christian terms. In Jewish terms, we were responsible for redeeming the land and the people. Yes, I felt privileged in a way to be part of that particular generation, but only as it related to being chosen to answer the challenge of the particular tasks at hand.

BILL: I can understand that and still be troubled by the triumphalism of the religions that say, "We are God's people."

ROBIN: But to be chosen as God's people, to be the beloved of God, is to be treated very harshly.

BILL: Rebekah certainly pays a price for being beloved, for being chosen.

LEON: When God enacts the covenant

with Abraham, it's a specific responsibility—"Walk before me and be wholehearted" and, later, "I've chosen him so that he shall teach righteousness to his children." There's a specific content to this responsibility. Right after the circumcision and the covenant, the very next story involves Abraham's meeting with the strangers. The question is: Will the covenant lead him to be hostile to strangers, or is he going to show that notwithstanding that he has the covenant, he is somehow open to those who are not his own?

NAOMI: And there's the story of Sodom and Gomorrah, where he argues with God for the sake of utter strangers.

LEON: Yes, there's a specific moral and political task in the world made necessary by the kind of world it is, a world filled with strangers.

BILL: What's the difference between the blessing and the birthright in this story?

ROBIN: The birthright automatically comes by virtue of birth order. The fact that Esau gives it up does not remove the character of birthright. It's still there. He simply tosses it away because of his immediate hunger. The blessing, though, seems to have been taken and acted upon. To be wholehearted, which is what Abraham is asked to do, is the blessing that's carried on. It's very difficult to be wholehearted. It means not to worship idols, especially the idol of one's own being. And it means to accept and to deal realistically with one's own human features and the human fea-

tures of those around us. What blessing really means is human love. Human love is not possible without it. Idolatry is possible, and slaughter is possible, but human love is not. Real love is not possible without having acquired human features. That seems to be what the blessing is about.

LEON: What does it mean when parents pronounce a blessing upon their children?

NAOMI: In observant Jewish homes, on Friday night, both parents reenact Jacob's blessing of Joseph's children by putting their hands on their children's heads and reciting a blessing. By internalizing the blessing of our parents' love, we acquire self-esteem, self-confidence, and a deep sense of security. Their blessing tells us we matter, that we are valued. All his life Jacob yearns for the genuine blessing he never got from his father Isaac.

BILL: And at the end, he says, "My years have been few and evil."

JEAN-PIERRE: When Latino children leave the house, every time they step out the door, the parent touches the child and grants the child a blessing so the child can go forth blessed.

NAOMI: What is the child walking away with?

JEAN-PIERRE: The presence of God.

NAOMI: So the child is being blessed not because he or she is better than any

Lorenzo Lippi, *Isaac Blessing Jacob*, ca. 1650

other kid on the block, but because in relation to the mother or the father, that child is special. In a way, this echoes the theme we get in the first chapter of Genesis, where God blesses us and says, "You are made in my image. I'm endowing you with spiritual identity so that whatever happens to you, you carry that inner knowledge that you're special to me."

BILL: But unlike the story of Esau and Jacob, the blessing is given to every child, so no one is upset.

ELAINE: It would be a wonderful change in the story if Isaac could bless Jacob and then give the same blessing to Esau.

BILL: Do you find it surprising that no moral judgment is rendered on any of these characters?

NAOMI: But there is a moral judgment here, and it's delivered in a subtle way. Deception begets deception. Jacob lies to his father in darkness, because Isaac is blind, both literally and figuratively. Later on in the story, Jacob is deceived by his uncle Laban, who promises him Rachel as a bride, but, under cover of darkness, sends her older sister Leah into the bridal chamber.

ELAINE: Part of the power of the story is that it's so morally complex. The good person does not necessarily get the good result. The story is really about Israel becoming God's favorite nation, and how that relates the people of Israel to all the other people who are brothers and sisters in fratricidal strife, all with the claim to be God's chosen. Second-century Christian Church fathers did the same, only they identified Esau as Israel and Jacob as the Church, which, they claimed, is now God's favorite, supplanting the older brother, Israel.

BILL: This may be a morally ambiguous story, but it is historically indispensable to the people of Israel. How does this influence the way the story is told?

ELAINE: The ancestral stories of every people I can think of place their own people at the center of the universe, claiming the place of greatest importance. This story, which is adopted by our culture, embodies a claim of divine favoritism.

STEPHEN: Sometimes this kind of extreme inflation of the importance of the self, whether that self is personal or national, can be very touching when it's carried out with a certain lightness and kindness. The Pueblo people whom Jung visited would get up every morning before dawn to perform a certain ritual so that the sun could rise. They thought they were doing this for the sake of all people; they just happened to be the ones who had been given that task. But the idea of being God's favorite is a very dangerous idea.

BILL: It also involves pain, as we've said. If I were given the choice of being Israel, I would say, "Are You kidding, God? Not me. You're asking me to take the responsibility of suffering. I don't want it."

STEPHEN: God's favoritism, from Cain and Abel onward, causes great pain. If you've had even a glimpse of God, you can't possibly imagine that God shows that kind of preference. Later, the prophet Amos tries to dance around the idea by having God say, "Aren't the Ethiopians, the Egyptians, the Philistines my children, too?"

LEON: In the beginning, God tries a universal way, and then, after the Flood, he tries another universal way with Noah and his sons. That falls apart in the first generation with the rebellion of Ham against his father. Then there is the universal way of the city of Babel, in which humans attempt to make themselves into God. At that point, God gives up on the universal way—although not the universal intention—and elects one man, Abraham, and one nation, Israel, to be the carrier of God's new way, with the intention of carrying this way, eventually, to the world as a whole.

ELAINE: But this is still the story of the same people—this is not the way the Egyptians would tell the story or the Arcadians or the Babylonians.

Marc Chagall, *Before Eating, Isaac Blind, Blesses His Second Son Jacob*, 1956

LEON: Yes, but on the other hand, international strife was not invented by the Bible. The question is: Can that strife be turned to good?

BILL: But if the Jews believe that they're the chosen people, and the Christians believe that they're the new chosen people, and the Muslims think that, too, how do we ever achieve any kind of peaceful coexistence?

STEPHEN: We don't.

ELAINE: There's no model in this story for that.

NAOMI: I think there's a misunderstanding here about choice. Take marriage, for example. I've chosen a particular man, and he's chosen me. That doesn't mean my husband is superior to every other man in this room. It merely means that for the purpose of being my partner in marriage, he's been chosen. And so have I. I believe that every nation and person has a particular task in life. Perhaps as Americans, we've all been chosen, or have accepted the challenge of being a pluralistic society. That doesn't mean we're inherently better than any other society. Perhaps the Italians have been chosen to create great opera and art. The British have created an extraordinary literary culture. But if you shirk the responsibility of fulfilling the specific task you've been chosen for, then you lose the privilege of being chosen.

JEAN-PIERRE: But what is the task?

NAOMI: The task is the birth of monotheism!

BILL: Why do you suppose God wanted things to be so complex?

JEAN-PIERRE: I'm actually more satisfied. There's a richness and an awesome beauty in the complexity of life and the uncertainty of the future. I think that's a blessing.

ROBIN: But it takes something to see that as a blessing because we begin by wanting things to be simple.

ELAINE: When we read these stories, we read into them our own complexity or our own issues. For example, in the story of the Garden of Eden, I'm interested in the dynamic between the serpent and the woman. But you could play with the story in a completely different way. For example, you could follow Valentinus, a Gnostic teacher who said that Adam represents the human body and Eve the soul. Eve is hidden within Adam the way that bone marrow is hidden inside the bone. It's a deep, hidden energy, of which Adam is completely unaware. I love this version of the story, which speaks of Adam's discovery of the spiritual energy that has been within him and of which he suddenly becomes aware. The discovery of that possibility hidden so deeply within us is just a delight. Maybe that's because I grew up in a self-consciously modern and "scientific" culture, in which biology and psychology were highly respected, and people thought that the life of the spirit was an embarrassment or an illusion.

LEON: But surely any reader of these stories has to wonder whether there isn't some mysterious source that lies behind them. If Homer can begin *The Iliad* by saying, "Sing, Muse," indicating that he's somehow a vehicle for something beyond himself, one has to wonder about these stories that so profoundly show us our life and guide us in ways that, left to our own devices, we might never discover.

STEPHEN: You can read these stories as dreams or patterns for the soul. And it's helpful, sometimes, to step into a story and notice where it is that we're standing. In the Garden of Eden story, for example, at what place in the Garden are we? Are we standing beside the serpent? Are we with Eve? In this story, I find myself standing beside Esau. His cry deeply touches my heart.

> *"You can read these stories as dreams or patterns for the soul."*

JEAN-PIERRE: Imagine how differently this story would read if it were told from the perspective of Esau. This would be the perspective of marginalized people around the world who rarely, if ever, have been able to tell their own story because their stories have been told on their behalf by those who were stronger or shrewder or more powerful in the ways of this world.

It's scary to discover that one has not been chosen in certain ways. It's a challenge, then, to find the ways in which one has been chosen. Jesus says, "Blessed are the poor," but the poor are not blessed in any apparent way. How are the poor blessed? Isaac reserves a blessing of sorts for Esau, a fairly peculiar blessing. But, ultimately, Esau is also chosen. He becomes a reconciler—a hesitant one, who comes to the task armed, but someone who embraces his own election in a very powerful way, a way that Jacob does not expect.

STEPHEN: You say, imagine if the story were told from Esau's perspective. But in a way, it is. That's the genius of these Genesis writers. We can feel the pain of Esau when he cries out loudly and bitterly and says, "Bless me, bless me too, Father." That cry echoes throughout eternity. The greatest consciousness in the Book of Genesis is not the consciousness of the God character but the consciousness of the writers, who include everything, and don't see the opponent as the enemy. This poisonous dualism appears later in the Hebrew Bible in the figure of a god who commands Joshua, for example, to slaughter the Canaanites—men, women, and children. It appears very often in the Gospels, where the Pharisees, or even the Jews as a whole, are seen as the enemy. But the Genesis writers have a generosity of spirit which includes the perspective of the defeated. That's a very moving quality of the text; it is a text that is filled with God's generosity.

JEAN-PIERRE: In an ancient hypothetical dialogue between a Christian and a

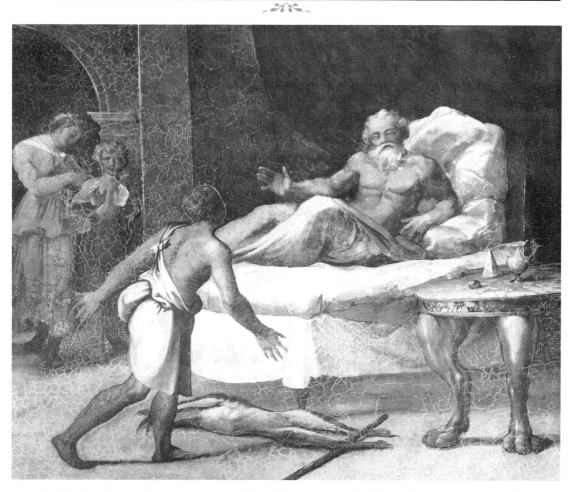

School of Raphael, *Esau Returning from the Hunt Demanding to Be Blessed by Isaac*, Vatican Palace, 1518–19

Jew, what makes it difficult for the Christian to relate to the Jew, who is standing in front of him, is his very proximity—how much they have in common. Their fights are sibling rivalries.

BILL: So you can't just paper over the differences. They are both profound and painful.

JEAN-PIERRE: A contemporary Christian theologian, Justo Gonzalez, speaks of our history as a "non-innocent history." This story of the blessing that Isaac bestows on Jacob is a terribly frank admission of the non-innocence of a people's history.

ELAINE: The early followers of Jesus

wanted so much to appropriate Jewish tradition. They're in love with it in a way, and want to claim it for themselves. That is also a non-innocent history.

BILL: If the story is a "non-innocent history," what is its point?

JEAN-PIERRE: "This is who we are," says the author. "There is where we have been. Now we have to deal with that as individuals, families, and peoples."

NAOMI: The whole story of Genesis, from Abraham on, is really a saga of four generations in a family that some today might call "dysfunctional." But in the end, what we always have to get to is the larger vision of the story—that the family revolves around a covenant, and that the covenant becomes the common denominator that holds them all together and allows them to prevail and transcend. As long as they transmit that, they have vitality and a sense of purpose, meaning, and values. When we come to the story of Joseph, with its dreadful example of sibling rivalry, there's a reconciliation at the very end—as long as you're able to transmit that identity, that set of values, that set of commitments, the family will continue. Even Isaac and Ishmael come together when their father is buried. We learn from this story that life is complicated and that our ancestors are not perfect.

BILL: Americans think of themselves as a chosen people, as "a city on the Hill."

NAOMI: You can't just be chosen. It's

an active relationship. Both sides have to work together for the choice to work. America has been chosen to be a pluralistic society, but we have to work on that. America is really like a family, where you want each sibling to keep his or her uniqueness and yet stay within the family.

STEPHEN: When I come to the stories in Genesis, I am working and struggling and loving with my ancestors. That is sometimes a painful process. Some of my Buddhist friends became Buddhists partly because of their problems with the Bible—appropriate problems! But sooner or later, they have to come back to the Bible and wrestle with God and, in the sense that Jacob does, *defeat* God in order to make the ancestors their own. In our culture, you can't avoid that wrestling because our language is a deeply Christian language. I have other ancestors. The Buddha is my ancestor. Lao-tzu is my ancestor. Jesus of Nazareth—the authentic Jesus—is my ancestor. But they don't cause pains in the way that these very unaware human ancestors do. They have transcended this kind of suffering and have become transparent, filled with the light and compassion of the God who is unnameable. But the god of this story is a different kind of god.

JEAN-PIERRE: Better this than nothing.

STEPHEN: *Is* the god of this story really better than nothing? "Nothing" is one of the *names* of God, according to the mystics. And a Zen master once said, "Even a good thing isn't as good as nothing."

LEON: "Nothing," the philosophers say, is unintelligible.

JEAN-PIERRE: But "nothing" doesn't have to be intelligible.

BILL: Whether we believe in the creator God or accept the Big Bang, the moment there is creation, "nothing" ceases to exist. We are constantly being driven back to these stories. What else is there?

JEAN-PIERRE: Part of the miracle is that God refuses to be limited by these stories.

ROBIN: We've been treating these stories as if they existed independently of the people who read and interpret them. But these stories are there because people *have* read and interpreted them in a certain way. We're simply adding another layer of interpretation, as we strive for a kind of community, which actually does exist here, as we become interpreters. But our interpretation ignores that in some sense the meaning of these stories already encloses the stories themselves because the meaning already exists in the lives of the people whom the story has already shaped.

LEON: Yes, the stories aren't self-interpreting, even though there is a meaning that encloses them. It's rare for the narrator's voice to intrude and pronounce a judgment. The stories, in all of their ambiguity, are simply there. What that says to me is that for these stories to live in the life of a people, they have to be appropriated by thought and conversation and by wrestling with the text and its meaning. When we take that task seriously, a kind of divine spark appears. So I'm happy that the stories are so ambiguous because that's the way they teach.

JEAN-PIERRE: And when we wrestle with these stories, a character like Rebekah ceases to be a mere character.

"When we wrestle with these stories, a character like Rebekah ceases to be a mere character."

LEON: She's here.

JEAN-PIERRE: She's here in this circle of persons.

ROBIN: And she blesses, too.

JEAN-PIERRE: And somehow our heirs and descendants are also participants in this conversation.

ויאבק איש עמו

IX

GOD WRESTLING

WALTER BRUEGGEMANN • ROBERTA HESTENES

JOHN S. KSELMAN • HUGH O'DONNELL

BURTON L. VISOTZKY • RENITA J. WEEMS

AVIVAH GOTTLIEB ZORNBERG

The stories of Genesis are about life in the making. They tell
us that we can change our lives. Even a scoundrel like Jacob,
wandering the desert with fear and trembling, becomes a new man.
His dreams make the difference—the first recorded dreams in the
Bible. We are told that "dreaming men are haunted men." This son
of Isaac was haunted right to the "gateways of heaven." He awoke,
no longer Jacob.

—BILL MOYERS

Jacob Wrestling with the Angel, Mahzor, Corfu, 1709

Yaakov went out from Be'er-Sheva and went toward Harran,
and encountered a certain place.
He had to spend the night there, for the sun had come in.
Now he took one of the stones of the place
and set it at his head
and lay down in that place.
And he dreamt:
Here, a ladder was set up on the earth,
its top reaching the heavens,
and here: messengers of God were going up and down on it.
And here:
YHWH was standing over against him.
He said:
I am YHWH,
the God of Avraham your father and the God of Yitzhak.
The land on which you lie
I give to you and to your seed.
Your seed will be like the dust of the earth;
you will burst forth, to the Sea, to the east, to the north, to the
    Negev.
All the clans of the soil will find blessing through you and
    through your seed!
Here, I am with you,
I will watch over you wherever you go
and will bring you back to this soil;
indeed, I will not leave you
Until I have done what I have spoken to you.
Yaakov awoke from his sleep
and said:
Why,
YHWH is in this place,
and I, I did not know it!
He was awestruck and said:
How awe-inspiring is this place!
This is none other than a house of God,
and that is the gate of heaven!
Yaakov started-early in the morning,
he took the stone that he had set at his head

and set it up as a standing-pillar
and poured oil on top of it.
And he called the name of the place: Bet-El/House of God . . .

And Yaakov vowed a vow, saying:
If God will be with me
and will watch over me on this way that I go
and will give me food to eat and a garment to wear,
and if I come back in peace to my father's house—
YHWH shall be God to me,
and this stone that I have set up as a standing-pillar shall become a
    house of God,
and everything that you give me
I shall tithe, tithe it to you. . . .

He arose during that night,
took his two wives, his two maids, and his eleven children
to cross the Yabbok crossing.
He took them and brought them across the river; he brought
    across what belonged to him.
And Yaakov was left alone—
Now a man wrestled with him until the coming up of dawn.
When he saw that he could not prevail against him,
he touched the socket of his thigh;
the socket of Yaakov's thigh had been dislocated as he wrestled
    with him.
Then he said:
Let me go,
for dawn has come up!
But he said:
I will not let you go
unless you bless me.
He said to him:
What is your name?
And he said: Yaakov.
Then he said:
Not as Yaakov/Heel-Sneak shall your name be henceforth
    uttered

but rather as Yisrael/God-Fighter,
for you have fought with God and men
and have prevailed.
Then Yaakov asked and said:
Pray tell me your name!
But he said:
Now why do you ask after my name?
And he gave him farewell-blessing there.
Yaakov called the name of the place: Peniel/Face of God,
for: I have seen God,
face to face,
and my life has been saved.
The sun rose on him as he crossed by Penuel,
and he was limping on his thigh.

—excerpts from *The Five Books of Moses*
(*Schocken Bible*, Vol. I), Chapters 28 and 32

BILL: Do any of you identify with Jacob?

WALTER: I think I identify with his incredible duplicities. I don't think it's possible for Jacob not to be duplicitous. Even after this last, wonderful vision, the very last thing Jacob does is lie to his brother. He says, "I'll meet you," and then he goes the other way. I don't know whether it's a habit of his to live this way.

AVIVAH: But Jacob doesn't actually believe in Esau's peacemaking.

BURT: I'm with Walter on this. When Jacob has stolen Esau's blessing and deceived his blind father, he flees for his life. That's where he has the first dream. You expect, at this juncture, for this to be a turning point in his life. He's going into exile—now maybe he'll have learned something from the experience. But when he reaches his Uncle Laban, the deceit starts all over again. He manages a six-year animal husbandry program where he is deceptive again. And then he comes back and has this great wrestling match. You think, "Oh, now he's going to change." Indeed, his name changes. But then he faces Esau and lies to him again and again, not just about where he's going but also about his children—"Well, the children are a little frail, and if we keep pushing on, all these cattle will die." Nothing about Jacob changes. In a way, that's what's so depressing. As a young man, he has a young man's dream—you know, everything is on the way up, and there are angels ministering to him. Then as a middle-aged man, he has a middle-aged man's dream—you know, twenty years pass, and you have four wives and twelve kids, and you just stay up all night wrestling. It's a very different take on the world. But despite the fact that as a young man, he has a young man's dream, and as a middle-aged man, he has a middle-aged man's dream, his habits remain the same. He doesn't change.

ROBERTA: I think that the elements of the essential person remain—at one level, we are who we are. But at another level, the story shows movement. In the beginning, Jacob's piety or spirituality is all external. It's all verbal. He puts on religious words in order to satisfy his father, and he'll pretend to be anything. His spirituality is surface—it doesn't go anywhere deep inside of him. But by the end of the story, he has come to a spirituality that's vulnerable.

WALTER: Yes, it's terribly important that these experiences happen at night, when Jacob is vulnerable.

ROBERTA: And if you look at the content of Jacob's prayer, you see that he's saying, "I'm afraid." He's naming something he's never named. He's saying, "I don't know what to do. I need . . ." in a way that he never has before.

WALTER: But there is duplicity even in that prayer, because he says to God, "You said to me, You promised me . . ." But if you look back, God never promised that. He holds his God and Protector, his Adversary, to a word that his Protector and Adversary never promised him.

AVIVAH: Yes, but he doesn't have a tape recorder.

WALTER: Which gives him great freedom.

AVIVAH: What he remembers is God saying, "I'll be very good to you." God never used that word "good." And why is that important for Jacob? Because throughout his life, Jacob is dogged by the sense of evil. The word "evil" is constantly used of Jacob. For him, the word "good" is the lodestone. It's a passion, it's not duplicity.

BILL: Do you find Jacob to be an admirable fellow?

AVIVAH: I don't find him duplicitous—but I know I'm sticking my neck out.

BILL: He's cunning.

AVIVAH: It's interesting how the Jewish sages translate those rather damning words that Esau cries out in betrayal—"He's outsmarted me twice!" He literally says, "He's out-*yakov*'ed me," or "He's Jacobed me twice!" The translation of the sages is "He's been too clever." The word used is fairly neutral, even a good word, one that is used for "wisdom."

BILL: He's "out-politicked" me?

AVIVAH: He's outwitted me. Outwitting is part of being witted.

BILL: Cunning as a virtue.

AVIVAH: The word I would use is "subtle."

BILL: But when we meet him, he is a thief, a coward, and a fugitive. He has stolen a birthright and is running for his life from his brother because he's afraid of his brother.

AVIVAH: Is it cowardly to be afraid?

ROBERTA: It's probably a realistic response. He wanted the blessing. One of Jacob's characteristics all the way through the story is that he's hungry for the blessing. Now what he understands by that seems to shift in the text. In the beginning, it's power and money, and he keeps caring about those things. But like all of us, Jacob struggles with his own myth of perfectibility. Somehow, because Jacob has an encounter with God, which does change him, we expect him to be a perfect person all of a sudden. I think the story tells us that the encounter with God changes us, but not to perfection. We are still human. We still bear the marks of everything we are. But Jacob is a different man after that encounter.

"Like all of us, Jacob struggles with his own myth of perfectibility."

JOHN: Yes. He comes away wounded, limping. That reminds us that encounters with God are very serious experiences, and we will come away wounded—but believing.

RENITA: What makes Jacob's story so incredibly engaging, and what inspires the energy we feel now, is that he's the first character in the Genesis story with so many dimensions. Here we finally have someone we use adjectives for— "deceptive," "clever," "shrewd," "subtle," whatever. Before Jacob, the characters are mostly one-dimensional. They pretty much do what God says, even though they may protest a little here and there. But if the Jacob story had fallen later in the text— for example, somewhere in the Book of Kings—I wonder whether we would have this strong reaction, because by the time we get to Kings, we've met so many clever, shrewd, duplicitous people, Jacob might have paled for us. In Genesis, we say, "Aha!" because this is someone who's human. This is a person we can all identify with.

BILL: I get a sense that this family could end up on *Oprah* or *Donahue*—you know, people who dream about confronting the hidden God and having four wives— something like that. But while you obviously found him intriguing, did you find him admirable?

RENITA: Admirable he is not. It's not what he does, but what life does to him. What makes it so incredibly intriguing to me is that Jacob is someone who seems to

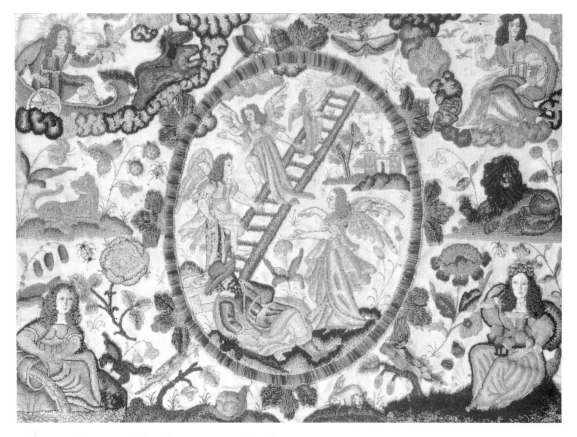

Jacob's Ladder, raised silk embroidery, England, ca. 1660

take things into his own hands, but, at the same time, he seems fated. I think that is the human predicament. In part of our lives, we have control; and in other parts, we absolutely do not have control. That's what makes this story so familiar to me.

BURT: In some ways, Jacob attempts to assert control at all times—and sometimes he is stunningly naive in this attempt. He has this incredible vision where God says, "I'll protect you, I'll take care of you." His response is a whole series of "if" clauses. He says, "Okay, You wanna make a deal? Great!" It's as if he doesn't understand what is at stake here or who his partner is in the covenantal relationship. He doesn't understand that God is holding all the cards. He says, "Okay, well, if You give me food and clothing, and if You protect me, and if You make sure I get home, then maybe You'll be my God." To which the rabbis quite cleverly respond, "And if not, He won't be God?" What could Jacob possibly be thinking?

HUGH: Jacob is pure genius. He's human genius.

BILL: How so?

HUGH: Jacob is a real hero in this story because he's cursed with a kind of active monkey brain and incredible invention and intellect. It keeps him awake. He can't get any rest or any peace. He's sent running through the world, and God comes down and gives him help. He gives him more help than just "Things are going to be okay, so go forth and do this or that." He actually shows him the pathway to heaven. He shows him the structure of how to do it because the man has the intellect and equipment to be able to do something with it.

BILL: What does this tell you about God? Here's this young man who's stolen his family's birthright, abused his brother, and he's on the run, afraid for his life.

HUGH: He's a typical second-born son, right? He's emerged with this equipment, and he's got this wild brother, and he knows, through the support of his mother, that he really is the one who has to save God's vision and the covenant.

BILL: I don't think he knows that.

HUGH: He knows he's only a child, but even then he has an unconscious vision. He is alert, and his mother knows he will be able to look after the covenant better than his brother.

BILL: But in spite of all his imperfections, God comes to him and pats him on the back. I would have expected God to be more severe with a twenty-year-old who is on the lam like this. But instead of saying,

"Wait a minute," God says, "It's okay, boy, I'm going to look after you. You just don't worry about anything."

AVIVAH: Yet there is no overt criticism in the whole story of what he did.

BURT: But he is criticized. Esau says explicitly that Jacob has tricked him twice. Esau even pronounces a death sentence on Jacob. This is his own brother—and not just any brother, but a twin that he's ready to kill.

AVIVAH: But that's not the voice of the author in any sense.

BURT: You know, I think we always give Esau short shrift. He has had it very bad for an awfully long time. I read that story and think of the two brothers in that twenty-year span. Ironically, Esau is the one who's grown. At the beginning of the story, Esau is so concerned about his stomach that he's willing to sell his birthright for a bowl of lentils. My God, he's just such a boor, you know—"Feed me." And yet, twenty years later, when Jacob returns, Esau has grown enormously. He's got lots of wealth. And he's utterly forgiving. He sees his brother and runs to greet him. He throws his arms around Jacob, kissing him and hugging him, and they cry.

BILL: But you're evading the harder question that Avivah posed: Why doesn't God demand more of Jacob or be more severe with him?

BURT: I think God exacerbates the problem. God is like parents who say, "Don't worry, sweetie pie. Whatever you do, I'll be here." And meanwhile the kid's standing there, having drawn on the wall. In a way, God makes Jacob worse and leads him to more duplicity.

ROBERTA: It's not necessary for God to do that, because in the world of consequences, you see God concerned about the covenant. God is concerned not with this person alone, but about all of the families on earth. You know, God's purpose is bigger. It involves the one, but it reaches to the all.

BILL: So God uses crooked sticks to draw straight lines?

HUGH: Absolutely.

ROBERTA: Actually, what God uses is blessing and grace and promise and covenant, in order to encourage this person to become the best he can be. And the circumstances of his life and the consequences of this deceit will work themselves out in history.

BURT: I couldn't possibly disagree more. I think God unlinks consequence from the action. This, in a way, is the disservice God does for Jacob. God essentially says, "You can behave however you want. I'm going to bless you, I'm going to protect you." God does this immediately after all the duplicitousness. Had God said at that point—"You know, you can't steal the blessing like that. You think you have a blessing? Well, I'm going to take it away from you"— Jacob would have thought twice before he did it again.

BILL: Why did God do it? Is God saying, "The end justifies the means"? That "my covenant, my purpose with Israel, my long-range historic aim justifies my using a dolt like this"?

BURT: Well, God certainly doesn't say anything like that in scripture.

BILL: Okay, throw out that translation.

BURT: It doesn't mean that it's not implied there. But still, the moral implications are very disturbing. That chosenness can in some way free you from moral obligation is a terrifying thought. In some way, it replicates what we saw with Abraham. Abraham does all kinds of things that are not quite on the up-and-up, and God rewards him. Now, two generations later, we go through the same thing. Jacob is duplicitous again and again, and God stands by. Now it's a nice message, I suppose, that God will always be with you—but you'd like there to be some link between your action and the consequence.

WALTER: Burt, earlier you said that Jacob did not have all the cards. Could it be that the narrator wants to say to us, "God doesn't have all the cards"? When we were talking about creation, we fudged a little about the issue of God's sovereignty. Has the narrator discovered that some other character holds some of the cards, a character who is Jacob, who is us, who is this family of blessing—and that, speaking of cards, God has got to deal a little bit?

BILL: You know, I haven't done well at all defining this dilemma because I think this is one of the most powerful and disturbing passages in the whole of the Hebrew Bible. Earlier God has been so angry at what people are doing on the earth that He decides to wipe them out and start over. He destroys Sodom and Gomorrah, innocent women and children, in His anger. This is a wrathful God of vengeance. Now, all of a sudden, after destroying Sodom and Gomorrah, and after destroying the earth with the Flood, God finds this duplicitous fellow on the run, who has cheated his family and continues to deceive, and God pats him on the back and says, "That's okay. That's okay." Suddenly there's a mercy here that was not available to the innocent.

HUGH: Well, you can say that all those other people have been living in the dark. Now Jacob comes along and gets some equipment from God in order to be able to really pass something on that can be of vital use.

BILL: What is that equipment?

HUGH: Implicit in the vision of the ladder is a working technology for being able to pass on to culture the relationship to God. It's a way of speaking through the covenant back to God. You know, the fact that God has human genius on His hands here is extremely important.

JOHN: To me, the art of the story is precisely that we are left with Jacob and God, to make our own judgments with the information from the conversation that the author gives us. So I don't think the autho-

rial intent is to portray a nonduplicitous Jacob, guided by God, but rather a person like me, who struggles with duplicity, and with calculating, bargaining prayer.

WALTER: Or at least cleverness.

AVIVAH: I think it's a person like me, who is both Jacob and Esau. Jacob recognizes the Esau in himself.

WALTER: If you were a Christian reader, I would say you were trying to whitewash and clean up the text. Traditional Christian readers want to impose a kind of nice morality on this story. I'm not saying you want to do that, but the direction you're going in can so easily be heard in a Christian context as saying, "These are all nice little boys and girls." And indeed they are not.

AVIVAH: No, absolutely not.

HUGH: This is about survival, isn't it?

BILL: Whose survival?

HUGH: They said it was about the survival of the tribe and the survival of the culture and the survival of vision.

BILL: So is God, in effect, saying that survival justifies everything?

HUGH: Not everything—not, for example, absolute and abject cruelty to other people.

BILL: When Harry Wu, an American citizen, was held in a Chinese jail on espionage charges, he signed a confession. When he got out, he called the confession a lie. He had lied to his captors because, he said, anything is justified in those circumstances. Is that what you're saying here?

ROBERTA: No, he said, "I lied to liars." They lied. I lied.

BURT: That was a very disturbing morality—and I find this morality disturbing, too. I don't think we can justify this. I don't think that survival of the tribe justifies immorality. If immorality is what it takes for this tribe to survive, my question is: Why bother?

HUGH: Morality isn't a question of life. Life is voracious, and you have to make really, really clever decisions on what is going to grow and what is not.

BILL: Are you saying that once God chooses this family—Abraham, Isaac, and Jacob—God is stuck with them, no matter what?

The Dream of Jacob, Gutenberg Bible, 1450–55

HUGH: Right. God starts the ball rolling, and He creates human genius. He's going to be constantly reflecting on that genius.

BILL: So once God chooses these people, God surrenders His own free will?

HUGH: Yes.

WALTER: So God doesn't have all the cards.

HUGH: Well, God has His creation.

BILL: And His creation is?

HUGH: Us.

BILL: Us. And we are—?

ROBERTA: —imperfect. For me, it's very important that Jacob not be whitewashed, because if the hidden assumption here is that God should work only with people who are perfect, or that God is somehow immoral, then I'm doomed. All of us are out of it. But God doesn't work only with perfect people. The fact that God works with this person, with all of his conflicting pushes and drives and struggles, is a sign of hope that God actually works with human beings.

AVIVAH: I absolutely agree. The drama is there—but Jacob starts off by being an *ish tam*, a simple whole—a term you could almost translate as "perfect." A perfect person. That's what he's called in the text. At the beginning of the story, he's con-

trasted with Esau. But he grows out of that.

BURT: Boy, does he! Yeah!

AVIVAH: That's what's so striking. He grows beyond that specious simplicity. This pale student, who has nothing to do with the dirty stuff in life, comes to recognize the necessity of having some of Esau in him, some of the way Esau lives in the world in himself. Jacob reconstructs himself in a much more complex and reproachable mode. I think the first movement is a movement downward.

BURT: The rabbis very naturally—and the Christian Fathers, too—make oppositions. Jacob's over here, and Esau's over there. They are really opposite types. And yet, in some way, the Bible doesn't do that. The Bible reminds us that they are twins. They come out of the same womb at almost the same moment, holding on to one another. I like very much what you said, Avivah, that you are both Jacob and Esau. Whatever opposition there may be, we have to recognize that we are both. God isn't just the God of Jacob. God is also the God of Esau. God doesn't just prefer genius, God also prefers the brute. God is the God of imperfection as well.

BILL: You remind me of something I read that said when Jacob and Esau came out of the womb, Jacob was grasping Esau's heel. "Grasping" is not a nice word. It's an odious word.

AVIVAH: It's not an odious word in Hebrew.

BILL: But this is a scheming, conniving, avaricious, ambitious kind of guy.

AVIVAH: I can't follow that because the Hebrew doesn't allow for such a dramatic understanding. It's simply that Jacob is fascinated by Esau. That's the way I would read it. From the beginning, Esau has come first. Jacob is behind. His eyes are filled with Esau's strength, his vitality, his prominence.

HUGH: He's his big brother, after all.

AVIVAH: His fantasies are full of Esau, and he constructs himself always in reference to Esau. It's absolutely there in the text. The classic distinction—that Esau is a hairy man and Jacob is a smooth man—is not supported in the text. The text says that Esau is hairy, but doesn't say anything about Jacob. Jacob says, "I am a smooth man" by contrast.

ROBERTA: Perhaps in the beginning, Jacob takes on an identity that is not his own. He takes on Esau's identity. That way he thinks he's going to get a blessing.

WALTER: Would you call that clever, or would you call that duplicitous?

ROBERTA: I wouldn't use either of those words right now. He's simply trying to figure out who he is and how to get what he wants. He wants the blessing from his father, but to get it, he has to be something he's not. Then you move on in the story, and you have the wrestling with the angel. In the wrestling comes the question: "Who

are you?" And then Jacob no longer answers, "I am Esau," but "I am Jacob." Then God gives him a new name: Israel. That's a movement of self-discovery. Do I make my way in the world by pretending to be somebody else?

HUGH: Isn't this about making civilization? When God says, "You are Israel. You are no longer Jacob," Jacob is being given the name of a whole people. He is a representative, a leader.

BILL: Let's come back to the seminal event of the dream of the ladder, which comes earlier than the wrestling, where Jacob becomes Israel. What do you think the dream says and means to Jacob?

AVIVAH: For me the dream is a dream about the connecting of heaven and earth. It's about angels who rise up from the earth and come back down from heaven. They start from earth, and they go up, and then they come down.

BILL: Angels being—?

AVIVAH: —angels being emanations of Jacob himself. They're expressions of Jacob himself, going up and down. The midrash offers a wonderful image for this. What are the angels doing? They're going up and looking at a kind of transcendent image of Jacob up above, and then they come down to the bottom of the ladder and see the real Jacob lying there, disgracefully sleeping in a holy place. If it's a holy place, he shouldn't be sleeping there. The ladder is Jacob himself. It's the connection between who he is as a recumbent body, just lying there on the ground, unconscious, and the great Jacob, the one you call the ''genius.'' The midrash has the angels rejoicing on the one hand and chiding and disapproving on the other. They're going up and down the ladder. In some way, Jacob's consciousness is full of the sense of the two levels of his being. On the one hand, he is here, and on the other level, he is there. And how is he ever going to create a real sense of integrity?

BURT: Before we take off on the dream, I'm still mulling over this business of how Jacob defines himself against others. I was very intrigued to hear Roberta and Avivah talk about how Jacob sees himself vis-à-vis Esau. That's something I hadn't fully appreciated until now. Since I'm a little brother, maybe my attention was captured by how much Jacob defines himself against Esau. Certainly, throughout his whole childhood, he measures himself against Esau. He sits in the tent while his big brother hunts. Although he's not really that much older, Esau looms large in Jacob's imagination. Always, even after twenty years, after four wives, after twelve children, when he comes back, he has never lost sight of Esau. Esau, meanwhile, gets over his rage and forgets all about Jacob. Jacob's not an issue for him. Esau goes his merry way. He's got his own power and his own issues. Jacob can never lose sight of that. In some way, he can never become whole until he can separate somehow from that twin.

BILL: But isn't the dream the beginning of the separation? Isn't the dream about the identity that he begins to achieve over time?

ROBERTA: In a sense, the angels are messengers. But the really surprising thing is that the Lord God is right in front of Jacob. He's not at the top of the ladder. That God is right with Jacob in that place is what makes the place holy. I don't think it was a holy place before and that Jacob was sleeping in the wrong place. I think it's because God is there with Jacob that it becomes a holy place, which is then recognized that way. In a sense, heaven has come to earth, and God is with Jacob.

BURT: And you know, Roberta, every place has God in it. In other words, every place is holy.

ROBERTA: When your eyes are open.

BURT: Yes, it's only when you recognize it—that God is standing right there in front of you. When you wake up from the dream.

RENITA: There's nothing like being confronted with the reality. There's nothing like the experience of knowing that, deep within. When you've had some kind of experience where you know that God is accessible, then heaven is accessible.

BILL: If you don't mind my asking a personal question: Have you had that experience?

RENITA: I've had that experience. They

happen every several years—you know, they're not regular experiences. But they're just powerful enough to keep you on the journey. They are so incredibly rare, but they're just enough. And then when they go, they vanish. But you never forget.

BILL: Are they interior experiences? Are they external events?

RENITA: They can be either one. I remember when I was in college, seriously contemplating suicide. I'll never forget one time, studying with some other students. I was wailing and crying about whatever it was. I was just at the point of contemplating suicide, when suddenly it was like something lifted. I don't even know what. I didn't say anything to anyone. I was just sitting there in the study carrel, along with other students, and I was crying and crying, when all of a sudden, something lifted. I knew that it was God, and that God was speaking to me. I don't know what God said, but all of a sudden, I didn't want to kill myself anymore. Since then, maybe I've had two more experiences like that.

BURT: Are they always out of depression?

RENITA: Oh, no, I'm rarely that depressed. When it comes to being about to kill yourself, that's just a good one to call up. But they're not always out of depression. The last one was a little less than a month ago. I was in a very good mood then. I was in the midst of a worship service. That was the rarest experience of all. I was in a church in Houston, during the

offering. Would you believe that? You know how mundane that moment is, when everything crashes. We were in the midst of the offering, and I was saying something—when all of a sudden, this presence came across in the worship experience. It was one of those moments when, thank God, I wasn't the only one who experienced it. You know, you can always sit back after it's over and say, ''You were just depressed'' or whatever. But in a congregation of two thousand people, when everyone there knows that something has changed—well, that's different. We did the call to worship, and nothing showed up. There was all the other gracing, and nothing showed up. But then, during the most mundane moment, the moment all worship crashes, the moment of offering, something happened in that worship experience, and everyone cried.

BURT: I'm intrigued by how God's presence is manifest. In both of your instances, people were around you. Jacob seems to have had his God experience very much alone.

RENITA: That's what I don't like about this story.

BURT: I think a lot of us have our God experiences very much in community.

ROBERTA: We have our experiences in different ways. I think back to my time in a college dormitory where, sitting in quiet, I said yes to God in a way that I didn't even understand then—I didn't know what I was doing. But I woke up the next morning

Elijah Pierce, *Climbing Jacob's Ladder*, 1965

with an incredible awareness of the reality of God near. And one of the things in the Jacob story that touches me is that this is so unexpected. He doesn't program this. He doesn't make this happen. He doesn't manipulate anything. He goes to sleep.

BILL: Walter said earlier that both of the moments of trauma occurred when Jacob was most vulnerable.

WALTER: We have our worst nightmares when the daytime is very troubling to us. At night, our defenses are down, and we lose the initiative for our existence that we can maintain all day long, when our guard is up.

AVIVAH: The Hebrew says that the night fell unexpectedly. The sun set before the proper time. When Jacob comes to the place, the Hebrew says he "collides" with a place—and suddenly, before he knows it, the place has taken him over.

BURT: And the word for "place" is a name for God. God is the omnipresent. God fills that place.

RENITA: We asked earlier: Why doesn't God judge Jacob and punish him or chastise him in some way? But sometimes an experience like this is enough to prostrate you. Sometimes the worst thing that God can do is show up and do something merciful to you. There have been times when I've been engaged in something depraved—don't use your imaginations!—or I've done something duplicitous, and I knew it was wrong. Then the next moment or within another week or two, something happens that's so glorious, so miraculous—something I just don't deserve. That in and of itself is enough sometimes to prostrate you.

HUGH: And sometimes when you get these wonderful gifts, it just ups the ante.

God has given you a bit more, and so you have more to do.

RENITA: The burden becomes greater.

JOHN: The story isn't about morality, though. It's about grace—the unexpected and unearned. To me, that's the wonder of this story. It's about free gifts given to the most undeserving people. I still think Jacob is duplicitous. But that encourages me— that unworthy folk can be the recipients of God's grace and God's mission.

> *"The story isn't about morality, though. It's about grace—the unexpected and unearned."*

BILL: Hugh, you said that the angel is the most important figure in the story. Why?

HUGH: I can think of lots of examples when grace or intuition has come to me and opened up heaven's gates. It's hardly to the same extent as this story, because this is about huge earthshaking events. But I can think of very small events that have been the opening of heaven's gates.

BILL: And angels?

HUGH: And it's angels every time, isn't it? We're talking about agency. Whenever heaven's gates open, it's because of an agency, which is not the person you think is driving. It's something like a lodger that lives inside you and takes over, thank God. Once, when I made a separation of my own kind, I moved into a state where I couldn't sleep for about five years. Every night was a terrible ordeal. In calling up what you think you have to call up in order to deal with the situation you are confronting, you call up more than you need. Sometimes God has to take hold of you and just wring it out of you. You learn grace.

BILL: You *learn* grace? Or you *receive* grace?

HUGH: You receive it when you give it up. When you finally surrender. When you are in such a state of surrender that the other part of you can come through— that's the opening of heaven's gate. Once I wanted to paint the rose window of Lincoln Cathedral. I wanted to get something of the sensation of a huge space filled with light, and I didn't know how to do it. I felt totally inadequate about it. Coincidentally, I developed a cyst in my eye where I had to have one eye closed up. I was in the hospital with one eye closed up and the other eye in overload, so everything was distorted. I thought, "Forget it. Not only am I inadequate to do this, now I'm handicapped." So I just gave up. I went back to my room and opened the door and saw the sun coming through the red curtain. The entire room was filled with red light. It was absolutely clear to me then what kind of painting I needed to do in order to embody the sensation of a rose light in a room.

BILL: We have to change our definition of angels from the heritage of Christian art—the celestial being with wings and a little halo. You're not talking about that kind of thing, are you?

HUGH: No, I'm talking about an extra-agency in your life that is connected to you and is not in your normal awareness but that comes through when you create space and ask for it to come through.

WALTER: Avivah, I was surprised to hear you say that the angels in this story were emanations of Jacob. I would have thought that they were the agents of God, inexplicable and irresistible, bringing a surplus into one's existence. The Bible seems to struggle with how to talk about that sort of "invasiveness" that is not a part of me but comes from outside me and impinges upon me with something of God's holiness or God's mercy. So I would link the angels much more to the coming of God than I would to the ideal self.

AVIVAH: The problem with that is that the angels begin on earth, not in heaven.

WALTER: Well, but that's all right—God is there, on earth.

AVIVAH: Yes, but why, then, does the ladder not begin in heaven and go from the top downward?

WALTER: That may be a problem—but in the next verse, with the utterance of God, you understand that this story surely has to do with the intrusiveness of God in this life.

AVIVAH: Absolutely.

WALTER: You used the word "connect." Those angels in that vision are connectors. And this man in exile is disconnected, and what he discovers in his vulnerability is that he is connected.

BILL: John, have you ever been touched by angels—whatever that term means? Has something happened that you could only explain by ascribing it to the touch of angels?

JOHN: No, but I've experienced the touch of God, which, for me, is the more important reality. If angels symbolize that, fine, but for me they are a bit of an obstacle as well.

BILL: For me too—I've never had this kind of experience.

JOHN: Yes—but once, recently, something like this happened in my daily life. I was getting ready to meet with another priest for what we call "spiritual direction." I was sitting at my desk in my office, thinking about the meeting, when suddenly I felt myself being held like—I don't know how to describe it. It was momentary. But that was the touch of God for me. I can't interpret it any other way. The experience was saying, "It's all right. It's all right. Be who you are." That is what the Bible offers me, not angels and intermediaries.

BURT: But I think that's already in the Bible. Jacob lies down, has a vision, wakes up, and says, "God is in this place, and I didn't even know it."

BILL: Has that ever happened to you?

BURT: I have had these kinds of experiences. Inevitably, they're stunningly mundane and yet, at the same time, very profound. Once I was with a friend, driving between New York and New Jersey. My friend was really depressed, and he was smoking away in the car, covered with ashes. He said, "I'm so depressed. Here I am, like Job, sitting here, feeling lousy and beaten, and covered in ashes. You know, if only I could have a sign from God." I was just about to turn to him and say, "Martin, it's just not gonna happen quite that way," when an enormous black Cadillac whizzed by us on the New Jersey Turnpike, and we both saw the same thing. Martin pulled over to the side of the road and turned to me. "Did you see those license plates?" "Yes." The license plate, a New Jersey plate, said "G-O-D." If I hadn't seen it and he had told me he had, I would have said, "No, no, no, no, no." But we both clearly saw it. Neither of us, of course, had the courage to call the License Bureau and ask whether they would give a vanity plate like that. We didn't want to find out. But what a ridiculous experience—on the New Jersey Turnpike, with a black Cadillac. But there it is. So how do you interpret it? I'm inclined to say, "Okay, it's bordering on the absurd, but the message is there."

RENITA: As you say, these things happen in stunningly mundane moments.

We're describing profound experiences, but they're not concocted moments. They're moments of everydayness. For Jacob, of sleeping. For you, of driving down the turnpike. For Abraham, just sitting around.

BURT: Yes, he's sitting at the tent, and three men show up.

ROBERTA: But our response to these moments takes us out of our routine life. One of the translations says Jacob is terrified. Our response to this sense of the realization of God is such that the angels often say, "Fear not, fear not." Angels are not these nice, chubby friends that make people feel good. They're forces that bring terror and awe . . . and humility.

"Angels are not these nice, chubby friends that make people feel good. They're forces that bring terror and awe . . . and humility."

HUGH: But sometimes they are chubby forces that make you feel good, too.

ROBERTA: Well, but not usually in the Bible.

AVIVAH: It reminds me of a tradition that the place where Jacob lay was the same place where Isaac was bound. Jacob deliberately aims for that place because he is haunted by it. He is a victim of his father's binding. That's the first place he goes to when he leaves his family and is on his own. That's where he has the dream and that's where God assures him, "I'll be with you"—in spite of the terror of his father's experience.

BILL: For me, this dream would be a nightmare. Knowing what happened to the people after they were chosen, I would say, "Oh no, not me! Take Esau!" As a consequence of the call, the mission, this is a haunted family. If I had been Jacob, I would be running away from that birthright.

HUGH: Well, yes—if you have a father you can't quite come to terms with, you have to create a greater father, or a clearer vision of a greater father. You need a physical father and a metaphysical father. That necessity propels Jacob's vision.

WALTER: And if it is that ominous, that would also illuminate why Jacob issues these conditions before he signs on. He's saying, "I don't want this big destiny unless there's some maintenance that comes with it."

BILL: "You'll be my God if I prosper"?

WALTER: Yes.

BILL: I can understand that.

AVIVAH: Jacob never refers to the God of his father without talking about fear. He swears by "the fear of my father, Isaac."

BILL: So if this is the spot where Isaac was offered as a sacrifice, there would be an enormous subterranean memory erupting here.

AVIVAH: Absolutely.

JOHN: There was an angel in that situation, too, who held back the hand of Abraham as he was about to sacrifice his son.

AVIVAH: In Hebrew, when Jacob gets up after the dream, he is described as "lifting up his legs." It means that he gets himself together and goes. The midrashic commentary is that Jacob has become lightfooted. He discovers a certain energy after lying all night in the place where his father, who was bound hand and foot, couldn't use his legs.

BILL: Fascinating. I'm reminded of Forrest Gump. Great things were happening to him beyond his knowledge, which he didn't understand at the time. And he becomes lightfooted at a moment of crisis. The other night, John, you referred to the story of Jacob as the *Rumpelstiltskin* story of the Bible. What did you mean by that?

JOHN: Well, there are elements in the wrestling that are folktale elements and that possibly point to the use of the story before Israel, which then incorporated the story into its own tradition. These particular folktale elements are also in *Rumpel-*

stiltskin. Until the name is learned, the princess will not be released. So the name has power. Knowledge of the name gives power to the person who overhears it and is finally able to reveal the name. The fact that dangerous adversaries or forces of night lose their power at break of dawn is another folktale element. So there are things in this story that are part of world literature.

RENITA: Another kind of universal theme we find here is the classic male come-of-age story about a man who leaves his family, and especially women, to discover himself. This has always been one of the most troubling aspects of the story for me—this notion of going away, of being alone, of hearing God and finding oneself separate and apart from a family. In Genesis, most of the women, like Hagar, experience God above the din of crying children. Leah, in the midst of having a number of children and being unloved, experiences God. But Jacob has the "luxury" of running away, or leaving mother and father and having this experience. It's the classic patriarchal story of a man who finds himself away from women and away from the family.

AVIVAH: But surely he's on his way to marry when he has the dream.

RENITA: Oh, that's true, too. But not yet married.

Title page with Jacob's dream, Book of Blessings, Fürth, Germany, 1735

BURT: It's an apposite dream for him at that point in his life. You're right, Renita, it's a coming-of-age story. Later, when he returns with a family and all the burdens of middle age—children, wives, all this responsibility—he knows he's going to inherit the farm, as it were. He's going back to the promised land. At that point, he has a very different kind of experience. We always refer to Jacob wrestling with the angel. That's not what the text says. The text says: "Jacob wrestled with a man." I

think this is something that we have to recognize in Genesis continually. It's very hard to know when a man is a man, and when a man is an angel, and when, in fact, an angel is God. So Jacob dreams of angels going up and down, wakes up, and there's God standing right there. He wrestles with a man, and when the wrestling match is over, whatever it is he's wrestled with says, "You have wrestled with a man and with God." That image of God is very much in human form. Genesis is so anthropomorphic that way—that is, we imagine God in human form. We imagine ourselves very clearly in God's image, so that when we wrestle, even with ourselves, there's God-wrestling going on.

WALTER: It's also the way dreams and nightmares work that when you have an adversary in a dream, that adversary has many identities, from many times and places, and these identities merge, so that when you wake up, you can't quite sort out who it was.

HUGH: I challenge this point about anthropomorphism because the biggest revelation in my life has been the ability to accept the rest of creation as not necessarily anthropomorphic. In my experience of this wrestling, I didn't wrestle with an anthropomorphic angel, I wrestled with a dog. I was in a state of insomnia, lying in bed, when I heard a noise in the room over by the door. A black shadow came into the room and walked right around the room, slowly. I was sitting up in bed, thinking, "Oh, no." And then, suddenly, the dog was on the bed. I was struggling with this thing, while at the same time thinking, "This is ridiculous. What am I doing fighting with this dog when I should be sleeping?" The dog just vanished, and I fell asleep. This happened before I was to make an important painting. It doesn't necessarily manifest itself as a golden angel or an ideal form, but as an embodiment of what you're actually thinking.

BURT: Did you limp the next morning?

HUGH: Everything that's happened to me in my work has always left a trace that never goes away.

BURT: You're right, there is a trace. But it's not a golden angel that Jacob wrestles with. Quite the contrary. It's a pretty nasty fight he has. When the angel or person can't prevail, he wounds Jacob. It's almost dirty fighting.

BILL: Remember that Jacob is returning home to face the brother he hasn't seen for many years, the brother from whom he stole the birthright. Maybe he has in mind the story of Cain and Abel, and he's imagining reuniting with Esau, troubled about whether there can really be a reconciliation and fearing what might happen. Is it possible that this encounter was his anticipated struggle with Esau as he comes back?

WALTER: Oh, I think there's no doubt of that, because right before the dream, the word "face" is used five times with reference to Esau. After the dream, Jacob says to his brother, "Seeing your face is like seeing the face of God."

BURT: And he names the place where he had the struggle *Pnel El*, "the face of God."

WALTER: That's right. So there's no doubt that part of whoever this wrestler is, is certainly Esau. Jacob is working out his forebodings about what he has to do the next day.

ROBERTA: One of the realities of a broken relationship is that if there's no move to healing, if what you do is run away from it, then that moment gets frozen in time and perhaps even amplified. Jacob has had twenty years to replay Esau's hatred, to replay fleeing as a fugitive, to do the "what-if" kind of story. So in turning around to go back, it was as if twenty years hadn't happened.

BILL: Haven't you had the experience of trying to return to someone who is an adversary, or with whom you have a broken relationship, and of being absolutely gripped by fear?

ROBERTA: Oh yes. It blows up and is magnified, and the anxiety chews at you in a deeper kind of way. The longer it is, the worse it can be.

RENITA: But you also find that in running away, you're running toward. Running away from your adversary, you're always en route to the adversary. Running away from God, you're always running toward God.

AVIVAH: And displaying a tendency always to be at the back.

WALTER: Where it's safe.

HUGH: But resistance is useless.

AVIVAH: As Jacob runs, the word that's used constantly is *ahar*. He is behind, he's born behind, he's in the back.

ROBERTA: He runs away, but he takes himself with him. So he deceives Laban and breaks that relationship, too.

AVIVAH: But isn't it interesting that when he's wrestling with the man, he says, "I will not let you go." It's almost like an anti-*Rumpelstiltskin* story, John. It doesn't say, "I will not let you go till you tell me your name," but "I will not let you go till you bless me." So what he wants is not necessarily control at this point. What he wants is a blessing.

BURT: He still wants a blessing.

RENITA: And what is this blessing?

AVIVAH: If one acknowledges that Esau is involved in this, then what Jacob wants is some kind of reconciliation—that Esau will grant him his own space on the earth.

JOHN: And Esau becomes the agent of reconciliation.

AVIVAH: Yes, it must come through Esau.

WALTER: Might he want the blessing that he stole in his subtleness, now given to him freely and ultimately?

AVIVAH: Well, that's an interesting combination because he does actually give a *berakha*, a present, to Esau. He gives a gift—but the word also means "blessing."

BILL: How do you read that?

AVIVAH: The rabbis read it as an acknowledgment. Jacob is saying, "I know you've got something against me, and in any way I can, I would like to give back the material benefits."

BILL: Some psychologists have suggested that Jacob was struggling with the dark side of his nature, with this confused ego that has been driving him to do these things all of these years. There's this wonderful image in Hinduism of the god Shiva, who's performing a great, glorious, liberating dance. If you look at Shiva's feet, you see that they're planted on a dwarf. In Hinduism, that dwarf represents the ego. The point of the symbolism is that, in order to fly, in order to dance, in order to be in the world joyfully, you have to step on your ego and keep it under control. Do you think this wrestling might be an account of Jacob wrestling with his ego, with the dark side of his nature?

AVIVAH: The problem I have with that again is the Hebrew word. *Vayeyaveyk*, "to wrestle," as the classic commentaries point out, is "to embrace." To wrestle is to embrace. It's a very intimate bodily encounter, legs around legs, and arms around arms, intertwined.

BILL: It's the embrace of adversaries, though. It's not love.

AVIVAH: But there's an erotic element in it, and if one is talking about Esau, who is part of Jacob—his twin brother—then it's not as simple as saying, "I put my foot on you, and I crush you." I don't think that's the symbolism there.

BURT: No. It's the same embrace Jacob had in the womb with Esau before either of them took precedence. This is something I just don't know what to do with. Esau is Jacob's twin. I don't think we should ever lose sight of that. You know, he's a *doppelgänger*, the mirror image. If we were to film this, how would we cast it? Everybody says, "Esau is hairy, and Jacob is smooth." But, in fact, the text doesn't make that distinction. That's Jacob's own reading of the distinction. Sometimes I wonder if they're not identical twins, so that any time Jacob looks at Esau, or vice versa, they see themselves.

ROBERTA: But this story doesn't have just one character—or even two, Jacob and Esau. This story also has the character of God.

BILL: And Jacob says, "For I have seen God face to face, and yet my life is preserved." He's not saying he saw his other self or his twin brother or his psychological mirror. He's saying, "I have wrestled with God face to face."

ROBERTA: And as he interprets his experience, he knows that the encounter that he's had is more than an encounter with himself or with his fears. He has had an encounter with the divine—with a force, a power, which is the covenant-making God, the promise-making God, and he's hungry in a way that we've seen when he wanted the blessing of Isaac and when he encountered God at the ladder. Jacob is hungry for the favor of God. What God will give to him, he wants. And he wants it so fiercely that he struggles to gain it.

RENITA: Someone said that our encounters with God are usually mediated through our encounters with other people—

BURT: —and also with our own selves.

BILL: I'm struck by my own experience here. I often don't know whether I'm struggling with God or with myself. And if I'm struggling with myself, I'm struggling with both the demonic and the divine in me. That's why, for me, this is the most resonant story in the whole of the Hebrew Bible.

RENITA: Yes, and it teaches us, too, about the distinction between mercy and grace. Mercy is not getting what you deserve; grace is getting what you don't deserve. Here we find both elements. Jacob, who should have received the judgment of God, receives mercy. In addition, he receives a blessing and encounters with God that he didn't deserve at all.

WALTER: That's what drives him crazy—that he finally has to receive it, even though he is always taking. It must come from the other side.

HUGH: Yes, but it comes from the other side of his life. Heaven's gate is contained within each individual. We have the key to open it—because it's always open.

WALTER: I don't believe that.

HUGH: But if the kingdom of heaven is within—

WALTER: —among. The kingdom of heaven is not "within" us, but "among" us.

BILL: I hope I'm not trespassing here, but if I am, the two of you can put up a sign, and I'll turn back. But I've sensed from the beginning a real tension between the two of you. I haven't known exactly what it is, except that theologians and artists compete over the patent for the interpretation of experience.

WALTER: I think that's true.

BILL: But I've sensed something, and it's even more evident now. Hugh, you said, "I don't accept the authority of God." Then Walter said, "I know you don't accept the authority of God." Why did you know that before we even came in here?

WALTER: Because earlier, Hugh told us a story about his father that set up a problem of authority. We all have problems with authority that take many different shapes—but, Hugh, yours looms large in how you think about these matters.

BILL: For people who may not have heard this story, could you tell us about wrestling with your father?

Jusepe de Ribera, *Jacob's Dream*, 1639

HUGH: When Jacob steals the blessing from his father, he has to get it by hook or by crook. When I was sixteen and wanted to separate from my father in order to claim authority over my own life and become an artist, I had to wrestle it out of him.

BILL: Physically?

HUGH: Yes, physically. I had to overpower him because until then, he had overpowered me.

BILL: A real wrestling match, then.

HUGH: There were no two ways about it—it had to be done. It couldn't be done in a reasonable way. It had to be done physically. He had to be overcome in a way in which he understood authority. It didn't come to anything death-defying, but it came to the point where he recognized my independence.

BILL: This was not playful wrestling?

HUGH: This was drawing blood. But when this occurred, he immediately arrived at a state in which he could say, "You are free—and free with my blessing." It wasn't

"Get the hell out of here and never darken this door again!"

BILL: He let you go be an artist?

HUGH: Yes—but nevertheless, the sense of having done that still stays with me as a kind of crime. My brother was also an artist, but he was never able to make that separation. He's still an artist, but he's not completely free, and he's ruled by the memory of his father. So when you take the blessing from the firstborn, you take on a double quest. You are upping what is really coming to you, so the burden becomes great.

AVIVAH: Isn't it very poignant with Jacob, then?

HUGH: I think it's extremely poignant. I've got great sympathy for the man. Jacob has an absolute void in him. He doesn't know how to reconcile himself with what he's done because he's done something that is greater than his awareness of himself. He has moved into his destiny. This need shapes his vision of moving into God as the next father.

AVIVAH: I think it's worth noticing that from the time Jacob comes back to the land of Canaan, he's supposed to go home to his father. That was a vow he made. The rabbis point out that it takes Jacob a terribly long time to get back. He really delays and defers.

HUGH: It's an entire life. I remember Goethe's story about a young man who asks a famous artist, "How come you do such wonderful stuff?" The artist replies, "Well, it's just pure genius." And the young man says, "Well, where did you get it?" "I got it from my father." "Well, where did he get it?" "He got it from his father." "And where did he get it?" "He took it!"

BURT: It's fascinating to me the extent to which Isaac and Rebekah replicate themselves in very subtle ways in Jacob's actions. Right before and after Jacob's famous wrestling match, he's facing the fact that he's going to cross the river and meet Esau. He's got this whole troop of family with him, and he's terrified. But the way he deals with this terror is, to me, horrifying. He divides his family into groups. He puts the concubines and their children up front, and then he puts Leah and her children behind them, and then Rachel and Joseph he keeps at the back. Then he actually even says out loud, "Well, you know, if somebody's got to go, let it be the front troops. We'll save the guys in back." I think to myself how horrifying it must have been for Gad and Asher and Naftali and Dan to hear their father say, "Okay, you guys, you're in the front lines, you're cannon fodder. If you die, it's not so terrible, as long as the boys in the back are saved." When I realized the horror that they must have felt, I recognized that, in fact, that is what Jacob and Esau hear from their parents. Rebekah prefers Jacob to the exclusion of Esau. Isaac prefers Esau to the exclusion of Jacob. And Jacob, when his turn comes, reproduces that terrible preference of children.

BILL: But this is not a God, Burt, Who cares much for ethical imperatives or moral orders. This is a God Who—well, remember the story of Lot, and Sodom and Gomorrah? Lot offers his daughters to the strangers. God makes no judgment on Lot. He makes a judgment on Sodom and Gomorrah, but not on him. This is not a God Who's got an ear attuned to the moral niceties that concern us.

BURT: I'm less concerned about God's role here than I am in what the psychiatrist Nancy Chodorow calls "the reproduction of mothering"—how, willy-nilly, we reproduce the sins of our parents.

BILL: Throughout Genesis, God is the Father, the patriarch of a dysfunctional family.

ROBERTA: But to take on your point—and it's most provocative—to say that God does not care about morality or those kinds of things is to misread the whole biblical narrative. It isn't a moralistic narrative—that is, it doesn't tell the story and then tack a little moral onto the end of it and tell you what to think and feel all the way through it. You understand God as a covenant-making God, a God of care, a God of promise-making, Who keeps His promises. And that's the fundamental basis of morality—to give your word and keep your word. The particular stories of Genesis are set within this larger narrative of the creative and covenant-making God. To say that because there is not a judgment made explicitly in the text is to misread the way in which the text conveys the truth.

JOHN: But that's to miss the other side of God, the terrifying side of God. I would like your picture of God to be like the God in the Bible, but as I read it, that's only half the picture. The other half is that He's a mysterious, terrifying, wounding Adversary against whom we all struggle. The God Whom Jacob confronts terrifies him.

AVIVAH: Yes, and, as I said, Jacob swears by "the fear of my father, Isaac." It strikes me as very arresting that the rabbis don't criticize Jacob for taking the blessing, but they do criticize him for not paying his vow to go back to his father in peace. He delays going back so long that God finally has to say to him, "Get up and go there!" He delays until the very last minute, and as soon as he gets there, Isaac dies.

BILL: You've completed the circle for me in taking us back to the father. Hugh, you withdrew your assent to God's authority because of the struggle with your father. But that might take you back to the ultimate father, if God is the Father of us all.

HUGH: Yes, the struggle with the authority of the father reminds me of the Greek myths—think of Prometheus, stealing fire from the gods. Or the fairy tales—we talked about *Rumpelstiltskin*, but what about *Jack and the Beanstalk*, where you take the wealth from heaven and then have to cut down the ladder in case the giants come to take it back? But, you know, you have to be sure you're talking to God before you absolutely give away your authority. And when you do finally give your

Jacob Epstein, *Jacob and the Angel*, 1940

authority to God, you're really giving through the best part of yourself.

BILL: What do you mean?

HUGH: I think that when we come to know God, we come to know a bigger idea of what we are. I had respect for my father and love for him. One day we were driving in a car, and I was trying to impress him with the world of art. He was a farmer, and he wasn't impressed with the world of art. I was telling him about Botticelli's *Venus*—this wonderful thing—and he said, "I don't know what you're talking about." Then he pointed out of the window of the car at a plowed field and said, "Now, *that* is beautiful." I thought, "What a jerk!" And then, later on, when I realized what he was saying, I felt so ashamed of thinking that.

BURT: And now you spend your time up in Connecticut, looking at the trees and the fields—

HUGH: —rescuing my father.

BILL: Whatever our interpretation of the story, isn't this really about the moment that Abraham's children, the chosen people, the people of God, are named Israel? Jacob loses his identity and emerges as the receiver of the covenant, the receiver of the blessing, whether he deserves it or not, and Israel emerges as a people.

AVIVAH: Except that he doesn't quite lose the name of Jacob. When Abram becomes Abraham, he's no longer Abram.

But Jacob always remains Jacob. He's referred to as Jacob many more times than he's referred to as Israel. He has two names from now on, and that's what makes him so fascinating. His identity is complex. He's constantly in a struggle between the two sides of his identity. It's not a transformation but an evolution. Something has opened up in him, but it's a resource, not something that will absolutely define him.

BILL: What does it mean for Israel that as a people, they emerge from a struggle with God?

JOHN: That's the story of this human community of the people of Israel—that their history is a history of a struggle with God, of opposition to God, of being wounded by God in the struggle, and yet of being blessed by God, too. The story encapsulates all of that. Think of what this story must have meant when Israel was in exile in Mesopotamia and in Babylon, as Jacob was. This story would tell them that as our ancestor Jacob met God in the night, so we can still meet God in the long night of our exile.

BILL: What's the importance of the wound? Jacob limps away from this wrestling match with a wound that is not just a bruise but a permanent injury. He never forgets it, nor are the people of Israel allowed to forget it.

JOHN: I think it's the text's way of saying that when you encounter God, when you wrestle with God, you're not going to leave that encounter unchanged. And the change can be a hurtful change. Any change or moment of transition in life can be painful because it means leaving something behind and moving forward. The wound symbolizes that. This encounter with God has meant pain for Jacob and pain for the people of Israel as well—the pain of struggling with God, of experiencing God as the Adversary. We often talk, and I think quite properly, of God as Father and of God as Protector. But what about God as Adversary? There's a long biblical tradition in the Book of Job and other places of God taking an adversarial position. But the mystery is that even the Adversary continues to love the one with whom the Adversary struggles.

> *"Any change or moment of transition in life can be painful because it means leaving something behind and moving forward."*

AVIVAH: Midrash says that Jacob demands a blessing "because you have injured me." There's a connection between the pain and suffering and the moral right to ask for a blessing. This relationship with God is so intimate and vulnerable that I can ask for a blessing.

ROBERTA: But the blessing is not for Jacob or Israel alone, it's for all the families of the earth. In the Abrahamic words of blessing—"blessed to be a blessing." And yet, to be a blessing to others does not mean being unwounded or invulnerable. Rather it is the wounded one who is the blessing. As Christians, we talk about the wounded healer and the fact that the way in which we are blessed to be a blessing, sharing in that covenant promise, is not out of perfect strength or infinite wisdom, but out of our vulnerability and our woundedness.

WALTER: If one extrapolates from the personal woundedness to the sense of community, it means that the community—whether Israel or the Christian Church—is never going to be the beautiful people. They're always going to be weird and odd misfits. I think that's a peculiar problem for Christians in the United States and in the West, because we are the dominant religious community. We are the establishment, and therefore we imagine that we ought to have it right. What is now being rediscovered, as the Church is being disestablished in the West, is that we are having to face up to our weirdness and the sense of being a misfit in the world. I suppose we always chafe against it, but it seems to me it's a given in the nature of this community of faith.

BILL: Perhaps Christians could profit from learning what it means to be Jews—perpetual outsiders. This would place us not in the seats of power, but rather against the seats of power.

WALTER: Which I suspect is the only effective way to be a blessing in the world.

RENITA: When the disciple Thomas is confronted with Jesus after the Resurrection, he says, "Show me your wounds"—as though woundedness authenticated that Jesus was, in fact, Jesus. Sometimes people want to know our wounds as a way of authenticating our own faith and our own struggle. There is something all right about struggling with God and having been wounded by God—so we don't have to be afraid of struggling. Hugh, I was thinking about your struggle with your father and how it symbolizes a struggle with God. For some people, that would be frightening. They would say, "I can't struggle with God. I must relent, I must do whatever . . ." And listening to the provocative conversation between Walter and you, I can't help thinking that there's something very masculine about all of that, and something very masculine about this story. This issue of struggling and fathers and wanting a blessing and separating and leaving people behind and sending the children away—

WALTER: It's not sending the children away; it's putting them up front in the line of fire.

RENITA: But remember, even in the second dream, Jacob has sent everybody away so that he is alone. As we talk about this story, I think to myself, "I don't particularly care about the Jacob story. It doesn't move me one way or another." I can *get* moved by this story, but I'm not *naturally* moved by it. But I think there's a feminine resonance to this story in the earlier story of Hagar, who is banished. She too sees the face of God or sees something that she thinks is the face of God. "Have I indeed seen God and still live?" Or, in the NIV translation, which I love to hear—"I have seen the One who sees me." Already in Genesis there's the image of a woman who has heard God above the noise of a crying child. She puts the child away from her—but not very far. She has to hear God above the voices of children, of crying. So there's not this kind of separation, of willfully leaving someone, that we find in the stories of men coming of age.

HUGH: But one of the things that's not explicit for women is the physical torture that men are constantly proud of—you know, it's their trophy. "I got wounded!" Women are touched in other ways. And we don't hear enough about that.

BILL: Except maybe in childbirth.

HUGH: Childbirth—that's fine, but there are other ways we can struggle.

RENITA: Oh, gee, the way you said that—childbirth, naaah. You need to go through that to know it's not a mild thing.

HUGH: Giving birth is without doubt the most spectacular physical act of creation that there is—but it's a biological act. My point is that spiritual creation is also within human possibility. Spiritual birth and genesis is something that needs to happen continually, in everybody's lives. Our society places too much emphasis on physical dominance, but as an artist, I know that a state of vulnerability is as dynamic as any overt act of aggression. Our society does not give enough acknowledgment to sensitivity and spiritual attainment. Trophies are awarded to the hunter-killers, and they are usually men.

ROBERTA: I want to tell a story about learning about vulnerability. It's a story that comes from an experience of trying to be tough. When I went to a famine camp for the first time, I told myself in advance that I was going to be strong and that I was going to be centered on problem solving. I was not going to get enmeshed in the horrible pain. As I stood in the famine camp, bodies of babies were piled up to my shoulder height—and that was just that one day's group of babies who had died. I was handed a child that looked to be about eighteen months old—thin, emaciated, weak. I was told this child was five. It was so malnourished and on the edge of dying—and I found myself unable to keep my original intention. I found the tears coming, and I was weeping there. The next day I went to a ''business meeting'' of Africans dealing with the problem of ''What should we do about this famine and that war that is part of it?'' I wondered how I would be introduced. An African man stood and said, ''Brothers and sisters, our sister has wept.'' And that gave me my credentials for being a part of that particular situation. Vulnerability is the way in which we connect our humanity with each other. For Jacob and for Israel to be vulnerable and to have Jacob seen as the vulnerable leader says

something about what it means to be human and how we are to live with each other.

AVIVAH: The story ends with the words ''the sun rises, and he limps.'' There's an illumination of the limping, a great consciousness about the fact that he's limping. It's not just that he's limping.

BILL: Didn't the Jews follow up on that with an injunction?

AVIVAH: Yes, there's a dietary restriction—we don't eat the sciatic nerve, which is a nerve in the side of the animal.

BURT: Which means we don't get to eat filet mignon.

BILL: And the purpose of that is remembrance—which, as the rabbi said, is the secret of redemption.

AVIVAH: Remember that Isaac's legs were bound, and that Jacob walked so lightfootedly in his youth. Then, in this more mature stage, he knows the wound in the leg. This is a mature awareness of himself.

BILL: A Jewish friend of mine said recently, after we had discussed this story, ''I wish Jacob had lost.'' He really meant it—he was not being facetious. ''I wish Jacob had lost. I wish he had not emerged the victor''—which he obviously was because he took the blessing and went on— ''because our people have paid a price far greater than that wound on the thigh. It isn't worth it to have been chosen. I wish that Jacob had lost." Do you ever feel that?

AVIVAH: We've cried many tears. But there's always something in me and, I think, in many Jews, that says "in spite of everything." In spite of everything, there is something we wouldn't have given up on. There's just this sense of an ability, a grandeur—something built into our condition that has to do with our suffering. We can't have one without the other.

RENITA: Yes, what Walter said is so. What I fear within modern Christianity is this quest for power and position, for returning America to Christianity. We're becoming so concerned about power and politics that we're losing touch with the fact that Christianity emerged out of marginality and suffering. To be a Christian now means to be prosperous, rich, politically established—to win.

WALTER: Well, the wound in the Christian tradition has been transposed into the cross. And what you're talking about is a Church that is increasingly embarrassed about the cross or postures itself as though you can have the gospel without the cross—as though you can have the blessing without the wound.

BILL: What do you think is the point of this story? Why is it included in the Bible?

WALTER: Well, it's obviously included because they loved it—precisely because it is so dense and complex. As our discussion of it indicates, it is inexhaustible. This com-munity kept returning to it and received something always fresh and energizing about its life in the world. I don't imagine it was preserved and canonized because it made this point or that. But it is the convergence of all those points that delivers Jews and, subsequently, Christians from a simplistic, one-dimensional self-understanding.

AVIVAH: That comes out very clearly in the answer to the question Jacob asks. He asks, "What is your name?" And he's brushed off. He's not going to know the name. And that confirms for the reader that we're not going to know. We can speculate. But, finally, we are not going to know, and that's what we're left with.

JOHN: What a wonderful thing, as you say, to begin by struggling with an adversary, only to discover that you are in the embrace of a lover. Maybe, in a certain sense, that's one of the transformations in this story, too. The man becomes the source of blessing—but this is not only wrestling, it is embrace.

"What a wonderful thing . . . to begin by struggling with an adversary, only to discover that you are in the embrace of a lover."

BILL: Walter, I remember something you wrote years ago about this story confirming the choice of Jacob as the anointed. No doubt about it, Jacob is the one. And there seems to be absolutely no moral basis for that choice.

WALTER: That's right. I suppose this says that the love that is driven by authority and resolve and generosity doesn't have anything explainable behind it beyond the determined act itself.

HUGH: What about sacrifice? Aren't we talking about self-sacrifice here? If you're doing anything that is life-affirming, you literally have to give your life. There's nothing else that you can do of any value in your life other than to give it up.

WALTER: That's right. But I thought Bill was asking what is it that's coming from God's side about all of this?

BILL: The people who put this in the Bible had to be trying to explain something about God's motive.

WALTER: I don't think they explain. I think they witness to it, and they confirm it every time they retell the story—but there's not a shred of explanation.

BURT: I think Walter's point is well taken—that one of the points of the story is that you don't get the blessing without getting wounded, and that even God's unconditional love for Jacob actually winds up costing Jacob something physically. I was sitting here earlier, kind of getting the creeps, I confess, listening to everyone show their wounds. Not the personal wounds so much as the Christians claiming, "We have our wounds." It suddenly dawned on me that what we're talking about is the cross. As a Jew, it makes me uncomfortable to see the cross there in the Hebrew Bible.

WALTER: No, I wasn't suggesting that.

BURT: But I think your point was well taken. The fact is that Christians have had their wounds just as Jews have. In some ways it's easier to hear Renita talk about it because the African American community is still fresh with wounds. Walter says that white Protestant Christians are in danger of forgetting that they carried the cross once. Judaism, I think, is in that moment as well. Certainly, we can all remember fifty years ago—the Holocaust. That was an enormous wound. But since 1967, with the power of the state of Israel and the wealth of the American Jewish community, we're also in danger of forgetting that we once were an oppressed people, and that whatever blessing we have, there are wounds, and there are always costs. Maybe God's love isn't quite as free as we like to think it is.

ROBERTA: I don't think Jacob is just arbitrarily chosen. You can see in the text that God is serious about the covenant and that when he is chosen, Jacob becomes serious about the covenant. With all of his failings, Jacob is someone who can be trusted. God cares about something—and what He cares about is the well-being of the whole planet. He chooses not a particularly moral or righteous character but someone to fulfill His purpose in history. The stories, as they unfold, are very much about God as the Actor, working out a purpose in history through the covenant. Jacob is a respondent to and participant in that purpose.

RENITA: Throughout Genesis, God continues to choose scoundrels. So what's the point of trying to do right if God continues to use the Jacobs of the world? And history seems to prove this text correct—God does seem to use scoundrels—myself included, I must admit.

JOHN: But doesn't that make it a better story? A story about people who play the margins is just a better story. What do we watch on television?

HUGH: But this is about the cost of leadership, too—those scoundrels, or people, who have to take the biggest risks with themselves and their own confused sense of their morality. They have to go out there without following the rules.

BILL: Every time you say "scoundrel," Avivah blanches.

RENITA: Messy people.

WALTER: Subtle people.

BURT: The interesting thing is how Jacob perceives himself in all of this. He has done whatever it took to get the blessing and the birthright, to wrestle with God,

and to grow quite wealthy. And at the end of the Book of Genesis, when he goes down to Egypt to be reunited with Joseph, he even blesses the Pharaoh. The Pharaoh asks him, "Tell me about your life. How many are the days and years of your life?" And this is Jacob's response: "The days and years of my life are thirty and one hundred. Few and ill-fated have been the days and years of my life." In the end, he seems to see himself as a pathetic character. That never ceases to amaze me. I used to get angry that he couldn't see the blessing. Now I'm starting to think that he has no other way to view himself. He's so constricted.

AVIVAH: Well, he's just emerged from the twenty-year trauma of the Joseph experience. After such an experience, it wouldn't be surprising if someone felt that life was a bleak affair.

"Faith is being willing, able, gutsy, vulnerable, and courageous enough to let go of the safety and security of the swinging bar, in the middle of the air, in order to take the hand of the one who will meet you."

BILL: After reading stories like this, what does faith mean to you? What is faith to you, personally?

ROBERTA: At one level, the story of Jacob unfolds for me in the interplay between his prayers and his experiences. Earlier he has a kind of foxhole faith. Prayer involves a kind of bargain—"Lord, get me out of this mess. Help me out here." The wonderful thing is that God stays with him, even though that is the kind of faith he has. I don't see faith as a once-for-all kind of thing. By the time Jacob engages in the wrestling match, he's done everything he knows how to do and he's been as clever as he knows how to be, and he knows that he's at the end of himself. Faith is a turning to God—and that reality. Basically, faith is a crying out to God that says, "God, You are. Here I am. You know my circumstances and need. I am looking to You." So faith is a kind of looking, a reaching out, a response. There's one other image that embodies faith for me and that is the image of the trapeze artist. What is faith? Faith is not the safe climbing of the ladder. Faith is being willing, able, gutsy, vulnerable, and courageous enough to let go of the safety and security of the swinging bar, in the middle of the air, in order to take the hand of the one who will meet you.

BILL: Have you ever let go and there's nothing there?

RENITA: Yes, many times. Faith is what you do between the last time you experienced God and the next time you experience God. I think it's that interval right

there—that "in the meantime." And it can be a long time. It can be twenty years, Jacob says.

> *"Faith is what you do between the last time you experienced God and the next time you experience God."*

WALTER: When you're in free fall.

RENITA: It is the daily things that you attend to, the ritual things, that keep you going. Flannery O'Connor said that every day she would get up early in the morning and go downstairs to her typewriter and sit before it, so that just in case something came, she would be there to receive it. Now many times I have mounted a pulpit or gone into a classroom and even written books when I was enraged with God, when I hadn't heard from God, and was not even on speaking terms. But still I mount the pulpit.

BILL: Why?

RENITA: Because in case God wants to speak, I'll be there to listen. I think that's the beauty of ritual. It's routine. It's boring. But every so often, if you're in the right place—Jacob went to "a certain place," it says—God shows up and whispers something, maybe enough to keep you going for another twenty years. Every night my daughter wants to hear the same story. I have nineteen books for this two-year-old, but she wants to hear the same story. And each night the story is different. In the dailiness—or nightliness—of telling that story, in the ritual, I do hear something. And in the dailiness, God shows up in those smaller ways.

HUGH: Without expectations?

RENITA: Without expectations. Yes.

BILL: What does this story demand of us?

WALTER: I think it demands engagement with God's holiness, which is always troubled by and never resolved with ingredients of submissiveness and assertiveness. In Jacob, you get larger doses of assertiveness than you do submissiveness, but they're both there. I believe that after the long establishment of Christianity, what the Church in the West is now having to relearn is that this engagement with the holiness of God is endlessly troubled and troublesome, and it cannot be any other way.

JOHN: I like Renita's point about faithfulness as part of faith. Sometimes it's hard for someone like me and others here who study the Bible professionally. That has to be an alienating experience because the Bible becomes an object for interpretation. It's only if I am faithful to that task that the Bible can once again speak to me and wound me. I have to remain open to God's voice in that text.

BILL: Doesn't the text also demand that our obsession with our well-being, our status, our power, our position, our ambition, not be the center of our concerns? Jacob had a mission larger than his own prosperity.

WALTER: I think that's right. But the narrative suggests that, willy-nilly, even when we are obsessed with those things, we are not finally going to avoid the nighttimes of vulnerability when these other things intrude upon us.

BILL: You keep saying this is real night work.

WALTER: Yes, and the reason I say it's real night work is that I'm so damn good at daytime work. I've got it all figured out. I can manage it. I can pay all my foreseeable bills. But that isn't what my life is about. What my life is about are those troublesome intrusions that call all of this into question and place it in jeopardy. Now that may just be the state of a sixty-two-year-old man who's had his youthful encounter and is now at the other end of the tale.

RENITA: What part of the tale is that?

WALTER: The part of the tale of having it all managed during the daytime, but then spending more time pondering the undercurrents that cannot be tamed. The

Jacob's Vision of the Heavenly Ladder (top); *Jacob Wrestling with the Angel, Munich Psalter*, England, before 1220 (bottom)

dream, or the nightmare, or whatever it was, seems to me to be that kind of undercurrent. What preoccupies me, not only personally, but in terms of the Church in the United States, is that my kind of established Church has got the daytime all figured out. It's very seductive to belong to a technological culture and to be a part of the white upper middle class, where you can program it all out. But what the Church in the United States is having to ask is: What about those undercurrents that remind us that all of this is really kind of phony and brutal, and that you can't live your life in terms of these things?

HUGH: Do you have any experience in your waking life where you know you've made a deal with God and that He will show up if you show up?

WALTER: Oh, I think so—but that gets stirred and reshaped in the nighttime.

RENITA: But what does it mean to experience God at sixty-two instead of at forty or twenty? What is the blessing a sixty-two-year-old wants that may be different from the blessing that a forty-year-old wants or that a twenty-year-old wants, such as food, clothing, and success?

WALTER: I don't know how much one can generalize because everybody is at a different place. But it is the transition from having to being. When you're on the down slope, about all you've got left is your life. The rest of it is less and less important.

ROBERTA: A friend of mine in his fif-ties has just worked it out under the rubric of moving from success to significance. The issues now are no longer those of success but of meaning and significance. Does my life count for anything?

WALTER: I have an older brother, and while we've never been alienated, lots of times we haven't bothered particularly. But my relationship to him now becomes much more important than it has ever been since childhood.

RENITA: And I can see where Jacob's relationship with Esau would be much more important than it was.

BILL: I really hear you, Walter. I've had it all right during the day—the résumé grew, the experiences, the acclaim. That's what I thought at forty was necessary to indicate that I was doing good. Good work. But the nights—the time of vulnerability, as you say, told me otherwise.

HUGH: If you had been snatched away at forty, would you have felt incomplete?

BILL: I'd have felt dead—and incompletely dead!

WALTER: But probably not feeling incomplete because those categories of awareness were not operative.

BILL: It's the awareness that time gives you—time, loss, pain, the experience of the suffering of other people. You put your finger on it, Mr. Theologian. It's the awareness that you don't have at forty. At forty, you have the acceptance. This is it. I've got it. Now go do something with it.

BURT: So what happens at sixty? Is it the birthday that does it? Is it some physical event? Is it some wrestling in the night?

BILL: Well, I had bypass surgery. I woke up in the hospital three days after the surgery, back in my room, having come from intensive care. It was midnight. The night nurse had left the TV set tuned to the public television station and fallen asleep. Beethoven's *Fifth* was playing. Now I've heard Beethoven's *Fifth* all my life—that is, I've listened to it. But this night I experienced it. I can't summon the words to tell you what it was to experience this music. I was aware in a different way.

BURT: But it is an awareness of mortality—

BILL: No—no, I was aware of the experience of the music.

BURT: And, Roberta, you experienced a heart attack less than a month ago.

ROBERTA: Yes, there's a heightened awareness of being intensely alive, in part because you've faced the fact that you might not be. It's as if every pore of your being is alert and tingling. I came home from the hospital and the first thing I did was to sit in the place where I sit each morning to read my Bible and pray. I watched the birds, especially a red cardinal, and it was like an epiphany. I didn't think, "Oh, maybe I could have died" or "I will

die, therefore I'm going to notice this." It's just that every part of me was more conscious because of that experience.

BILL: As the two of you talk, Jacob becomes a part of this circle. At forty, I wasn't wounded. I did more wounding at forty than I was wounded—parents, brother, wife, children. I was not so aware of it, but at forty, I was a wounder. At sixty, I'm wounded. Once you are wounded, you can see why the Jacob story is in the Bible. Once you are wounded, you don't want to wound anymore. You want to heal.

HUGH: And is this when you can say, "I'm now in the House of God—this is heaven's gate"?

BILL: Only God can say.

HUGH: Ralph Waldo Emerson said that when you see through the eyes of the soul, you feel as if you're on another planet. You're in the same place, but suddenly you say, "What's this? What have I not been looking at?"

RENITA: And if there are angels, they are indeed those messengers who bring us precisely this kind of awareness. That's certainly what the angels do in Jacob's story—bring him to a new level of awareness and insight.

ROBERTA: "I don't want to wound anymore" speaks to me very, very deeply. It was part of my own conscious awareness coming out of this experience that I want to be part of the healing of the world rather than a wounder. I wouldn't want to make too much of this, but the Jacob story doesn't end with the part we looked at. Very soon after this part, the sons are engaged in acts of violence and desecration that are just awful. We see Jacob—and he is not cheering them on. He is not entering into the wounding. He is reproaching, with tragic sadness. He sees the pain that has been inflicted and the price that will be paid for that pain by ongoing generations. And I think there is a sense that in being wounded, he does not want to wound.

JOHN: But think of the story from the point of view of the sons, when they come back to Jacob with the story of Joseph's death, and Jacob laments, as if he had lost his only son, in the presence of the other sons. Maybe that wasn't an intentional wounding—but they must have been so wounded. So Jacob continues to be Jacob.

WALTER: Bill said one doesn't *want* to wound. He didn't say he *didn't* wound.

BILL: Isn't it remarkable that even as we talk about this shadowy figure, thousands of years old, that he does indeed seem to emerge here in the midst of our conversation.

JOHN: Every time you go back to these stories, something new is revealed—something about you, something about God, something about the relationship between you and God, something about the community in which you experience God, the people of Israel, or the Church—

RENITA: —and something about reading and hearing and thinking about these stories in a community. I can't say that when I sat down last night and read this story on my own that I heard all of *this* conversation. There's something about reading with others and hearing other experiences that make this story just so precious. I had the experience the other week of reading what to me was a good novel, and I asked myself, "What makes a good novel?" I decided that a good novel is one whose characters live in my head for days after. When I read this good novel, I kept saying, "No, see, if I were that character, I would have done this. And then I would have done that. And why didn't she do this? I mean, how dare she!"

HUGH: That's agency, as opposed to angel—put on a smaller level. But this is one of the most crucial ways people need to be unlocked. People feel as if they're prisoners in their own skin.

RENITA: And there are degrees to being locked. For example, in this conversation there were times when we were all locked into "What does it say?" Then there were other times when we were a little freer, playing with what it says and how we experience what it says and what it does not say.

HUGH: And that ladder is Jacob, seeing himself stretch all the way to heaven. He's that large.

RENITA: I'm glad we had an artist like

Hugh in the group—because, Hugh, I don't think I've seen a thing that you've said.

HUGH: That's what the Bible's saying.

RENITA: But I couldn't see it unless you were here.

BURT: Here we are sitting around and studying an ancient text and bringing it to our own lives. But it isn't that there are just eight voices here. There's yet another voice. You could say it's the voice of the text. This is an old rabbinic concept, and every time this happens to me, I'm stunned that they got it. In some profound way, it's the revelatory voice of God. You asked earlier how we experience God. I think study, particularly study in the community of people who are likewise seekers, who are willing to take risks and to wrestle, who are willing to be wounded, brings us great bless-

ing. And the blessing is that, in some small way, God is revealed.

AVIVAH: There's a classic idea in Jewish thinking that a certain part of Torah never was said until you said it now. The Torah is always incomplete until this moment.

BURT: It's a conversation. The late Rabbi Louis Finklestein said it very poignantly. He said, "When I pray, I talk to God. And when I study, God talks to me."

RENITA: It may be that this time we've had together has been study as worship. That is a radical thought for many of us in our tradition.

BILL: Well—if this is worship, on public television, it may be unconstitutional.

X

EXILE

Dianne Bergant • Norman J. Cohen

Francisco O. García-Treto • P.K. McCary

Seyyed Hossein Nasr • Phyllis Trible

Burton L. Visotzky

We learn in life that most blessings are mixed blessings. Joseph, who is precocious, learns it early. He is blessed with the gifts of reading dreams, physical beauty, and his father's love. But these very gifts cause his downfall, and he winds up in slavery and exile. Our discussions of Genesis began with the story of Abraham on the move toward the promised land. We end with Joseph in a foreign land. But far from home, he is never far from his roots. This is a familiar refrain in Genesis, from beginning to end.

—Bill Moyers

Zulaykha Seizing the Skirt of Joseph's Robe, Yusuf and Zulaykha by Jami, Iran, ca. 1540

Now Joseph was taken down to Egypt, and Potiphar, an officer of Pharoah, the captain of the guard, an Egyptian, bought him from the Ishmaelites who had brought him down there. The LORD was with Joseph, and he became a successful man; [he found favor in his master's sight, and Potiphar made him overseer of his house . . .]

Now Joseph was handsome and good-looking. And after a time his master's wife cast her eyes on Joseph and said, "Lie with me." But he refused and said to his master's wife, "Look, with me here, my master has no concern about anything in the house, and he has put everything that he has in my hand. He is not greater in this house than I am, nor has he kept back anything from me except yourself, because you are wife. How then could I do this great wickedness, and sin against God?" And although she spoke to Joseph day after day, he would not consent to lie beside her or to be with her. One day, however, when he went into the house to do his work, and while no one else was in the house, she caught hold of his garment, saying, "Lie with me!" But he left his garment in her hand, and fled and ran outside. When she saw that he had left his garment in her hand and had fled outside, she called out to the members of her household and said to them, "See, my husband has brought among us a Hebrew to insult us! He came in to me to lie with me, and I cried out with a loud voice . . . He left his garment beside me, and fled outside." Then she kept his garment by her until his master came home . . .

When his master heard the words that his wife spoke to him, saying, "This is the way your servant treated me," he became enraged. And Joseph's master took him and put him into the prison, the place where the king's prisoners were confined . . . But the LORD was with Joseph and showed him steadfast love; he gave him favor in the sight of the chief jailer . . .

After two whole years, Pharoah dreamed that he was standing by the Nile, and there came up out of the Nile seven sleek and fat cows . . . Then seven other cows, ugly and thin, came up out of the Nile after them . . . The ugly and thin cows ate up the seven sleek and fat cows. And Pharoah awoke. Then he fell asleep and dreamed a second time; seven ears of grain, plump and good, were growing on one stalk. Then seven ears, thin and blighted by the east wind, sprouted after them. The thin ears swallowed up the seven plump and full ears. Pharoah awoke, and it was a dream. In the morning his spirit was troubled; so he sent and called for all the magicians of Egypt and all its wise men. Pharoah told them his dreams, but there was no one who could interpret them to Pharoah. Then the chief cup-bearer said to Pharoah . . . "Once Pharoah was angry with his servants, and put me and the chief baker in custody . . . A young Hebrew was there with us, a servant of the captain of the guard. When we told him, he interpreted our dreams for us . . ." Then Pharaoh sent for Joseph, and he was hurriedly brought out of the dungeon. When he had shaved himself and changed his clothes, he came in before Pharoah. And Pharoah said to Joseph, "I have had a dream, and there is no one who can interpret it. I have heard it said of you that when you hear a dream you can interpret it."

Joseph answered Pharoah, "It is not I; God will give Pharoah a favorable answer . . ."

Joseph said to Pharoah, "Pharoah's dreams are one and the same; God has re-vealed to Pharoah what he is about to do. . . . There will come seven years of great plenty throughout all the land of Egypt. After them there will arise seven years of famine, and all the plenty will be forgotten in the land of Egypt; the famine will consume the land . . . Now therefore let Pharoah select a man who is discerning and wise, and set him over the land of Egypt . . . Let them gather all the food of these good years that are coming, and lay up grain under the authority of Pha-roah for food in the cities, and let them keep it. That food shall be a reserve for the land against the seven years of famine that are to befall the land . . ." So Pharoah said to Joseph, "Since God has shown you all this, there is no one so discerning and wise as you. You shall be over my house . . ." Removing his signet ring from his hand, Pharoah put it on Joseph's hand; he arrayed him in garments of fine linen, and put a gold chain around his neck . . . Thus he set him over all the land of Egypt . . . Joseph was thirty years old when he entered the service of Pharoah king of Egypt . . . Joseph had two sons . . . Joseph named the firstborn Manasseh, "For," he said, "God has made me forget all my hardship and all my father's house." The second he named Ephraim, "For God has made me fruitful in the land of my misfortunes."

—excerpts from *New Revised Standard Version*
(The Holy Bible), Chapters 39 and 41

BILL: Why is the story of Potiphar's wife in this narrative?

P.K.: Because it's the story of beginning manhood—all the temptations of youth.

FRANCISCO: I can't forget that Joseph is a slave in that household, and that Potiphar's wife is attracted to him. She doesn't try to persuade him, she just says, "Lie with me." It's an imperative. She's trying to use him sexually. He gets caught in this trap of power abuse, as so many people have been, whether male or female.

NORMAN: I read it differently because Joseph is in a position of power in that house. He's second in command and has all the luxury that goes with that. The only thing kept from him is the woman. Yes, he doesn't have his freedom in the sense that he can't simply up and leave, but he's in a position of some control.

FRANCISCO: What I don't see in the narrative is any attraction on the part of Joseph for her. It's a moral issue, a religious issue for him.

DIANNE: The story of Joseph is an entirely different kind of story than those of the other ancestors. It belongs to the tradition that asks, "What is a righteous man? Who is the wise man?" Now, one of the attributes of a wise and discerning man, as you read in Proverbs, is that you avoid the foreign woman. It's not just sex. Sex is part of what it means to be wise and discerning. Joseph is wise enough to avoid the foreign woman.

BILL: For what reason?

DIANNE: To avoid bringing foreign influence into the community, as Solomon did when he brought in his foreign wives with their worship and their gods.

FRANCISCO: But Joseph marries a foreign woman, Asenath, the daughter of a priest of On. So what do you make of that?

HOSSEIN: It's a question of morality, as you said, not just of being foreign. The fact is that this woman is someone else's wife. But there's another very important element. Some of the greatest literary masterpieces of the Persian language are about the love of Joseph and Zulaykha, Potiphar's wife. This love is mentioned in the Qur'an. Among the prophets, Joseph represents beauty, and that beauty is a double-edge sword, as beauty is in this life. Beauty can lead us to God, but it can also land us in difficult situations. In this story, it's the source of great temptation. Zulaykha too is extremely beautiful. Joseph must choose between human beauty and divine beauty. That is a profound choice we have in this life. The beauty of Joseph is not accidental but a very central aspect of God's creation. Joseph appears in this story as the great prophet of beauty, rather than the bringer of law, which Moses was, or the asserter of the unity of God, which Abraham was. A person who possesses beauty and is also spiritually inclined is always in the middle of a great tension between human and divine love.

BILL: Does the Islamic story suggest that Joseph loves Potiphar's wife?

HOSSEIN: It suggests that he was deeply attracted to her, so it was a difficult choice.

BURT: In rabbinic readings of this story, for reasons that aren't entirely clear to me, Joseph is seventeen years old. The rabbis paint him in almost gaudy colors. He is very attractive to men and women alike, and he knows how to use this beauty. It's really God's grace. Physical beauty is something that comes to you as a gift. But although Joseph knows how to use his charm, he doesn't appreciate its power at first. I think he's just foolish enough as a young man to flirt with this woman and draw her attraction, not understanding, until it's too late, that her attraction is the last thing he needs.

P.K.: That's precisely what this part of Joseph's story with Potiphar means to me. I'm teaching the story to young men and women who are wrestling with puppy love and physical attraction, and how far to go with it. You get the sense that Potiphar's wife is older, more sophisticated, more worldly than Joseph. He probably looks at Potiphar as a father and has deep loyalty to him. It becomes a question of what is the right thing to do in this situation.

NORMAN: There's more. The text doesn't simply say, "How can I do this terrible thing because I owe fidelity to my master." Look at the phrase that's added on—"I will sin against God." Suddenly Joseph recognizes God's presence in his life. And where? When he's alone, in exile!

BURT: Yes, this story is such an interesting read. The rabbis play with this because they appreciate Joseph's youth. He's foolish and charming and knows the full heat of a seventeen-year-old. How could he have resisted the charms of Potiphar's wife? And the rabbis appreciate the terror of a seventeen-year-old, too. He's damned if he does, damned if he doesn't. On one hand, she's his boss. He's a slave, and when she tells him to lie with her, as Frank pointed out, she's commanding him, not asking him. He's supposed to obey her. On the other hand, he knows there's another boss in the house who may have a little more clout. I don't think it ever dawns on Joseph that she's going to destroy him either way. During the course of this story, Joseph learns a powerful lesson about what to do with charm. He was put in the pit earlier, but, apparently, not long enough to learn the lesson. Later, when Potiphar has thrown him in prison, he thinks he's going to charm his way out by interpreting the cup-bearer's dream, but the cup-bearer forgets all about him. His charm isn't quite sufficient at the moment. But when the Pharaoh asks him to come into court, Joseph takes the trouble to shave and change his clothes. He looks good, but he never takes credit himself. In front of the Pharaoh, the first thing he says is "God will give you a good answer."

NORMAN: You could look at this episode with Potiphar's wife another way, too. When Joseph spurns her advances, he begins to learn about himself and his own power as well.

BURT: But do you imagine this is the first time Joseph says no? It strikes me as very odd that this is a kid who's used to getting everything he wants, any whim, and now, maybe for the first time in his life, he's faced with a very delicious choice, and he actually says no. And then he winds up in jail for saying no.

PHYLLIS: Look, I just can't take any more of this story. It's misogynist. Outright misogynist. Where shall I start? If you look at the stories of the other ancestors in Genesis, women are prominent in them: Sarah, Rebekah, Rachel, Leah, Hagar. But in this story, from beginning to end, there are only two women. One is Ms. Potiphar, and the other is Joseph's wife, whose name is there, and she never says anything. She's simply the prize given to him by the Pharaoh because he did what the Pharaoh wanted. The story is practically devoid of women. It's a terribly patriarchal story and has no resonance with those of us who are not males, unless you ignore the fact that sexism and misogyny are important issues. Ms. Potiphar is a good example of what Proverbs wants to do to women. Proverbs has only two places for women. It's a book of instructions or teachings for young men—how to live in the court, how to get along in society. It's sociology, psychology, etiquette. But the young men are not interested in these things, they're interested in the little girls who are walking down the streets of Jerusalem. So they have to be taught not to pay attention to those girls. Now, what is a symbol of great evil? The symbol of great evil could be the woman, but not just any woman—the foreign woman. You get otherness in a double

way—the foreigner and the female. If you're going to take that away from the young in school, what can you give them? Well, give them wisdom. How can we make wisdom attractive? Who cares about being wise if you're a little boy and have these sexual interests? Ahhh, make wisdom a woman. And that's what happens. The positions for women in patriarchy are pedestal or gutter. Ms. Potiphar is—

DIANNE: —both.

PHYLLIS: Exactly. She has her own status in her society, but she is still the foreign woman, and she is the one who's trying to seduce. Almost everybody here has been taking the story at face value, and we haven't even talked about the misogyny of the story. To use the modern language that everybody likes now, the story is racist, sexist, and elitist.

BILL: But it's not a modern story.

PHYLLIS: No, but we talk about it in modern terms, and in one sense, it is a modern story. It is the projection of sexuality onto the female, thus keeping the male pure. So Joseph can have it both ways. He can be attractive, charming, beautiful, but although he does not succumb, he can also be seduced by a woman.

NORMAN: Let's push this issue a little bit. You're right—in its context, the story is misogynist, written by males for a particular kind of audience and all the rest. But as a feminist reader, what are you going to do with the story? Are you simply going to reject the story out of hand and say, ''It

The Story of Joseph (detail),
Morgan Old Testament,
France, ca. 1250

doesn't speak to me because it's prismed through a value system that we no longer hold''? Or can you resurrect something from the story that can ultimately be meaningful to you?

PHYLLIS: The first thing I'm going to do with the story is what I'm doing right now. It's clear from this conversation that very few people here are at the level of seeing the misogyny in the story. So we have to talk about the meaning of the misogyny in the story, and how come the story's so different from all the others.

BILL: And by misogyny, you mean—

PHYLLIS: —hatred of women.

BILL: You sense that Joseph hates this woman?

PHYLLIS: No, but the narrator is shaping a story in which women are objects of hatred, with sexuality and the evils of sexuality projected upon them. I think there's a sense in which the story echoes even Adam. In the Garden story, the serpent approaches Eve, and they have this conversation. As the text makes clear, the man is there with her. Most people think he's out farming or something so that he's released from being blamed. But he's right there with her. After the serpent slithers away, she's left to contemplate the tree, and Adam is with her. She sees that the fruit is physically desirable and that it would taste good. It's a beautiful fruit, and it would make her wise. Only then does she eat. Then she gives some to Adam, and what do we read? Did he contemplate it and think it was beautiful? Did he think it was sapientially transforming? Oh, no. "And he ate." He's belly-oriented. Totally. In the Joseph story, what is the one thing Potiphar does after he puts Joseph in charge of everything? What does the text say? "He eats." Oh, my goodness, this is like the first man. "And he eats." In the story in Genesis 3, you have the serpent, who is the seducer, despite what tradition wants to say about the woman being the seducer. But you also have the serpent engaging the woman. What this Ms. Potiphar story does is to collapse those two things. Like the serpent, she is the seducer; but she is also the foreign woman. So this story just reeks of misogyny.

HOSSEIN: Let me talk as an outsider for a moment. If these stories are so misogynistic, why do people read them? Why is there interest in the Bible? Why not throw this book away? You could dismiss it as the product of a patriarchal society, which late-twentieth-century America—although not the whole of the globe—doesn't accept any longer.

DIANNE: Many *have* thrown it away.

HOSSEIN: But why haven't the rest? Why is it that one must torture a story? It's like saying, "I hate baseball, but I'm rooting for the New York Yankees." This doesn't make any sense. So I want to turn to another case. In the Islamic world, many women are called Zulaykha, the name of Potiphar's wife. She is a heroine. Three blocks from here, in the Metropolitan Museum of Art, you can see some of the greatest Persian miniatures, and a good number of them depict the love of Joseph and Zulaykha. She is always depicted in a very positive sense. She's not hated, by any means. There is no misogyny, as far as the story is concerned. When Zulaykha's friends complain that she is succumbing to Joseph's attractions, she places Joseph in front of them. They are all peeling fruit, but when they see the beauty of Joseph, they are so distracted that they cut their hands. And this brings us back to the question of beauty. The deepest meaning of this story is precisely the significance of beauty in human life. Potiphar's wife is depicted as someone who has the eyes to appreciate God's most beautiful creation, and, therefore, she is a heroine. She's one of the major romantic heroines of Islamic literature.

DIANNE: Well, I think that's a perfect example of how we may read the same story but at the same time be reading it from entirely different social situations. You read it from your culture, Hossein, and it opens up in a wonderful way. You read it from the rabbinic perspective, Burt, and it opens up other things. And Phyllis and I read it from a feminist perspective, and we see other things. So it's not merely a matter of which is right, but where do you stand when you read it. Your question, Hossein, is: "How do we save such a text? How is it redeeming?" But I would ask: "Redeeming for whom? For the ancient world?" The text originated in a patriarchal society and is told from a male perspective. In such a society, even stories about women are told from the man's point of view. But do we have to replicate the world view of a patriarchal society? We can't really replicate that world view.

HOSSEIN: Why not?

DIANNE: Because we're in another world.

NORMAN: And because we don't choose to.

DIANNE: We're in a twentieth-century world—perhaps a twenty-first-century world. The challenge is: How does a religious tradition or text that originated elsewhere become religiously meaningful in another place?

BILL: Let me put it this way. If you are a believer, how do you read this text and find a revelation of God in it?

DIANNE: That's precisely what I'm asking. It's not by repeating or reinterpreting what this story meant for the ancient world that we find revelation, but by discovering what it means for us. I think there is a dynamic in the Joseph story that appears twice. It is not simply that somebody falls from grace, but that somebody rises. Joseph goes into the pit twice and rises.

He's put into the pit by his brothers, and he rises. He's put in the pit again—prison this time—and rises. The dynamic is that those who are lowly are raised up. So reading this text we are moved to ask, "Who in our society are the lowly ones?" The lowly ones may be women who will be raised up. The lowly ones may be people of color who are raised up. The lowly ones may be people of a lower class who will be raised up. That I find revelatory.

BILL: You're saying God is on the side of the underdogs?

DIANNE: I think the story says that.

BILL: But in this story, Joseph is not a lowly, disadvantaged—

DIANNE: —but he's raised up from the pit.

NORMAN: The text says, "God is with Joseph." He is subservient to the power of the Pharaoh, but he has God with him, and the Pharaoh will come to know of God because of Joseph. In that sense, Dianne is right. It's right there from the very outset of the story.

BURT: Phyllis, does it work from a feminist perspective to say that because Joseph is the lowly one and because, quite frankly, he's being sexually harassed by one of his employers—

PHYLLIS: No. How do you know he's being harassed? You assume the point of view of the narrator. In the early days of feminism, when Philip Roth's *Portnoy's*

Complaint became a point of discussion, one feminist wrote _Ms. Portnoy's Complaint._ We don't have Ms. Potiphar's story, we have words put in her mouth by the narrator, whose sympathy is with Joseph—and who is a Hebrew at that. We don't have Ms. Potiphar, the Egyptian woman, speaking her story.

B U R T : But because Joseph is so sexually ambiguous that he appeals to both men and women, is it possible for women to identify with him in that position? That, like women, he is the one who gets caught in the trap?

P H Y L L I S : For me, never.

B U R T : It won't work for you?

P H Y L L I S : It will not work for me. No.

B I L L : So, looking at this from within a faith tradition, Phyllis, what does it say to you? What is revealed here about God and God's workings?

P H Y L L I S : A couple of things. First, I understand what Dianne is doing, and that is a level of interpretation in which you move from the specifics of the text to the realm of themes. You draw out of the story certain themes, which you can then appropriate for people for whom the story is not directly concerned. I understand the value of that, but I also resist it because I respect the specificity of the text and its particularities, and I recognize that some texts just won't work like this. God is in the details, and the devil is in the details. We have to

talk about the details. If you go to the level of themes, then you can forget the misogyny. We wouldn't talk about that as a theme. We'd talk about how the lowly get lifted up. I think Dianne has a point, although I don't see Joseph as an underdog and therefore God being on his side. Even if you do see Joseph as an underdog, you have a larger concern, namely, that in Genesis, the patriarchs are not underdogs, yet God is on their side. God is on the side of Abraham, and God is not on the side of keeping Hagar within the fold.

P . K . : There are some interesting dynamics going on, even among us. Unfortunately, unless the narrator tells everybody's side of the story, we get the story only from the male perspective. One minister has said that Joseph is actually very cunning, but he couldn't outsmart someone who was a little more sophisticated. That was the lesson Joseph was learning. He charmed the pants off everyone in Potiphar's house.

D I A N N E : Interesting image.

P . K . : He charmed everyone and never realized that being charming could get him into a whole lot of trouble. The other thing for me is that we tend to think God controls the events of our lives. I don't think that. The events of our lives happen, and as we get more spirited and more in tune with what God would have us do, the circumstances surrounding the events in our lives begin to change. That's what Joseph learns—what happens to you when you're charming but don't look farther than the

Joseph's Dream, Haggadah, Spain, ca. 14th c.

nose on your face. This is precisely the lesson I want to get across to young men and women.

BILL: Which is?

P.K.: Well, that all that glitters ain't gold. That what looks good and feels good for the moment may hurt you farther on down the road. Adam and Eve knew the rules, but here was something delicious, fruitful. They never thought past the noses on their faces. And Abraham lying—"This is my sister, not my wife"—so he doesn't get into any trouble. But he does get into

trouble. These are people who never think ahead. And young people are like that.

BILL: You've been quiet, Norman. Is this one of your favorite stories?

NORMAN: Not at all. From a literary perspective, of all the stories in Genesis, it's one of my least favorites. Elie Wiesel described it so wonderfully in his book *Messengers of God*. It's a slow-paced, monotonous, overdetailed, overwritten story with redundancies that can put the reader to sleep. Starting from that perspective, then, one has to question, "Why this text?"

Maybe the key is that in spelling out so many details, the narrator reminds us that this is a story about real life. It's the fabric of a multiplicity of details of the redundancies of life. And we, like Joseph, have to learn how to rise from a position of constraint to a position of wholeness. Looking at the text through years of interpretive tradition—in the church, in the mosque, in the synagogue—might be helpful here. The rabbinic tradition, which is certainly misogynist, written from a male point of view for over two thousand years—

P H Y L L I S : —Let's make one clarification. When I use the word "misogyny," I do not equate it with being written from a male point of view. It's worse than that. And patriarchy is not necessarily misogynist. Misogyny is the hatred of women, which is not necessarily the same as patriarchy.

N O R M A N : I think Phyllis is correct. All I'm saying is that when we ask the question about reading the text from the perspective of a particular religious tradition, we have to understand that we're seeing it through generations of interpreters, and this can help us begin to access the story in ways that if we just came *de novo* to the biblical text, we couldn't.

D I A N N E : But sometimes these interpretations just add layer upon layer of misogyny. That's my experience of the tradition.

B U R T : One of the traditions of interpretation has to do with the question: Why

doesn't Potiphar have Joseph killed instead of just putting him into prison? The rabbis say that when Potiphar's wife grabs at Joseph's clothing, she, in effect, leaves her fingerprints on the scene of the crime. She leaves evidence because his clothing is torn from behind. It's proof to Potiphar that Joseph was fleeing, not advancing. Potiphar understands the situation, but then that puts him in an awkward position. His wife has been shamed. He knows that she has not been behaving as a wife should behave. But he wants to save her face. On the other hand, maybe Joseph isn't as guilty as is claimed, and he doesn't want Joseph's blood on his hands. So Potiphar imprisons Joseph rather than killing him. That's also in the Qur'an.

H O S S E I N : There's a great deal about Joseph in the Qur'an. He is a young person who possesses great beauty and is attractive to others. Yet he is also responsive to divine law. The Ten Commandments have not yet been revealed, but there is a divine law, and one of the great lessons of this story is that God's law pertains to everyone, at all ages, no matter how gifted one is physically. The story of Joseph begins in the Qur'an with God saying to the prophet and to human beings that "Verily, we shall now recount for you the most beautiful of all stories." There's no story that is more beautiful in the Qur'an. To this day, when Muslim women get married, they open the Qur'an to the story of Joseph. What this story says is that the attraction of the male and female for each other comes from the realization of beauty, which has a divine element in it. The attraction between Poti-

Fere Seyon, *Abraham with Isaac and Jacob* (right panel from *Patriarch Panels*), Central Ethiopia, 1440–80

Jusepe de Ribera, *Jacob Receives Isaac's Blessing*, 1637

Rembrandt van Rijn, *Jacob Wrestling with the Angel*, ca. 1636

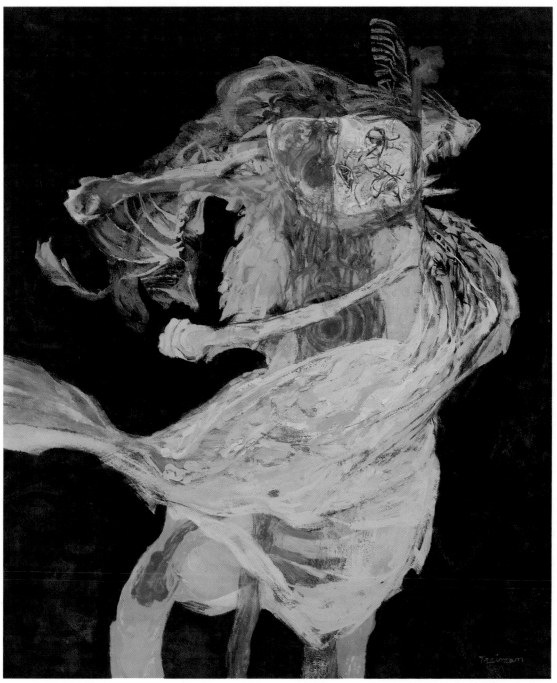

Joyce Treiman, *Jacob, Man, Angel*, 1956

Jacob's Ladder, Haggadah, Spain, 14th c.

Paul Gauguin, *The Vision After the Sermon*, 1888

Jacob's Ladder, School of Avignon, France,
ca. 1490

Gabriel Voel, from
Almen, *Jacob's Ladder*,
A Book for a Mohel,
Amsterdam, printed
1745, illustrated 1786,
1806

Jean Fouquet,
The Story of Joseph,
from Josephus,
Jewish Antiquities,
ca. 1420

Joseph Explains Pharaoh's Dream, Naples Bible, late 14th c

Francesco Xanto Avelli, *Joseph and Potiphar's Wife*, majolica plate, Urbino, 1537

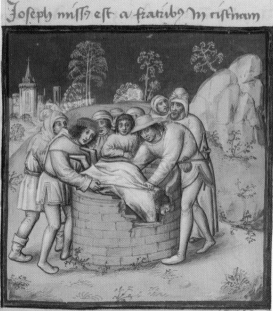

Joseph Cast into the Well,
Mirror of Human Salvation,
Flemish, 15th c.

Yusuf and Zulaykha Holding Hands,
Yusuf and Zulaykha by Jami,
Judeo–Christian
translation ca. 1853

Yusef Talks with His Brothers, Qisas al-Anbiya (Legends of the
Prophets), Iran, 1577

phar's wife and Joseph in the Islamic account always has the third dimension, which is the divine presence.

B I L L : So is that divine presence the reason Joseph refuses to enter an adulterous relationship?

H O S S E I N : Exactly. Because it is adulterous.

B U R T : And yet they have a platonic love.

H O S S E I N : That's right. It's a love that's never realized on the human plane but nevertheless represents the intensity of attraction.

N O R M A N : I want to suggest a different perspective that perhaps contrasts the rabbinic to the Muslim tradition. At the denouement of the story in the rabbinic tradition, the rabbis say that Joseph envisions the presence of his father, which dissuades him from continuing. So here is a wonderful tension. Is it a sense of God's presence and what God wants of us that ultimately impels us to act in a particular way? Or—not mutually exclusive, however—is it a sense of what our parents expect of us that guides our behavior? What is most attractive to me about this rabbinic reading of the text is that here is Joseph, isolated in Egypt, years removed from his parents, and yet the rabbis see him as carrying with him his parents' values, which are guiding principles.

B I L L : Joseph just does the right thing it

seems to me. He ascribes it to God. He doesn't betray his—

F R A N C I S C O : But wait a minute. I think you have a really human Joseph. Joseph is away from home and on his own. In this particular instance, he knows what's wrong. On the one hand, there's a natural sense of loyalty to a master who's been good to him. On the other hand, he has a natural sense that there's something wrong here, and he ascribes this sense to God. It's often pointed out that, unlike the other Genesis stories, in the story of Joseph, God does not appear. Well, God's not in the story as a *character*, but God's not in my life or your life as a character, either. God is in my life—and this is one of the reasons I like the Joseph story—as feelings, promptings, inclinations, the kind of thing you can easily miss in a moment of attraction for something or another. I see Joseph picking up on the right vibes and saying, "No, it's wrong."

"It's often pointed out that, unlike the other Genesis stories, in the story of Joseph, God does not appear."

B I L L : You're putting in a good word for this story.

FRANCISCO: I'm putting in a good word for the whole Joseph story. But I'll tell you the truth. I used to hate this story when I was a kid in Sunday school. I found it boring. But in my life—well, perhaps I should say I'm an exile myself. I live in a country where I was not born. Like Joseph, I didn't come here as a baby, I came as a boy. I was close to seventeen when I first came to this country. The last time I went home to Cuba was in 1960. I've raised a family and become an academic. I have a good life here. I don't run San Antonio, but, you know, I don't want to, either. But I can see both sides of exile. I think the people who wrote this story were people for whom exile was the dominant experience. In many ways, I see exile as the great paradigm for human existence that speaks to us in the Bible. Definitely the Joseph story speaks to us that way.

> "In many ways, I see exile as the great paradigm for human existence that speaks to us in the Bible."

PHYLLIS: But you say "the people." They're always the male people. How would this story work for a woman in exile?

FRANCISCO: Okay, you have a very good question, Phyllis. But there is so much

that is wrong in our culture because of misogyny and racial hatred and all kinds of human traits. If we were just to identify those in every story, in every work of art, in every cultural experience, we would just be focused on what's wrong, on the poison, and I don't know what I would turn to. You see, I have to deal with the Joseph story. I have to deal with the Bible. It's part of my tradition.

BILL: And for you it is still the revelation of God?

FRANCISCO: Yes, it is. Now, I recognize the misogyny. I see much there that I reject. But as Dianne said, we have to learn to read these stories setting that aside.

DIANNE: No, not "setting it aside." I didn't say that. I said "admitting it first."

FRANCISCO: Well, admitting it—

DIANNE: and then going beyond it.

FRANCISCO: Okay, admitting and going beyond it. In other words, how does an exiled woman read this?

HOSSEIN: I think it's wrong to identify every character according to sex. Joseph is also a human being.

PHYLLIS: Yes, but in the Potiphar story, Joseph is a male.

HOSSEIN: That's right. But in the aspect we're talking about now, he's not simply a male, he's a human being in exile.

Properzia de' Rossi, *Joseph and Potiphar's Wife*, Basilica of San Petronio, Bologna, 16th c.

NORMAN: Joseph represents the human condition that can play out in a multiplicity of ways. It's not only Joseph as a metaphor for the Cuban-American here, or the fact that Hossein is sitting here, and in 1979 he had to leave his home in Iran. In a more subtle way, it's my son who is living in Pensacola, Florida, at the University of West Florida, in an environment that's very different from the one in which he was raised. And it's us, every one of us. It's Norman Cohen fifteen years ago, going through a divorce, sitting in a small, dingy, sublet apartment a few blocks from here. I had nothing of my own. I had to face the question of how it felt to be utterly alone. To have nothing. I had to ask myself, "Is there hope that I can hold on to, that can bring me back from the place of alienation and otherness and separateness?" I think this story speaks to every single person.

FRANCISCO: Well, I'd like to shift the ground a little bit away from the issue of gender to the issue of power and power relationships because there both men and women can identify with this kind of story.

BILL: But Phyllis is looking very uncomfortable. Before we move on to power and exile, I want to make sure I understand something that Phyllis has caused us all to think about. Reading this story through the eyes of a modern woman, Phyllis, does it still signify for you religiously, in your own faith journey?

PHYLLIS: May I put that in a larger context? The Bible is not a sanitized book. It does not have a single point of view. It comes to us full of conflicts and contradictions and problems. Now, the canonizers, the redactors, the editors tried to harmonize it and make it all look right. But they failed. We see behind it and in front of it all these conflicted ways of looking at human life. And biblical people didn't agree with one another. To me, this is one of the great blessings of the Bible. It is an authentic document precisely because of that, among other reasons. It can speak authentically to human existence out of its conflicted nature. No one text must ever become idola-

trous. A text may one day be the word of God and another day it may not be the word of God.

"The Bible is not a sanitized book. It does not have a single point of view. It comes to us full of conflicts and contradictions and problems."

HOSSEIN: I don't agree with that.

PHYLLIS: Of course you wouldn't. But let me finish. A lot of the text is put in the mouth of Moses, and you agree with him?

HOSSEIN: Yes.

PHYLLIS: In the Book of Deuteronomy, Moses said, quoting God, "Lo, I set before you life and death, blessing and curse. Choose life that you and your descendants may live." Now, that to me is the paradigm for what the Bible is. It is a book that sets before us life and death, blessing and curse. And it does not always tell us which is life and which is death, which is blessing and which is curse. So I don't take a yellow pad and my number one pencil and draw a line down it and say, "These are the texts for blessing, and these are the texts for curse, and now I've got it all settled." Because something in the right column may one day be in the column on the left, and vice versa. There is no final way of settling this. This is the grandeur and the glory and the redemptive value of the Bible.

H OSSEIN : Well, that doesn't destroy its being the word of God. Both life and death are part of our human life, but both, for those who believe, come from God. The fact that a different message is given in the Bible doesn't mean that some of it is the word of God and some of it isn't.

F RANCISCO : I think I see what you're saying. If someone were to read the story of Joseph in Potiphar's house in such a way that the message was "Women are sexually aggressive, oppressive beings"—a misogynistic reading—that would, of course, not be the word of God. I would agree with you. On the other hand, that's part of the Joseph story, so we can't very well excise it. It's there. And yet the Joseph story has other things to say that certainly have given great meaning to my understanding of my own existence.

B URT : To some extent, classical midrash—the way the rabbis read the story over the centuries—would agree with you. We can't say that one day this text is the word of God and the next day it's not. The text is always there. The words don't change. They're always the same words, whether it's Deuteronomy or Genesis. What changes is the way we read. What's important is how God's word is heard. God's word isn't just in a static book. My friend Ed Greenstein says, "You open the

Joseph, Potiphar's Wife, and Her Friend, Siddur, Germany, ca. 1300

book up—it doesn't talk." The words are just there on the page. But as communities of readers, we get together and when we talk, when we debate, when we get heated, that's when we hear the word of God.

"The words don't change. They're always the same words, whether it's Deuteronomy or Genesis. What changes is the way we read."

That's when the text becomes revelation. Revelation, which can happen in a secular community as well as a religious community, is a very powerful thing. It's that lightbulb going on over your head. You hear someone else with a different point of view, and that person doesn't even have to convince you so much as to show you that there's more than one reading of the text.

DIANNE: And something can mean different things in different communities at the same time—for example, "Blessed are the poor." In a poor community, that's hope. In a privileged community, that's challenge.

NORMAN: But the irony is that it can mean different things to the same person at different times.

BILL: How many times as a boy in East Texas did I hear this story presented as the importance of resisting temptation. It was also presented as inspiration. "You can go and do great things, too." This young Jewish boy was taken as a slave and—

NORMAN: —became a success.

DIANNE: Were you taught to be wary of the woman, too?

BILL: No, I never heard the story quite this way until today—which is why I agree with you about its being a moment of revelation when people are talking together. Look at how this one little story has triggered all of this intensity and passion among us. Why?

BURT: I think Norman's point is right, that you identify with the story in different ways. In the synagogue we read through the Five Books of Moses annually. That means I hear this Joseph story once a year. Every year the words are the same, but I hear a different story. Certainly, throughout my youth, I identified with the youthful Joseph. But, as I get older, I'm identifying more and more with Joseph coming to terms with power, with Joseph in the court, with Joseph as an adult. So it's funny. Unlike a lot of you in this circle, I always identified with the Joseph story. I was raised to be a very charming kid, to smile, thinking that would get me by. I also learned along the way that this gets you into trouble, too. Now I'm learning to move past that. The identification with Joseph is a very powerful one, but year by year it changes.

P.K.: As a mother talking to children, I tell them Joseph was raised right. He had to get that home training from somewhere. In an African American community, it's real important that when you go out into the world, you remember your home training. Somewhere Joseph got a sense of what was right and what was wrong. There was something Joseph wouldn't do to himself as well as to Potiphar because of his religious upbringing.

FRANCISCO: But look, there's a beautiful thing right here, and it's Joseph's developing sense of common humanity. He's loyal to an Egyptian who happens to be his master. He could have said, "I'm oppressed, and I'm going to rip this guy off, if not with his wife, then in other ways." But Joseph reaches a kind of maturity. He looks across at the humanity of Potiphar, who has power over him, and says, "No, I can't do that to him. He's a human being, too. He's someone I owe something to above and beyond this position of power." I think that's a beautifully human and mature thing. There was a developing conscience coming from home, as P.K. says. Who knows who his teachers were? But somehow he had a sense of constraint.

P . K . : And he was a brash brat when he came to Potiphar's house.

B I L L : What does this story say to you about keeping faith in exile?

N O R M A N : For me, from a Jewish perspective, it's the paradigmatic story. Egypt is the quintessential exile. You could say that going down to Egypt is going down to death. When Jacob hears of Joseph's disappearance, he says, "I'm going down

Nöel Hallé, *Joseph Accused by Potiphar's Wife*, ca. 1740–44 mourning to Sheol, to the netherworld.'' And he goes down to Egypt. In a sense, that's what Egypt is for him—the place of alienation, of lost identity, just as the pit is a place of lost identity for Joseph. He's out of sight; he's not remembered; he's not seen. But the question is: Can you survive that place of alienation, of exile, of otherness when you're absolutely alone? Rachel said it best in the words echoed in Jeremiah, Chapter 31, when she weeps for her children who have gone into exile and are no more. She says they are *ainenu*, or ''gone''—the very word Jacob uses about his son Joseph. But there's the other side as well. Can there be hope in exile? For me, the one line in the entire Joseph story that jumps off the page, because it summarizes its essence, comes in the very next line after Chapter 41. Jacob sees that there is grain in Egypt. The word for grain is *shever*. But this word has other meanings as well. *Shever* means ''break''; it means ''calamity,'' ''disruption,'' ''fragmentation.'' But the word is also a play on a Hebrew word *sever*. If you move the dot in Hebrew from one side of the letter to the other, you get a *sh*-sound instead of a *s*-sound. The word *sever* means ''hope.'' The question is: Is there calamity and loss in Egypt, or is there hope in Egypt? That point speaks to every single person. In a context of feeling lost and fragmented, can we point to something that gives us hope? The Joseph story does.

B I L L : So Egypt is the second pit in Joseph's experience?

N O R M A N : Exactly. The word used for the pit into which he's thrown is the same word in Hebrew for the prison in Egypt. I think Egypt is the pit. But there is something else. Joseph names his second child *Ephraim*, ''God made me fertile.'' Where? ''—in the land of my affliction.'' There you get the tension. He's fertile. He rises. He finds himself in the land of his affliction. So you can become fertile and creative and come to wholeness, even in the place of alienation. This speaks to the soul of every single human being.

F R A N C I S C O : Before we go in that direction a little too far, we should remember that Joseph saves Egypt. Egypt prospers because of Joseph's acumen and vision, his activity and energy. Remember the blessing of Abraham? This is a clear case where the seed of Abraham is a blessing for all kinds of people who don't even realize it. Here is someone who comes to Egypt as a slave, who goes into that pit and fills it with grain. And Joseph saves Egypt's life and that of his family and countless others. What's the lesson? There is this reaching out to be a blessing to all humanity. Egypt may literally be the pits, but here is Joseph blessing Egypt, as it were.

B U R T : It's more than that. Pharaoh has to get some credit here. The King of Egypt is willing to take a risk with a foreigner, an alien, an immigrant. The stranger is put in charge and thus saves Egypt. It's a very different Pharaoh that we see in the Book of Exodus. There he's xenophobic. He doesn't like strangers and thinks the Jewish community is going to rise up against him. As a result of enslaving them, the Pharaoh destroys Egypt. Two very different points of view here.

FRANCISCO: The Pharaoh who did not know Joseph.

BURT: Right. The good Pharaoh is the one who takes the risk that the immigrant community can contribute, can become part of a greater enterprise.

BILL: Now, this takes on some very modern aspects. The world is on the move. Immigrants everywhere.

HOSSEIN: Do you know that Joseph's success in Egypt had a lot to do with the later Islamization of Egypt? People do not pay attention to this, but Joseph is a great prophet as presented in Islam. To this day, the Egyptians are very proud that Joseph came to Egypt. Driving through the streets of Cairo, you can see posters with the verse of the Qur'an that says this was the land to which God sent Joseph.

BURT: Joseph slept here!

HOSSEIN: It's more profound than that. There is a hill outside Cairo that is called al-Mugattam. Anyone who's visited Cairo knows it. For the last fourteen hundred years, Islamic mystics, the Sufis, have

Jean Adrien Guignet, *Joseph Interpreting Pharaoh's Dreams*, 1848

gathered here. That mountain is where Joseph is supposed to have stayed. So to this day there's an important relationship between Joseph and a country of sixty million people. By going beyond your own land to identify yourself with another people and serve them, you break racial barriers. And there's something else—this very profound theme of exile. Despite the fact that the success of Joseph has had a profound effect upon the spread of Islam in Egypt, throughout the history of Islam, Canaan is still seen as the original abode. Paradise is where we came from and to which we will return. So, despite the success of Joseph in Egypt, he is always seen as being in exile. The great sorrow of his father, Jacob, who, according to the Qur'an, cries until he becomes blind, is that his son is in exile. Now here is the prototype of our own exile in this world. By definition, the spiritual person is always in exile in this world.

"A person who has a yearning for the spirit feels like an exile in this world, no matter how much he serves it."

BILL: "This world is not my home."

HOSSEIN: Yes, all of the different religions have emphasized that. The Qur'an tells a beautiful story which shows this deep nostalgia. Joseph has another shirt besides the one grabbed by Potiphar's wife, and he sends this shirt, which contains his scent, to his father in Canaan. When this scented cloth is put on the blind Jacob's eyes, Jacob begins to see the light. It's a very profound and beautiful story. It presents our plight in nostalgia. A person who has a yearning for the spirit feels like an exile in this world, no matter how much he serves it.

BILL: So the question remains, from the Garden of Eden onward: How do you live permanently in exile in this world and retain the core of your identity?

FRANCISCO: There are plenty of things I don't find so congenial about America, but one of the things I do find congenial here is that if you dig deep enough, everybody's from somewhere else. FDR hit it right when he began a speech, "Dear Fellow Immigrants." The experience of so many people I know, of being from somewhere else, raises a different kind of consciousness, for this country particularly, because we always feel as if we have roots in an idealized place. I've never been to Ireland, but I bet it's nowhere near as beautiful as Irish-Americans paint it. I know that Cuba is not as idyllic as my friends in the Calle Ocho of Miami paint it. If you want to go to Old Havana, go to Miami. They've tried to reconstruct it there. So you always have this nostalgia, this sense of being fallen from paradise, no matter how good it is here.

BILL: Have you had a hard time holding on to your identity?

FRANCISCO: Yeah. Here we are, speaking in English, which for me is an acquired language. Joseph had to speak in Egyptian, I'm sure. In fact, it's an element in the story. At the end, he disguises himself from his brothers by speaking Egyptian and using a translator. I hope all of you have the experience of knowing another language, because you think in different ways. You organize reality in different ways.

BURT: I grew up with English as my first language, but as a Jew, I had to acquire my mother tongue, which was Hebrew.

NORMAN: I think there's more here. The rabbis tell a wonderful story about Joseph as he goes back to Canaan, carrying Jacob's bones with him, to bury his father in Canaan. He passes the very pit into which he had been thrown by his brothers, and he stops to make a blessing over that pit. It's just so astounding to think of Joseph blessing the pit, that place of downtroddenness, of ignominy. Then you begin to understand that the pit is really the place that saved his life. Had he not been thrown into the pit, maybe his brothers would have murdered him. Can the pit be transformed into a place of redemption? Ultimately, the question becomes: Can Egypt—*mitzrayim*, which signifies "the narrow places"—can the place of confinement, where we feel persecuted and alone, be a birth canal through which we are reborn?

P.K.: Well, I do this thing called "a blessing party." I bless those people who make me feel the angriest because I feel that if I bless them, maybe things will change for the better between us. At least the next time I meet them, I won't have that anger toward them. I ran away from home when I was young and only recently returned. I understand what Joseph does to his brothers when they finally meet, that feeling of paying them back. So for me, this is a beautiful story for young people.

HOSSEIN: But to go back to the whole question of the ambivalence of exile. Frank pointed out earlier that you can be successful in exile and, at the same time, never forget where you came from. Frank and I are the only people here who are in exile because of political circumstances. If you asked me the question you posed to Frank—"How do you fare as a person in exile?"—I would think of myself as a person very deeply attached to Persian culture, a person who was at the center of activities of my culture. But I would also always remember the first meaning of exile, the spiritual meaning of exile, that we are all in a sense exiled in this world. It's this knowledge that permits me to function in exile as a teacher and writer, participating in the life of this country without losing my original identity. That is why the story of Joseph speaks so deeply to me. You know, it's not accidental that this aspect of the Joseph story is now resonating much more than it did, let's say, in the nineteenth century. There's a big difference between American society and other societies. In the old days, when people went into exile, very few became successful, like Joseph. They usually remained in an exiled community, a ghetto. America is one of the very few places where

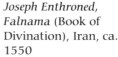
Joseph Enthroned,
Falnama (Book of
Divination), Iran, ca.
1550

a Joseph can be successful. It's not certain that if Frank had migrated to Poland or Egypt or even to Japan, he would have become a successful professor.

FRANCISCO: The good thing about being in exile, about being of two cultures, is that it allows you to look at yourself and others from the point of view of the Egyptians, as it were. You begin to realize how much you have in common and how much of what this society affirms about the other is not so.

BURT: I can speak to that as a member of the American Jewish community. We went through a long period of time that we wanted to be Americans. It took us a couple of generations to realize that what being a good American meant was being a good

Jew. That was okay in America because that's how it works.

BILL: It seems to me that Joseph does make an enormous accommodation while he's in Egypt. He remains Hebrew, but he takes on many of the attributes of the Egyptian world. How much accommodation can one accept and still be true to oneself in exile?

DIANNE: I think there are many different levels of that. We've been talking about it as an ethnic issue. But in my situation, as a member of a religious community, one of the most difficult things we're facing is: How can one be faithful to the vows of poverty, chastity, and obedience in a society that doesn't understand these vows or even value them? I don't have an answer, but that's the crux, as far as I'm concerned. How does one live *in* the world and not *of* it, especially when the world is not outside us, but inside? Egypt is within. I'm a product of my culture. How can I also be faithful to my religious traditions?

BILL: How do you take a vow of poverty in a society that is so materialistic, so affluent, where advertising is always beating the message into you?

DIANNE: Yes. When I took the vow, it wasn't as hard because we were living in an enclosed society. But once we moved out after the Second Vatican Council, and became much more involved in the lifestyle of the world, it became a constant struggle. It's not merely "How much money do I have?" That's not the problem. For me, the problem is "How much contemporary electronic information do I need?" Do I have to get on to the internet? On the one hand, I'm a professor, and I need that information. But do I need a laser printer? Those are real issues for me.

BILL: Well, have you reconciled them?

DIANNE: Are you asking whether I have a laser printer? No, I don't have a laser printer, but that doesn't make me poor. I don't want to resolve these issues because by that time, I would have moved to one side or the other. In this world, I don't know if we can make such a movement.

BILL: You're in permanent exile then?

DIANNE: Yes, and struggling constantly, as Joseph was.

FRANCISCO: But listen, you've just brought up something important. Obviously my struggle is with my own culture. To be specific, I come from a culture that is very family-oriented, where you would expect the extended family to be present throughout your whole life. Now, here I am in San Antonio. My sister lives in Los Angeles, and we can't have that kind of interaction. The real question for me is: How you remain faithful to those values in a situation where you can't live in an extended family anymore?

PHYLLIS: I must say that while the Joseph story does not speak to me in any deep ways, the theme of exile does. Women in the Church—whether they're in a religious community, like Dianne, or are laywomen, whether they're Roman Catholics or Protestants—have been in exile for years. Centuries. And it's not getting any better. Some women have said, "I don't need this. I'll just exile myself to a better way of being."

BILL: Well, there are some Protestant churches that do ordain women today.

PHYLLIS: It highlights the exile.

DIANNE: That's right. It's the same structure, so it doesn't necessarily put them into a better situation.

BILL: So do you still feel an exile in this world?

PHYLLIS: Oh, yes.

BILL: As a woman?

PHYLLIS: Yes, as a woman and, also, as Hossein was saying, in the mystical, spiritual sense of anyone who is rooted in transcendence and understands creation as the work of a transcendent God and knows we are in the world, but not of it.

BILL: Can you help me understand why, given the obvious concerns you have with these texts, you remain in the Church if the Church continues to be, as you've described it, dominated by an alien culture?

PHYLLIS: Well, some people may question whether I remain in it. I've never repudiated it, so if that means remaining in it, then I remain in it. But I have long ceased to find it a home. I cease to make it a big issue for myself because I do not seek ordi-

nation and religious trappings of that sort. You would understand this, Bill. We both come from a free-church tradition. There's something liberating about a free-church tradition because you can find a local church in which to be, whereas your denomination might be horrendous. So that helps.

FRANCISCO: Listening to this, I'm remembering the story and Joseph's ability to interpret the Pharaoh's dreams. I think he could do this because he was the outsider. The Egyptian dream interpreters are so committed to pleasing the Pharaoh that they will not give him bad news. The Pharaoh, in his very person, represents the power of fertility, and his country is about to go through the worst famine ever. His courtiers are not about to give such bad news to the Pharaoh. But Joseph is looking at the situation as an outsider. Remember, he's just come out of prison. He's come out of Canaan. He knows famine first-hand because it's a fact of life in Canaan. He sees it for what it is, and he will tell it for what it is.

BILL: Interesting. In President Johnson's official court, no one really foresaw disaster in Vietnam. It was the outsiders, the dissenters, the protesters, those who were not part of the official culture, who first raised the warning signs.

HOSSEIN: Let me say something about the art of interpreting dreams, which has been absent from Western civilization for the past few centuries. It's now coming back with a vengeance through Jungian psychologists and others. Now, in Islam the

Prophet said that there would be no prophecy after him—that is, that the Prophet of Islam would be the last prophet in this period of human history—except that one-fortieth of the prophecy would be preserved in dreams. In the ancient world, the interpretation of dreams always had to do with having direct contact with God. It was a prophetic and sometimes priestly function. The fact that Joseph is able to interpret these dreams is one of the most significant aspects of this story. It's perhaps the most interesting of all the stories of the Bible, not from an ethical point of view, but from the psychological point of view. What do dreams mean, and what is their significance? This opens up a vast subject. Joseph was not only an outsider, he was given by God the science of dream interpretation.

P.K.: And he was given this gift early. The difference between Joseph at age sixteen telling a dream and now Joseph at thirty is his ability to realize how divine in nature this gift really is. When he tells his dreams to his brothers, he's really a braggart. He doesn't know what to do with his gift, and he doesn't recognize the importance of his power.

FRANCISCO: Going around bragging about that power when he's a kid—that's what gets him into trouble in the first place.

NORMAN: There's one other aspect here which is secondary, but still important. When Joseph is confronted in the first set of dreams by the cup-bearer and the baker, he sees them and asks, ''Why are you so downtrodden today?'' He looks at their faces and sees who they are. Thomas Mann says, ''The test of Joseph is to learn to read the faces of other people.'' Joseph gains a sense of who these people are. The spirit of God is in him in the sense that he sees through the eyes and hearts of other people. That speaks to us. We learn about the nature of life as we listen to other people and respond to them.

PHYLLIS: But those dreams aren't very interesting. They're pretty obvious. It doesn't take a whiz kid to interpret them. Let me ask you, Burt: Why does the tradition not have women interpreting dreams?

BURT: I don't know the answer to that. But I disagree with you about Joseph's reading of the dreams. You're right that the dreams are simple. The rabbis agree with Islam, Hossein, although the fraction is different, in saying that a dream is one-sixtieth prophecy. The rabbis also say that the trick to dreams is that dreams follow their interpretations. On its own, a dream is inert. When it is interpreted, it happens. So you have to be careful how you interpret dreams. Joseph's genius is not in reading the dream, you see. Anybody could say, ''Oh, yes, there's going to be seven years of plenty.'' That's easy to say to the Pharaoh. The genius is in saying, ''Of that plenty, we must put aside a certain amount.'' Now that takes courage. It takes enormous courage to be able to say, ''In the midst of all this wonderful productivity, there has to be a very serious tax because without putting this aside, we have no future.''

FRANCISCO: And then there's the

touch of practically writing your own job description!

B I L L : A big question did drop through the floor here. Phyllis asked Burt, "What does the tradition tell us about why there are no women interpreters of the dreams?" Talk about that.

B U R T : This is a very hard issue for me because I'm a rabbi, and I have a vested interest in promoting rabbinic tradition. But even as I do that, I recognize that friendliness to women is not a part of the tradition—although this tradition is no more or less unfriendly than any other culture. It couldn't have been fun to be a woman in the third or fourth century of the common era. You're right, Phyllis. There's this enormous gap—half of the population more or less brushed under the rug. Not good.

P H Y L L I S : You do have Hagar, the first woman to receive a divine messenger. That's marvelous. The messenger comes to an Egyptian woman at that! So women can receive divine revelation. Women can be prophets—Deborah, Miriam, and all the rest. Women are also sages. There's the wise woman of Tekoah, for instance. And women sing songs on various occasions—victories in battle and mourning rites. So women do a variety of things. But I cannot think of an example of a woman interpreting dreams.

B I L L : As we come to the end of the Joseph story, we confront an inescapable irony. It's that Joseph's success in Egypt leads ultimately to the enslavement of his people. He becomes the unwitting agent of

their downfall—because, thanks to Joseph, Egypt has grain in this time of famine. They come down to Egypt seeking food and wind up in slavery. What do you think of that?

H O S S E I N : That question has a very clear answer, I think, that brings up an important lesson for the modern world. That lesson is that too much success in the world will lead to enslavement. The very success of Western civilization in dominating nature puts the whole natural environment at risk. That's one of its lessons. The fact that Joseph is successful, that he becomes viceroy, that he brings plenty back to Egypt, and that the Egyptians don't all starve leads to the enslavement of his people. This is a very profound story for modern civilization.

"Too much success in the world will lead to enslavement."

N O R M A N : For the Jew living in America today, this is our repeated story—the story of the refugee who doesn't know anybody, has no connections, but adapts to a new environment, a new culture, has tremendous success, and rises to power. Several generations later, it's Egypt for us on some level. Our identity as Jew is now threatened because of our acculturation. It's a challenge: How do we survive that acculturation and hold on to our traditional

Jacob Blesses the Sons of Joseph, Ephraim and Manassah, Naples Bible, late 14th c.

values and customs? Language and culture and customs are so easily dissipated.

HOSSEIN: Yes, a Jewish friend told me that among the greatest challenges Judaism has ever faced is precisely this success in the world. And this is a challenge for the six million Muslims in America, too. Holding on to our faith is a major challenge for the younger generation, especially when they are successful in this society. This challenge makes life in exile even more difficult and is one reason why the Joseph story is so powerful in the context of the American experience.

BILL: I think there's something beyond the challenge to tradition and that is the tendency of American presidents and electorates to interpret the dream with only fat cows in it. We don't face up to the racial fissures, we don't see the destruction of nature, we don't see the growing inequality. Well, we see and acknowledge it, but we don't act on it. We seem to think this dream will always produce fat cows.

BURT: Well, even when it is producing fat cows, we are particularly bad at recognizing that seven years down the road there may be famine and we've got to save so we are ready for that.

BILL: Where are you, Joseph, now that we need you?

EPILOGUE

You can do this, too.

Now that you have read this book and perhaps watched the PBS series, I want to encourage you to convene a Genesis group of your own.

Indeed, my hope for the series and book was that they would encourage others to do what we attempted in these conversations—to read and talk about the stories of Genesis for the experience itself and as a way of opening one's mind to what we can learn from each other.

If you do create or join such a group, you will be able to draw on your experiences, your memories, your ideas in talking about the stories of the Bible. The wonderful thing about this process is that we all have insights that will enrich a discussion—not only about the stories in the Bible but about our own lives and the lives of our families and communities. To facilitate these discussions, Doubleday is publishing "Talking About Genesis: A Resource Guide." Filled with questions, essays, commentaries, and activities, I hope this book will serve as a catalyst for conversation.

Genesis discussions can be held anywhere, but I would suggest that you bring some structure to them, by arranging to conduct them at specific times in a location where you will not be disturbed. You might gather on a weekly basis with your immediate or extended family; you might want to form a group made up of neighbors or friends at work; you might want to contact organizations that already have ongoing discussions. These might include temples, churches, and mosques, community adult education centers, continuing education departments at community colleges, libraries, YMCA/YWCAs, YMHA/YWHAs, the National Conference (formerly the National Conference for Christians and Jews), the American Association of Retired Persons, or similar groups. If you belong to a book discussion club, you might wish to make Genesis your topic. If you work with youngsters at risk, or prison inmates, or with people who are abusing alcohol and drugs, you might want to form a Genesis group. It is important to include members of a faith different from your own.

Dialogue is about telling and listening. As I participated in these discussions, I noticed several things that contributed to the pleasure and excitement. People listened to one another without censure and disagreed without denunciation. No one tried to mask his or her own religious beliefs, but respected the integrity and boundaries of the religious traditions of all others in the group. A generosity of spirit prevailed in the circle, even when, say, a Muslim and a Christian were in strong disagreement about the character of Abraham, or when one participant declared the story of Joseph and Potiphar's wife to be misogynist, making for a lively few minutes on how each of us reads the Bible through the lens of our own experience.

Furthermore, although some participants were ordained or formally trained in biblical scholarship, no one resorted to expertise to claim authority over the others. Participants approached the story in the spirit of the great theologian Martin Buber, who urged people "to read the Bible as if they had never seen it." Even the most faithful believers kept themselves open to surprise; the admission of not knowing exactly what the passage means made possible an unexpected visitation, a revelation.

Planning for your session is important. I suggest that you devote one short meeting to developing a standard agenda. It might include asking people to read the chapter in this book, to watch the television program, or to read the appropriate Bible passage. Have a different person read the text aloud each session. Switch Bibles from week to week, so that the group is exposed to various translations. We sent our participants four different versions—Everett Fox's stunning new translation, *The Five Books of Moses*, also known as the *Schocken Bible*, which in its deep poetic power echoes the Hebrew tongue; the revered *King James Version*, which has so profoundly influenced our language and discourse; the *New Revised Standard Version*, my personal choice for its contemporary prose; and W. Gunther Plaut's very helpful commentary, *The Torah: A Modern Commentary*. My colleagues and I then read and reread the stories ourselves, met for days to determine the themes that invited the most promising and contemporary relevance, and talked with the participants by phone to solicit their thoughts on how to approach the text, although we never discussed in advance the actual questions I might introduce once the discussion began. You obviously do not need to go to such lengths for your sessions, but even in private and informal discussions, homework makes a difference.

Be sure to establish the rules for discourse. It is essential that everyone be given the opportunity to speak and that the speaker be allowed to finish what he or she has to say. But no speeches, please; a dialogue will die if people start holding the floor longer than three minutes. Insist that people look at one another when they talk and that they respond to the point just made. In the beginning try asking everyone to give an opinion for each question. And don't let the sessions turn into group therapy.

Urge your participants to share their own experiences as commentary on the story. For example, in "Call and Promise" Eugene Rivers, who works with street kids in Boston, talked about the incident in which his home was fired on and how his family had to struggle to decide whether to stay in that community. This was *their* call, as real to them now as Abraham's was to him long ago. When we came to the story of Joseph in Egypt, I was impressed at how many in the circle talked about their own exile—from Cuba, Iran, and India, among others—and the challenge to their faith in a foreign land. You will be surprised at the range of experiences in your own group.

You will need a facilitator—someone to set up the meetings, establish the ground rules, and to solicit and suggest questions for discussion. The role could be filled by a different person every week.

I believe you will find it helpful to watch the PBS program about the story your own group is discussing. Follow the viewing with an open discussion of what you just saw. Ask each one in your circle for his or her reactions. With whom on the panel did they agree? Disagree? Then you can ask the same questions that we asked—you can find them by turning back to the chapters in this book—or move on to your own questions and those of your group.

We hear a lot these days about "dialogue and democracy." Concerned about falling voter participation, nasty political campaigns, and a declining sense of community, various organizations are convening thinkers and doers to address issues of civic renewal. Surely religion belongs in that conversation—religion as a wellspring of values and ideas reflecting different aspirations for a moral and political order, religion as the exercise of men and women to bring form to their lives from the chaos around them; religion as the interpretation of experience itself.

Some of the most interesting stories of our time are emerging in the intersection between the secular and the spiritual. One is the attempt to find a new vision for America that has the authority and power of a religious vision but that is inclusive, not sectarian, one that encourages an ethic of cooperation to balance the economics of raw competition. We can see what happens when a leader such as Nelson Mandela offers a vision so inclusive that an entire nation creates a revolution no one thought possible. It succeeded with the help of Mandela's old adversary, the white South African F. W. de Klerk, who was moved by his religious faith to risk all; he too had a vision. At its best, religion's great accomplishment has been to create social bonds based on love and justice and mutual respect, providing a moral and ethical underpinning to necessity and law. In a pluralistic society containing many diverse factions of the faithful, how are we to recover an energizing and organizing vision, so that our pride in our country can be justly sustained and our hunger suitably filled?

A second story is emerging on a more personal level: How can we be properly enthusiastic—that is, filled with God, *ne-theos*—without denying mind or matter? What does it mean to be inspired?

My determination to persist with this series—it took five years to raise the funds—was spurred by an experience early in 1994. I awoke after midnight on a Friday and could not get back to sleep. Turning on my bedside radio for company, I found myself listening to a call-in show devoted mainly to current events. The discussions were so perfunctory that they had the effect of a sedative on me, and I began to drift back into unconsciousness. But then a plaintive voice caught my ear and I heard a young man telling the host, "This is my birthday. Here I am three hours into my eighteenth year and I need help to know how to live in a world that is disintegrating."

The host, momentarily taken aback, tried a wisecrack. "No," the young man said, "I'm really serious. I'm scared. I'm starting my eighteenth year in a world that makes no sense to me."

"Are you thinking about checking out?" the host blurted. There was a long pause before the young man answered: "I don't know. All I know is this world I'm living in is a shambles and I don't know how to put it together."

Other callers chimed in to talk about how awful things are, and the young man's voice was soon lost in the chorus. Whether he got any help from the exchange he had provoked among strangers in the night, I don't know. I lay there, though, thinking about him. Gabriel's line from Green Pastures came to me: "Everything that's tied down is coming loose." I thought of the chaos in the lives of the characters in the play *Angels in America*, where disease, despair, and cynicism threatened to make wrecks of health, hope, and love. We were working at the time on a series about youth violence, and my desk in the study was piled high with research about the brutalities of American life, including those that constantly assault the imagination. Getting out of bed, I went to my desk and thumbed through the titles of comic books that we had collected—comic books with names like *The Warlock Five*, *The Avengers*, *Gun Fury*, *The Blood Sword*, *Swamp Thing*—which promulgate a paranoid view of reality and tell youngsters that the initiation of violence is their only protection against those plotting their doom.

Shortly before dawn I fell asleep, still thinking of that young man's lament: "I'm starting my 18th year in a world that makes no sense to me . . . I don't know how to put it together."

A few days later I fell into conversation with a young woman, a television executive, who, hearing me talk about my hope of basing a series on Genesis, told me that she belongs to a study group that gathers informally but regularly to read and discuss the Bible. They were then working their way through Genesis, engaging each other in trying to apply its insights to their own experience. Among the questions they had confronted were these: Why did God create creatures in God's own image with the freedom of choice if God knew that we would sin? Why was sin permitted? Is sin different today, and if indeed, as Genesis tells us, "it is crouching at your door desiring to have you," how are we to master it? Can you trust a God Who asks a father to put the knife to his son? What does it mean to trust what we cannot see? Do we, like Jacob and Esau, have a spiritual birthright? How do we get the chance to "come into our own?" Is it fate? Or is it Providence? And what about the great message of forgiveness in the story of Joseph? Why is forgiveness so hard for us? Is this unwillingness to forgive at the heart of our social predicament today, our jugular politics? What does it mean to be bold in forgiveness?

She described how a discussion about Noah and his sons and Lot and his daughters led her group into a vigorous debate over whom to believe in disputes over sexual abuse. And the stories of Abraham, she said, prompted sustained argument over the nature of doubt, the definition of faith, and the meaning of God's promises to humanity. Listening to her accounts of the dialogue inspired by these Genesis stories, I wished that I knew the name of the eighteen-year-old caller to the midnight talk show so that I might find and persuade him to join this company of sojourners. In a living conversation about these old stories, he might have found help and hope no talk-show host could give him.

The participants in *Genesis* demonstrate that it is possible to talk about such matters from profound religious convictions with respect, nonetheless, for those who differ. At this moment between two centuries, as one millennium gives way to another, we Americans need a new story about what it means to be a nation, about our identity as a people. How are we to write this new story for ourselves unless we learn to talk about our deepest religious beliefs with people not like us?

When we were beginning production of our series, I informed the new president of PBS, Ervin Duggan, about the enterprise. He wrote me a letter, which I then read to our participants before each session. He said:

> The great temptation in our secular age is to sanitize religious themes—to discuss "the Bible as literature," for example—in a well-intentioned effort to be "pluralistic." In fact, the well-intentioned effort does the opposite; it secularizes the subject matter, disenfranchises those who are religious, and betrays the ideal of pluralism. For pluralism, if it is to have any meaning, means honoring and including all groups; allowing them to express themselves; trying to understand what makes them tick—even if, horrors, they happen to be religious folk who approach Genesis not as "literature" but as a source of faith—of ultimate grounding in Truth, with a capital T.
>
> Most people instinctively know there is more than one valid way of knowing; of apprehending truth. When we read Emily Dickinson's great death-witness poems, for example, we know that they are true, in some deep, elemental way. When we hear Schiller's *Ode to Joy*, the great choral finale to Beethoven's *Ninth Symphony*, we experience truth at the soul's bottom and become deeper, more aware human beings.
>
> Similarly, there is a valid *religious* way of knowing. When we read the Book of Genesis

with its profound accounts of human fallenness, we experience truth unless we're made of stone. When we hear a great sermon or read Francis Thompson's *The Hound of Heaven*, we open ourselves to the apprehension of truth through this way of knowing. Perhaps one reason our epoch has no Leonardo is that we don't allow people to be like Leonardo. His achievements, remember, were religious and artistic (*The Last Supper* and *The Virgin of the Rocks*) but also scientific (his achievements in empiricism, mathematics, and mechanics still underlie modern scientific thinking). How could he be such a polymath? In part, I submit, because his age accepted each path to truth and encouraged people to be geniuses upon those varied paths.

Can it be that our age is less tolerant than his?

Sadly, one reason for the intolerance is religion itself. The Bible can be a stumbling block to conversation because it rubs old wounds or opens new ones; so much of religious history has been an exercise in atrocity, from human sacrifice and scapegoating to fanaticism and persecution, from crusades and holy wars to the Inquisition and Holocaust. "The Bible has too often been used as a wedge to drive people apart," Rabbi Visotzky writes. In founding the Genesis seminar, he hoped his participants would read the Bible "to encourage a sense of community, tolerance, and diversity. Especially now, with America's many cultural groups flying off into fragments, the Bible can be a common ground for discussion. The message of Genesis is that God has a relationship with all of us."

May the conversation continue.

— BILL MOYERS

ADDITIONAL READING

In preparation for these conversations, we asked our participants to read the Genesis stories in four different translations:

- *King James Version*
    The Holy Bible, 1611. Revised in 1881–85, 1902, and 1953.

- *New Revised Standard Version*
    The Holy Bible, 1989.

- *Schocken Bible*
    Fox, Everett. *The Five Books of Moses.* New York: Schocken, 1995.

- *The Torah*
    Plaut, W. Gunther. *The Torah: A Modern Commentary.* New York: Union of American Hebrew Congregations, 1981.

For your own pleasure and continuing conversation, we asked the participants for their recommendation of additional reading. Here are their suggestions:

Alter, Robert. *The Art of Biblical Narrative.* New York: Basic, 1981. "Literary analysis of the biblical text, based on a discriminating reading of the Hebrew text and informed by interesting interpretation." (A. Zornberg) "A perfect introduction to literary appreciation of the Bible." (B. Visotzky)
———. *Genesis: A New Translation with Commentary.* New York: Norton, 1996. "The translation seeks to reproduce in English more of the stylistic features of the Hebrew than are evident in existing English translations, and the commentary concentrates on literary aspects of the stories." (R. Alter)
Bachelard, Gaston. *On Poetic Imagination and*

Reverie: Selections from the Works of Gaston Bachelard. Trans. Colette Gaudin. New York: Bobbs-Merrill, 1971. (H. O'Donnell)
———. *The Poetics of Space.* 1958. Trans. Maria Jolas. Boston: Beacon, 1969. (H. O'Donnell)
Bailey, Lloyd R. *Genesis, Creation, and Creationism.* New York: Paulist, 1993. "Solid research on biblical creationism from the viewpoint of the text of Genesis itself." (A. Di Lella)
Barr, James. *The Garden of Eden and the Hope of Immortality.* London: SCM, 1992. "A stimulating study of the Adam and Eve story, which is interpreted not as a Fall, but as a chance for immortality that was lost, and of the Noah and Flood story, which tells of human alienation from God." (A. Di Lella)
Brueggemann, Walter. *Genesis: A Bible Commentary for Teaching and Preaching.* Atlanta: John Knox, 1982. (D. Bergant)
Cassuto, U. *A Commentary on the Book of Genesis.* 2 Vols. Jerusalem: Magnes, 1961. "Of the modern scholarly commentaries, this is the most helpful. There are wonderful discussions of difficult linguistic and structural problems." (L. Kass)
Cohen, Norman. *Self, Struggle, and Change: The Family Conflict Stories in Genesis and Their Healing Insights for Our Lives.* Woodstock, Vt.: Jewish Lights, 1995. (B. Visotzky)
Comfort, Philip Wesley. *The Origin of the Bible Commentary.* Wheaton, Ill.: Tyndale, 1992. "A companion for teaching." (P. K. McCary)
Dennis, Trevor. *Sarah Laughed: Women's Voices in the Old Testament.* Nashville: Abingdon, 1994. (D. Bergant)
Dresner, Samuel H. *Rachel.* Minneapolis: Fortress, 1994. "This is a beautiful book exploring the life and legacy of the matriarch Rachel in both biblical and postbiblical

sources." (L. Kass) (Also recommended by D. Bergant)

Fokkleman, J. P. *Narrative Art in Genesis*. Amsterdam: Von Gorcum, 1975. "An excellent literary critical analysis of many parts of Genesis." (N. Cohen)

Friedman, Richard. *Who Wrote the Bible?* New York: HarperCollins, 1989. "A layman's guide to modern critical study of the Bible." (B. Visotzky)

Fromm, Erich. *You Shall Be As Gods: A Radical Interpretation of the Old Testament and Its Traditions*. New York: H. Holt & Co., 1991. "An intriguing interpretation of the Biblical text, from a humanistic psychoanalytical point of view." (N. Rosenblatt)

Hartman, Geoffrey H., and Sanford Budick. *Midrash and Literature*. New Haven, Ct.: Yale Univ. Press, 1986. "A collection of articles on the relation between literary interpretation and midrash." (A. Zornberg)

Hirsch, Samson Raphael. *The Pentateuch with Commentaries*. New York: Judaica, 1990. "The Torah with comments by the nineteenth-century German Jewish scholar, one of the most erudite thinkers in Jewish history." (F. Kellerman)

Hyde, Lewis. *The Gift: Imagination and the Erotic Life of Property*. New York: Vintage, 1979. "This book deals with how an individual must create space for creation to be possible." (H. O'Donnell)

Jeansonne, Sharon Pace. *The Women of Genesis: From Sarah to Potiphar's Wife*. Minneapolis: Fortress, 1990. (D. Bergant)

Josipovici, Gabriel. *The Book of God: A Response to the Bible*. New Haven, Ct.: Yale Univ. Press, 1988. "A sensitive literary reading of the Bible that argues for its distinctiveness, while showing connections with certain rare modern writers who ask us to look at the world in new terms." (R. Alter) " 'Relates the Bible to the deepest pains and happinesses of the modern soul'—John Drury." (A. Zornberg)

Kikawada, Isaac, and Arthur Quinn. *Before Abraham Was*. New York: Parthenon, 1985.

"A superb analysis of the creation and Noah stories, which helps the reader to grasp the coherence and moral power of the narrative." (B. Greenberg)

Levenson, Jon D. *Creation and the Persistence of Evil*. New York: Harper & Row, 1988. "An outstanding, fresh commentary that illuminates the mythic-yet-relevant dimensions of the Bible and the remarkable covenantal role of God and human beings in the world." (B. Greenberg)

Life Application Bible for Students: The Living Bible. Wheaton, Ill.: Tyndale, 1992. "A must for any young person studying the Word." (P. K. McCary)

Lings, Martin. *Muhammad*. Cambridge: The Islamic Texts Society, 1991. "The most authentic biography in English of the Prophet of Islam and his relation to Abraham and other ancient prophets." (H. Nasr)

Mann, Thomas. *Joseph and His Brothers*. New York: Knopf, 1944. (N. Cohen)

Marshall, Celia Brewer. *A Guide Through the Old Testament*. Louisville: John Knox, 1989. "A wonderful workbook/study book." (P. K. McCary)

Meyers, Carol. *Discovering Eve: Ancient Israelite Women in Context*. New York: Oxford Univ. Press, 1988. (D. Bergant)

Mitchell, Stephen. *Genesis: A New Translation of the Classical Biblical Stories*. New York: HarperCollins, 1996. (E. Pagels)

Nachshoni, Y. *Studies in the Weekly Parashah*. New York: Mesorah, 1988. (F. Kellerman)

Newby, Gordon Darnell. *The Making of the Last Prophet: A Reconstruction of the Earliest Biography of Muhammad*. Columbia, S.C.: Univ. of South Carolina Press, 1989. "Chapters on 'Creation, Adam and Eve,' 'Abraham, the Friend of God,' and 'Joseph' present valuable compilations of early Islamic traditions about these subjects." (F. García-Treto)

Newsom, Carol A., and Sharon H. Ringe, eds. *The Women's Bible Commentary*. Louisville: John Knox/Westminster, 1992. (D. Bergant)

Pardes, Ilana. *Countertraditions in the Bible: A Feminist Approach*. Cambridge, Mass.: Harvard Univ. Press, 1992. (D. Bergant) "The one feminist reading of the Bible that manages to open up new perspectives without special pleading, pro or contra." (R. Alter)

Pitzele, Peter. *Our Fathers' Wells*. San Francisco: Harper San Francisco, 1995. (N. Cohen)

Rilke, R. M. *The Selected Poetry of Rainer Maria Rilke*. Ed. and trans. Stephen Mitchell (1982). New York: Vintage, 1989. "Rilke has created poems that are an education of the senses. He teaches us to lend ourselves in a partnership of communication with animate and inanimate phenomena. There is a deep sympathy in his work for animal and plant life. I know of no better poet who has articulated ways in which imagination helps us to converse with other life forms." (H. O'Donnell)

Rosenberg, Joel. *King and Kin*. Bloomington: Indiana Univ. Press, 1986. "A subtle literary analysis of the Garden of Eden and Abraham stories as a reflection on the life cycle of human beings." (B. Greenberg)

Rosenblatt, Naomi H. and Joshua Horwitz. *Wrestling With Angels: What Genesis Teaches Us About Our Spiritual Identity, Sexuality and Personal Relationships*. New York: Doubleday, 1996. "A comprehensive framework for exploring human nature. By exploring the saga of the first family of the Bible, we discover how their conflicts and transcendental spiritual vision reflect our own contemporary search for purpose and meaning." (N. Rosenblatt)

Rumi, Jalal al-Din. *The Mathnawi*. Trans. R. A. Nicholson. London: Luzac, 1982. "Contains many stories about the prophets and brings out the esoteric and spiritual significance of their lives and actions from the Islamic point of view." (H. Nasr)

Sacks, Robert D. *A Commentary on the Book of Genesis*. Lewiston, Me.: Mellon, 1991. "This is a remarkable political-philosophical commentary on the entire book, chapter by chapter, line by line. There are provocative suggestions and revealing discoveries on virtually every page." (L. Kass) (Also recommended by J. Barth)

Sarna, Nahum. *Understanding Genesis*. New York: Schocken, 1966/1970. "A lucid and balanced scholarly introduction to Genesis that alerts readers to the relevant comparative materials from the ancient Near East." (R. Alter) "Useful, instructive treatment in the light of extra-biblical sources relevant to Genesis." (A. Zornberg)

Sheres, Ita. *Dinah's Rebellion: A Biblical Parable for Our Time*. New York: Crossroads, 1990. (D. Bergant)

Speizer, Ephraim. *Genesis*. (Anchor Bible Commentary). Garden City, N.Y.: Doubleday, 1964. (B. Visotzky)

Spiegel, Shalom. *The Last Trial: On the Legends and Lore of the Command to Abraham to Offer Isaac as a Sacrifice*. Trans. with Intro. and Pref. by Judah Goldin. Woodstock, Vt.: Jewish Lights, reprint 1993. "A classic, luminous presentation of the Aggadic tradition concerning the binding of Isaac." (F. García-Treto)

Steinmetz, Devora. *From Father to Son: Kinship, Conflict and Continuity in Genesis*. Louisville: Westminster/John Knox Press, 1991. "An erudite literary analysis of Genesis from the point of view of family dynamics and continuity." (N. Cohen)

Steinsaltz, Adin. *Biblical Images: Men and Women of the Bible*. New York: Basic Books, 1984. (N. Cohen)

Sternberg, Meir. *The Poetics of Biblical Narrative*. Bloomington: Indiana Univ. Press, 1985. "Though some of the technical literary analysis will be too elaborate for the general reader, the volume offers some brilliant close readings of biblical stories, including several from Genesis." (R. Alter)

Strauss, Leo. "On the Interpretation of Genesis," *L'Homme* 21.1 (1981): 5–20. "A most remarkable analysis of the first chapter of Genesis, for its content, structure, and intention. It also contains a brief but profound discussion of the second creation story and its relation to the first, as well as a marvelous interpretation of the transgression." (L. Kass)

_～2I～_

Suzuki, Shunryu. *Zen Mind, Beginner's Mind.* Ed. Trudy Dixon. New York: Weatherhill, 1970. ''I think of this book in relation to the question of subduing the earth. The Zen practice of bringing quiet to the mind is built on an earlier Shinto practice called 'quieting the land.' Rituals of bringing order to chaos are here discussed as a guide to ethical behavior and preparation for the creative act.'' (H. O'Donnell)

Teubal, Savina. *Hagar the Egyptian: The Lost Tradition of the Matriarchs.* San Francisco: Harper, 1990. (D. Bergant)

———. *Sarah the Priestess: The First Matriarch of Genesis.* Athens, Ohio: Swallow/Ohio Univ. Press, 1984. (D. Bergant)

Trible, Phyllis. *God and the Rhetoric of Sexuality.* Philadelphia: Fortress, 1978. (D. Bergant)

———. *Texts of Terror: Literary Feminist Readings of Biblical Narratives.* Philadelphia: Fortress, 1984. (D. Bergant)

Vawter, Bruce. *On Genesis: A New Reading.* Garden City, N.Y.: Doubleday, 1977. ''A popular and readable commentary on the complete text of Genesis.'' (A. Di Lella)

Visotzky, Burton L. *The Genesis of Ethics.* New York: Crown, 1996. ''A conversation on the ethics of Genesis and how we learn to be ethical by discussing the family stories in Genesis.'' (B. Visotzky)

———. *Reading the Book: Making the Bible a Timeless Text.* New York: Doubleday/Anchor, 1991; Schocken reprint, 1996. ''A user-friendly guide to midrash (the rabbinic readings of the Bible).'' (B. Visotzky)

Waskow, Arthur. *Godwrestling.* New York: Schocken, 1976. ''A modern midrashic treatment of the stories in Genesis by a creative modern Jew.'' (N. Cohen)

———. *Godwrestling—Round Two: Ancient Wisdom, Future Paths.* Woodstock, Vt.: Jewish Lights, 1996. (N. Cohen)

The Weekly Midrash. New York: Mesorah, 1994. (F. Kellerman)

Westermann, Claus. *Creation.* Trans. J. J. Scullion. Philadelphia: Fortress, 1974. ''A brilliant essay on the doctrine of creation in Genesis.'' (A. Di Lella)

———. *Genesis: An Introduction.* Trans. John J. Scullion, S.J. Minneapolis: Fortress, 1992. (D. Bergant)

———. *Genesis: A Practical Commentary.* Trans. D. E. Green. Grand Rapids, Mich.: Eerdmans, 1987. ''A popular presentation of the author's three-volume scholarly study of Genesis.'' (A. Di Lella) ''My translation of Genesis is deeply indebted to the three-volume commentary by Claus Westermann [*Genesis 1–11*, *Genesis 12–36*, and *Genesis 37–50*—English translation published by Augsburg Publishing House]. This is the greatest work of biblical scholarship I have ever studied: judicious, exhaustive, subtle, meticulous, and especially acute in disentangling the various layers of the text.'' (S. Mitchell)

Wiesel, Elie. *Messengers of God: Biblical Portraits and Legends.* New York: Random, 1976. ''An exquisite mixture of classic rabbinic tradition and modern interpretations of key characters in the Bible.'' (N. Cohen)

Wildavsky, Aaron. *Assimilation versus Separation: Joseph the Administrator and the Politics of Religion in Biblical Israel.* New Brunswick, N.J.: Transaction, 1993. ''This is a thoroughgoing examination and critique of the career of Joseph. Wildavsky makes a powerful case to show that Joseph is an antihero in Israel, a perfect foil for Moses.'' (L. Kass)

Zornberg, Aviva Gottlieb. *Genesis: The Beginning of Desire.* New York: Jewish Publication Society, 1995; reprint, Doubleday, 1996. ''An excellent new commentary that combines a grand and sweeping vision of the sacred with a microscopic view of the most intimate of human relationships.'' (B. Greenberg) ''This is a book that scrapes the film of familiarity from these stories by subjecting them to a heady mix of scholarship, ranging from ancient to postmodern.'' (R. Goldstein) (Also recommended by B. Visotzky and S. Mitchell)

PICTURE CREDITS

CHAPTER 1

1. The Schocken Institute for Jewish Research of the Jewish Theological Seminary of America, Jerusalem (Ms.14940)
2. Bibliothèque Municipale, Moulins, France (Ms.1F.4v.), Giraudon/Art Resource, N.Y.
3. Museo del Prado, Madrid, Spain, Foto Marburg/Art Resource, N.Y.
4. Alinari/Art Resource, N.Y.
5. The Metropolitan Museum of Art, N.Y., Gift of Mrs. Frederick F. Thompson, 1915 (15.76.3)
6. Jewish Museum/Art Resource, N.Y.
7. Courtesy of the Arthur M. Sackler Gallery, Smithsonian Institution, Washington, D.C. (S86.0254)
8. Collection Chuck and Jan Rosenak

CHAPTER 2

1. Courtauld Institute Galleries, London
2. Jewish Museum/Art Resource, N.Y.
3. Courtesy Phyllis Kind Gallery, N.Y.
4. Jane Voorhees Zimmerli Art Museum, Rutgers, the State University of New Jersey, the Norton and Nancy Dodge Collection of Nonconformist Art from the Soviet Union
5. Fitzwilliam Museum, Cambridge, England
6. Foto Marburg/Art Resource, N.Y.
7. Spencer Collection, the New York Public Library, Astor, Lenox, and Tilden Foundations
8. Z. Radovan, Jerusalem

CHAPTER 3

1. Scala/Art Resource, N.Y.

2. Courtesy the artist and Cameron Books, Scotland
3. Municipal Museum, Bruges, Belgium, Foto Marburg/Art Resource, N.Y.
4. Alinari/Art Resource, N.Y.
5. Ashmolean Museum, Oxford
6. Collection Hebrew Union College Skirball Museum, Los Angeles, photo Lelo Carter
7. Ronald Sheridan Photo Library/Ancient Art and Architecture Collection, London
8. By Permission of the British Library, London (OR 2884 Fol.3)

CHAPTER 4

1. Spencer Collection, the New York Public Library, Astor, Lenox, and Tilden Foundations
2. Erich Lessing/Art Resource, N.Y.
3. Collection Connie Tavel, Los Angeles, photo Ave Pildas
4. Neue Residenz, Bamberg, Germany, Giraudon/Art Resource, N.Y.
5. Z. Radovan, Jerusalem
6. Art Resource, N.Y., © 1996 Artists Rights Society (ARS), N.Y./ADAGP, Paris
7. British Museum, London, Foto Marburg/Art Resource, N.Y.
8. Cameraphoto/Art Resource, N.Y.

CHAPTER 5

1. Z. Radovan, Jerusalem
2. Österreichische Nationalbibliothek, Vienna (Cod. OR 31 Fol.IV)
3. Palazzo Rosso, Genoa, Scala/Art Resource, N.Y.
4. The Edwin Binney III Turkish Collection at the Los Angeles County Museum of Art

5. © Miriam Schapiro, courtesy Steinbaum Krauss Gallery, N.Y., Gift of Mrs. Beverly Dubin Lauren and Mr. and Mrs. Richard Rumick—commissioned for Temple Sholom, Chicago
6. Alinari/Art Resource, N.Y
7. Museum of Old Jewish Cemetary, Prague, Scala/Art Resource, N.Y.

CHAPTER 6

1. Bibliothèque Municipale, Moulins, France, Giraudon/Art Resource, N.Y.
2. Bayerische Staatsgemäldesammlungen, Munich.
3. Courtesy Marlborough Graphics, Ltd., London.
4. Klosterneuburg Abbey, Austria, Erich Lessing/Art Resource, N.Y.
5. Alinari/Art Resource, N.Y.
6. Pinacoteca di Brera, Milan, Scala/Art Resource, N.Y.
7. The Metropolitan Museum of Art, N.Y., Rogers Fund, 1938 (38.64)
8. Courtesy of the Library of the Jewish Theological Seminary of America (Yerushalmi Plate 45)

CHAPTER 7

1. Jewish Museum, Gift of Dr. Harry G. Friedman in memory of Dr. Murray Last (F 3546)/Art Resource, N.Y.
2. Foto Marburg/Art Resource, N.Y.
3. Musée Historique des Tissus, Lyon, France, Giraudon/Art Resource, N.Y.
4. Calouste Gulbenkian Foundation, Lisbon
5. Uffizi, Florence, Alinari/Art Resource, N.Y.
6. Jewish Museum/Art Resource, N.Y.
7. Z. Radovan, Jerusalem
8. Alinari/Art Resource, N.Y.

CHAPTER 8

1. Museo Civico, Cremona, Scala/Art Resource, N.Y.
2. The Granger Collection, N.Y. (Morgan Ms. 739)

3. The Pierpont Morgan Library/Art Resource, N.Y.
4. The Schocken Institute for Jewish Research of the Jewish Theological Seminary of America, Jerusalem (Ms. 24087), courtesy Mr. Nathan Rome
5. Alinari/Art Resource, N.Y.
6. Schloss Weissenstein, Pommersfelden, Germany, Foto Marburg/Art Resource, N.Y.
7. Art Resource, N.Y. © 1996 Artists Rights Society (ARS), N.Y./ADAGP, Paris
8. Alinari/Art Resource, N.Y.

CHAPTER 9

1. Courtesy of the Library of the Jewish Theological Seminary of America (N.Y. Ms.-8236)
2. Holburne Museum, Bath, Great Britain, Bridgeman/Art Resource, N.Y.
3. Art Resource, N.Y.
4. Private Collection
5. Jewish Museum, Gift of George and Bee Wolfe/Art Resource, N.Y.
6. Museo del Prado, Madrid, Spain, Alinari/Art Resource, N.Y.
7. Courtesy Granada Television Ltd.
8. Staatsbibliothek, Munich (Ms.CIM 835 F. 13r), Foto Marburg/Art Resource, N.Y.

CHAPTER 10

1. The Metropolitan Museum of Art, N.Y., Gift of Alexander Smith Cochran, 1913 (13.228.5)
2. The Pierpont Morgan Library (M.638 F.5)/Art Resource, N.Y.
3. Z. Radovan, Jerusalem
4. Alinari/Art Resource, N.Y.
5. Courtesy of the Library of The Jewish Theological Seminary of America, N.Y. (8972)
6. The David and Alfred Smart Museum of Art, the University of Chicago, Gift of the Mark Morton Memorial Fund and Mr. and Mrs. Eugene Davidson
7. Musée des Beaux-Arts, Rouen, France, Giraudon/Art Resource, N.Y.

8. Courtesy of the Arthur M. Sackler Gallery, Smithsonian Institution, Washington, D.C. (S86.0255)

9. Österreichische Nationalbibliothek, Vienna (Cod.1191 Fol.23)

COLOR

1. Z. Radovan, Jerusalem
2. Calouste Gulbenkian Foundation, Lisbon
3. Courtesy Museum of Fine Arts, Boston, Bequest of Maxim Karolik
4. Collection Glenn and Linda Smith
5. Laurie Platt Winfrey, Inc., N.Y.
6. Courtesy of the artists
7. Courtesy of the artist, photo © Paul Rocheleau
8. The Pierpont Morgan Library (PML 17917)/Art Resource, N.Y.
9. © Miriam Schapiro, Courtesy Steinbaum Krauss Gallery, N.Y.
10. Collection George and Sue Viener
11. Z. Radovan, Jerusalem
12. Coptic Museum, Cairo, Borromeo/Art Resource, N.Y.
13. © Rimma Gerlovina and Valeriy Gerlovin.
14. Courtesy Schmidt-Bingham Gallery, N.Y.
15. Österreichische Nationalbibliothek, Vienna (Cod. 1191 Fol.5V)
16. Courtesy Mary-Anne Martin/Fine Art, N.Y.
17. Scala/Art Resource, N.Y.
18. Courtesy Brewster Arts Ltd., N.Y.
19. Hildegard von Bingen, "Wisse die Wege. SCIVIAS," Otto Müller Verlag, Salzburg, 1987
20. Biblioteca Trivulziana, Milan (Ms. 2139) Alinari/Regione Umbria/Art Resource, N.Y.
21. Open Air Museum, Kizhi Island, Russia, Erich Lessing/Art Resource, N.Y.
22. Spencer Collection, the New York Public Library, Astor, Lenox, and Tilden Foundations
23. Collection George H. Meyer, photo Charles B. Nairn
24. Art Resource, N.Y.
25. Jüdisches Museum der Schweiz, Basel, Switzerland, Erich Lessing/Art Resource, N.Y.
26. Scala/Art Resource, N.Y.
27. Louvre, Paris, Erich Lessing/Art Resource, N.Y.
28. Photo © 1995 the Detroit Institute of Arts, Gift of Joan Lovell and James A. Tuck
29. Bibliothèque Municipale, Dijon, (Ms. 562) Erich Lessing/Art Resource, N.Y.
30. By Permission of the British Library (Ms. 27210 Fol.3)
31. The Pierpont Morgan Library (M.638 F.2v)/Art Resource, N.Y.
32. Photo © Paul Rocheleau
33. Cathedral, Gerona, Spain, Erich Lessing/Art Resource, N.Y.
34. Courtesy of the Freer Gallery of Art, Smithsonian Institution, Washington, D.C. (48.8)
35. Photo Malcom Varon, New York City © 1996 (Courtesy Institute of Ethiopian Studies, Addis Ababa)
36. Museo del Prado, Madrid, Giraudon/Art Resource, N.Y.
37. Bildarchiv Preussischer Kulturbesitz, Berlin
38. Courtesy Schmidt-Bingham Gallery, N.Y.
39. Z. Radovan, Jerusalem
40. National Gallery of Scotland, Edinburgh, Bridgeman/Art Resource, N.Y.
41. Musée du Petit Palais, Avignon, France, Giraudon/Art Resource, N.Y.
42. Hebrew Union College, Francis–Henry Library Collection, JIR-Los Angeles, photo John Reed Forsman
43. Bibliothèque Nationale, Paris, Bridgeman/Art Resource, N.Y.
44. Österreichische Nationalbibliothek, Vienna (Cod. 1191 Fol.19v)
45. Museo Nazionale del Bargello, Florence, Nimatallah/Art Resource, N.Y.
46. Musée Condé, Chantilly, France, Giraudon/Art Resource, N.Y.
47. Courtesy of the Library of the Jewish Theological Seminary of America, N.Y. (Ms. 1534, Fol.69v)
48. Spencer Collection, the New York Public Library, Astor, Lenox, and Tilden Foundations